International Conference on e-Learning 2017

Held at the Multi-Conference on Computer Science and Information Systems (MCCSIS 2017)

Lisbon, Portugal
20 – 23 July 2017

Editors:

Miguel Baptista Nunes
Maggie McPherson
Piet Kommers
Pedro Isaias
Luis Rodrigues

ISBN: 978-1-5108-6530-3

Printed from e-media with permission by:

Curran Associates, Inc.
57 Morehouse Lane
Red Hook, NY 12571

Some format issues inherent in the e-media version may also appear in this print version.

Printed by Curran Associates, Inc. (2018)

For permission requests, please contact International Association for Development of the Information Society (IADIS) at the address below.

International Association for Development of the Information Society (IADIS)
Rua Sao Sebastiao Da Pedreira
No. 100, 30, 1050-209
Lisbon, Portugal

Phone: 351 21 3151373
Fax: 351 21 3151244

secretariat@iadis.org

Additional copies of this publication are available from:

Curran Associates, Inc.
57 Morehouse Lane
Red Hook, NY 12571 USA
Phone: 845-758-0400
Fax: 845-758-2633
Email: curran@proceedings.com
Web: www.proceedings.com

INTERNATIONAL CONFERENCE

E-LEARNING 2017

part of the

MULTI CONFERENCE ON COMPUTER SCIENCE AND

INFORMATION SYSTEMS 2017

PROCEEDINGS OF THE INTERNATIONAL CONFERENCE

E-LEARNING 2017

Lisbon, Portugal
JULY 20 - 22, 2017

Organised by
IADIS
International Association for Development of the Information Society

Volume Editors:
Miguel Baptista Nunes and Maggie McPherson

Computer Science and Information Systems Series Editors:
Piet Kommers and Pedro Isaías

Associate Editor: Luís Rodrigues

TABLE OF CONTENTS

FOREWORD ix

PROGRAM COMMITTEE xiii

KEYNOTE LECTURE xv

FULL PAPERS

GAME CHANGER FOR ONLINE LEARNING DRIVEN BY ADVANCES IN WEB TECHNOLOGY 3
Manfred Kaul, André Kless, Thorsten Bonne and Almut Rieke

E-LEARNING INSTRUCTIONAL DESIGN PRACTICE IN AMERICAN AND AUSTRALIAN INSTITUTIONS 13
Sayed Hadi Sadeghi

A GAME BASED E-LEARNING SYSTEM TO TEACH ARTIFICIAL INTELLIGENCE IN THE COMPUTER SCIENCES DEGREE 25
Amable de Castro-Santos, Waldo Fajardo and Miguel Molina-Solana

THE NEXT STAGE OF DEVELOPMENT OF ELEARNING AT UFH IN SOUTH AFRICA 32
Graham Wright, Liezel Cilliers, Elzette Van Niekerk and Eunice Seekoe

EFFECT OF INTERNET-BASED LEARNING IN PUBLIC HEALTH TRAINING: AN EXPLORATORY META-ANALYSIS 39
Ying Peng and Weirong Yan

ENHANCING A SYLLABUS FOR INTERMEDIATE ESL STUDENTS WITH BYOD INTERVENTIONS 47
Ewa Kilar-Magdziarz

POST GRADUATIONS IN TECHNOLOGIES AND COMPUTING APPLIED TO EDUCATION: FROM F2F CLASSES TO MULTIMEDIA ONLINE OPEN COURSES 55
Bertil P. Marques, Piedade Carvalho, Paula Escudeiro, Ana Barata, Ana Silva and Sandra Queiros

TOWARDS ARCHITECTURE FOR PEDAGOGICAL AND GAME SCENARIOS ADAPTATION IN SERIOUS GAMES 63
Wassila Debabi and Ronan Champagnat

SEMANTIC MODELLING FOR LEARNING STYLES AND LEARNING MATERIAL IN AN E-LEARNING ENVIRONMENT 71
Khawla Alhasan, Liming Chen and Feng Chen

PHYSICAL INTERACTIVE GAME FOR ENHANCING LANGUAGE COGNITIVE DEVELOPMENT OF THAI PRE-SCHOOLER 80
Noppon Choosri and Chompoonut Pookao

FROM A CV TO AN EPORTFOLIO AN EXPLORATION OF ADULT LEARNER'S PERCEPTION OF THE EPORTFOLIO AS A JOBSEEKING TOOL 89
John Kilroy

THE EMOTIONAL GEOGRAPHIES OF PARENT PARTICIPATION IN SCHOOLING: HEADTEACHERS' PERCEPTIONS IN TAIWAN 97
Hsin-Jen Chen and Ya-Hsuan Wang

GEOPOLITICAL E-ANALYSIS BASED ON E-LEARNING CONTENT 105
Anca Dinicu and Romana Oancea

PREDICTORS OF STUDENT PERFORMANCE IN A BLENDED-LEARNING ENVIRONMENT: AN EMPIRICAL INVESTIGATION 113
Lan Umek, Nina Tomaževič, Aleksander Aristovnik and Damijana Keržič

PRACTICE OF ORGANISATIONAL STRATEGIES OF IMPROVING COMPUTER ROOMS FOR PROMOTING SMART EDUCATION USING ICT EQUIPMENT 121
Nobuyuki Ogawa and Akira Shimizu

WHY DO LEARNERS CHOOSE ONLINE LEARNING: THE LEARNERS' VOICES 130
Hale Ilgaz and Yasemin Gulbahar

ENHANCING INTERCULTURAL COMPETENCE OF ENGINEERING STUDENTS VIA GVT (GLOBAL VIRTUAL TEAMS)-BASED VIRTUAL EXCHANGES: AN INTERNATIONAL COLLABORATIVE COURSE IN INTRALOGISTICS EDUCATION 137
Rui Wang, Friederike Rechl, Sonja Bigontina, Dianjun Fang, Willibald A. Günthner and Johannes Fottner

SHORT PAPERS

EXPLORING CHARACTERISTICS OF FINE-GRAINED BEHAVIORS OF LEARNING MATHEMATICS IN TABLET-BASED E-LEARNING ACTIVITIES 149
Cheuk Yu Yeung, Kam Hong Shum, Lucas Chi Kwong Hui, Samuel Kai Wah Chu, Tsing Yun Chan, Yung Nin Kuo and Yee Ling Ng

BREAKING THE GENDERED-TECHNOLOGY PHENOMENON IN TAIWAN'S HIGHER EDUCATION 154
Ya-Hsuan Wang

ONTOLOGY-BASED LEARNER CATEGORIZATION THROUGH CASE BASED REASONING AND FUZZY LOGIC 159
Sohail Sarwar, Raul García-Castro, Zia Ul Qayyum, Muhammad Safyan and Rana Faisal Munir

LEARNING FACTORY – INTEGRATIVE E-LEARNING 164
Peter Steininger

INTERCULTURAL SENSIBILITY IN ONLINE TEACHING AND LEARNING PROCESSES 169
Eulalia Torras and Andreu Bellot

MOBILE LEARNING ON THE BASIS OF THE CLOUD SERVICES 175
Tatyana Makarchuk

PERSONALIZATION OF LEARNING ACTIVITIES WITHIN A VIRTUAL ENVIRONMENT FOR TRAINING BASED ON FUZZY LOGIC THEORY 179
Fahim Mohamed, Jakimi Abdeslam and El Bermi Lahcen

PROMOTING BEST PRACTICES IN TEACHING AND LEARNING IN NIGERIAN UNIVERSITIES THROUGH EFFECTIVE E-LEARNING: PROSPECTS AND CHALLENGES 184
Grace Ifeoma Obuekwe and Rose-Ann Ifeoma Eze

REFLECTION PAPERS

A CONCEPTUAL FRAMEWORK FOR WEB-BASED LEARNING DESIGN 191
Hesham Alomyan

THE KEY TO SUCCESS IN ELECTRONIC LEARNING: FACULTY TRAINING AND EVALUATION 196
Warren Matthews and Albert Smothers

USING GAMES, COMIC STRIPS, AND MAPS TO ENHANCE TEACHER CANDIDATES' E-LEARNING PRACTICE IN THE SOCIAL STUDIES 201
Nancy B. Sardone

SCANNER BASED ASSESSMENT IN EXAMS ORGANIZED WITH PERSONALIZED THESIS RANDOMLY GENERATED VIA MICROSOFT WORD 205
Romeo Teneqexhi, Margarita Qirko, Genci Sharko, Fatmir Vrapi and Loreta Kuneshka

DESIGNING A WEB-BASED ASYNCHRONOUS INNOVATION / ENTREPRENEURISM COURSE 209
Parviz Ghandforoush

SEMANTIC ANNOTATION OF RESOURCES TO LEARN WITH CONNECTED THINGS 213
Aymeric Bouchereau and Ioan Roxin

POSTERS

DEVELOPMENT OF A FRAMEWORK FOR MOOC IN CONTINUOUS TRAINING 219
Carolina Amado and Ana Pedro

INFORMATION LITERACY IN THE 21ST CENTURY: USEFULNESS AND EASE OF LEARNING 222
Patricia Fidalgo and Joan Thormann

DOCTORAL CONSORTIUM

E-LEARNING RESEARCH AND DEVELOPMENT: ON EVALUATION, LEARNING PERFORMANCE, AND VISUAL ATTENTION 227
Marco Rüth

AUTHOR INDEX

FOREWORD

These proceedings contain the papers of the International Conference e-Learning 2017, which was organised by the International Association for Development of the Information Society, 20 - 22 July, 2017. This conference is part of the Multi Conference on Computer Science and Information Systems 2017, 20 - 23 July, which had a total of 652 submissions.

The e-Learning (EL) 2017 conference aims to address the main issues of concern within e-Learning. This conference covers both technicai as well as the non-technical aspects of e-Learning.

The conference accepted submissions in the following seven main areas: Organisational Strategy and Management Issues; Technological Issues; e-Learning Curriculum Development Issues; Instructional Design Issues; e-Learning Delivery Issues; e-Learning Research Methods and Approaches; e-Skills and Information Literacy for Learning.

The above referred main submission areas are detailed:

Organisational Strategy and Management Issues
- Higher and Further Education
- Primary and Secondary Education
- Workplace Learning
- Vocational Training
- Home Schooling
- Distance Learning
- Blended Learning
- Change Management
- Educational Management
- Continuous Professional Development (CPD) for Educational and Training Staff
- Return on e-Learning Investments (ROI)

Technological Issues
- Learning Management Systems (LMS)
- Managed Learning Environments (MLEs)
- Virtual Learning Environments (VLEs)
- Computer-Mediated Communication (CMC) Tools
- Social Support Software
- Architecture of Educational Information Systems Infrastructure
- Security and Data Protection
- Learning Objects
- XML Schemas and the Semantic Web
- Web 2.0 Applications

e-Learning Curriculum Development Issues
- Philosophies and Epistemologies for e-learning
- Learning Theories and Approaches for e-learning
- e-Learning Models
- Conceptual Representations
- Pedagogical Models
- e-Learning Pedagogical Strategies
- e-Learning Tactics
- Developing e-Learning for Specific Subject Domains

Instructional Design Issues
- Designing e-Learning Settings
- Developing e-Learning Pilots and Prototypes
- Creating e-Learning Courses
    - Collaborative learning
    - Problem-based learning
    - Inquiry-based learning
    - Blended learning
    - Distance learning
- Designing e-Learning Tasks
    - E-learning activities
    - Online Groupwork
    - Experiential learning
    - Simulations and Modelling
    - Gaming and edutainment
    - Creativity and design activities
    - Exploratory programming

e-Learning Delivery Issues
- e-Delivery in different contexts
    - Higher and Further Education
    - Primary and Secondary Schools
    - Workplace Learning
    - Vocational Training
    - Distance Learning
- Online Assessment
- Innovations in e-Assessment
- e-Moderating
- e-Tutoring
- e-Facilitating
- Leadership in e-Learning Delivery
- Networked Information and Communication Literacy Skills
- Participation and Motivation in e-Learning

e-Learning Research Methods and Approaches
- Action Research
- Design Research
- Course and Programme Evaluations
- Systematic Literature Reviews
- Historical Analysis
- Case Studies
- Meta-analysis of Case Studies
- Effectiveness and Impact Studies
- Evaluation of e-Learning Technologies
- Evaluation of Student and Tutor Satisfaction
- Learning and cognitive styles
- Ethical Issues in e-learning

e-Skills and Information Literacy for Learning
- Teaching information literacy
- Electronic library and information search skills
- ICT skills education
    - in schools and colleges

- for business, industry and the public sector
  - in adult, community, home and prison education
  - informal methods (peer groups, family)
- Education for computer-mediated communication skills
  - Netiquette
  - Online safety for children and vulnerable users
  - Cybercrime awareness and personal prevention
- Student production of online media
  - Web design
  - Digital storytelling
  - Web 2.0 tools
  - etc.
- Digital media studies

The e-Learning 2017 conference received 102 submissions from more than 30 countries. Each submission has been anonymously reviewed by an average of four independent reviewers, to ensure that accepted submissions were of a high standard. Consequently only 17 full papers were approved which meant an acceptance rate of 17 %. A few more papers were accepted as short papers, reflection papers, posters and a doctoral paper. An extended version of the best papers will be selected for publishing as extended versions in the Interactive Technology and Smart Education (ITSE) journal (ISSN:1741-5659) and also in the IADIS International Journal on WWW/Internet (ISSN: 1645-7641). Other outlets may also receive extended versions of the best papers, including journals from Inderscience.

Besides the presentation of full papers, short papers, reflection papers, posters and a doctoral paper the conference also included one keynote presentation from an internationally distinguished researcher. We would therefore like to express our gratitude to Professor Thomas C. Reeves, Professor Emeritus of Learning, Design and Technology, College of Education, The University of Georgia, USA, for being the e-Learning 2017 keynote speaker.

A successful conference requires the effort of many individuals. We would like to thank the members of the Program Committee for their hard work in reviewing and selecting the papers that appear in this book. We are especially grateful to the authors who submitted their papers to this conference and to the presenters who provided the substance of the meeting. We wish to thank all members of our organizing committee.

Last but not the least, we hope that everybody will have a good time in Lisbon, and we invite all participants for the next edition of this conference.

Miguel Baptista Nunes, School of Information Management, Sun Yat-Sen University, Guangzhou, China
Maggie McPherson, University of Leeds, United Kingdom
e-Learning 2017 Conference Program Co-Chairs

Piet Kommers, University of Twente, The Netherlands
Pedro Isaías, The University of Queensland, Australia
MCCSIS 2017 General Conference Co-Chairs

Lisbon, Portugal
July 2017

PROGRAM COMMITTEE

E-LEARNING CONFERENCE PROGRAM CO-CHAIRS

Miguel Baptista Nunes, School of Information Management, Sun Yat-Sen University, Guangzhou, China
Maggie McPherson, University of Leeds, United Kingdom

MCCSIS GENERAL CONFERENCE CO-CHAIRS

Piet Kommers, University of Twente, The Netherlands
Pedro Isaías, The University of Queensland, Australia

E-LEARNING CONFERENCE COMMITTEE MEMBERS

Adamantios Koumpis, Universität Passau Fakultät für Informatik und Mathematik, Germany
Airina Volungevičienė, Vytautas Magnus University, Lithuania
Andreas Bollin, Klagenfurt University, Austria
Andrew Lian, Suranaree University of Technology, Thailand
Antoanela Naaji, Vasile Goldis West University of Arad, Romania
Antonio Hervás-Jorge, Universidad Politécnica de Valencia, Spain
Antonio Navarro, Universidad Complutense de Madrid, Spain
Antonio Panaggio, Italian Ministry of Education, Italy
Apostolos Gkamas, University Ecclesiastical Academy of Vella of Ioan, Greece
Avgoustos Tsinakos, Eastern Macedonia and Thrace Institute of Technology, Greece
Benedict du Boulay, University of Sussex, United Kingdom
Carmen Holotescu, University Politehnica Timisoara, Romania
Cecilia Ruiz, University of Murcia, Spain
Charalampos Karagiannidis, University of Thessaly, Greece
Christina Gloerfeld, Fernuniversität In Hagen , Germany
Christos Bouras, University of Patras, Greece
Claudia Steinberger, Klagenfurt University, Austria
David Guralnick, Kaleidoscope Learning, USA
Demetrios Sampson, Curtin University, Australia
Dessislava Vassileva, Sofia University “St. Kliment Ohridski”, Bulgaria
Dimitra Pappa, National Center for Scientific Research – Demokritos, Greece
Dimitris Fotiadis, University of Ioannina, Greece
Egle Butkeviciene, Kaunas University of Technology, Lithuania
Eliza Stefanova, Sofia University, Bulgaria
Elvis Mazzoni, University of Bologna, Italy
Erick Araya, University Austral of Chile, Chile
Esteban Vázquez Cano, Spanish National University of Distance Education, Spain
Eugenia Kovatcheva, University of Library Studies and Information Technologies, Bulgaria
Eva Jereb, University of Maribor, Slovenia
Foteini Grivokostopoulou, University of Patras, Greece
Francesca Pozzi, Instituto Tecnologie Didattiche – CNR, Italy
Fridolin Wild, Oxford Brookes University, United Kingdom
George Palaigeorgiou, University of Western Macedonia, Greece
Giuliana Dettori, ITD-CNR, Italy
Giusy Cannella, Indire, Italy

KEYNOTE LECTURE

HUMAN LEARNING, MACHINE LEARNING, AND E-LEARNING: CONFLICT OR CONFLUENCE?

Professor Thomas C. Reeves, Professor Emeritus of Learning, Design and Technology, College of Education, The University of Georgia, USA

ABSTRACT

The technologies underlying machine learning are developing so rapidly that huge swaths of career paths previously open to university graduates are being assumed by algorithms and robots. These are not just easily-automated manual labor jobs such as filling orders at online stores, but high cognitive demand professions such as those of pharmacists and journalists. Meanwhile, politicians around the world promise to bring back high-paying manufacturing jobs and voters naively believe them, seemingly unaware or unwilling to acknowledge an emerging "techno-feudalism" wherein many, perhaps most, people will have few options other than minimum wage work or government subsistence payments in the form of a "guaranteed minimum income." Amid this economic and social devolution, higher education institutions continue to offer degree programs in professions that may soon disappear or be drastically reduced in numbers. This keynote presentation will explore the implications of machine learning for human learners, and more specifically, for designers and providers of e-learning.

Full Papers

GAME CHANGER FOR ONLINE LEARNING DRIVEN BY ADVANCES IN WEB TECHNOLOGY

Manfred Kaul, André Kless, Thorsten Bonne and Almut Rieke
Hochschule Bonn-Rhein-Sieg, University of Applied Sciences, 53757 Sankt Augustin, Germany

ABSTRACT

Almost unnoticed by the e-learning community, the underlying technology of the WWW is undergoing massive technological changes on all levels these days. In this paper we draw the attention to the emerging game changer and discuss the consequences for online learning. In our e-learning project "Work & Study", funded by the German Federal Ministry of Education and Research, we have experimented with several new technological approaches such as Mobile First, Responsive Design, Mobile Apps, Web Components, Client-side Components, Progressive Web Apps, Course Apps, e-books, and web sockets for real time collaboration and report about the results and consequences for online learning practice. The modular web is emerging where e-learning units are composed from and delivered by universally embeddable web components.

KEYWORDS

web technology, modular web, web components, client-side component model, mobile web, embedded collaborative learning

1. INTRODUCTION

The initial development of the big e-learning platforms such as Moodle, Blackboard or the German open-source platform ILIAS started over 20 years ago. The underlying web technology is the LAMP architecture (Linux, Apache, MySQL and PHP) or Java or similar server-centric architectures. Since then many technological revolutions have taken place on all levels: Even on the lowest level, the underlying Internet communication protocol HTTP has changed into SPDY, becoming HTTP/2. HTTP/1 being client pull only, with HTTP/2 server push enters the stage. Additionally, new Web protocols like Web Sockets have emerged. The web programing language JavaScript began as a little scripting language for event handlers in a single web page and has never been designed for large systems programming. Nowadays, JavaScript is the most used programing language on the web (W3Techs 2017), and large systems with millions of lines of code have been built successfully with JavaScript. The innovation rate in the JavaScript language standard ECMAScript itself has increased to a new release every year. A new JavaScript library is released every 8 minutes somewhere around the world (npmjs 2017). The JavaScript package manager npm is offering nearly half a million packages by now, with almost half a billion downloads every day (npmjs 2017). The standards body for web technology, the World Wide Web Consortium (W3C) is hardly keeping up with the technological advances of the big technology leaders in industry, so that the browser vendors started their own consensus platform, the WHATWG, (WHATWG 2017). Many new web technologies arise constantly in all subparts of the Web. The WWW is a completely different technology today, but the former big e-learning platforms are very hard to change and to adapt to the rapid advances in Web technology. Legacy systems become a bottleneck for innovation demands in e-learning for the same reasons.

In 2015, OECD marked the current state of e-learning technology as ineffective in improving student learning outcomes (OECD 2015). The Horizon Report (NMC 2015) argues, that course apps (apps dedicated to a single specific course) are the new way to go, because current e-learning platforms are too limited and inflexible. In order to push the boundaries of what is possible, course apps provide more features and a richer environment on mobile platforms for anytime anywhere learning experience: On mobile devices, cameras, microphone, GPS and additional sensors are available to enrich the learning experience. Social and interactive capabilities lead to a richer engagement and active learning. The underlying technologies of mobile web and mobile apps have a deep impact on online learning, teaching tools, learning habits, and teaching and learning workflows.

In our e-learning project "Work & Study", funded by the German Federal Ministry of Education and Research (Work & Study 2017), we have experimented with several new technological approaches such as Mobile First, Responsive Design, Mobile Apps, Web Components, Client-side Components, Progressive Web Apps, Course Apps, e-books, and web sockets for real-time collaboration. In this paper, we report about the results of our research and consequences for online learning practice, and how they change the online learning and teaching experience.

2. GAME CHANGER

In this chapter we address the most important game changer for online learning driven by advances in web technology.

2.1 Advances in Web Technology

When Tim Berners-Lee invented the World Wide Web (WWW) in 1989, he had an open, democratic, distributed platform for reading hypertexts in mind helping the scientific community to organize large volumes of rapidly changing texts on the Internet (Berners-Lee 2010). Starting from this first read-only system, the WWW has taken a tremendous journey towards a dynamic, readable and writable world wide platform not only for texts, but for all kinds of media and software. Today, the WWW is a *software on demand* delivery platform: With a web page, the browser also loads the appropriate software turning static text into engaging interactive media. This development took several steps and is still continuing to change the WWW as we know it. The world witnessed the beginning of dynamic web applications with web forms, into which the user fills in data. This data is uploaded to the server and processed by server-side engines (mostly PHP and Java), storing data into a server database. In the "LAMP age" dynamic behavior was server-side. Today, the WWW architecture turns to the "JavaScript age" with most dynamic behavior being client-side in the browser and even the server turning to JavaScript (Driscoll 2011).

Tim Berners-Lee being the Director of the WWW Consortium (W3C 2017) realized the importance of standardization of the browser in order to defeat cross-browser issues. Thereby, all software delivered to any browser of any vendor has a standard interface. In contrast, the server-side has never been standardized in such a fundamental way. Therefore, there is no general vendor neutral standard interface for web server plugins. Nevertheless, the e-learning community has continued to deliver e-learning content to server platforms.

The big e-learning management systems (LMS) such as Moodle, or the German open-source platform ILIAS or OLAT (Online Learning and Training) from Switzerland were developed more than 20 years ago in the LAMP age, and are server-centric. The e-learning community has produced a lot of software, teachware and learnware on these platforms with server-side integration. But without server-side standards, software remains bound to a single platform or vendor. This is well known as platform or vendor lock-in. Exchange across platform or vendor boundaries is hard and very costly. Server-to-server platform exchange formats such as SCORM often turn out to be too limited (Born 2015).

In the WWW industry the browser is the common standardized delivery platform and is rapidly enhanced by new features built directly into the platform. The need for additional libraries is decreasing at an enormous speed, because the needed features are built into the browser directly. "#UseThePlatform" is a popular Twitter hash tag in the web developer community reminding of the native capabilities of the browser: The browser supports more and more features natively. This reduces the need for additional platforms.

Therefore, in this paper we propose a focus shift from the "e-learning server platform" paradigm to the paradigm "The browser is the main platform": The browser has become so powerful, that the main part of the functionality can be implemented there. Thereby, cross vendor and cross platform issues are shifted to and resolved by W3C browser standards on a global industry scale. The e-learning industry can benefit from this paradigmatic shift by reducing own standardization burden.

Along with this shift, the amount of client software (JavaScript delivered to the browser via the web page) has increased dramatically. In order to manage the ensuing large scale of complexity, modularization is urgently needed. Unfortunately, the founders of the web did not foresee this new turn in the evolution of the web; the web standards did not embrace modularization at all. In the beginning, web pages were seen as rather limited text with very little JavaScript helpers. Therefore, the need for modularization was not envisioned.

Partitioning large scale web software into tiny reusable components is the next step. The W3C fosters this step via the W3C web components standard "v0" that started in 2011 and "v1" in 2016 (WebComponents.org 2017). W3C web components lay the groundwork for browser software modularization. The web components consists of four features which can be used independently or all together: (1) Custom Elements (2) Shadow DOM (3) HTML Template and (4) HTML imports. With (1) the markup language HTML with tags such as <h1> for first level header, <p> for paragraph etc. can be extended by your own custom tags like <login-button>, <my-navigation>, <my-quiz> or <my-lecture>. HTML has become extensible. With custom elements, the e-learning community creates its own specific HTML extensions for its own e-learning needs. Thereby a "*Domain Specific Language for e-learning*" (E-Learning DSL) is constructed as HTML extension. In this DSL, complex e-learning applications are easily composed from basic e-learning building blocks, just as web pages are composed from nested HTML tags. (In our project, we have already started to develop several custom elements for e-learning and composed complex learning units from them, as described in the next chapter.) With (2) the shadow DOM the document object model is encapsulated and scoped. For details see (WebComponents.org 2017).

The semantics of your own custom element is given by your own web component implementation. The implementation of a custom element needs programming skills, whereas the use and remix of web components become as easy as using HTML tags. The complexity of web components is hidden behind custom tags. Publishing web components on a marketplace (WebComponents.org 2017), programers upload their web component software and e-learners use the web components simply via custom element and HTML import. For mere usage, no programing skills are needed. Both tasks are separated clearly, programing and usage.

Meanwhile, Internet usage has changed completely since the advent of the mobile devices such as the smartphone. Mobile Internet usage tripled in 5 years and 2013 surged 54%. Proportions are shifting more and more towards mobile ever since (comScore 2016). Apple generates more revenue via iPhone than all other products. Google´s CEO declared "Mobile First!" as the new company strategy. Web products have been designed for mobile devices in the first place, but also adapt themselves dynamically to other devices with other screen sizes. Using Responsive Design, the adaptation process works continuously starting from smallest screen sizes up to largest wall displays smoothly without friction.

Besides the mobile web, native apps installed from app stores and running natively on the mobile hardware have become commonplace and even surpasses the usage of the mobile web: On mobile devices, native apps generate 87% of internet traffic and the mobile web via browsers only 13% (comScore 2016). Apps being closed environments solely governed by their vendor, a huge threat to the open and democratic nature of the WWW has emerged. One reason for this disaster was, that web apps had poor performance compared to apps. Even worse, native apps only had full access to the device hardware (camera, micro, geolocation, etc), whereas web apps were restricted (sandboxed). This severe disadvantage of the mobile web led to the mentioned serious drawback in usage numbers. Therefore, leading browser manufacturers started to develop advanced browser technology to keep up with modern mobile device capabilities and native app performance. The umbrella term for the advanced browser technology is *Progressive Web App* (PWA), (Google 2016). With PWA, the exclusive advantages of native apps vanished: The mobile web became as performant and feature rich as native apps: PWA include offline mode, add-to-homescreen, push notifications, caching, pre-fetching, fast start-up and more features without any needed installation (Google 2016). The mobile web is striking back and regaining its battlefield.

A PWA has a large sophisticated software base that can best be managed by composing it from loosely coupled modular units. Here web components come in once more, returning the open and democratic nature of the web again inviting everybody to contribute.

The up coming modular web is a big game changer in digital learning as well as in the web in general. It introduces a new way of thinking about learning contents, applications, packaging and delivery. Instead of big monolithic platforms which wall learning contents and applications inside their borders, web components introduce an open way of packaging contents with application software deployable to every LMS with HTML support, to any web page or even HTML-based e-book, e.g. in EPUB3 format. The web components approach to e-learning is similar to the learning objects approach (Beck 2008), but is solely based on web standards. Packaging learning contents with application behaviour (via the underlying JavaScript software), web components are self-contained: each component can be taken independently. Contents can be delivered cross platform and cross vendor. Even inter-platform communication and realtime collaboration become feasible. They are reusable: a single component may be used in multiple contexts for multiple purposes. They can be aggregated: components can be grouped into larger collections of content, including traditional course structures. In figure 1, a complex e-learning component which contains a video, a quiz, commenting and rating, is aggregated from basic web components, each containing encapsulated HTML, CSS and JavaScript, just like Lego® building bricks.

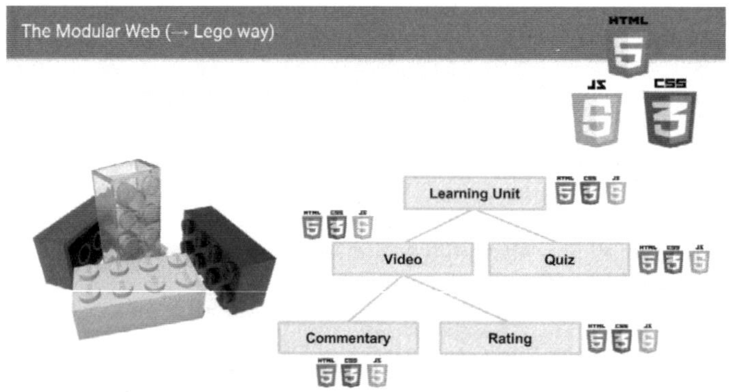

Figure 1. The Modular Web

In comparison to learning management systems (LMS), our web components based approach to learning contents, applications, packaging and delivery has several advantages: An LMS is no longer required, but when working with an LMS, or with several LMSs, web components fit in nicely: They enhance the platform via embedded components, but do not disturb the normal operation of the LMS. Even inter-LMS communication and collaboration become feasible via web components: For example, embedding the same chat component in different, heterogenous LMS enables students to chat across LMS borders, still remaining in their old well-known learning environment. In international projects this situation occurs quite often: Partner universities use different LMSs, thereby hindering students to collaborate seamlessly across borders.

Table 1. Comparison of the LMS and Web Components Approach to E-learning

	LMS	**W3C Web Components**
Standardization	SCORM, AICC, PENS, ...	W3C-Standard
software architecture	monolithic	loosely coupled web components
Component Market	LMS specific, if any	components used via markets
Reusability of Components	low, restricted to LMS, if any	high, across LMS
cross platform delivery	via SCORM, if available	directly deliverable
inter platform communication	via AICC, if available	directly available
inter platform collaboration	N/A	directly available
Composability of aggregates	LMS specific, if any	directly available via standard

LMS contents may be standardized by SCORM, AICC or PENS, but cross platform delivery is still complicated and platform dependent, as shown in our migration study (Born 2015). On the other side, W3C browser standards are developed on a global industry scale and after a small delay of engineering work, they are implemented in most modern browsers. Cross-browser incompatibility was a painful issue back in the last decade, but for several years now, major browser vendors have invested heavily in unification via WHATWG and standardization via W3C. Standardization of JavaScript is continuously refined on a yearly basis by ECMA (TC39 2017). However, in case of old browsers, small JavaScript libraries called "polyfills" are available to redeem the gap (Lawson et al. 2011). It is important to highlight that the cross platform issues no longer have to be solved by the LMS community, but are redeemed on a larger industry scale by browser manufacturers.

There already are some successful markets for learning components. For example, "learningapps.org" is a very successful marketplace for learning components with nearly 2.3m components and almost 1.7m registered users. Over 200 million learning apps have already been downloaded(LearningApps 2017). But learningapps.org was founded in 2010, when web components were not yet available. Therefore, the technology of learning apps is restricted to iFrames only: Every app is isolated within its iFrame and cannot communicate with other learning apps or the surrounding context, the web page and its CSS style rules. This restricts composability drastically: Complex web components as shown in fig. 1 cannot be composed from this kind of learning apps. Nevertheless, the huge success of learningapps.org is an excellent proof of the learning apps concept, which also contributed to our own concept.

Compared to LearningApps.org being based on iFrames, our own approach is based on the latest W3C web components standard. Since 2011 the web standard "v0" for W3C Web Components has been work in progress. The consensus of all browser vendors was finally achieved in 2016 with the "v1" web component standard, (WebComponents.org 2017). A highly advanced solution and concrete implementation of the component based approach is our own JavaScript framework for building and running web components, called *ccm*. Since 2015 we have already implemented seven complete semester e-learning courses taught at our university using *ccm* as a basis and many web components were built with *ccm* to meet e-learning needs.

2.2 Client-side Component Model (CCM)

The "Client-side Component Model" (CCM) is a model for composing, embedding and running web components inside the browser. Our implementation *ccm* consists of a single JavaScript framework *ccm* and many *ccm* components. In order to work smoothly in most browsers without polyfills, *ccm* uses only two W3C "v1" web component standards: Custom Elements and Shadow DOM. In this chapter *ccm* is explained in detail.

The *ccm* framework provides two services, one for embedding *ccm* components inside any web-based content and the other service for data management. The framework is delivered as a tiny JavaScript file (24kB minified, 9kB zipped), uses standard JavaScript (ES5) and has no dependency to other resources or frameworks. The *ccm* framework is published as free software under MIT licence (github.com/akless/ccm). It is loaded automatically when a *ccm* component is used.

A *ccm* component is a tiny JavaScript file which works with standard HTML, CSS and is based on the *ccm* framework. It may be composed of other *ccm* components and use other JavaScript frameworks. From multiple *ccm* components, complex components and web apps can be constructed. There are no restrictions in complexity and application domain. Every *ccm* component is embeddable in every web-based content.

With a *ccm* component, content as well as the underlying software for rendering and running is packaged in a single unit. The content maybe e-learning content or general web contents.

ccm components for quiz, fill-in-the-blank text, chat, team building, slidecast, commentary, rating, user input, user authentication, data logging and unit tests have already been developed and tested. All these components are published as free software under MIT Licence.

A marketplace has been developed as *ccm* component itself where all published *ccm* components are collected and information about them presented. This information contains basic metadata like author, licence, version and the public URL of the component JavaScript file.

There are three different ways to use a *ccm* component, which are described in detail: (1) Declarative via HTML Tag, (2) Functional via JavaScript, (3) Interactive via Bookmarklet. (1) Declarative via HTML Tag: This works in two steps. Firstly, the *ccm* component must be loaded using a HTML <script> tag. This introduces in a new HTML tag representing the new W3C Custom Element. Secondly, the custom tag is put at any place inside the web page any number of times, thereby embedding the custom element(s) into the web page. The component specific HTML attributes of the tag and the component specific inner HTML tags are used for setting up the configuration data. If the configuration data is stored in a database or a JSON file and the URL is specified as attribute, it is loaded directly.

```html
<!DOCTYPE html>
<script src="js/ccm.unit.js"></script>
<script src="js/ccm.video.js"></script>
<script src="js/ccm.comment.js"></script>
<script src="js/ccm.rating.js"></script>
<script src="js/ccm.quiz.js"></script>

<ccm-unit>
 <h1>Learning Unit 1: WWW</h1>
 <ccm-video key="cuoZenpQveQ">
   <ccm-comment></ccm-comment>
   <ccm-rating></ccm-rating>
 </ccm-video>
 <ccm-quiz key="WWW"></ccm-quiz>
</ccm-unit>
```

Figure 2. The e-learning DSL-representation for fig. 1 becomes valid HTML via *ccm*

(2) Functional via JavaScript: This works in two steps. Firstly, the *ccm* framework must be loaded using a HTML <script> tag. Secondly, the *start* method of the *ccm* framework is called for starting a *ccm* component. The method *start* needs the URL of the selected component JavaScript file and its configuration data.

(3) Interactive via Bookmarklet: A bookmarklet is a browser bookmark enriched by JavaScript. Our *ccm* marketplace provides a bookmarklet for each published component. So a web user can use such a bookmarklet on any web page to add a new draggable and resizable web page area with the embedded component in it by a simple drag-and-drop action.

A *ccm* component is embeddable on-demand and cross-domain inside any web-based content. On-demand means that a component is not only embeddable when a website is loading, it can also be included later. Cross-domain means that components must not be located on the same server where the actual website comes from, but it can be located on any other web server. With both aspects, any web user is able to embed a component in any currently viewed web page. The embedding of a *ccm* component works without iFrame. The CSS, JavaScript and HTML ids and classes are capsuled in Shadow DOM.

Like the Lego system, *ccm* components are recombinable. This results in a dependency tree. For example, the component for rendering a learning unit reuses the components for quiz and video and the video component reuses components for commentary and rating (fig. 1). These dependencies are automatically solved recursively and asynchronously by the *ccm* framework at runtime. The framework ensures that all dependent resources are loaded in parallel and no resource is loaded twice. Any dependent resource and data can be loaded cross-domain.

The *ccm* framework and all *ccm* components are versioned and use Semantic Versioning (semver.org). The same *ccm* component can be embedded multiple times in the same web page and also different versions of a component without any conflicts and side effects. That is because each component and version has its own namespace inside a web page. It is also possible to use different versions of the *ccm* framework in the same web page; this ensures backward compatibility.

Each *ccm* component can be provided as mobile web app in two steps: The component is embedded inside the <body> tag of a blank web page. Appropriate HTML <meta> tags to display the web page on mobile devices as native app are added. Then, a user can open the web page and store it as mobile web app on the home screen of a mobile device. In modern browsers the web app specification is stored in a separate standardized manifest file instead of the <meta> tags.

The *ccm* framework provides a service for component developers for data management. It allows the usage of *ccm* datastores. A *ccm* datastore can manage datasets in one of three data levels and can also be used autonomously of *ccm* components for easy data management. The different data levels are described below. *ccm* datastores are intended to be universal and provide a simple uniform API for basic CRUD operations to create, read, update and delete data sets. On the first level the data will be managed in a local object. Then all managed datasets are fugitive data which are gone when leaving the website. On the second level the data will be managed in a client-side database. Than all managed data are still there after page reload. This is specially interesting for offline functionality. On the third level the data will be managed in any server-side database of choice. The server must have a *ccm* compatible interface. Then all managed datasets are stored persistently on a server and they are not bound to a specific client. Different network protocols are possible for communication between client and server. In case of real time communication with the WebSocket protocol for a *ccm* datastore with data level 3, the server informs every active client about changing data sets. Then a *ccm* component which uses such a datastore can react according to these changes, mostly by updating the frontend immediately.

If *ccm* components are using the same *ccm* datastore with data level 3 and WebSocket protocol, then the components are able to exchange data in real time. If the *ccm* components are used in different domains or web-based platforms, this real time communication is cross-domain. This is the technical groundwork for digital learning defined as *Embedded collaborative learning* (ECL): Think of a learning unit that is developed in form of a *ccm* component, so it can be used inside any web-based content. That means it can be embedded inside different virtual learning environments like web-based learning platforms, mobile web apps and websites. Say the learning unit reuses a *ccm* component like chat or team building which is using cross-domain real time communication. This implies that we have real time collaboration between students and educators across virtual learning environments. For example, one student uses the learning unit from the educator website, another one from the university learning platform, another one from a mobile web app and a last one from the actual opened website via Bookmarklet. Despite the different access points, the students can collaborate in real time, which results in embedded collaborative learning across different platforms and devices.

ECL Definition: Embedded collaborative learning is digital learning with learning modules being used collaboratively and autonomously of the platform. The modules are embeddable in any web-based learning environment. Thus, collaboration can occur between all users independently of the web-based learning environments itself (Kless 2015).

Publishing these learning units under a free licence results in an interactive and collaborative Open Education Resource (icOER). Every *ccm* component published as free software can be used in OERs and enrich them with that interactive or collaborative elements. If an icOER uses ECL, a web user can participate in the collaboration from wherever the icOER is used. That means the collaboration is not limited to a single web-based environment, for example a website, an app, a course or even an e-learning platform.

Educators need a way to build web applications for digital learning without the need of computer science knowledge. For this reason, a component developer can build an input mask, in which educators specify configuration data for the component. These input masks are packaged as *ccm* component themselves and are retrieved and used as the other *ccm* components as well. We call these components *factory components*. For every component, a separate factory component serves the need for input of configuration data. Additionally, an educator can also build learning apps in the declarative way by using *ccm* component specific HTML custom tags and attributes.

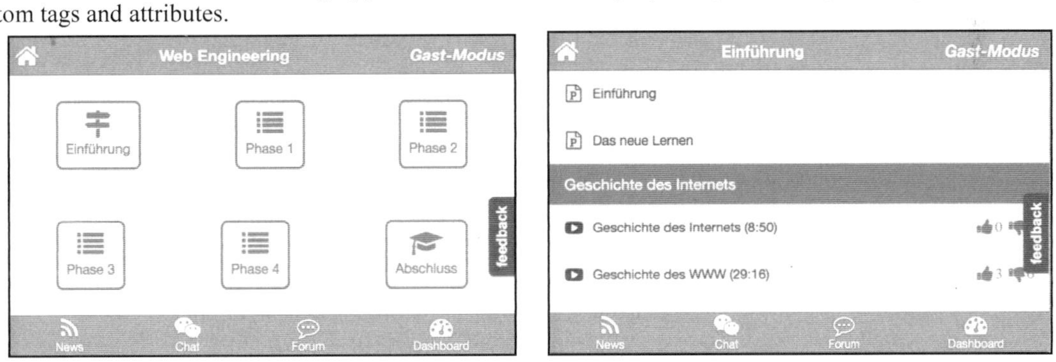

Figure 3. Web Engineering WebApp as *ccm* component aggregated from many *ccm* components

Ccm components are so powerful as one can build complete web apps from them. In our project we have built two course apps as *ccm* component by aggregating existing *ccm* components, specifically components for chat, user input, forum, menu, posts, pie chart, quiz, kanban board, team building, video and rating. A course app is a web app specifically dedicated to a single course. In CCM, a course app is built as a *ccm* component and at the same time a stand-alone mobile web app that can be loaded in any browser just like a web page. Links to the according web apps are http://kaul.inf.h-brs.de/ccm/klr_guest.html and http://kaul.inf.h-brs.de/ccm/we_guest.html. Students can access the course app inside the university learning management system (LMS) or directly via mobile web app or simply via the website. Real time collaboration via chat, kanban board and team building works across all different access points. That means, the course apps realizes ECL.

From *ccm* components complex course material can be aggregated. In our project we developed some OERs based on *ccm* components. The following link is a website where all OERs developed in our project are embedded: akless.github.io/akless/we/.

In our project four universities with different LMSs develop a joint online study program. To overcome the heterogeneity *ccm was the best solution. Ccm* components are reusable in every web-based learning platform, even if the platform does not know it. This was implemented in both legacy web-based learning platforms of our partnering universities, ILIAS and OpenOLAT, in parallel. Figure 4 shows the usage of the *ccm* component for kanban board in both LMSs. The changed content inside the kanban board in ILIAS is immediately updated cross-plattform in realtime at the corresponding kanban board in OpenOLAT.

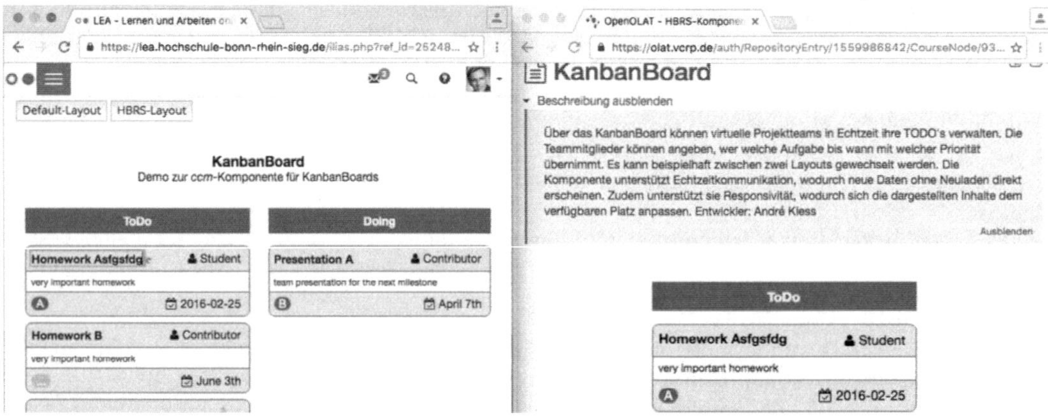

Figure 4. *ccm* component for kanban board embedded in two different LMSs, ILIAS and OpenOLAT

Legacy platforms typically offer some kind of plug-in application programming interface (API) for extending their functionality or for customizing the platform. Plugins were heavily used at our university for customizing the central e-learning platform which serves all educators and students on campus. Unfortunately, with every new release of the platform all custom plugins have to be re-engineered, which turns out to be a very costly procedure. Therefore, our e-learning administrators had to reduce the custom plugins to a bare minimum, which stands in stark contrast to the urgent demand of educators and students who want even more functionality of their platform. Our many years of experience in e-learning support shows that plugins are a too expensive for customizing or extending our platform.

Our solution is the use of HTML5 technology instead. In the HTML5 pages *ccm* components are embedded, thereby, extending the functionality of the legacy platform without necessarily using its API. The new functionality is added to the platform without altering the platform itself. A user cannot distinguish between functionality delivered by the platform and those functions delivered by *ccm* components. As an additional benefit, when changing the underlying platform the HTML5 pages and the *ccm* components can be migrated to the new platform without any re-engineering. If multiple platforms are used, *ccm* components can be used across platforms. In addition, in our project there was a special demand for the use of a best-of-breed wiki platform, because the wiki of the standard e-learning platform was not sophisticated enough. Therefore, all e-learning components, all quizzes and fill-in-the-gap games had to be migrated to the best-of-breed wiki. By using *ccm* components, this task could be achieved without any re-engineering. By focusing on the browser as the target platform instead of the e-learning server platform, technology becomes much more standardized, loosely coupled and can be migrated between different projects, contexts and platforms without re-engineering.

2.3 Apps, Course Apps and interactive E-Books

One of our first course apps we composed from *ccm* components as basic building blocks was for a course in Managerial Accounting in 2015. By using the *ccm* framework we reused *ccm* components that were previously developed for other courses or other purposes. This specific app includes course content quizzes, a forum to communicate with others, a team building component to ensure that participants in the course can find other teammates easily and also focusses on videos that are embedded as the main format to provide the course content. We chose videos as the leading format, because we believed that the success of massive open online courses on platforms like Udacity or Coursera is driven by this visual format.

In 2017 the course evaluations showed the following results: The students were very excited about using a course app. However, they preferred not to use the videos as provided, but additional textbooks for learning. Based on the evaluations and personal feedback, we saw a need to develop a new more text-oriented format for this Managerial Accounting course. The idea of creating an e-book was born. But most e-books are read-only texts with few interaction. We also wanted to offer videos, quizzes, the possibility to give feedback or marks and to communicate with other students or educators within the e-book. Therefore, we developed a course app with the look-and-feel of an e-book instead. According to (NMC 2015), the key features of course apps are mobility, interactivity, engaging design, and integrated analytics. In order to gain experience with other frameworks and to compare it to *ccm*, the open source framework Ionic based on Angular 4 was chosen. Our course app built in Angular combines e-book functionality with interaction components. Ionic enables the development of native apps for all major app stores and PWAs using a single code base. In the pilot version of our e-book, we included videos and quizzes, a forum, a function to write notes and offered links that were embedded directly in the text.

The pilot version of the app was named "@boox" and can be found under "atboox" in the app stores (Apple, Google), which is also available as PWA under www.atboox.de/app. At the time of writing, we are evaluating the use of the app in two courses with about 60 students. Only two participants had actually requested a paper version of the e-book content. Nearly all of the students are nomadic learners who prefer using apps from the stores. Some students preferred to use the PWA on their laptops for working at home or at the university. All in all, evaluations showed a very positive acceptance of this new type of format.

Compared to *ccm*, Angular is much more complex. Angular comprises both, a module and a component concept. Both concepts are solely for decomposing app complexity top-down, not for bottom-up reusability. Angular is about conquering complexity, *ccm* about avoiding and hiding complexity. Transfer of components between Angular projects turned out to be more difficult than between *ccm* projects. Our *ccm* approach is much more oriented towards global reusability and bottom-up design: *ccm* apps are composed bottom-up from reusable *ccm* components offered on a global component marketplace. This fits well with the typical workflow of educators, who have no programming skills: Educators (1) first look on the *ccm* market place for suitable *ccm* components, (2) adapt them via factory components according to their needs and (3) aggregate them building up a composed learning unit. Instead, designing and programming a complex Angular app would not be feasible for them.

2.4 Changes in Learning Environments

The aim of our e-learning project „Work & Study" is developing a new bachelor's degree in Business for non-traditional students.. Four universities of applied sciences in Germany are involved in this research project committed to developing blended learning modules. The challenge encountered was that all partner universities are using different learning management systems or even other platforms: e.g. OpenOLAT, ILIAS or PbWorks, a commercial wiki system. This kind of heterogeneity does not contribute to a convenient teaching and learning environment.

By using *ccm* we were able to develop online learning content and applications that are available in all virtual learning environments. Educators just have to develop their content once with *ccm* and can use it in any platform if needed. *ccm* components can also be combined with each other, quite contrary to apps. This allows educators to go beyond the constraints of one institution and empowers the individual educational setting, giving new freedom to place or move assignments to any place on the web. Embedded collaborative learning is reality in „Work & Study". ECL is needed not only between partner universities but also in international projects, in today´s work settings and in lifelong learning: The digital world forces a new set of skills for learning in both educational and work settings (*digital literacy*). The demand is continuously increasing for highly skilled tasks, for problem solving capabilities and interpersonal skills. Andrew Palmer states "Technological change demands stronger and more continuous connections between education and employment" (Palmer 2017). Lifelong learning is essential nowadays and will continue to play a role in the future. This demands a new technology enabling learning to take place at anytime, anywhere across devices and platforms, across institutional boundaries and work environments.

Ccm provides web components for teaching and learning media that can easily be placed anywhere on the web via *embed code*. This process is easy and sustainable: Once a learning module unit has been developed, the embed code is ready for use on the web. This kind of embedding is well accepted by YouTube users and bloggers. With *ccm* all other kinds of interactive media become embeddable as well. Compared to YouTube that provides a video player, *ccm* offers a universal *web component player*.

Ccm also provides a modular solution to *Learning Analytics*: A *ccm* component for logging browser events can be flexibly combined with any learning component, thereby tracking, filtering and storing browser interactions of this learning component. The collected data can be analyzed with the usual statistical tools afterwards. We are also planning *ccm* components that display analytics for educators.

3. CONCLUSION

The latest advances in web technology have dramatic impact on the way we can search, retrieve, edit, package, recombine, deliver and run e-learning content and applications. Based on the latest W3C standard for web components, we propose a modular kind of e-learning, concerning content, application and media and software packaging as well, which we implemented via our *ccm* framework developing many *ccm* components dedicated to e-learning. From these *ccm* components as basic "Lego-like" building blocks, we have aggregated complete semester courses, course apps and interactive and collaborative Open Educational Resources (icOER). Embedding *ccm* components in web pages, LMSs or e-books results in cross-platform deployment of interactive e-learning content and applications as well as inter-platform collaboration between heterogeneous platforms, yielding embedded collaborative learning (ECL) .

ACKNOWLEDGEMENT

The authors thank their colleague, Regina Brautlacht, for improving the English of the paper, and the German Federal Ministry of Education and Research (BMBF) for funding our research, ref. no. 16OH21056.

REFERENCES

Beck, R., 2008. "What Are Learning Objects?", in: *Learning Objects*, Center for International Education, University of Wisconsin-Milwaukee, http://www4.uwm.edu/cie/learning_objects.cfm?gid=56 on 31 May 2017.

Berners-Lee, T., 2010. Long Live the Web; in: *Scientific American*, Dec. 2010.

Born, C., 2015. *Migration from the ILIAS LMS to the Drupal CMS*, Bachelor Thesis, H-Bonn-Rhein-Sieg.

comScore, 2016. *The State of The U.S. Mobile Market*, 2016 report, http://www.aaaa.org/.

Driscoll, M., 2011. *Node.js and the JavaScript age*, https://gigaom.com/2011/04/11/node-js-and-the-javascript-age/.

Google, 2016. *Progressive Web Apps*, https://developers.google.com/web/progressive-web-apps/ on 1 July 2017.

Kless, A., 2015. *Eingebettetes kollaboratives E-Learning,* Master Thesis, Univ. of App. Sci., Bonn-Rhein-Sieg.

Lawson, B.; Sharp, R., 2011. *Introducing HTML5*, Introducing Polyfills, pp. 276–277.

LearningApps, 2017. *Operation Statistics*, http://verein.learningapps.org/, 1 July 2017.

NMC, 2015. Course Apps, An NMC Horizon Project Strategic Brief, *The New Media Consortium, Volume 2.4*, October 2015, https://www.nmc.org/publication/2015-nmc-strategic-brief-course-apps/ , 25 May 2017.

npmjs, 2017. *Node Package Manager*, https://www.npmjs.com/ .

OECD, 2015. *Students, Computers and Learning: Making the Connection*, OECD Publishing, Paris.

Palmer, A., 2017. Lifelong learning is becoming an economic imperative, in: *The Economist*, 12 Jan 2017.

Pichai, S., 2017. *Google I/O 2017 Keynote*, https://www.youtube.com/watch?v=TUyY2Ng0Yjc , on 25 May 2017.

TC39, 2017. *TC39 - ECMAScript®*, http://www.ecma-international.org/memento/TC39.htm.

WebComponents.org, 2017. *Web Components*, https://www.webcomponents.org/ on 31 May 2017.

WHATWG, 2017. *Web Hypertext Application Technology Working Group (WHATWG)*, https://whatwg.org 1 July 2017.

Work & Study, 2017. *Work and Study - offene Hochschulen Rhein-Saar*, joint project of the universities of applied sciences Koblenz, Worms, Bonn-Rhein-Sieg, Saar; Federal Ministry of Education and Research, ref. no. 16OH21056, http://www.work-and-study.info .

W3C, 2017. Tim Berners-Lee, https://www.w3.org/People/Berners-Lee/ .

W3Techs, 2017. https://w3techs.com/technologies/overview/client_side_language/all .

E-LEARNING INSTRUCTIONAL DESIGN PRACTICE IN AMERICAN AND AUSTRALIAN INSTITUTIONS

Dr Sayed Hadi Sadeghi
Faculty of Education and Social work, The University of Sydney, Asutralia
Project Director of the University of Tehran's human resource development project

ABSTRACT

This research study provides a comparative understanding of instructional design e-practice in an Australian and an American university. This comparative study identifies information relating to the current status of instructional design e-practice that will be of assistance to Australian universities to improve their existing online programs. The study investigated two universities using a quantitative methodological approach. Participants were students, lecturers and admins of one Faculty in an Australian university and one Faculty in an American university engaged with e-learning programs. The instructional design variables, namely clarifying expectations, personalization, learning scenarios, organizing resources and accuracy of materials were investigated for e-practice. The results showed that there were no significant differences in evaluation of the sub factors between Australian and American students and lecturers. American admins evaluated the sub factors of personalization, organizing resources, and accuracy of materials higher than Australians; however, Australian admins evaluated the sub factor of clarifying expectations higher than the Americans. The evaluations of instructional design practice and its sub factors were above average in general in both countries; however, the sub factor of organizing resources was evaluated as poor in the Australian sample and poor and average in the American sample. This indicates that this sub factor needs to improve in both countries.

KEYWORDS

Instructional Design, e-Practice, Australian Institutions, American Institutions

1. INTRODUCTION

According to the latest reports of e-learning status, while the rapid pace of online learning growth has moderated, it still accounted for nearly three-quarters of all US higher education's enrolment increases last year and the education system has strategic plans for the future of it (Allen and Seaman, 2015); for example, Pennsylvania's State System of Higher Education will strive to achieve outcomes by 2020 which include increasing the number of students in online learning to 53,000 (PASSHE, 2014).

Similarly, in Australian institutes, there are many statistics and reports in relation to e-learning growth rate which show that between 2009 and 2014 the online education industry in Australia experienced an annual growth of 14.4% with estimated revenue of over 6 billion dollars (IBS World, 2014). Australian higher education's embrace of the use of e-learning as a vehicle to enhance teaching opportunities and improve learning outcomes is one of the strongest among developed countries in the globalization era. Open universities and distance learning institutions continue to offer students e-learning, using a diverse range of institutional policies to support the promised benefits (Bates, 1997). The providers and educational policy-makers are able to demonstrate that their processes in regard to online learning as a mode of delivery for their programs are sound and effective (Hosie, Schibeci, & Backhaus, 2005; Oliver, 2005). It can be concluded that adoption of online teaching and learning in the Australian higher education sector has been widespread and is now found across a range of disciplines (e.g., business, education, health, psychology, and accounting and information technology) and a range of program levels.

To conclude, with due attention to fast-growing e-learning programs in institutional and pedagogical structures, there is no doubt that comparative studies on virtual learning environments will lead to fundamental change in the educational process, because focusing on a variety of opinions and experiences in different systems and cultures will enable the identification of strategic issues (strength, weakness, opportunity, and threat). Also "the use of comparative studies has become a prominent feature in policymaking and related processes which is characterised by increased technological, information and pedagogical transfer" (Adamson, 2012, p. 641).

According to the evidence, e- practice which is based on instructional strategies can support online courses by developing a standards-based design path (Sadeghi, 2015). The issue of instructional design is "the first important one related to usability and efficiency of a user interface" (Skalka, Drlik & Svec, 2012, p.3). Those e-practices based on instructional design which frame all the elements of the learning process in order to optimise learning and teaching environments are among the most effective (cf. Phipps & Merisotis, 2000; Finger, Jamieson-Proctor & Watson., 2006; Putnam & Borko, 2000; Marshall, 2012). Instructional design e-learning has five sub-factors:

Clear expectations: Learning audiences tend to focus more on learning when e-learning programs are organized with clear expectations (Ku, Akarasriworn, Rice, Glassmeyer, & Mendoza, 2011). Clear explanation is a key to successful e-learning programs because clear explanation helps to prevent misunderstanding of content of learning and tasks (Lee, 2014). Clear objectives, expectations and syllabi prefigure unity between learning activities by describing the learning content, the actions to be taken or performed and how these will be assessed (cf. Phipps & Merisotis, 2000; Holsapple & Lee-Post, 2006; Kala, Isaramalai & Pohthong, 2010; Khan & Granato, 2008; Marshall, 2012; Lee, 2014)

Learning scenarios: Present scenarios of e-learning programs are taking advantage of online web technologies to connect learners and facilitate sharing information in an interoperable way for satisfactory learning experience based on effective scenarios (Santos and Boticario, 2015). As Marshall (2006) explained, the online scenario, which can be considered to be an educational technique, can shape and influence every part of the learning process, both as a means of understanding how students learn and as a tool for guiding the design and aligning learning activities and practices (Masoumi, 2010). The scenarios of online learning should be selected based on the goals of the course, content of modules and effective instructional strategies (cf.Chickering & Gamson, 1987; Duffy, Lowyck & Jonassen, 2012; FitzPatrick, 2012; Kala et al., 2010; Oliver, 2001).

Accuracy of resources: The accuracy of resources sub factor is an important one which is related to the reliability of the instructional materials in e-learning (cf. Phipps & Merisotis, 2000; Holsapple & Lee-Post, 2006; Zhao, 2012).

Organizing resources: Organizing resources incorporates different activities and practices, e.g. sorting or grouping resources of interest in a personal classification system, storing of organized content, at least for the time of use and sharing of the arranged content with peers (Seidel, 2014, p. 6). According to Oliver (2001), Holsapple & Lee-Post (2006) and N. Lee & Rozinah (2009), the main quality issues concerning organizing and structuring learning resources can ultimately determine the effectiveness and efficiency of the learning environment (Masoumi, 2010).

Virtual personalization: In order to improve success in e-learning practice, additional interventions in online programs need to be explored, including those that increase student motivation via personalization (Pemberton & Moallem, 2013). As Martinez (2010) explained, "personalization uses student-specific approaches to address individual needs and expectations to support and promote individual learning success" (Pemberton & Moallem, 2013, p. 908). In fact students' motivation increases as a result of a personalized link between the students and the content, and is directly affected by the manner in which the content is presented to the students (Wlodkowski, 1999). Virtual environments based on students' needs and interests directly affect the learning and teaching process (Klašnja-Milićević, Vesin, Ivanović, & Budimac, 2011; Marshall, 2012; Weld, Adar, Chilton, Hoffmann & Horvitz, 2012; Pemberton & Moallem, 2013).

2. METHOD

A total of 215 participants from an Australian Institute and an American Institute were recruited to take part in this research through an online invitation email asking for volunteers. Of the sample of 215, 99 participants were from an Australian Institute and 116 participants were from an American Institute.

The primary independent variables in this research were the academic positions of participants. The dependent variable was instructional design e-practice. Table 1 is a summary of the demographic makeup of the participants of both countries.

Table 1. Demographic information based on Country

Country	Gender	N	Age	N	Position	N	Experience	N
AUS	Female	59	20 to 30	57	Student	71	Blended and online	62
	Male	40	30 to 40	20	Lecturers	20	Fully online	37
	---	---	40 to 50	22	Admins	8	---	---
	Total	99						
USA	Female	70	20 to 30	42	Student	78	Blended and online	93
	Male	46	30 to 40	48	Lecturers	25	Fully online	23
	---	---	40 to 50	26	Admins	13	---	---
	Total	116						
All Total						215		

The instrument used was a questionnaire self-constructed by the researcher. Exploratory factor analysis was applied to test the validity of the constructed questionnaire.

Participants answered each question by using the Likert scale (1 = Extremely Poor, 2= Poor, 3= Average, 4= Good, 5= Excellent). It is worth mentioning that three versions of the instructional design e-practice questionnaire were presented to participants based on their positions. The factor of instructional design e-practice has 5 sub factors elicited by the items set out in the table below: clarifying expectations, personalisation, learning scenarios, organizing resources, and quality and accuracy (Finger et al., 2006; Marshall, 2012; Phipps & Merisotis, 2000; Putnam & Borko, 2000)

Table 2. Sub-factors, Items and Questions of instructional design e-practice

Sub-Factors	Items
Clarifying expectations	Clear objectives and expectations The outline and syllabus
Learning scenarios	The content of modules Effective instructional strategies
Quality and accuracy	Resources of instructional Reliable materials
Personalization	Personalization
Organizing rescores	Organizing online materials

After obtaining ethical approval, the study was conducted by creating an e- questionnaire of instructional design e-practice using Lime Survey software. The e-learning centres of the Institutes then sent the link of the survey to those lecturers, admins and students who were engaged with online courses. The participants responded to the questionnaire voluntarily.

3. RESULTS OF CURRENT STATUS OF INSTRUCTIONAL DESIGN E-PRACTICE

The instructional design e-practice factor was measured by 5 sub factors namely: clarifying expectations, personalisation, learning scenarios, organizing resources, and quality and accuracy. In this section, the results of each sub factor based on academic position of participants in Australia and America engaged in e-learning courses are reported. Finally the total results of all sub factors of the main factor, instructional design e-practice, are reported.

Clarifying Expectations: Table 3 reports the means and standard deviations regarding the clarifying expectations sub factor based on answers obtained from the academic participants of one faculty in an Australian university and one faculty in a US university. As can be seen in this table, the highest mean, for Australia, belonged to admins (M = 8.37, SD = 0.51). After them, the lecturers reported the clarifying expectations sub factor (M = 7.85, SD = 1.08) as high and the lowest score was reported by students

(M = 7.69, SD = 0.99). To investigate if there are any differences in evaluation of this sub factor between students, lecturers and admins, ANOVA was applied. The results showed that there was no significant main effect of academic position on evaluation of the clarifying expectations sub factor by participants of one faculty in an Australian university [F (2, 98) = 1.79, p = .17]. The results showed that Australian students and lecturers believed clarifying expectations was above average. Also, the admins believed there were excellent clarifying expectations.

Table 3. Mean, SD, and F value of evaluation of clarifying expectations

Country	Students		Lecturers		Admins		*F*	*P*
	M	*SD*	*M*	*SD*	*M*	*SD*		
AUS Participants	7.69	0.99	7.85	1.08	8.37	0.51	1.79	0.17
USA Participants	7.69	0.79	8.04	0.93	5.46	0.96	44.97	.00***

****p*<.001

In one faculty in a US university, as can be seen in this table, the highest mean of answers to the clarifying expectations sub factor belonged to lecturers (M = 8.04, SD = 0.93). After them, students reported this factor next highest (M = 7.69, SD = 0.79) and the lowest score was reported by the admins (M = 5.46, SD = 0.96). To investigate if there are any differences in evaluation of the clarifying expectations sub factor between American students, lecturers and admins, ANOVA was applied. The results showed that there was significant main effect of academic position on evaluation of the clarifying expectations sub factor by participants of one faculty in a US university [F (2, 115) = 44.97, p = .00]. An LSD test showed that admins evaluated this sub factor significantly lower than students and lecturers. There were no differences between the evaluation of lecturers and students. The results showed that American admins believed clarifying expectations to be average. However, the students believed this sub factor was above average. On the other hand the lecturers believed there were excellent clarifying expectations.

Comparing the answers of participants of one faculty in an Australian university and one faculty in a US university showed that there were significant differences in evaluation of the clarifying expectations sub factor between Australian and American admins [F (1, 20) = 60.94, p = .00]; Australians significantly evaluated it higher than Americans. However, the results of ANOVA revealed that there was no significant difference in evaluation of this sub factor between Australian and American lecturers [F (1, 44) = 0.42, p = .51]. An ANOVA test showed that there was no significant difference in evaluation of the clarifying expectations sub factor between Australian and American students [F (1, 148) = 0.00, p = .99].

Overall, as shown in Figure 1, American and Australian students believed clarifying expectations to be above average. On the other hand, the American lecturers assessed this sub factor as excellent but Australian lecturers assessed clarifying expectations as above average. Surprisingly, the American admins gave an average assessment to clarifying expectations but Australian admins believed clarifying expectations was excellent.

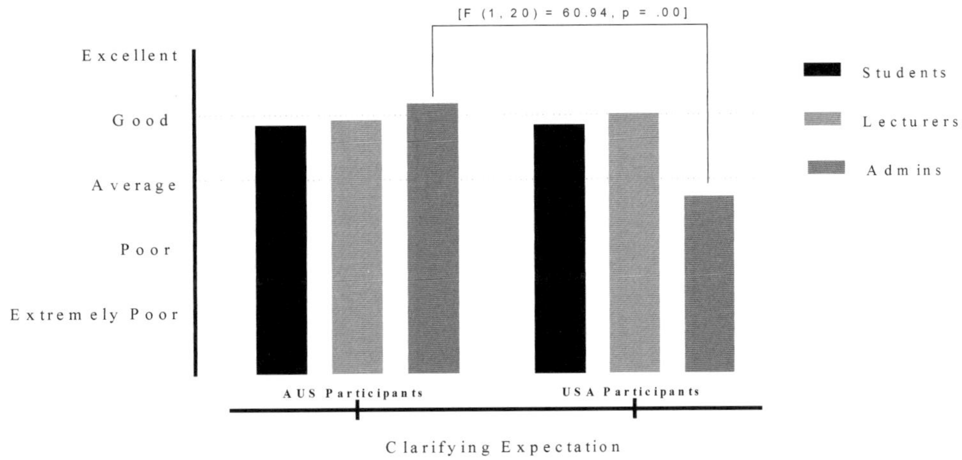

Figure 1. Mean level of clarifying expectation

Virtual Personalization: Table 4 reports the means and standard deviations of the personalization sub factor based on the academic participants of one faculty in an Australian university and one faculty in a US university. As can be seen in this table, the highest mean of the personalization sub factor belonged to admins (M = 3.37, SD = 0.51). After them, the students reported the personalization sub factor (M = 2.98, SD = 0.58) as high and the lowest score was reported by lecturers (M = 2.70, SD = 0.57). To investigate if there are any differences in evaluation of the personalization sub factor between students, lecturers and admins, ANOVA was applied. The results showed that there was significant main effect of academic position on evaluation of this sub factor by participants of one faculty in an Australian university [F (2, 98) = 4.29, p = .01]. An LSD test revealed that lecturers evaluated this sub factor significantly lower than admins and students; however, there were no differences in evaluation of this sub factor between students and admins. The results showed that Australian students and lecturers believed personalization to be at an average level. However, the admins believed that personalization was above average.

Table 4. Mean, SD, and F value of evaluation of Virtual Personalization

Country	Students		Lecturers		Admins		*F*	*P*
	M	*SD*	*M*	*SD*	*M*	*SD*		
AUS Participants	2.98	0.58	2.70	0.57	3.37	0.51	4.29	.01*
USA Participants	3.11	0.62	2.44	0.69	4.23	0.43	34.98	.00***

*p<.05
***p<.001

In one faculty in a US university, as can be seen in this table, the highest mean of responses to the personalization sub factor belonged to admins (M = 4.23, SD = 0.43). After them, students reported this factor next highest (M = 3.11, SD = 0.62) and the lowest score was reported by the lecturers (M = 2.44, SD = 0.69). To investigate if there are any differences in evaluation of the sub factor between American students, lecturers and admins, ANOVA was applied. The results showed that there was a significant effect of academic position on evaluation of the personalization sub factor by participants of one faculty in a US university [F (2, 115) = 34.98, p = .00]. An LSD test showed that admins evaluated the personalization sub factor significantly higher than students and lecturers. Also, students evaluated this sub factor significantly higher than lecturers. The results showed that all participants of one faculty in a US university had different assessments. The students believed it to be above average, the lecturers believed average and the admins believed excellent.

Comparing the answers of participants of one faculty in an Australian university and one faculty in a US university showed that there were significant differences in evaluation of the personalization sub factor between Australian and American admins [F (1, 20) = 16.47, p = .001]; Americans significantly evaluated it higher than Australians that shown in Figure 2. However, the results of ANOVA revealed that there was no significant difference in evaluation of this sub factor between Australian and American lecturers [F (1, 44) = 1.67, p = .20]. An ANOVA test showed that there was no significant difference in evaluation of the personalization sub factor between Australian and American students [F (1, 148) = 0.00, p = .99]. Overall, comparing the results showed that Australian and American lecturers believed personalization practice to be average. The American students assessed it as above average but Australian students placed it at an average level. On the other hand, American admins assessed this sub factor as excellent while Australian admins assessed it above average.

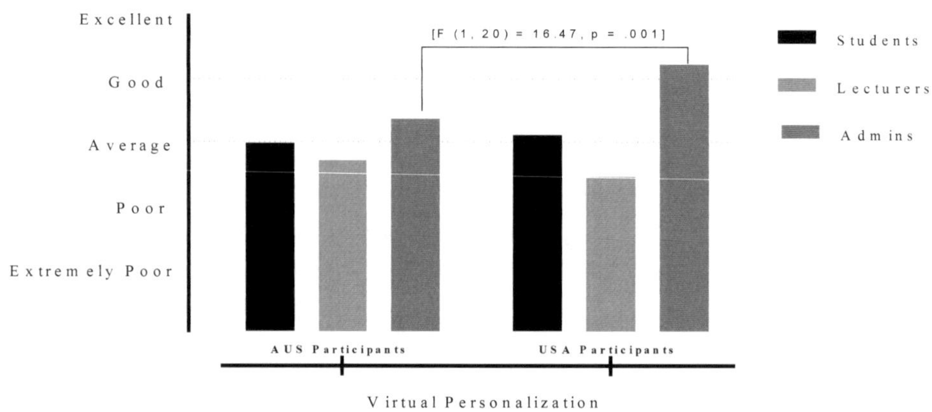

Figure 2. Mean level of virtual personalization

Learning Scenarios: Table 5 reports the means and standard deviations regarding the learning scenarios sub factor based on the academic participants of one faculty in an Australian university and one faculty in a US university. As can be seen in this table, the highest mean of the learning scenarios sub factor belonged to admins (M = 7.12, SD = 1.12). After them, the lecturers reported this sub factor (M = 6.95, SD = 1.35) as high and the lowest score was reported by students (M = 6.63, SD = 1.04). To investigate if there are any differences in evaluation of the learning scenarios sub factor between students, lecturers and admins, ANOVA was applied. The results showed that there was no significant effect of academic position on evaluation of the learning scenarios sub factor by participants of one faculty in an Australian university [F (2, 98) = 1.14, p = .32]. The results showed that all participants of one faculty in an Australian university believed learning scenarios to be above average.

Table 5. Mean, SD, and F value of evaluation of learning scenarios

Country	Students		Lecturers		Admins		*F*	*P*
	M	*SD*	*M*	*SD*	*M*	*SD*		
AUS Participants	6.63	1.04	6.95	1.35	7.12	1.12	1.14	.32
USA Participants	7.18	0.98	8.00	0.91	6.61	0.65	10.97	.00***

***p<.001

In one faculty in a US university, as can be seen in this table, the highest mean of responses to the learning scenarios sub factor belonged to lecturers (M = 8.00, SD = 0.91). After them, students reported this factor next highest (M = 7.18, SD = 0.98) and the lowest score was reported by the admins (M = 6.61, SD = 0.65). To investigate if there are any differences in evaluation of this sub factor between American students, lecturers and admins, ANOVA was applied. The results showed that there was a significant effect of academic position on evaluation of the learning scenarios sub factor by participants of one faculty in a US university [*F* (2, 115) = 10.97, *p* = .00]. An LSD test showed that lecturers evaluated the learning scenarios sub factor significantly higher than students and admins. Also, students evaluated this sub factor significantly higher than admins. The results showed that American students and admins believed learning scenarios to be above average. However, the lecturers believed learning scenarios were excellent.

Comparing the answers of participants of one faculty in an Australian university and one faculty in a US university showed that there were no significant differences in evaluation of the learning scenarios sub factor between Australian and American admins [*F* (1, 20) = 1.75, *p* = .20]. However, the results of ANOVA revealed that there was significant difference in evaluation of it between Australian and American lecturers [*F* (1, 44) = 9.58, *p* = .003]; Americans evaluated this sub factor significantly higher than Australians. An ANOVA test showed significant difference in evaluation of the learning scenarios sub factor between Australian and American students [*F* (1, 148) = 11.09, *p* = .001]; American students evaluated this sub factor significantly higher than Australian students that shown in Figure 3. Overall, comparing the results showed that all participants of one faculty in an Australian university and American students and admins believed learning scenarios practice was above average. However, the American lecturers believed learning scenarios practice was at an excellent level.

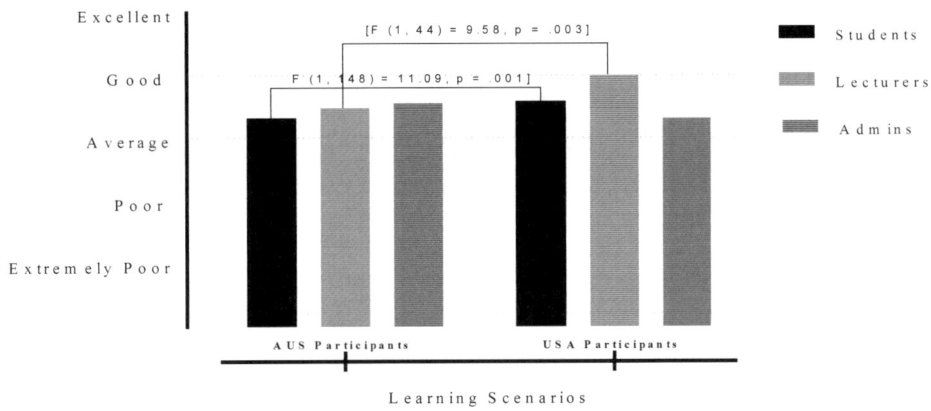

Figure 3. Mean level of learning scenarios

Organizing Resources: Table 6 reports the means and standard deviations of the organizing resources sub factor based on the academic participants of one faculty in an Australian university and one faculty in a US university. As can be seen in this table, in Australia, the highest mean of the organizing resources sub factor belonged to admins (M = 3.87, SD = 0.35). After them, the lecturers reported this sub factor (M = 3.25, SD = 0.85) as high and the lowest score was reported by students (M = 3. 22, SD = 0.65). To investigate if there are any differences in evaluation of the organizing resources sub factor between students, lecturers and admins, ANOVA was applied. The results showed that there was a significant effect of academic position on evaluation of the organizing resources sub factor by participants of one faculty in an Australian university [F (2, 98) = 3.26, p = .094]. An LSD test showed that admins evaluated this sub factor significantly higher than lecturers and students. However, there were no differences in evaluation of this sub factor between students and lecturers. The results showed that all participants of one faculty in an Australian university had the same assessment namely that organizing resources were poor.

Table 6. Mean, SD, and F value of evaluation of organizing resources

Country	Students		Lecturers		Admins		*F*	*P*
	M	*SD*	*M*	*SD*	*M*	*SD*		
AUS Participants	3. 22	0.65	3.25	0.85	3.87	0.35	3.26	.094
USA Participants	3.39	0.62	3.45	0.46	4.61	0.50	24.76	.00***

***p<.001

In one faculty in a US university, as can be seen in this table, the highest mean of responses to the organizing resources sub factor belonged to admins ($M = 4.61$, $SD = 0.50$). After them, lecturers reported this factor next highest ($M = 3.45$, $SD = 0.46$) and the lowest score was reported by the students ($M = 3.39$, $SD = 0.62$). To investigate if there are any differences in evaluation of the organizing resources sub factor between American students, lecturers and admins, ANOVA was applied. The results showed that there was a significant effect of academic position on evaluation of the organizing resources sub factor by participants of one faculty in a USA university [F (2, 115) = 24.76, p = .00]. An LSD test showed that admins evaluated it significantly higher than lecturers and students. There were no differences between the evaluations of lecturers and students. The results showed that American students and lecturers believed organizing resources practice was poor. However, the admins believed organizing resources practice was at an average level.

Comparing the answers of participants of one faculty in an Australian university and one faculty in a US university showed that there were significant differences in evaluation of the organizing resources sub factor between Australian and American admins [F (1, 20) = 13.05, p = .002]; Americans significantly evaluated this sub factor higher than Australians that shown in Figure 4. However, the results of ANOVA revealed that there was no significant difference in evaluation of the organizing resources sub factor between Australian and American lecturers [F (1, 44) = 1.04, p = .31]. Also, an ANOVA test showed that there was no significant difference in evaluation of it between Australian and American students [F (1, 148) = 2.60, p = .10]. Overall, comparing the results showed that all participants of one faculty in an Australian university and American students and lecturers believed organizing resources practice was at a poor level. However, the American admins believed organizing resources practice to be average.

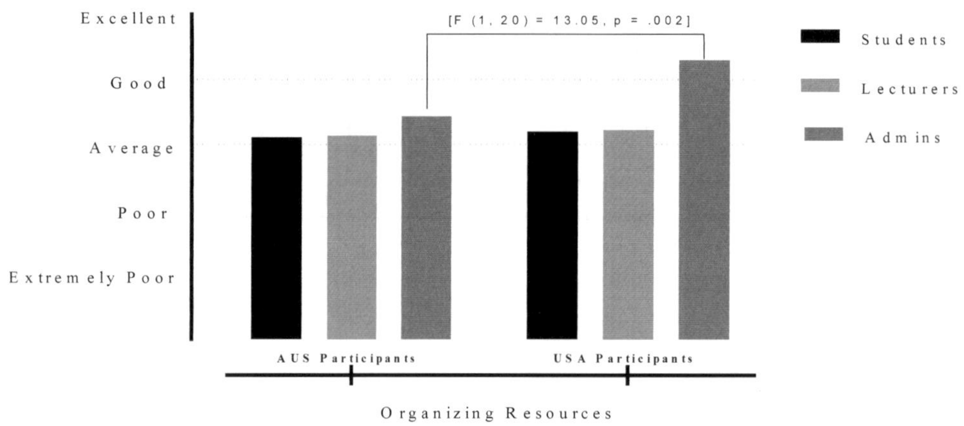

Figure 4. Mean level of organizing resources

Quality and Accuracy Materials: Table 7 reports the means and standard deviations of the accuracy materials sub factor based on the academic participants of one faculty in an Australian university and one faculty in a US university. As can be seen in this table, in Australia, the highest mean of accuracy materials belonged to admins ($M = 7.00$, $SD = 0.92$). After them, the students reported accuracy materials ($M = 6.14$, $SD = 0.94$) as high and the lowest score was reported by lecturers ($M = 5.75$, $SD = 1.33$). To investigate if there are any differences in evaluation of accuracy materials between students, lecturers and admins, ANOVA was applied. The results showed that there was a significant effect of academic position on evaluation of accuracy materials by participants of one faculty in an Australian university [F (2, 98) = 4.19, p = .01]. An LSD test illustrated that admins evaluated this sub factor significantly higher than students and lecturers; however, there were no significant differences on evaluation of this sub factor between students and lecturers. The results showed that Australian students and admins believed that accuracy materials are at an above average level. However, the lecturers believed accuracy materials were only average.

Table 7. Mean, SD, and F value of evaluation of accuracy materials

Country	Students		Lecturers		Admins		*F*	*P*
	M	*SD*	*M*	*SD*	*M*	*SD*		
AUS Participants	6.14	0.94	5.75	1.33	7.00	0.92	4.19	.01*
USA Participants	6.20	0.76	5.11	1.19	8.46	0.96	60.24	.00***

*$p<.05$ ***$p<.001$

In one faculty in a US university, as can be seen in this table, the highest mean of answers regarding the accuracy materials belonged to admins ($M = 8.46$, $SD = 0.96$). Next highest came students' reports of this factor ($M = 6.20$, $SD = 0.76$) and the lowest score was reported by the lecturers ($M = 5.11$, $SD = 1.19$). To investigate if there are any differences in evaluation of accuracy materials between American students, lecturers and admins, ANOVA was applied. The results showed that there was a significant effect of academic position on evaluation of accuracy materials by participants of one faculty in a US university [F (2, 115) = 60.24, p = .00]. An LSD test showed that admins evaluated accuracy materials significantly higher than lecturers and students. Also, students evaluated this sub factor significantly higher than lecturers. The results showed that American students believed this sub factor was at an above average level, the lecturers believed it was at an average level and the admins believed accuracy materials practice was excellent.

Comparing the answers of participants of one faculty in an Australian university and one faculty in a US university showed that there were significant differences in evaluation of accuracy materials between Australian and American admins [F (1, 20) = 11.66, p = .003]; Americans significantly evaluated accuracy materials higher than Australians that shown in Figure 5. However, the results of ANOVA revealed that there was no significant difference in evaluation of accuracy materials between Australian and American lecturers [F (1, 44) = 2.85, p = .09]. To continue, an ANOVA test showed that there was no significant difference in evaluation of accuracy materials between Australian and American students [F (1, 148) = 0.21, p = .64]. Overall, comparing the results showed that Australian students and lecturers as well as American students and lecturers had the same perspective in that they believed accuracy materials practice to be above average. The Australian admins believed accuracy materials practice was above average however, the American admins believed there was an excellent level of accuracy materials.

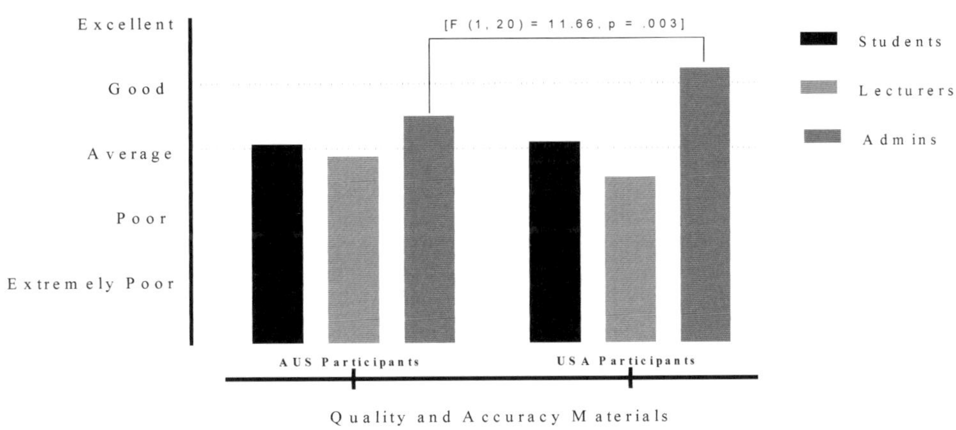

Figure 5. Mean level of quality and accuracy materials

4. FINAL RESULT AND CONCLUSION

Table 8 reports the means and standard deviations of the instructional design practice factor based on the academic participants of one faculty in an Australian university and one faculty in a US university. As can be seen in this table, the highest mean of instructional design practice belonged to admins (*M* = 29.75, *SD* = 1.83). After them, the students reported instructional design practice (*M* = 26.67, *SD* = 2.50) as high and the lowest score was reported by lecturers (*M* = 26.50, *SD* = 2. 60). To investigate if there are any differences in evaluation of instructional design practice between students, lecturers and admins, ANOVA was applied. The results showed that there was a significant effect of academic position on evaluation of instructional design practice by participants of one faculty in an Australian university [F (2, 98) = 5.83, p = .004]. An LSD test showed that admins evaluated this factor significantly higher than students and lecturers but there were no significant differences in evaluation of this factor between students and lecturers. Overall, regarding the level of practice assessment, it seems that all participants of one faculty in an Australian university had the same assessment placing it in an above average level.

Table 8. Mean, SD, and F value of evaluation of instructional design e-practice

Country	Students		Lecturers		Admins		*F*	*P*
	M	*SD*	*M*	*SD*	*M*	*SD*		
AUS Participants	26.67	2.50	26.50	2. 60	29.75	1.83	5.83	.004**
USA Participants	27.59	2.23	27.06	2.21	29.38	1.75	5.01	.008**

**p<.01

In one faculty in a US university, as can be seen in this table, the highest mean of responses to instructional design practice belonged to admins (*M* = 29.38, *SD* = 1.75). After them, students reported this factor next highest (M = 27.59, SD = 2.23) and the lowest score was reported by the lecturers (M = 27.06, SD = 2.21). To investigate if there are any differences in evaluation of instructional design practice between American students, lecturers and admins, ANOVA was applied. The results showed that there was a significant effect of academic position on evaluation of instructional design practice by participants of one faculty in a US university [F (2, 115) = 5.01, p = .008]. An LSD test showed that admins evaluated this factor significantly higher than students and lecturers but there were no significant differences in evaluation of this factor between students and lecturers. The results showed that all participants of one faculty in a US university gave it the same assessment namely above average.

Comparing the answers of participants of one faculty in an Australian university and one faculty in a US university showed that there were significant differences in evaluation of instructional design practice between Australian and American admins. Furthermore, the results of ANOVA revealed that there was no significant difference in evaluation of instructional design practice between Australian and American lecturers. However, ANOVA test showed that there was significant difference in evaluation of instructional design practice between Australian and American students; American students evaluated instructional design practice significantly higher than Australian students. All participants of one faculty in an Australian and one faculty in a US university gave the same assessment namely that instructional design practice was above average.

According to the result of this study the evaluations of instructional design practice and its sub factors were above average in general in both countries; however, the sub factor of organizing resources was evaluated as poor in the Australian sample and as poor and average in the American sample. This indicates that this sub factor needs to be improved in both countries. American students evaluated the factor of instructional design e-practice higher than Australian students, however, lecturers and admins evaluated this factor in both countries the same. Also, American students and lecturers evaluated the sub factor of learning scenarios higher than Australians. There were no significant differences in evaluation of the remaining sub factors between Australian and American students and lecturers. American admins evaluated the sub factors of personalization, organizing resources, and accuracy materials higher than Australians; however, Australian admins evaluated the sub factor of clarifying expectations higher than the Americans. Based on these results it seems that the quality of instructional design e-learning practice in America is higher than in Australia.

AUTHOR'S DECLARATION

This research meets the University of Sydney's Human Research Ethics Committee (HREC) requirements for the conduct of research. Project Approved Number: 2013/669
The authors declare that they have no conflict of interest.

REFERENCES

Adamson, B. (2012). International comparative studies in teaching and teacher education. *Teaching and teacher education*, *28*(5), 641-648.

Allen, I. E., & Seaman, J. (2015). Grade level: Tracking online education in the United States. *Babson Park, MA: Babson Survey Research Group. Accessed March, 10*, 2015. Retrieved from http://www.onlinelearningsurvey.com/reports/gradelevel.pdf

Bates, T. (1997). *Restructuring the university for technological change* (pp. 78-101). Murdoch University.

Chickering, A. W., & Gamson, Z. F. (1987). Seven principles for good practice in undergraduate education. *AAHE bulletin*, *3*, 7.

Duffy, T. M., Lowyck, J., & Jonassen, D. H. (2012). *Designing environments for constructive learning*. Springer.

Finger, G., Jamieson-Proctor, R., & Watson, G. (2006). Measuring learning with ICTs: an external evaluation of Education Queensland's ICT curriculum integration performance measurement instrument. In *Proceedings of the Australian Association for Research in Education Annual Conference (AARE 2005)*. Australian Association for Research in Education.

FitzPatrick, T. (2012). Key Success Factors of eLearning in Education: A Professional Development Model to Evaluate and Support eLearning. *Online Submission*.

Holsapple, C. W., & Lee-Post, A. (2006). Defining, Assessing, and promoting e-learning success: an information systems perspective. *Decision Sciences Journal of Innovative Education*, *4*(1), 67-85.

Hosie, P., Schibeci, R., & Backhaus, A. (2005). A framework and checklists for evaluating online learning in higher education. *Assessment & Evaluation in Higher Education*, *30*(5), 539-553.

IBS World. (2014). *Online education in Australia*: Market research report. In a. X008 (Ed.), Retrieved from http://www.ibisworld.com.au/industry/default.aspx?indid=1907

Kala, S., Isaramalai, S.-a., & Pohthong, A. (2010). Electronic learning and constructivism: A model for nursing education. *Nurse Education Today*, *30*(1), 61-66

Khan, B. H., & Granato, L. A. (2008). Program evaluation in e-learning: Retrieved from http://asianvu.com/bk/elearning_evaluation_article.pdf

Klašnja-Milićević, A., Vesin, B., Ivanović, M., & Budimac, Z. (2011). E-Learning personalization based on hybrid recommendation strategy and learning style identification. *Computers & Education, 56*(3), 885-899.

Ku, H. Y., Akarasriworn, C., Rice, L. A., Glassmeyer, D. M., & Mendoza, B. (2011). Teaching an online graduate mathematics education course for in-service mathematics teachers. *Quarterly Review of Distance Education*, *12*(2), 135.

Lee, J. (2014). An exploratory study of effective online learning: Assessing satisfaction levels of graduate students of mathematics education associated with human and design factors of an online course. *The International Review of Research in Open and Distributed Learning*, *15*(1).

Lee, N., & Rozinah, J. (2009). Developing and validating an instrument to assess the e-learning environment at a public higher education institution in Malaysia. *Measuring Business Excellence*, *12*(3), 56-75. Retrieved from http://www.emeraldinsight.com/doi/abs/10.1108/13683040810900403

Marshall, S. J. (2006). *eMM version two process assessment workbook.* Report to the New Zealand Ministry of Education, Wellington: Victoria University of Wellington.

Marshall, S. J. (2012). An analytic framework to support e. learning strategy development. *Campus-Wide Information Systems*, *29*(3), 177-188.

Martinez, M. (2010). Adaptive and personalized learning: Supporting individual learning differences. *The Training Place.* Retrieved from http://www.trainingplace.com/source/research/masspersonalization.htm.

Masoumi, D. (2010). *Quality in e-learning in a cultural context: The case of Iran*. Department of Education, Communication and Learning; Institutionen för pedagogik, kommunikation och lärande.. Retrieved from https://gupea.ub.gu.se/bitstream/2077/22173/1/gupea_2077_22173_1.pdf.

Oliver, R. (2001). Developing e-learning environments that support knowledge construction in higher education. In S. Stoney & J. Burn (Eds). *Working for excellence in the e-conomy*, 407-416. Churchlands: Australia, We-B Centre. Retrieved from http://ro.ecu.edu.au/ecuworks/4766/

Oliver, R. (2005). Quality assurance and e-learning: blue skies and pragmatism. *Research in Learning Technology*, *13*(3).

PASSHE . (2014). *Strategic Plan 2020 (Rising to the Challenge).* Pennsylvania's State System of Higher Education.Retrieved from http://www.passhe.edu/inside/bog/Documents/Strategic%20Plan%202020%20Rising%20to%20the%20Challenge_10-14.pdf

Pemberton, A. & Moallem, M. (2013). The impact of personalized learning on motivation in online learning. In R. McBride & M. Searson (Eds.), *Proceedings of Society for Information Technology & Teacher Education International Conference* ,907-914. Chesapeake, VA: Association for the Advancement of Computing in Education (AACE).Retrieved from http://www.editlib.org/p/48228/

Phipps, R., & Merisotis, J. (2000). *Quality on the line: Benchmarks for success in internet-based distance education.* The Institute for Higher Education Policy, 1-45. ERIC. Retrieved from http://eric.ed.gov/?id=ED444407

Phipps, R., & Merisotis, J. (2000). *Quality on the line: Benchmarks for success in internet-based distance education.* The Institute for Higher Education Policy, 1-45. ERIC. Retrieved from http://eric.ed.gov/?id=ED444407

Putnam, R. T., & Borko, H. (2000). What do new views of knowledge and thinking have to say about research on teacher learning?. *Educational researcher*, *29*(1), 4-15.

Sadeghi, S. H. (2015). The current status of pedagogical e-practice in an Australian university context. *International Journal of Advanced and Applied Sciences*. *2*(10), 70-74. Retrieved from http://www.science-gate.com/IJAAS/Articles/2015-2-10/08%202015-2-10-pp.70-74.pdf

Santos, O. C., & Boticario, J. G. (2015). User-centred design and educational data mining support during the recommendations elicitation process in social online learning environments. *Expert Systems*, *32*(2), 293-311.

Seidel, N. (2014). Interaction design patterns for design and development of video learning environments. In *Proceedings of the 19th European Conference on Pattern Languages of Programs, 20*. ACM.

Skalka, J., Drlik, M., & Svec, P. (2012). E-learning courses quality evaluation framework as part of quality assurance in higher education. In *Interactive Collaborative Learning (ICL), 2012 15th International Conference on, 1-5*. IEEE. DOI: 10.1109/ICL.2012.6402173

Weld, D. S., Adar, E., Chilton, L., Hoffmann, R., & Horvitz, E. (2012). Personalized Online Education—A Crowdsourcing Challenge. *Paper presented at the Workshops at the Twenty-Sixth AAAI Conference on Artificial Intelligence*.

Wlodkowski, R. (1999). *Enhancing adult motivation to learn: A comprehensive guide for teaching all adults.* San Francisco, CA: Jossey-Bass Publishers.

Zhou, Y. (2012). Towards Capability Maturity Model of e-Learning Process. *Intelligent Information Management*, *4*(4).

A GAME BASED E-LEARNING SYSTEM TO TEACH ARTIFICIAL INTELLIGENCE IN THE COMPUTER SCIENCES DEGREE

Amable de Castro-Santos[1], Waldo Fajardo[2] and Miguel Molina-Solana[3]
[1]*Universidad de Granada, Granada, Spain*
[2]*Universidad de Granada Dept. Computer Science and Artificial Intelligence, Granada, Spain*
[3]*Data Science Institute, Imperial College, London, UK*

ABSTRACT

Our students taking the Artificial Intelligence and Knowledge Engineering courses often encounter a large number of problems to solve which are not directly related to the subject to be learned. To solve this problem, we have developed a game based e-learning system. The elected game, that has been implemented as an e-learning system, allows to develop Artificial Intelligence Decision Making Systems of very diverse complexity level. The e-learning system discharges the students of doing work not directly related with the Artificial Intelligence and Knowledge Engineering problems. This way, students can try their development and self-evaluate their progression level. The results obtained after using this e-learning system with the students (during the Artificial Intelligence and Knowledge Engineering course) show a substantial improvement in students' learning outcomes.

KEYWORDS

E-learning, Collaborative Learning, Problem-based Learning, Game-based Learning, Artificial Intelligence Learning

1. INTRODUCTION

Computer science students are usually very willing to study subjects related to software development but when they deal with subjects with more abstract content, such as Artificial Intelligence and Knowledge Engineering, they often struggle. This means that the students usually require a greater number of hours for their learning, so the application of distance education systems in these subjects is clearly indicated, since they provide the student with a greater temporal availability of information.

However, given the type of subject to which we refer and the type of skills to be acquired, it is not enough for this distance learning to use a classic tool that is limited to improving access to content or providing exchange information forums. Recently the concept of community within the courses has been taking force. These communities enhance the collaborative learning. In this way, the students themselves actively participate in the training by providing information and valuing the work of their peers (Fajardo et al. 2015).

The present work describes the initial assessment, the development, and the final results from the innovation project carried out in the context of the Artificial Intelligence and Knowledge Engineering courses, within the Computer Engineering degree. The implemented platform enables students to develop and test their work, in individual and cooperative ways, on intelligent systems for decision making. The advantages of using a game as the platform are, among others, a higher motivation from students and a limited domain that does not need external experts.

After using the e-learning systems (developed to address the practical contents of the courses), the results from evaluations clearly justify the work carried out.

This paper is organized as follows. Firstly, in Section 2 we provide some background about both Artificial Intelligence and Knowledge Engineering which are the subjects for which the e-learning system have been developed. This section also introduces the characteristics of the game elected to develop the system. In section 3, we briefly explain the game based e-learning system, its operation and the benefits that it brings to students. Section 4 presents the academic results before and after the students use the developed system. Finally, Section 5 points out some conclusions and further developments.

2. BACKGROUND

Artificial Intelligence aims to reproduce human behavior through computational systems. In this way, it tries to obtain systems that are able to respond to consultations or situations as if they were a human being.

Artificial Intelligence reached great achievements with the development of Expert Systems (Ignizio, 1991). Knowledge Engineering is the area of Artificial Intelligence that works on the development of Expert Systems or Systems Based on Knowledge (Frost, 1986). Knowledge Engineering focuses its efforts on the development of high performance systems specializing in certain professional domains and researches methods and techniques to develop man-machine systems with expert problem solvers.

Feigenbaum presented the following two fundamentals ideas in the International Joint Conference on Artificial Intelligence of 1977 (Feigenbaum, 1977):

- The power of an expert system derives from the knowledge it possesses, not from the particular formalisms and inference schemes it employs.
- Expert knowledge provides the key to high productivity, while knowledge representations and inference schemes provide the necessary mechanisms for their use.

Traditionally, for the coursework of the Knowledge Engineering course, students develop prototypes of systems capable of performing decision-making using context information. These assignments have the following problems:

- There are no human experts who students could apply techniques of acquisition of knowledge for the later modeling of a system.
- It is necessary to choose an area of knowledge in which to make decisions. As they are real areas of knowledge, they are not bounded. For this reason, a lot of time is spent in the work of information retrieval and little in the development of Artificial Intelligence techniques.
- Students spend a lot of time developing visual interfaces. This interface is not the fundamental part of his work for this course but it is a necessary part to assess the proper functioning of his work.
- Usually, the motivation of the students reflects on their interest for the elected topic to develop the prototype, and not all the topics proposed by students are equally valid for the development of the practices.

To tackle these problems, we have decided to change the work to develop and in this change one of the priorities is to do more attractive the work to develop to pass the course.

2.1 Games, Artificial Intelligence and Engineering

Traditionally, game playing has been an area of research in Artificial Intelligence. Games such as checkers and chess have been used to prove the power of Artificial Intelligence methods since the beginning (Schaeffer, 2008). There are references of this research since the 50s (Copeland, 2000). To highlight the achievements of these works we can mention the defeat of Garry Kaspárov by IBM's Deep Blue computer in 1997 (McCorduck, 2004).

From the early days to the present, Artificial Intelligence in games has evolved notability. Today is unthinkable to develop a game that does not have any Artificial Intelligence in it. The use of Artificial Intelligence in videogames is making a better user experience. Now, the quality of Artificial Intelligence is a high-ranking feature for game fans in making their purchase decisions and an area with incredible potential to increase players' immersion and fun (Nayerek, 2004).

The use of Artificial Intelligent in the software development gets results that are far from repetitive models and patterns. For this reason, Artificial Intelligence techniques are used every day in any area that aims to simulate human behavior, from video games to computer animation. Scenes of movies as famous as The Lord of the Rings or Avatar include Artificial Intelligence in their development.

In addition to the previous information we can say that games have been used in the education of engineering students and professionals for decades (Hauge et al., 2012). Similarly, a variety of games have been developed and proved successful for the mediation of skills in complex systems (Windhoff, 2001).

After these reasons, using games as a tool to teach Artificial Intelligence and Knowledge Engineering is clearly justified. But we also think that games are highly attractive to students, both from the perspective of the game itself, and from the perspective of doing the work to get specific milestones.

In this way, we have changed the work to pass the subject's coursework. Now the student should develop a prototype of intelligent player of a tactical game. This idea is based on the fact that games have traditionally been of fundamental importance in the research of Artificial Intelligence. The development of a game is reduced to a set of decisions making in a bounded environment, depending on the information provided throughout the game. The complexity level of the universes where the games run can be very different. Games can also reproduce environment and situations with a high level of realism and, in addition, it is a well-known fact the addiction that games can generate on their players.

For these reasons, we have designed and developed a parametric game based e-learning system to use for the coursework of the aforementioned courses. In this system, the game is the main component. This e-learning system enables the interaction between humans and automatic gamers (prototypes of decision making systems) developed by the students.

2.2 The Elected Game

To implement the coursework over a game, we have to guarantee that it fulfills a set of fundamental characteristics. The chosen game must be attractive (addictive if it is possible), complex enough to ensure that the student may develop such sophisticated systems as their personal capacity will allow, and parametric to ensure that the game features change for different years.

To meet our needs, we have chosen a tactical game in which a set of robots fight a battle on a particular terrain. At each moment of the game, players must make decisions based on the terrain, the state of the robot and its location on the map.

We can see that the use of the chosen game as an environment for the realization of the subject's practices guarantees the solution to the problems previously discussed because now:

- Instructor and students themselves become experts, so students can apply knowledge acquisition techniques for later develop making decision systems.
- Now the scope is clearly bounded, so students can spend much more time applying artificial intelligence techniques.
- As the e-learning system has an interface, the students do not need to develop it. Again, the students have more time to spend developing the artificial intelligence techniques for their own decision-making system.
- Usually a game is an interesting topic to develop thus achieving greater student motivation. As the game has been specifically chosen for this coursework, it is appropriate to teach decision making systems to the students, and it has the same complexity level to all of them.

3. THE GAME BASED E-LEARNING SYSTEM

For all the above, the main goal has been to develop and introduce a specific e-learning system to be used for the coursework of the Knowledge Engineering course. The system takes the form of an on-line game with a graphical interface that allows to the students to test their pieces of coursework in an individual and cooperative form. This way, coursework changes from developing an intelligent decision-making system in an unspecified domain to developing an intelligent player capable of make decisions in the on-line game. For this, the students develop a multiagent system (Wooldridge, 2009) that is later uploaded by a web interface to our e-learning system.

The game has been developed over a web system. In this form, the students can test the performance of their coursework in an interactive way at any time and place, with the only restriction of needing a network connection. This fact makes it easier for the students to develop their work for the subject, adjusting to their own rhythm of study, without temporal or physical limitations, even allowing the students to dedicate additional time to the coursework.

Another additional goal of the e-learning system is that students can test the performance of their intelligent players against players developed by other colleagues, in a healthy competition among peers that allows them to deepen in the goals of the subject.

The game platform developed is fully parametric, enabling the instructor to change some features of the game to obtain substantially different problems to solve. We can assign different coursework to students each academic year. These parameters are set at the beginning of the academic year, before the beginning of the course. After this, the students must study the settings of the game being used and adjust their developments to those characteristics. This software feature assures that coursework is not copied from one call to another, and forces the students to understand the presented problem and its context.

When the game start, the system runs the players' software and shows the game progress in the screen (Figure 1). The students can see how their robots (their Artificial Intelligent System) make decisions.

In a detailed form, the operation within the system is described next.

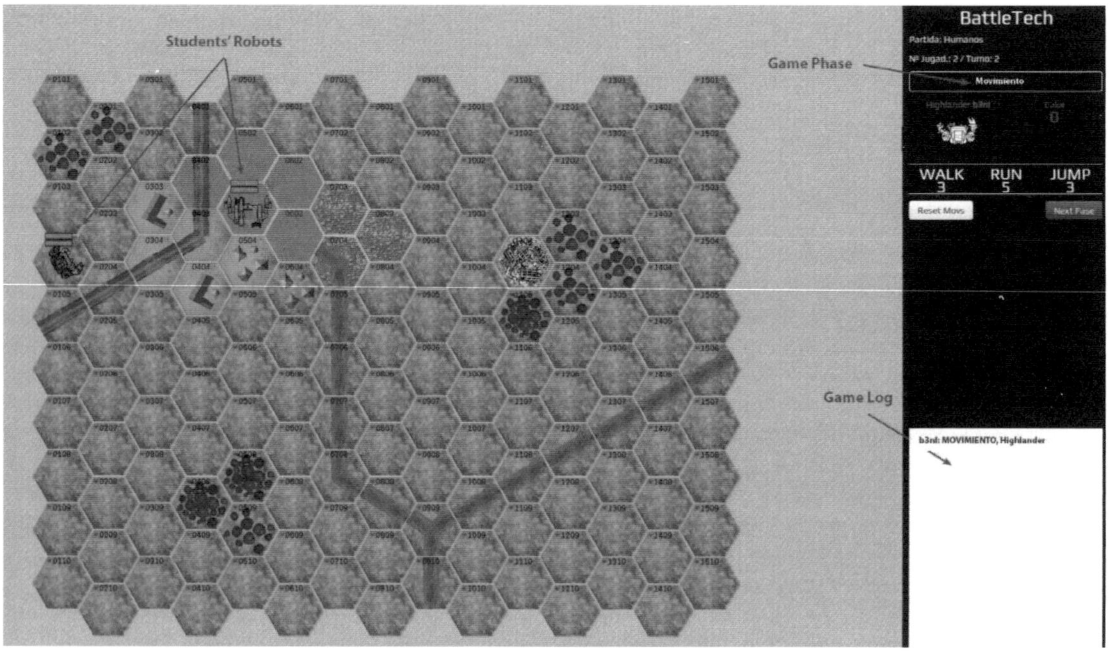

Figure 1. Screenshot showing the game board with trees, lakes and elevations, and two players' robots

- The student logs in the e-learning system. After this, the e-learning system shows the active games. The student can select to play an active round, to create a new game or to manage his Artificial Intelligence System (Figure 2)
- If a student selects to manage her Artificial Intelligence Systems, she can upload new Systems (the Artificial Intelligence Systems are developed by students using Python), update existing Systems, see errors of the last run or delete Systems.
- If a student decides to select the new game option, an interface gives her the necessary tools to generate a new game. The new game will be configured as a battle with the intervention of two or more players, and can be a closed game (only the players selected during the game creation can play) or an open game (the e-learning system permits that any user can later join the battle).

Usually in the first stages, students define battles of two players where a player is his Artificial Intelligence System and the other player is himself (It is possible to play in an interactive form using an interface). In this form, when the user plays against his System, she can evaluate the quality of her own work.

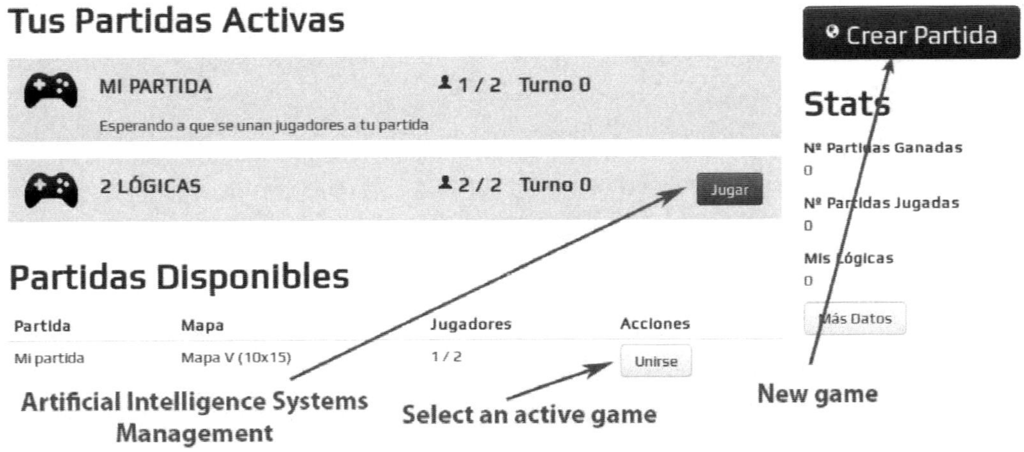

Figure 2. Game selection

When the students have theirs Artificial Intelligence Systems in advanced stages of development, they often begin to generate games with lots of players (open or closed) using the Artificial Intelligent Systems stored in the e-learning system.

This way, students have two self-evaluation levels:

- A first level, when they compete again themselves (student vs. her Artificial Intelligent System)
- A second level, when they compete against other students (student's Artificial Intelligent System vs. other students' Artificial Intelligent Systems).

The feedback achieved when the student competes against herself is the most important, because when a student gets a System that can beat her, she has really achieved an Artificial Intelligent Systems that plays as herself (or even better!).

It may seem that the feedback achieved in the second level (vs. others) only gets the student and her Artificial Intelligent System (if she uploads it) to play better.

But this second level of evaluation makes the student part of a cooperative system, since the improvements made in her software (software that she later uploads to the e-learning system for testing) are contributions that help to the improvement of their peers' systems.

Obviously, there is a large part of the system designed to control battles. These modules must ask the players (software or human) for the movements and other actions for combat, verify their legality with respect to the configuration established for the game, manage the results of all the actions of the players and show all the information through the system interface.

4. ACADEMIC RESULTS

The e-learning system has been fully deployed in the teaching of the Knowledge Engineering course. Since the students started using the system, they have achieved a deeper understanding of the contents of the course and have more easily reached the competences of the subject. This is mainly due to the new platform encouraging a greater temporal dedication to the learning of the specific content of the subject and to the practice of the associated skills, removing other tasks not directly related to the course. This has resulted in an increase in the success rate of students in the course.

These assessments are demonstrated through a notable improvement in the students' marks, achieving an increase in the success rate of the students compared to the levels of the previous years. The students themselves value very positively the realization of the coursework using the gaming platform, and recommend it to be used in subsequent years.

As we can see, the percentage of students evaluated that passes the coursework of the subject is, after the implementation of the e-learning system, clearly higher than in a previous course (Figure 3).

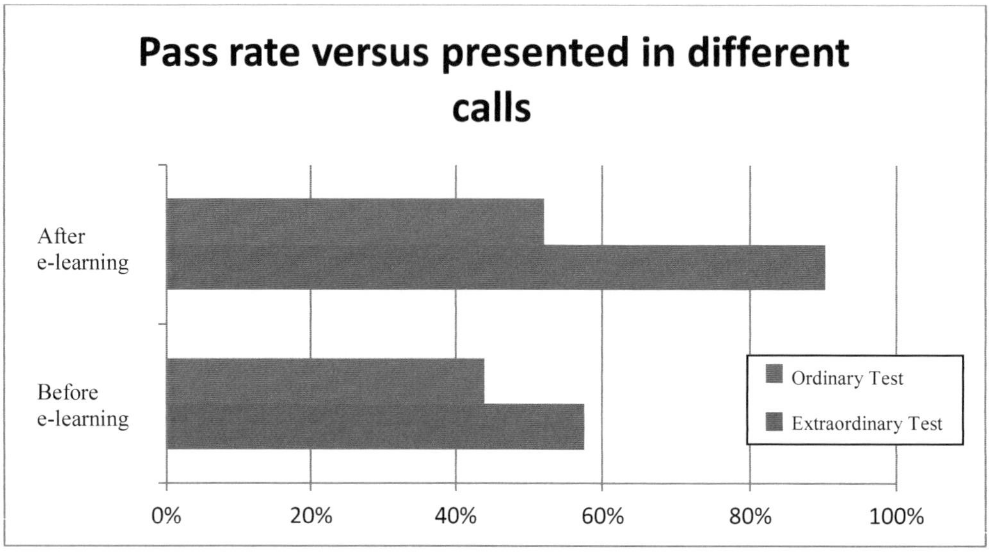

Figure 3. Rate of success in the practices of the subject (students approved on students presented).

5. CONCLUSION

This work shows the teaching innovation made in the course Knowledge Engineering of the degree in Computer Engineering.

The coursework for this course focus on building an intelligent system for decision making. However, several aspects made the academic progress of the students not appropriate to the goals of the subject. Among the main problems were the diversity of work domains, the lack of motivation of the students in the specific problem, or the need to develop additional software components that had nothing to do with the subject, but were necessary to achieve the objectives.

After identifying such problems, we have developed a game-based e-leaning system, on which students must develop intelligent players. Additionally, the e-learning system prevents students from having to develop additional tools for their coursework and facilitates that they focus their work efforts on the objectives of the course in an individual and cooperative form.

The interest shown by the students has increased significantly since a game is used to develop and evaluate the practices of the subject.

The use of new methodologies to teach computer science, as well as to do it from a didactic and practical perspective, is in accordance with the principles expressed by the National Agency for the Evaluation and Accreditation (ANECA) for the Degree in Computer Science (ANECA, 2005), agreed by all the Spanish universities that teach said studies.

The results of use the e-learning system during the last courses of the subject have been very positive, both for the students and the teachers.

ACKNOWLEDGEMENT

The authors thank the Secretariat for Teaching Innovation of the University of Granada for the funding provided for the development of this project.

REFERENCES

ANECA, 2005. *Libro Blanco del Título de Grado en Ingeniería Informática*. ANECA, Madrid. Spain

Copeland, J. 2000, *AlanTuring.net A Brief History of Computing*. Alanturing.net, http://www.alanturing.net/turing_archive/pages/Reference%20Articles/BriefHistofComp.html [Accessed 31 May 2017].

Fajardo, W., 2010, Diseño y desarrollo de un entorno de juego para desarrollo y prueba interactiva y cooperative de prácticas de sistemas inteligentes, *III Jornadas de Innovación Docente de la Universidad de Granada*. Granada, España.

Bailón, B., Fajardo, W., Molina-Solana, M., 2015 Intelligent Tutoring System, Based on Video E-learning, for Teaching Artificial Intelligence. In: Bajo J. et al. (eds) *Trends in Practical Applications of Agents, Multi-Agent Systems and Sustainability*. Advances in Intelligent Systems and Computing, vol 372. Springer, Cham, Germany.

Feigenbaun, E. A., 1977, The Art of Artificial Intelligence: I. Themes and Case Studies of Knowledge Engineering, *Proceedings of the 5th international joint conference on Artificial intelligence*, Cambridge, USA, pp. 1014-1029.

Frost, R.A., 1986, *Introduction to Knowledge Base Systems.*Collins, London, Great Britain.

Hauge, J.M.B., Pourabdollahian, B., Riedel, J.C.K. H., 2012, The Use of Serious Games in the Education of Engineers, *IFIP International Conference on Advances in Production Management Systems, APMS 2012: Advances in Production Management Systems. Competitive Manufacturing for Innovative Products and Services*, pp 622-629

Ignizio, J.P., 1991, *Introduction to Expert System*, McGraw Hill, New York, USA.

McCorduck, P., 2004, *Machines who think. A personal inquiry into the history and prospects of artificial intelligence.* A.K. Peters Publisher, Natick, USA.

Nareyek, A., 2004. AI in Computer Games, *Queue - Game Development*, Vol. 1, No 10, pp. 59-65.

Schaeffer, J. 2008, *One Jump Ahead: Computer Perfection at Checkers*, Springer, USA.

Windhoff, G. 2001. *Planspiele für die verteilte Produktion. Entwicklung und Einsatz von Trainingsmodulen für das aktive Erleben charakteristischer Arbeitssituationen in arbeitsteiligen, verteilten Produktionssystemen auf Basis der Planspielmethodik.*, Wissenschaftsverlag Mainz, Aachen, Germany.

Wooldridge, M., 2009, *An Introduction to Multiagent Systems*. John Wiley & Sons, USA.

THE NEXT STAGE OF DEVELOPMENT OF ELEARNING AT UFH IN SOUTH AFRICA

Graham Wright, Liezel Cilliers, Elzette Van Niekerk and Eunice Seekoe
University of Fort Hare
Oxford St, East London, South Africa

ABSTRACT

This paper is a review of eLearning using Blackboard as a Virtual Learning Environment (VLE) to identify the future development of the VLE within the Faculty of Health Sciences at the University of Fort Hare. The paper uses a case study approach to identify problems associated with the implementation of VLE's in Sub-Saharan Africa. Problem-Based Learning (PBL) and Case-Based Learning (CBL) are both based on a constructivist learning model that is used in many Health Faculties to underpin undergraduate and postgraduate education. All over the developed world, Higher Education Institutions (HEI) have introduced online learning systems, and this has been repeated in Sub-Saharan Africa during the last decade alongside student-focused curriculum designs. The challenges of producing harmony between the classroom and electronic learning environments are discussed within the case study. The paper concludes that there is a need to explore the tools and applications available to enable student focused and initiated interfaces with "Blackboard Learn" to support the implementation of an environment suitable for PBL and CBL.

KEYWORDS

Virtual Learning Environment, eLearning, Problem-Based Learning, Blackboard, Case-Based Learning, Sub-Saharan Africa

1. INTRODUCTION

Academics have been utilising online repositories to distribute learning material even before the advent of the World Wide Web (WWW) in 1993. Before the advents of web browsers were developed, internet systems such as Viewdata, Teletext and bulletin board system (BBS) had simple mail and file storage functions. In the developed world the advent of the personal computer (PC) and the WWW change the way in which academics could interact with each other and their student population. Availability gradually increased, and most students had either ownership or access to a computer during the 90's. Universities in the UK had the added advantage of the Joint Academic Network (JANET) while in the USA the Advanced Research Projects Agency Network (ARPANET) had been serving major universities until it was decommissioned in 1990.

None of these events had an impact on Education Institutes in South Africa which lack the connectivity to be involved before the linking of South African firstly by Rhodes University using Fidonet in 1998 followed by the other Universities and Science organisations which later connected via UNINET. South Africa was also by passed by the PC revolution and only a minority of academics in South Africa's universities had access to during connected computing during the PC revolution that brought the World Wide Web (WWW) to the rest of the world.

Following the advent of the WWW and proliferation of web browsers the access was limited in Africa; however, Telkom South Africa introduced an ADSL with download speeds of 512 kbps in 2002 and so the broadband era started in earnest within South Africa. Mobile Phones have become ubiquitous in South Africa, which is the economic leader of Africa. So a very different ICT landscape from other regions in the rest of the world but one which is now catching up on some of the computers systems but is utilising mobile phone technology rather than PC's for access.

1.1 Functions of Blackboard

Blackboard was first released in 1998 following the development of WebCT 1.0 (Goldberg, Salari, Swoboda, 1996) in 1995. Blackboard is an interactive eLearning platform that involves both the instructor and student to create, utilise and share digital contents (Kim, Do, 2016). They describe "the Homepage" of the programme as an interactive platform where course material, lesson notes and research material are made available to students. The major functions of Blackboard can be categorised into three sets of eLearning tools, namely interactive, resources and assessment tools, which El Zawaidy (2014) loosely describe as communication and content functions.

The communication function consists of interactive tools such as Announcements, Discussion Boards, Wikis, and Blogs (Kim, Do, 2016). Instructors typically post instructions on the Discussion Board for an upcoming lecture, while students post any queries they might have regarding assignments. The Discussion board is a tool allowing students to access it anywhere at anytime. Liaw (2008) stated that this 'chat-room' offers an ideal opportunity for students to maintain "up-to-date and regular communication" with instructors and peers from remote sites.

Students and instructors can send each other messages via the Discussion Board (El Zawaidy, 2014) while the resource function provides for content such as class notes, syllabus, videos and lecture slides. Assignments are loaded for students to complete and once completed; students return them to be assessed. The instructor grades the assignments and provides a mark, which is captured automatically into the Grade book. Lectures can also be video or sound recorded and loaded onto Blackboard so Students can view them in their own time.

The Assessment function within the Grade centre is used to create mark sheets, capture examination or test results and provide feedback to students. Multiple-choice tests can be administered on Blackboard and as the student completes the test the results are captured in the Grade book (Kim, Do, 2016). There is a Retention centre that monitors the students' progress and warns teachers if any of the students fail to submit assignments or if a student's average is below a pre-set percentage. An Achievement can also be reported in Blackboard. Through blackboard's reviewing systems, instructors can determine how many logins, time on tasks and which tools were the most used in courses (McCabe, Meuter, 2011).

2. BLACKBOARD LEARN

A search of Scopus, Pubmed and Google Scholar was conducted using the keywords:- eLearning, VLE's and Blackboard.

The use of VLE's by Universities around the world appears to focus on the administration and management of learning processes, with modules for timetabling, student performance, assessment and registration on module details.

Wright, Betts and Murray (2005) stated that it was important to take "a pedagogical rather than a technological approach to support students' learning" as it was essential to define the expected learning rather than just offer an eLearning portal to which students had access.

Betts and Wright (2002) suggested, as do many other eLearning practitioners, that human interaction is an important component of any learning process, at any academic level, and through any mode of delivery. Thus the interactive functions of the eLearning environment require staff to pay particular attention to their interactions with students online as well as in the classroom.

In a small study, Murray, Betts, Roberts and Wright (2003) found that respondents who were involved in using online learning systems thought "the simple delivery of materials was sufficient. Little reference was made to pedagogic underpinnings, to interactions among learners and teachers/facilitators" Is there evidence that such attitudes continue?

Certainly the use of phrases such as "Learning Management System" , "Blackboard Analytics" and "course management system" put yet another view of the important features to be found on the Blackboard website (http://uki.blackboard.com/about-us/index.aspx) for instance.

Blackboard is described as "a Web-based server software which features course management, customizable open architecture, and scalable design that allows integration with student information systems and authentication protocols. " ; On Google advanced search this exact phrase was found on 162 sites, including http://research.omicsgroup.org/index.php/Blackboard_Learn.

McLoughlin and Lee (2008) stated that "Currently, e-learning pedagogies at universities and colleges appear to be fuelled largely by learning management systems (LMS's) that replicate these traditional paradigms in an online setting. They conform to a "student-as information consumer" model, thus reinforcing instructor-centred approaches to teaching, learning and knowledge, as opposed to being conducive to constructivist modes of learning that enable a high degree of learner self-direction and personalisation."

Hughes (2008) wrote a whole paper on the subject ending with the statement that "Technology, without the pedagogy, can be a fetishised and empty learning and teaching experience – stylised but without substance or simply electronic information push." Thus many authors at the time were extremely concerned by the implementation of LMS's that focused on the management rather than the needs of students and the pedagogic underpinnings their learning environment.

Mlitwa and Van Belle (2011) note in their study that "the omission of the word learning" in these accounts, which questions whether learning is considered central to eLearning" and secondly that "these perceptions are function-based rather than pedagogy-focused." They go on to extemporise that not coming up with an articulated pedagogical direction leaves the staff focusing on mangement of student materials such that the students become passive consumers.

Okantey and Addo (2016) conducted a study in Ghana using a Technology Acceptance Model (TAM) adapted to also explore institutional factors. They found that Lecturers adoption of eLearning using Blackboard was related to Perceived Usefulness (PU) that is their perception of how useful Blackboard would be in their academic work. Their results also highlighted the relationship between eLearning and Perceived Ease of Use (PEOU) to be the weakest. How much of the VLE do staff need to understand to be able to use it effectively on a daily basis?

JISC (formerly the Joint Information Systems Committee) is the UK higher education, further education and skills sectors' not-for-profit organisation for digital services and solutions. Amongst its many publications is a short guide (https://www.jisc.ac.uk/guides/technology-and-tools-for-online-learning/virtual-learning-environments) regarding VLEs that stated that "One advantage of using VLEs is that institutions can train all staff to make the most of their particular system. However, VLEs have been criticised for not inspiring innovative curriculum design, or offering flexible ways for learners to engage with content." And that "Staff can be tempted to simply upload all their existing content, rather than consider how they could use technology to change the design of the curriculum. "

2.1 A case Study of VLE's in Sub-Saharan Africa

Sub-Saharan Africa has adopted online learning, but the process is still in its infancy (Kotoua, Ilkan & Kilic, 2015). The first online university was founded by the World Bank in Africa in 1996. It was based at the University of Kenyatta, Kenya, but involved four other African countries namely Ghana, Kenya, Uganda and Zimbabwe. Today the university offers science, engineering, business and vocational course making use of a variety of technologies including a learner management system (Kotoua, Ilkan & Kilic, 2015).

With the advent of eLearning, there has been increasing adoption and use of various Learning Management Systems (LMS) in higher education of Sub-Saharan countries. These systems provide the lecturer with a variety of tools to deliver course content and include audio, video, and text as well as commutation tools (chat, discussions forums, email, and whiteboards), and assessment tools (Mtebe & Raisamo, 2014). The most popular systems deployed in several institutions in Sub-Saharan countries are: Blackboard, Moodle, Atutor, Sakai, and Kewl (Ssekakubo et al., 2011). Moodle seems to be the most popular as Ssekakubo et al (2011) and Hoosen and Butcher (2012) found that HEIs in several countries in Sub-Saharan Africa (South Africa, Zambia, Kenya and Uganda, Mozambique, Tanzania, Ghana, Nigeria) made use of this system.

The cost of procuring, installing and maintaining an LMS can be seen as prohibitive, but has been supported by several international agencies such as the World Bank, Swedish International Development Cooperation Agency (SIDA), United Nations Educational, Scientific and Cultural Organization (UNESCO), United Nations Development Programme (UNDP), and United States Agency for International Development (USAID) are supporting various eLearning initiatives in Africa (Farrell & Isaacs, 2007).

However, despite the financial support of these agencies, the majority of LMS implemented in Sub-Saharan countries has not been successful. Ssekakubo et al. (2011) reported that the majority of users in HEIs in Sub-Saharan countries do not use the LMS installed in their institutions. For example, the Makerer University reported only 60 registered users on the LMS, the university of Nairobi only 10 active users, 87% of instructors at the Open University of Nairobi and 74% of instructors at HEIs in Zimbabwe reported that they have never used Blackboard since they were trained (Ssekakubo et al., 2011; Bhalalusesa, Lukwaro, & Clemence, 2013).

GHANA. The Ghanian government has made eLearning a priority in their HEI. The government has entered into a partnership with the private sector to import computers without any tax implications in order to improve the Information and Communication Technology (ICT) infrastructure in the country (Kotoua, Ilkan & Kilic, 2015). Despite these concessions, the growth of online education and the use of LMS in Ghana have remained stilted. While most universities offer Internet access half of the students do not have access to the Internet off campus. For this reason, most students in Ghana prefer traditional face-to-face classes as they cannot access the educational resources on the LMS (Kotoua, Ilkan & Kilic, 2015).

TANZANIA. Lwoga (2014) investigated an LMS at a HEI in Tanzania and found that seven variables will contribute to the adoption of these systems. These variables include information quality, system quality, service quality, instructor quality, perceived usefulness, user satisfaction and continual usage intention. System quality was found to be the most important of these factors.

Characteristics of the LMS that determine system quality was found to be guaranteed response time, interactivity, user interface and better design functionalities. Students in general perceived the LMS as useful with easy and user-friendly operations (Cheng, 2012). Instructor quality was also found to be a significant predictor of both perceived usefulness and user satisfaction and include the ability to respond to students' queries and good communication skills. Service quality had insignificant association but technical guidance and support play a key role in enhancing learners' eLearning acceptance (Cheng, 2012).

SOUTH AFRICA. In South Africa, at the University of Fort Hare the Academic Development Centre of the institution identified Blackboard as an appropriate LMS to be used by the institution in 2008. In 2009, the Blackboard server was installed at the University and training commenced. Over the next four years the use of Blackboard increased steadily. The advantages of the LMS for teaching as reported by the lecturers included efficiency of communication, storage of materials, access to materials, discussion classes, engagement, instant feedback, and out of class interactions. Area of concern reported by the staff included the user-friendliness of the system and navigation problems (Nkonki, Ntlabathi & Mkonqo, 2013). Isabirye and Dlodlo (2014) found that lack of eLearning and ICT support, lack of awareness amongst lecturers and management about the benefits of eLearning lead to negative attitudes among lecturers and students were barriers in South Africa to overcome.

2.1.1 Problems

Andersson and Grönlund (2009) provide a framework to explain challenges for LMS as part of eLearning in Africa. These challenges can be summarised as follow:

- Individual challenges include both the student and teacher. Factors such as motivation, age, time, qualification, competence, academic and technological confidences are found in this category. The social problems that inhibit the growth of eLearning include the 'brain drain' from Africa to developed countries. University staff that are trained to make use of LMS and eLearning are lost as they move abroad to access better salaries and working conditions (Adeyinka, 2013). Mlitwa and Van Belle (2011) found that individual challenges of computer literacy, in addition to the resistance to change were also a barrier to the implementation of LMS in South Africa.
- Course challenges include curriculum, pedagogical issues, subject content flexibility and localisation and the proper support to make use of ICT resources.
- Contextual challenges such as knowledge management of teaching content, funding, training and the attitudes of both student and teacher to use eLearning.

- Technological challenges such as lack of infrastructure facilities such as computers, high cost of ICT infrastructure and internet access, connectivity, electricity and limitations in bandwidth (Abdelfatah, 2016). Some universities also rely on foreign donors for funding to implement eLearning facilities and resources, which mean that the program is prone to collapse once these donors withdraw (Kotoua, Ilkan & Kilic, 2015).

2.2 Pedagogy

The university of Fort Hare launched a new Faculty of Health Sciences as part of its centenary celebration. The faculty started with five departments and five research centres. The faculty has to respond to the South Africa's National Development Plan (NDP). The NDP requires development of human resources for health which results in health professionals being developed who can think critically, solve health care problems, function independently and provide leadership in clinical care. To strategically meet this demand the Faculty has been guided by Boyers Model of scholarship development that highlights the focus on the concepts of scholarship of Discovery (research), Teaching, Integration and engagement (Badat, 2010).

The introduction of innovative methods including Problem Based Learning (PBL), Community Based Education (CBE) and Case-Based Teaching (CBT) in the Faculty of Health Sciences assist in reflecting the University of Fort Hare's response to the challenge of transformation in higher education and national health policy.

2.2.1 Problem-Based Learning- Community Based Education (PBL-CBE)

Within the Faculty of Health Sciences, University of Fort Health the pedagogical approach of PBL-CBE has been integrated in professional health programmes for teaching undergraduate students.

ELearning, Problem Based learning (PBL) – Community Based Education (CBE) and Case Based Teaching (CBT) are based on the constructivist learning model which according to Ellis and Wright (2013) gives the learners the opportunity to:

- To learn to embrace complexity;
- To find relevance in their learning as it applies to the programme they are following;
- To be prepared for the type of problem-solving they will be expected to use in the work-place; and
- To enhance their capacity for creative and responsible real-world problem solving

PBL-CBE can be considered to be the founding paradigm on which other learner-centred approaches such as Case-Based Learning have been developed.

2.2.2 Case-Based Learning

Case-Based Learning using well developed and realistic cases help to develop critical thinking and which enables students to differentiate realistic and informed from false or flawed logic. Case Based Learning takes postgraduate learners through a voyage of discovery and provides insight into the discipline and terminology of the subject as well as the relationships and concepts within the case study. In a case there are usually explicit and implicit leadership and management issues to be confronted. A case is defined by "a description of an actual situation, commonly involving a decision, a challenge, an opportunity, a problem or an issue faced by a person (or persons) in an organization" (Jonassen, 2010)

Barnes, Christensen and Hansen (1994) of Harvard Business School define a case as: "a partial, historical, clinical study of a situation which has confronted a practicing administrator or managerial group. Presented in narrative form to encourage student involvement, it provides data – substantive and process – essential to an analysis of a specific situation, for the framing of alternative action programs, and for their implementation recognizing the complexity and ambiguity of the practical world"

This is the definition used by the Albertina Sisulu Executive Leadership Programme in Health (ASELPH Fellowship) programme by its partners Harvard T.H. Chan School of Public Health (Harvard), University of Pretoria (UP), University of Fort Hare (UFH) and the South African National Department of Health.

3. CONCLUSION

There would appear to be a need to explore the implementation of the use of "Case studies" and PBL as a teaching strategy in the Faculty post-graduate programmes in Public Health using Blackboard as the Learning Environment. Also given the nature of the ASELPH fellowship programme, there is a need to ensure competent mentorship is provided alongside and within that environment. These challenges are in addition to those identified and summarised earlier in this article. Introducing such innovative pedagogy requires curriculum review and capacity building of faculty members which can be enabled through on-site training of staff, visit local and international higher education institutions with more experience and expertise. Faculty members can understudy guest presenters who have specific areas of expertise and use coaching through eLearning and interactive media such as videoconferences, Skype and Blackboard.

Tsai and Chiang (2013) undertook a review of the literature on PBL and eLearning and came to the conclusion that "Underpinned by the Constructivist Approach, PBL is one of the methods that could be applied in online learning environments" However this is little evidence that this has been successfully implemented on Blackboard Learn. Our next stage of work will be to explore the tools and applications available to enable student focused and initiated interfaces with Blackboard Learn to enable the implementation of an environment suitable for PBL and CBL For example Blackboard Learn has 227 Extensions that is module which extend the core functions or add new ones. A search of Google Scholar for 'Extensions "Blackboard Learn" ' reveals 326 papers for us to review.

REFERENCES

Abdelfatah, H. (2016). Cyber learning from reality through virtuality to holoportation: status-quo and a proposed model for closing the gap in africa. *ASRO Journal of Education*, 1(2), 28-38.

Adeyinka, A. (2013). Current problems of educational development in Nigeria. *Journal of negro education*, 1-82.

Andersson, A. S., & Grönlund, Å. (2009). A conceptual framework for e-learning in developing countries: A critical review of research challenges. *The Electronic Journal of Information Systems in Developing Countries*, 38.

Bhalalusesa, R., Lukwaro, E.E. & Clemence, M. (2013). Challenges of Using E-learning Management Systems Faced by the Academic Staff in Distance Based Institutions from Developing Countries: A Case Study of the Open University of Tanzania. *Huria Journal of OUT*, 14, 89-110.

Barnes, L.B., Christensen, C.R., Hansen, A.J., (1994) *Teaching and the case method: Text, cases, and readings*: Harvard Business Press.

Betts, H., Wright, G., (2002) *Virtual universities--the reality of e-learning?* 90:752.

Cheng, Y.Y. (2012), Effects of quality antecedents on e-learning acceptance, *Internet Research*,

Vol. 22 No. 3, pp. 361–390.

El Zawaidy, H. (2014) Using Blackboard in online learning at Saudi universities: faculty member's perceptions and existing obstacles. *International Interdisciplinary Journal of Education,* 3(7), 141-150.

Ellis, M., Wright, G., (2013) *The implementation of problem-based learning as a preferred teaching methodology: an action-research view1.*149.

Farrell, G. & Isaacs, S. (2007). *Survey of ICT and Education in Africa: A Summary Report, Based on 53 Country Surveys* (pp. 0–74). Washington, DC. United States. http://www.infodev.org/en/Publication.353.html

Goldberg, M.W., Salari, S., Swoboda, P. (1996) World Wide Web—Course tool: An environment for building WWW-based courses. *Computer Networks and ISDN Systems,* 28(7), 1219-1231.

Hughes, J. (2008) Letting in the Trojan mouse: Using an eportfolio system to re-think pedagogy.

Hoosen, S. & Butcher, N. (2012). ICT Development at African Universities: The Experience of the PHEA Educational Technology Initiative. Proceedings of e/merge 2012. http://emerge2012.net/proceedings/

Isabirye, A. K., & Dlodlo, N. (2014). Perceived Inhibitors of Innovative E-Learning Teaching Practice at a South African University of Technology. *Mediterranean Journal of Social Sciences*, 5(4), 390.

Jonassen, D.H., (2010) *Learning to solve problems: A handbook for designing problem-solving learning environments*: Routledge.

Kim, J., Do, J. (2016) Learning management system: Medium for Interactive communication. *International Journal of Applied Engineering Research,* 11(2), 1073-1076.

Kotoua, S., Ilkan, M., & Kilic, H. (2015). The Growing of Online Education in Sub Saharan Africa: Case Study Ghana. *Procedia-Social and Behavioral Sciences*, *191*, 2406-2411.

Liaw, S.-S. (2008) Investigating students' perceived satisfaction, behavioral intention, and effectiveness of e-learning: A case study of the Blackboard system. *Computers & Education,* 51(2), 864-873.

Lwoga, E. T. (2014). Critical success factors for adoption of web-based learning management systems in Tanzania. *International Journal of Education and Development using Information and Communication Technology*, *10*(1), 4.

McCabe, D.B., Meuter, M.L. (2011) A student view of technology in the classroom: Does it enhance the seven principles of good practice in undergraduate education? *Journal of Marketing Education*, 0273475311410847.

McLoughlin, C., Lee, M. (2008) Mapping the digital terrain: New media and social software as catalysts for pedagogical change. *Ascilite Melbourne*.

Mlitwa, N., Van Belle, J.-P., (2011) *Mediators For Lecturer Perspectives On Learning Management Systems At Universities In The Western Cape, South Africa.* 135.

Murray, P.J., Betts, H., Roberts, J., Wright, G., (2003) *E-learning in health informatics: trying to agree what we mean, attempting to determine the research priorities.*

Mtebe, J. S., & Raisamo, R. (2014). A model for assessing Learning Management System Success in higher education in sub-Saharan countries. *The Electronic Journal of Information Systems in Developing Countries*, *61*.

Nkonki, V., Ntlabathi, S., & Mkonqo, L. (2013, June). Explaining influences in the adoption of Blackboard at an institution of higher learning. *In International Conference on e-Learning (p. 301). Academic Conferences International Limited.*

Okantey, M., Addo, H. (2016) Effect Of Theoretical And Institutional Factors On The Adoption Of E-Learning. *European Scientific Journal,* 12(16).

Ssekakubo, G., Suleman, H. & Marsden, G. (2011). Issues of Adoption: Have E-Learning Management Systems Fulfilled their Potential in Developing Countries ? In *Proceedings of the South African Institute of Computer Scientists and Information Technologists Conference on Knowledge, Innovation and Leadership in a Diverse,Multidisciplinary Environment* (pp. 231–238). Cape Town, South Africa.

Tsai, C.-W., Chiang, Y.-C. (2013) Research trends in problem-based learning (PBL) research in e-learning and online education environments: A review of publications in SSCI-indexed journals from 2004 to 2012. *British Journal of Educational Technology,* 44(6), E185-E190.

Wright, G., Betts, H., Murray, P. (2005) Health Informatics Masters Education, Online Learning and Student Support. *IMIA Yearbook of Medical Informatics*.

EFFECT OF INTERNET-BASED LEARNING IN PUBLIC HEALTH TRAINING: AN EXPLORATORY META-ANALYSIS

Ying Peng and Weirong Yan
Department of Epidemiology and Biostatistics, School of Public Health, Tongji Medical College
Hangkong Road 13#, Wuhan,430030, China

ABSTRACT

Internet-based learning is increasingly applied in medical education, but its effect in the field of public health training is still unclear. This meta-analysis was undertaken to explore the impact of Internet-based learning on students/professionals' knowledge of public health compared with no intervention and with traditional face-to-face (FTF) formats. Two reviewers independently searched Medline, Web of Science, ProQuest, Google scholar, ERIC and Elsevier databases for relevant studies between 1st January, 1990 and 30th December, 2016. Studies in English language providing information on educational outcomes after Internet-based training in public health courses compared with no-intervention or a pre-intervention assessment, or with FTF control group were retrieved, reviewed, and assessed according to the established inclusion/exclusion criteria in the current study. There were 16 eligible studies with 1183 participants in total. Heterogeneity in results was detected across studies. A random effects model was used to pool effect sizes for knowledge outcomes. The pooled effect size (standardized mean difference, SMD) in comparison to no intervention was 1.92 (95% CI: 1.05 to 2.78; P<0.0001), favoring Internet-based interventions. Compared with FTF formats, the pooled effect size was 0.39 (95% CI: -0.06 to 0.83; P=0.09). The study suggested that Internet-based learning was superior to no-intervention in improving students/professionals' public health knowledge. Compared with traditional FTF formats, Internet-based learning showed a similar effect.

KEYWORDS

Internet-based learning; Public health training; Meta analysis

1. INTRODUCTION

Internet-based learning, which has been defined as using the Internet to deliver and access learning materials, to interact with peers and instructors and to enhance knowledge and performance (Wutoh et al. 2004), is increasingly applied in medical education over the past few decades. Compared to traditional learning approach, Internet-based learning has advantages in satisfying an extensive range of learning needs and permitting flexible learning transcending time and space (Cook et al. 2010; Greenhalgh 2001). Its growing spread has led to discussion, research, and debate over the effect of Internet-based learning compared with traditional face-to-face (FTF) instruction and no-intervention (Choules 2007; Greenhalgh 2001; Hemans-Henry et al. 2012).

Quantitatively summarizing these evidences could increase statistical power and is more convincible to inform educators and learners about the extent to which the Internet-based learning is effective. Currently, the reviews concerning the effect of Internet-based learning in medical education have mostly focused in the field of clinical medicine or basic medicine (Cook et al. 2008; Lahti et al. 2013; Lewis 2003). Cook DA and his colleagues reported positive results in their meta-analysis comparing Internet-based intervention to no-intervention in clinical medicine (Cook et al. 2008). Lahti M et al. reported that Internet-based learning is as good as traditional learning methods in nursing courses in a review (Lahti et al. 2013).

However, so far there is no quantitative pooling to estimate the effect of Internet-based learning in the field of public health. As Internet-based learning is a new field, interventions are not yet clear. According to the previous meta-analysis (Cook et al. 2008; Lahti et al. 2013), we expect large heterogeneity of studies, especially of intervention. Two meta-analyses were conducted in the present study, the first exploring Internet-based compared with no intervention or pre-intervention assessment, and the second summarizing the studies comparing Internet-based and traditional FTF instructional methods.

2. MAIN RESULTS

2.1 Data Sources

To identify the relevant studies, Medline, Web of Science, ProQuest, Google scholar, ERIC and Elsevier databases were searched. Key search terms included delivery concepts (such as "Internet, OR Web OR computer OR distance OR online" AND "learning OR instruction OR education OR training"), study design concepts (such as "evaluat* OR compar* OR pretest OR effect*"< * is a truncation symbol for searching. For instance, evaluat* would retrieve entries containing the words: evaluate, evaluation, or evaluative, etc>), and educational topics "public health/education [mesh]". To complement the search strategies, keyword searching of Google scholar was also conducted. The reference lists of retrieved articles were reviewed to identify any additional publication. More details on the search strategies were available upon request from the authors.

2.2 Search Results

The search strategy identified 709 studies from the databases. A review of the reference lists of the retrieved studies identified additional 13 potentially relevant articles. Out of the 722 publications, 109 potentially eligible articles were read in full text for further assessment. From these, 22 were considered appropriate for inclusion. After that, six studies were excluded due to insufficient data for coding quantitative outcomes. Thus a total of 16 studies were included in the quantitative analyses, among which four studies compared the Internet-based learning with both no intervention and traditional FTF instruction (Abdelhai et al. 2012; Hugenholtz et al. 2008; McGready and Brookmeyer 2013; Smits et al. 2012). Therefore 12 studies were contributed to meta-analysis of no-intervention comparison (Abdelhai et al. 2012; Aggarwal et al. 2011; Chung et al. 2004; Curioso et al. 2008; Farel et al. 2001; Hugenholtz et al. 2008; McGready and Brookmeyer 2013; Ried 2010; Sears et al. 2008; Smits et al. 2012; Steckler et al. 2001; Zahner 2006), and 8 contributed to meta-analysis of traditional FTF instruction comparison (Abdelhai et al. 2012; Campbell et al. 2008; Evans et al. 2007; Fayram and Anderko 2009; Hugenholtz et al. 2008; McGready and Brookmeyer 2013; Rose et al. 2000; Smits et al. 2012). The search flow was shown in figure 1.

2.3 Study Characteristics

The included 16 studies were published between 2000 and 2016. Table 1 summarizes key characteristics of the included studies. The sample size of the included studies varied from 13 to 138 participants, and the total number was 1183. Besides one study conducted in Egypt (Abdelhai et al. 2012), one in India (Aggarwal et al. 2011), the remaining 14 studies were in Europe and North America, including two in Netherlands (Hugenholtz et al. 2008; Smits et al. 2012), one in the United Kingdom (Campbell et al. 2008), one in Canada (Sears et al. 2008), and ten in the United States (Chung et al. 2004; Curioso et al. 2008; Evans et al. 2007; Farel et al. 2001; Fayram and Anderko 2009; McGready and Brookmeyer 2013; Ried 2010; Rose et al.

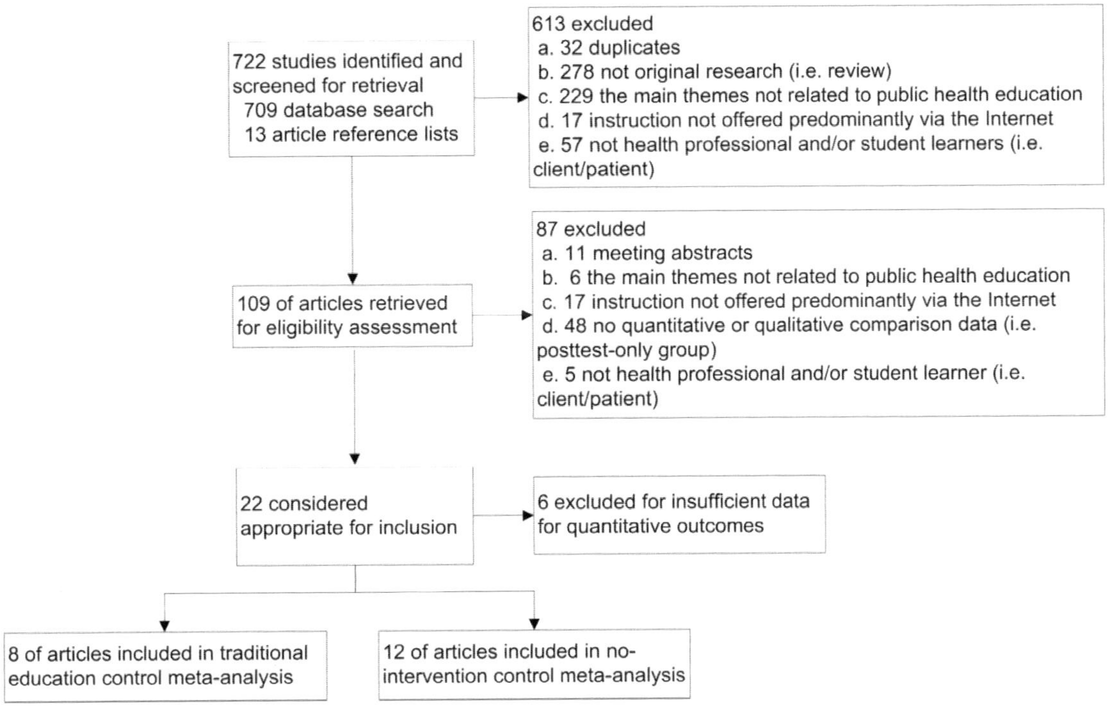

Figure 1. Flow diagram

2000; Steckler et al. 2001; Zahner 2006). Besides biostatistics and epidemiology courses (6/16), topics such as occupational health, community health, reproductive health, tobacco and public health, and quantitative and qualitative research methods were also addressed. In addition, review of the selected articles revealed big variations in the Internet-based education modalities, including tutorial, videoconference, case study and online discussion with peers and/or instructors, et al.

2.4 Quantitative Data Synthesis of No-Intervention Comparison

Twelve studies were included in the analysis (Fig 2). The pooled effect size of 1.92 (95% CI: 1.05 to 2.78, $P<0.0001$) significantly reflected a large effect according to Cohen's criteria (Cohen 1992), which suggested that Internet-based learning has a substantial benefit on learners' knowledge compared with no-intervention. However, there were large inconsistency across studies ($I^2=97\%$), and individual effect sizes ranged from 0.10 to 5.41. The test of funnel plot asymmetry indicated publication bias among studies (Egger's test $P=0.003$). We executed sensitivity analyses by sequential omission of individual studies to reflect the influence of the individual data on the pooled effect size and evaluate the stability of the findings. The results demonstrated that the sensitivity analyses would not considerably affect the conclusion.

Subgroup analyses were further performed and categorized by study design, methodological quality scale, and instructional design aspects to explore the sources of inconsistency. The effect sizes showed consistently positive number (favoring Internet-based learning) when conducting each subgroup analysis respectively, although some of the results became statistically insignificant (undergraduate degree courses, duration less than 1 week, absence of exercise, and with single access to course materials)(Table 2).

Table 1. Characteristics of the included study

Study characteristic	No-intervention control		Traditional instruction control	
	No. of studies	No. of participants	No. of studies	No. of participants
All studies	12	951	8	865
Design				
pre-posttest, 2 group	4	633	4	633
posttest, 2 group	0	0	4	232
pre-post, 1 group	8	318	0	0
Quality Newcastle scale				
≧4 points	9	558	5	493
≦3 points	3	393	3	372
Country				
USA	7	368	4	266
Netherlands	2	200	2	200
Egypt	1	295	1	295
Canada	1	59	0	0
UK	0	0	1	104
India	1	29	0	0
Degree				
undergraduate	3	527	3	474
graduate	3	225	5	391
not mentioned	6	199	0	0
Object				
student	4	665	4	612
professionals	8	286	4	253
Duration				
≧1 week	7	625	5	620
< 1 week	3	259	2	200
not mentioned	2	67	1	45
Exercise				
present	9	766	5	582
absent	3	185	3	283
Discussion				
present	5	536	4	569
absent	7	415	4	296

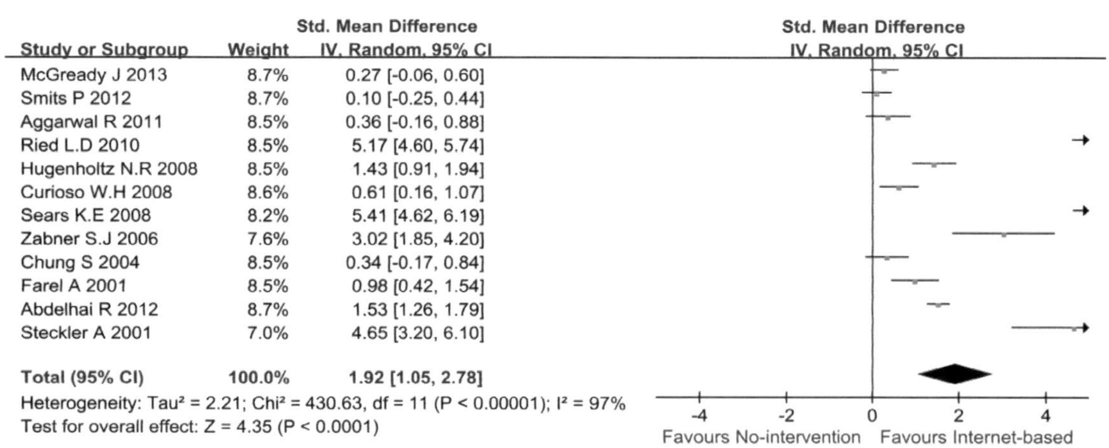

Figure 2. Forest plot for no-intervention control meta-analysis

Table 2. Pooled effect sizes (standard mean difference, SMD) for subgroup meta-analyses of Internet-based learning vs. no-intervention

Subgroup	No. of studies	No. of participants	SMD (95%CI)	I2	p-value
All studies	12	951	1.92(1.05, 2.78)	97%	<.0001
Design					
Pre-posttest, 2 group	4	633	0.82(0.05, 1.60)	95%	.05
Pre-posttest,1 group	8	318	2.53 (1.01, 4.05)	98%	
Quality Newcastle-scale					
≧4 points	9	558	1.74 (0.68, 2.80)	97%	.51
≦3 points	3	393	2.48 (0.53, 4.42)	97%	
Degree					
undergraduate	3	527	2.25 (-0.01, 4.51)	99%	.93
graduate	3	225	1.91 (0.35, 3.48)	95%	
not mentioned	6	199	1.74 (0.43, 3.05)	97%	
Participant					
student	4	665	1.75 (0.11, 3.39)	98.9%	.79
professionals	8	286	2.01 (0.93, 3.09)	96%	
Duration					
≧1 week	7	625	2.12 (0.87, 3.36)	98%	.07
< 1 week	3	259	2.29 (-0.29, 4.87)	99%	
not mentioned	2	67	0.76 (0.41, 1.11)	0%	
Exercise					
present	9	766	2.43 (1.31, 3.55)	98%	.002
absent	3	185	0.44 (-0.06, 0.95)	71%	
Discussion					
present	5	536	2.33 (0.94, 3.73)	98%	.47
absent	7	415	1.64 (0.37, 2.90)	98%	
Repetition					
persistent access	8	663	1.99 (0.93, 3.05)	97%	.86
single instance	4	288	1.79 (-0.02, 3.61)	98%	

2.5 Quantitative Data Synthesis of Traditional FTF Instruction Comparison

Eight traditional FTF instruction controlled studies were included in the present analysis (Figure 3). Although the random effect size showed some improvement associated with Internet-based learning compared to traditional FTF format, it was not statistically significant (SMD: 0.39; 95% CI: -0.06 to 0.83; P=0.09). Individual effect sizes ranged from-0.32 to 1.30. The heterogeneity amongst studies was large (I^2=88%), but the test of funnel plot asymmetry indicated no evidence of publication bias (Egger's test P=0.665).

Study or Subgroup	Weight	Std. Mean Difference IV, Random, 95% CI
McGready J 2013	13.9%	0.11 [-0.22, 0.44]
Smits P 2012	13.8%	0.03 [-0.32, 0.38]
Abdelhai R 2012	14.4%	1.30 [1.05, 1.55]
Fayram E.S 2009	9.9%	0.67 [-0.15, 1.49]
Hugenholtz N.R 2008	12.9%	0.08 [-0.38, 0.55]
Campbell M 2008	13.4%	0.63 [0.22, 1.03]
Evans S 2007	10.4%	-0.32 [-1.08, 0.43]
Rose M.A 2000	11.2%	0.47 [-0.20, 1.14]
Total (95% CI)	**100.0%**	**0.39 [-0.06, 0.83]**

Heterogeneity: $Tau^2 = 0.34$; $Chi^2 = 58.59$, df = 7 (P < 0.00001); $I^2 = 88\%$
Test for overall effect: Z = 1.71 (P = 0.09)

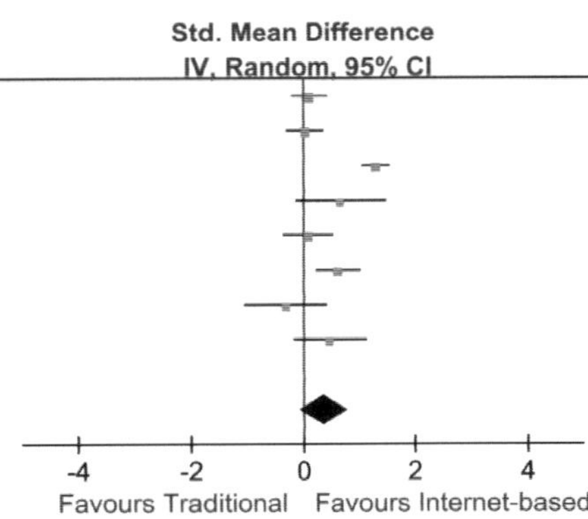

Figure 3. Forest plot for traditional F2F instruction control meta-analysis

Table 3. Pooled effect sizes for subgroup meta-analyses of Internet-based learning vs. F2F-intervention

Subgroup	No. of studies	No. of participants	SMD (95%CI)	I2	p-value
All studies	8	865	0.36 (-0.10,0.83)	89%	.12
Design					
Pre-posttest, 2 group	4	633	0.35 (-0.39, 1.10)	94%	.97
posttest,2 group	4	232	0.41 (-0.00, 0.82)	40%	
Quality Newcastle-scale					
≧4 points	5	493	0.16 (-0.10,0.42)	46%	.03
≦3 points	3	372	0.89 (0.29, 1.49)	70%	
Degree					
undergraduate	3	474	0.37 (-0.67, 1.41)	95%	.94
graduate	5	391	0.33 (0.07,0.58)	28%	
Participant					
student	4	612	0.31 (-0.46, 1.08)	94%	.77
professionals	4	253	0.43 (0.15, 0.72)	11%	
Duration					
≧1 week	5	620	0.51 (-0.10, 1.12)	90%	.26
< 1 week	2	200	0.05 (-0.23, 0.33)	0%	
not mentioned	1	45	0.47 (-0.20, 1.14)	-	
Exercise					
present	5	582	0.53 (-0.09, 1.15)	90%	.38
absent	3	283	0.17 (-0.34, 0.68)	72%	
Discussion					
present	4	569	0.68 (0.05, 1.32)	91%	.08
absent	4	296	0.07 (-0.18, 0.31)	0%	
Repetition					
persistent access	4	582	0.64 (0.02, 1.26)	91%	.10
single instance	4	283	0.07 (-0.19, 0.33)	5%	

In subgroup analyses, the effect sizes showed significantly positive number (favoring Internet-based learning) in studies of low quality score, delivering graduate degree courses, with public health professionals, the presence of discussion and ongoing access to learning materials (Table 3).

3. CONCLUSION

To our knowledge, this is the first meta-analysis to explore the effect of Internet-based public health training on participants' knowledge improvement compared to no-intervention and traditional FTF format. The results of the present study revealed that Internet-based learning in public health training has a large positive effect compared with no-intervention. In contrast, the pooled effect sizes of Internet-based learning in comparison with traditional FTF instructional formats were small and of no statistical significance. The findings indicated that Internet-based learning is educationally beneficial and can achieve similar effects as that of traditional FTF instructional approach in public health training context, which concurred with previous reviews regarding Internet-based learning in other health branches such as clinical context (Cook et al. 2008), basic medicine (Lewis 2003), and nursing courses (Lahti et al. 2013).

However, results suggested heterogeneity existed across studies. With reference to the preliminary evidence (Cook et al. 2010; Lahti et al. 2013), we hypothesized that the inconsistency might arise from the variations in study design, the involved education topics, participant type, and instructional design aspects of the retained studies. Yet the results of the subgroup analyses seemed only partially explaining such inconsistency.

The present exploratory meta-analyses have several limitations. Firstly, we chose to collect only published articles in English, which could bring publication bias, despite there being no significant evidence of publication bias detected in meta-analysis of traditional FTF control group; Secondly, the sample size of 1183 participants was relatively small, and the educational outcomes were restricted to knowledge level due to limited quantitative data in other outcome levels such as skills and practice. Thirdly, unexplained inconsistencies would allow us to make tenuous inferences.

In summary, despite conclusions could be weakened by the methodological limitations, heterogeneity across reviewed studies and the possibility of publication bias, meta-analyses of individual studies increased statistical power by reducing the standard error of the weighted average effect size. The synthesized evidence demonstrated that Internet-based learning appears to have a consistent positive effect as compared to no-intervention and have a similar effect to traditional FTF instruction methods in public health training context. Even the Internet-based learning is not superior to traditional FTF formats, it can, however, offer an alternative method of learning in public health training areas. In general, this review offers important information to increase knowledge about the effectiveness of the state-of-the-art education methods.

REFERENCES

Abdelhai, R., et al. (2012). An e-learning reproductive health module to support improved student learning and interaction: a prospective interventional study at a medical school in Egypt. BMC Med Educ, 12: 11.

Ades, A. E., Lu, G., & Higgins, J. P. (2005). The interpretation of random-effects meta-analysis in decision models. Med Decis Making, 25(6): 646-654.

Aggarwal, R., et al. (2011). A comparison of online versus on-site training in health research methodology: a randomized study. BMC Med Educ, 11(2011): 1-10.

Alexander, L., Igumbor, E. U., & Sanders, D. (2009). Building capacity without disrupting health services: public health education for Africa through distance learning. Hum Resour Health, 7: 28.

Campbell, M., et al. (2008). Online vs. face-to-face discussion in a Web-based research methods course for postgraduate nursing students: a quasi-experimental study. Int J Nurs Stud, 45(5): 750-759.

Choules, A. P. (2007). The use of elearning in medical education: a review of the current situation. Postgrad Med J, 83(978): 212-216.

Chung, S., et al. (2004). Efficacy of an educational Web site for educating physicians about bioterrorism. Acad Emerg Med, 11(2): 143-148.

Cohen, J. 1992. A power primer. Psychol Bull, 112(1): 155-159.

Cook, D. A., et al. (2010). Instructional design variations in internet-based learning for health professions education: a systematic review and meta-analysis. Acad Med, 85(5): 909-922.

Cook, D. A., et al. (2008). Internet-Based Learning in the Health Professions: A Meta-analysis. JAMA, 300(10): 1181-1196.

Curioso, W. H., et al. (2008). Evaluation of a joint Bioinformatics and Medical Informatics international course in Peru. BMC Med Educ, 8: 1.

Evans, S. R., et al. (2007). Evaluation of distance learning in an "introduction to biostatistics" class: a case study. Statistics Education Research Journal, 6(2): 59-77. http://eric.ed.gov/?id=EJ839969

Farel, A., Umble, K., & Polhamus, B. (2001). Impact of an online analytic skills course. Eval Health Prof, 24(4): 446-459.

Fayram, E. S., & Anderko, L. (2009). Applied epidemiology for public health and community-based nurses. J Contin Educ Nurs, 40(8): 361-366.

Greenhalgh, T. (2001). Computer assisted learning in undergraduate medical education. BMJ, 322(7277): 40-44.

Hemans-Henry, C., Greene, C. M., & Koppaka, R. (2012). Integrating public health--oriented e-learning into graduate medical education. Am J Prev Med, 42(6 Suppl2): S103-106.

Higgins, J. P., et al. (2003). Measuring inconsistency in meta-analyses. BMJ, 327(7414): 557-560.

Hugenholtz, N. I. R., et al. (2008). Effectiveness of e-learning in continuing medical education for occupational physicians. Occup Med (Lond), 58(5): 370-372.

Khan, K. S., et al. (2003). Systematic Reviews to Support Evidence-Based Medicine. How to Review and Apply findings of Health Care Research. London: Royal Society of Medicine Press.

Laczo, R. M., et al. (2005). A comment on sampling error in the standardized mean difference with unequal sample sizes: avoiding potential errors in meta-analytic and primary research. J Appl Psychol, 90(4): 758-764.

Lahti, M., Hätönen, H., & Välimäki, M. (2013). Impact of e-learning on nurses' and student nurses knowledge, skills, and satisfaction: A systematic review and meta-analysis. Int J Nurs Stud, 51(1): 136-149.

Lewis, M. J. (2003). Computer-assisted learning for teaching anatomy and physiology in subjects allied to medicine. Med Teach, 25(2): 204-206.

McDonagh, M., et al. (2008). Avoiding Bias in Selecting Studies.

McGready, J., & Brookmeyer, R. (2013). Evaluation of student outcomes in online vs. campus biostatistics education in a graduate school of public health. Prev Med, 56(2): 142-144.

Moher, D., et al. (2009). Preferred reporting items for systematic reviews and Meta-analyses: The PRISMA statement. Plos Medicine, 6(7): e1000097.

Morris, S. B., & DeShon, R. P. (2002). Combining effect size estimates in meta-analysis with repeated measures and independent-groups designs. Psychol Methods, 7(1): 105-125.

Ried, L. D. (2010). A distance education course in statistics. Am J Pharm Educ, 74(9): 172.

Rose, M. A., et al. (2000). Evaluation of the effectiveness of a Web-based graduate epidemiology course. Comput Nurs, 18(4): 162-167.

Sears, K. E., Cohen, J. E., & Drope, J. (2008). Comprehensive evaluation of an online tobacco control continuing education course in Canada. J Contin Educ Health Prof, 28(4): 235-240.

Smits, P. B., de Graaf, L., Radon, K., de Boer, A. G., Bos, N. R., van Dijk, F. J., et al. (2012). Case-based e-learning to improve the attitude of medical students towards occupational health, a randomised controlled trial. Occup Environ Med, 69(4): 280-283.

Steckler, A., et al. (2001). Can health professionals learn qualitative evaluation methods on the World Wide Web? A case example. Health Educ Res, 16(6): 735-745.

Stroup, D. F., Berlin, J. A., Morton, S. C., Olkin, I., Williamson, G. D., Rennie, D., et al. (2000). Meta-analysis of observational studies in epidemiology: a proposal for reporting. JAMA, 283(15): 2008-2012.

ENHANCING A SYLLABUS FOR INTERMEDIATE ESL STUDENTS WITH BYOD INTERVENTIONS

Ewa Kilar-Magdziarz
Dublin Institute of Technology, Ireland

ABSTRACT

Mobile devices such as tablets and smart phones have entered education and started being used by teachers and learners for studying. This evidence-based case study focuses on the enhancement of a syllabus with BYOD classes and the role it played in boosting motivation and classroom engagement. It shows how to enhance a syllabus for Intermediate level students of English and how to implement any syllabus changes, furthermore, it shows the impact of the changes on the staff members and learners. The study was carried out in an Irish, middle- sized language school, concluding that the enhanced syllabus had a positive impact both on the learners and the teachers.

KEYWORDS

BYOD; mLearning; TESL; syllabus design

1. INTRODUCTION

As the recent Docebo (2014) report informs us, mobile phones and technologies have entered all walks of life. This trend seems to be increasing every year as more and more people use smart phones for work and education, they are just a must for many (Cearley, 2014). With global access to the Internet, people study on the go, at any time and place.

Modern learners are called by some the *net generation* or *digital natives* (Hockly & Dudeney, 2010) referring to the ways the students cope with reality around them, study, work and build social networks. These students build their reality online and acquire new competencies and skills online. All of this leads to developing digital literacies feeding into building full digital citizenships (Alberta Education, 2012).

There are myriad ways of working with the current generation, and Bring Your Own Device (hereafter, BYOD) might have potential to help students increase their skills.

1.1 BYOD: Description and Discussion

The term BYOD is an acronym that stands for Bring Your Own Device (Disterer, 2013) and often is substituted by BYOT (Bring Your Own Technology), or just BYO (Bring Your Own). BYOD/BYOT emerged when more and more companies started to allow their employees to use their own laptops, notebooks, tablets, smartphones at work. The devices could be company owned as well as employee owned. In both cases there was a need for rules and regulations before embarking on the BYOD path (Disterer, 2013). With the majority of people having access to the Internet on-the-go, and the ubiquitous presence of smart phones, there is a tendency to use mobile devices over any others at work, and to study (Sweeney, 2012). Smart phones serve the purpose of communicating, looking for information, and recording findings in multiple ways so are fully fit for education. BYOD gives a lot of flexibility, increases efficiency, reduces the costs of training and maintenance and it seems to be a good move for many organisations. On the other hand, security of all data must be considered and regulated through policies, especially in education. It is a must to involve all parties involved in BYOD projects to protect the intellectual property of individuals, and prevent problems arising from any policy breaches (Beckett, 2014).

2. LITERATURE REVIEW

In Ireland BYOD has already entered public schools especially at primary level, but there have been no studies carried out in language schools with regard to it. Many brochures and guidelines were published for public schools outlining the implementation and procedures, but no formalised research has been carried out in the field of BYOD syllabus changes for Teaching English as a Second Language (hereafter TESL).

There are different models of managing and directing BYOD implementation in an educational context. The models vary depending on the organisational decisions but Alberta Education suggests five of them (the fifth one can be a hybrid of the other four) and they fall into the continuum ranging from high standardisation to high flexibility (Alberta Education, 2012 p.11). Whichever BYOD model is considered, we must acknowledge that the technology has entered our lives and the students we teach take it for granted. Therefore the use of Information and Communication Technology (hereafter ICT) in the ESL class is inevitable (Kolade, 2012). ICT in language education started in the early 1980s with Computer Assisted Language Learning (CALL), which evolved into Technology Enhanced Language Learning (TELL) in the 1990s, adding the use of projectors, Interactive Whiteboards and tablets in the class (Hockly & Clanfield, 2010).

Then the Internet entered schools with the 21st century and allowed for mobile or m-learning. This shift enabled students to study on-the-go and changed the static classroom environment to fluid personal spaces, which redefined the ways of communicating (El-Hussein & Cronje, 2010). Following the general trend, a new approach emerged in language learning i.e. Mobile-Assisted Language Learning called hereafter MALL (Kukulska-Hulme & Shield, 2008). MALL takes into account all mobile devices, excluding stationary desktops, which can be used for learning languages through the use of short messages systems (SMS), instant communicators, microblogging sites, augmented reality applications, GPS (Yang, 2013).

The integration of ICT and TESL has potential, but must be done through consideration of the educational aims, defining individual teaching models, organising the classroom, assessing the tools to be use and then revisiting them to review their validity (Lewis, 2009). Dudney, Hockly and Pegrum (2013) suggest using TPACK or SAMR frameworks to integrate ICT in TESL. TPACK is a widely known model, which has been taking shape over the last few years (Schmidt at al., 2009) and the acronym stands for teachers' integrated Technological, Pedagogical and Content Knowledge. The framework suggests that educators should not try to become IT specialists; technology is just an enhancement to the pedagogical and content knowledge they possess (Dudney at al., 2014). To complement the integration of ICT in English Classes, Puentedura (2014) proposes his SAMR model (2011), which initiates the changes in an educational process with just an enhancement to regular classes (Substitution and Augmentation), moving to the transformative process (Modification and Redefinition), which enables the teachers to create new tasks, inconceivable with older technology.

Al-Oklai (2013) has researched the use of personal devices by her students and her study indicated that students' engagement in the classes increased and that there should be more research done in this field. The study focused on the use of smartphones with multitude of applications. There are many applications that can be used for language learning ranging from managing systems to games, flashcards, crosswords and quizzes (Ballantyne, 2010, Sharma, 2013), but what has been suggested is the use of Device Neutral Applications (DNA), that can be used on any device and platform (Campo, 2013). Al- Olkai (2013) suggests two ways of approaching the issue of using mobile applications while teaching. First of all, a teacher must be fully flexible and accept students' choices. Secondly, assignments might be based on previous experience and feedback from students. Campo (2013) adds to this list the use of generic instructions, cross platform Web 2.0 tools, group in students to produce a satisfactory outcome and allowing some freedom in a tool they would use. Strasser (2012) suggests that following these guidelines will support the implementation of ICT in class and help teachers take advantage of it.

3. METHODOLOGY AND METHODS

The research was a case study, seeking an insight into the use of BYOD enhanced English lessons in TESL. Figure one shows the triangulation of research methods with reference to students' engagement (Online Questionnaire and Focus Group) and the staff involvement (Teacher Log).

3.1 Student Questionnaire and Focus Group

The first phase of the research was a two-part questionnaire. The questionnaire had 20 questions, and was piloted prior to being sent to respondents as suggested by Seliger and Shohamy (2011). The questionnaire aimed to get an insight into the way students react to the use of smartphones or mobile devices in the classroom.

The questionnaire was distributed to students in an electronic form through a free online survey tool (www.surveymonkey.com). The respondents were sent the link to the questionnaire via email, and they could also access it through Facebook. Each student could only use the link once, with no possibility to reuse a link. The questionnaires were completed before the introduction of the lesson plans for teachers.

The focus group took place at the end of the research project after lessons using the new materials had been completed. The focus group questions were semi-structured questions which triggered respondents to thorough thinking and elaboration within limits (Seliger & Shohamy, 2011 p. 167).

3.2 Teacher Participation and Selection

Initially the whole project was intended to be carried out by the researcher; however with a change of the position within the organisation, the researcher did not have the direct access to the students in classes. Therefore, English teachers were involved in the implementation phase. There were three teachers invited to take part, and all of them have extensive experience TESL. They were given pseudonyms Julia, Jenny and James. Teachers were fully informed about the project and provided with technical support while carrying out the project. Julia and Jenny stated that they were 'casual users' or technology, whereas James had a technical background so felt 'familiar with the use of IT in class'.

4. IMPLEMENTATION

4.1 The Questionnaires

The questionnaire took the students a maximum of 12 minutes to fill in and none of the students had any problems understanding and responding to questions. Fifteen students at an Intermediate level of English responded to the questionnaire.

4.2 Participation

The implementation phase of the research project was stretched over four weeks throughout which students were exposed to BYOD enhanced lessons called here interventions (total number of 8 interventions). Prior to each intervention teachers were provided with a lesson plan. Each lesson plan was designed according to the lesson plan model suggested by Harmer and included Presentation, Practice and Production (Harmer, 2001). BYOD activities were designed to substitute the traditional approach to teaching and introduce, practice or produce some pieces of the language being learned with the focus on vocabulary, grammar or language skills.

For this project the traditional lesson plan template also included a reference to anticipated problems and solutions as well as warm-up and follow-up activities. All lesson plans were shared with the teaching staff on Google Drive prior to the classes taking place and teachers were asked to analyse and prepare them for the class and contact the researcher in case of questions. Teachers then adapted the lesson plans to meet their needs, especially where they encountered something that was not appropriate.

As a follow up after each session there was homework assigned to the students, who could practice a bit more of the language. Students and teachers were encouraged to use a social networking site to share their projects and individual tasks. Therefore the implementation phase allowed the students to practice not only the language skills but also digital literacies. To access the eight lesson plans used in this research please go to: http://myesol.weebly.com/byod-enhanced-syllabus-for-an-intermediate-level.html.

After each intervention the teachers were asked to answer four questions in writing (via email). The first question was a reflection on the lesson plan design, its usefulness and relevance. The second question posed was to get an insight into the implementation phase and adaption to the use of BYOD. The third one focused on the language skills students were practising in class. Finally, the last one was a general comment on the lesson and a subjective opinion on the success of the class. Once the set of data was collected, it underwent an inductive procedure in which sets of categories were derived from the text, followed by the discovery of commonalities and patterns in the data (Seliger & Shohamy, 2011 p. 205).

4.3 Focus Group

Thirty students were invited to take part in the focus group after their classes but only four attended the meeting. The meeting was facilitated by an independent person trained and experienced in facilitating meetings.

The students who came to the meeting signed a consent form and were given the information on the project. There were no incidents during the meeting and students had no problems answering the questions asked. Focus group data was analysed though thematic coding.

5. FINDINGS

5.1 Questionnaire

There were fifteen responses to the questionnaire and the majority of respondents came from Latin America and were mainly females aged 20-35, at Intermediate Level of English (B1 CEFRL scale). European Council describes Intermediate students as those who can form longer sentences with some minor mistakes that do not impede communication, understand most of the written and spoken pieces of information and are able to react in different social situations and use a good range or grammatical and lexical structures (Council of Europe, 2011).

Although, studying English is a complex activity, the respondents managed to pinpoint the things they find easy and difficult when studying English.

Starting with easy of study, the most commonly mentioned were listening, reading and writing i.e. two receptive skills (listening and reading) and one productive (writing). Living in an English-speaking country allows students to practice their receptive skills all the time, whereas written production allows students to take time and analyse the language structures. One of the respondents said that writing is easy as she can understand all the words. On the other hand, this shows that the students still need to focus on speaking, vocabulary and grammar which can be practised in and outside of the class.

When asked about difficulties when studying English, the respondents commented on the above mentioned adding also pronunciation issues and struggles with long comprehension texts. This data shows that there is a need for an additional teaching focus on the areas that students have problems with, to give them extra motivation and encouragement when studying, and help them to progress.

The majority of respondents spend more than three hours a day online. The majority logs into social networking sites and looks for particular information online. This information can be of use when designing BYOD courses. When asked about studying online all of the respondents have done it or still do it and found it beneficial. They also use the Internet for entertainment, which is also now enabled by mobile devices. Traditional forms of communication and quality face to face time have been substituted by the virtual realm as one of the respondents uses the Internet to check my email account, listen music, watch video, find information and use online communicators. This could have implications for BYOD in the classroom, as students might expect to me more entertained whenever in class.

All students use their laptops, smartphones and mobile phones every day. The qualitative data showed they would like to use their devices for learning, which has a great potential for all educators. The majority of respondents agree that using mobile devices in the class is a good idea, as it motivates them more. One of the respondents said It will be dynamic, and it's nice we can use the technology to learn and study English [sic]. There is some negativity around the use of technology in the class that might stem from a personal preference of face-to-face classes or the possibility of distraction during classes. Although, the issue of distraction during class time has always been present in the field of education regardless of the use of technology.

Finally, the majority of respondents believe that technology is vital, fast, easy and fun saying "That's maybe funny!" and I think will be a great idea have examples, videos and actual material to improve the classes, could be good material to make the class more dynamic [sic]. They would appreciate some extra activities online that accompany the course materials. They really and like to use the Internet to search for information, translate words, find images and examples while in class.

5.2 Participation by Teachers

The teacher logs focused on their use of the pre-designed lesson plans. The feedback on the lesson plans was very positive with all commenting that the BYOD activities were nice and useful as follow-up or lead-in activities and that students found them motivating. Julia mentioned that the lessons were a success, students were interested throughout the lessons and loved using their mobile devices for an English language learning activity. All interventions were designed and timed, so no issues were observed with the implementation. Julia commented that everything was well-staged, clear and concise which made the lesson plans fully usable. In one situation Jenny stated that the lesson plan had to be stretched to the next class as the students could not finish the online activity on time because of a poor WIFI connection.

Teachers were then asked to comment on how they felt about introducing different parts of the lesson. Jenny said that the students were attentive and interested in the class as the class was a bit different. On the other hand teachers also encountered problems. A major problem mentioned a few times by teachers was the WIFI connection in the classrooms. In one instance some students could not access the Internet to download the applications which were supposed to be used and the students had to move to another room to get the connection. This issue was also resolved by James and Jenny by using the computer room and moving away from using mobile devices in the class. James stated I had organised to do the class in the computer room for the relevant sections. This way the students that had problems connecting to the app etc with their phones could use PCs. By doing this I felt confident giving the class. Teachers felt more confident with the familiar PCs which were giving them full control over the class.

Julia also said that giving students the name of a reliable website prevents wasting time. This way students do not have the option to choose a website they prefer, just to work on the websites prescribed by the teacher.

As the teachers teach in a communicative way they were asked about the content of their classes with the reference to language skills and competencies. As can be seen, teachers were focusing on vocabulary, pronunciation, speaking and grammar most of the time. In addition, we can see that the rest of language skills were also practised and were not neglected in the course of study.

Finally, teachers were asked about the success of their lessons enhanced with BYOD. Only positive comments were made such as the lesson was different than ordinary classes, bringing a new way of teaching and learning to life. The teachers stated that the BYOD lessons added some extra value to the class but what the students enjoyed the most was the possibility of sharing their work with their classmates, friends and families on the social networking site. They responded well to the idea of collaboration and for them it was really rewarding to see their artefacts online. What is important to note here is the increase in interaction among the students, albeit in a virtual setting.

5.3 Focus Group

Having attended the BYOD enhanced classes students were asked questions related to their past and present experience with learning a language as well as the future of education with ICT.

First of all, students were asked to comment on the ways they practice their language skills. All of them were mentioning the traditional (book, pen, paper) and modern methods (mobile devices, PCs, applications) of studying. Students practice speaking mainly in the street, student 1 said that she uses English when she asks for directions or is in a restaurant. Movies also play an important role for students as they watch and repeat what is said by the actors. Students pay attention to intonation and pronunciation patterns, which might differ across English speaking countries but can still be a good model to follow. Students also mentioned the importance of repetition and recording their voices. They stated that they like the applications that enable voice recordings as then they listen to the audio tracks and compare with the right patterns of pronunciation to copy the exact sentence.

Listening is a receptive skill might easier to practice as students are surrounded by English music and films. It can be connected with entertainment and allows students to practice without fully realising doing it. Some of the students mentioned listening to news on the radio, which involved more attention, but can be even more beneficial than just films and songs exposing students to more sophisticated and formal vocabulary. Furthermore, some respondents mentioned podcasts which can be listened to on-the-go and can be really interesting, as the listener chooses on the topic of interest. This information is crucial for BYOD projects as it directs educators into the field of personalised study, with the use of own devices for better results.

Apart from listening, another receptive skill is reading. Here students mention all traditional ways of studying including books, newspaper and journal articles. Through the study of the above mentioned, the learners can expand their vocabulary and also practice their grammar, and see how the real life language is used in a written form. On the other hand, students mention the use of websites and reading articles on the go. This is the new dimension of studying, and students resort to online texts in a natural way. They process the online information without even seeing a difference between the hard copies and electronic versions while studying.

Writing has always been a skill that required a lot of input from students. It is also time consuming. To practice the skill of writing students can write short sentences as well as the lengthy articles at different registers. Students mentioned that they only practice this skill in the class, when they have to write something for the teacher. They see only the potential of practising this skills outside of class while writing emails and texts as they have to communicate with other friends that do not speak their mother tongue. This might suggest using emails and online communicators for written assignments could be beneficial.

Similarly to writing, students do not tend to practice grammar outside of the class. They just do the exercises provided to them at school, and watch some films with subtitles as subtitles are better than just listening to people because they (actors) have good grammar and you can watch and see the spelling [sic], listen to songs and analyse the lyrics. It might be a traditional way, but could be easily enhanced by the use of e.g. some quiz-making applications, which can help the students grasp English grammar, provide them with some entertainment allowing peer correction or comments. Any online activities that involve inputting data would be perfect for grammar practice.

The analysis of the ways students study at the moment, gives an insight on how important it potentially is to introduce technology in teaching English. Students are already accustomed to ICT and the personalisation of their studies could have benefits. Students were also asked to comment on their preferred study methods and mentioned that a blended learning method is the most desired by them. At school they would like to use course books while outside of the school in the form of mobile devices. When talking about technology, they feel that translators can be really useful in class, when they need to look up a word quickly and the apps do not need the WiFi connection to work.

Apart from the functionality of mobile devices as translation tools, students mentioned that the lessons with mobile phones are less boring, as there is some variety. On the other hand, one student mentioned issues with the automatic error correction function when using translation tools and other editing applications. It was stated that auto correction makes you really indifferent and you just switch off your thinking and do not fully engage. It might imply that students do not really want to be spoon-fed with information, but would rather use technology for experimenting with the language, bringing it to life more. They want to be engaged and involved.

IT skills seem to be irrelevant for the students when using mobile devices. They all have different levels and abilities but feel that can manage mobile learning. In the focus group meeting there were students with high IT skills as well as with low IT skills. Low IT skills should not impede the production of language and the students can always learn from each other.

When introducing mobile learning (BYOD) for the purpose of the project there were some issues with the Internet connection. Students taking part in the meeting really enjoyed the BYOD lessons but stated that the problems with networks must be addressed prior to the commencement of the lessons enhanced with BYOD activities. Students enjoyed the multiple applications and websites used in the project, as they were practising many skills at the same time and some of them can be used in everyday situations. Students also mentioned that the educational organisation should always have some extra tablets and smart phones available for the students, if there are to be classes run with the use of mobile devices. When asked for preferences of applications, students liked the ones with the recording option as they could listen to what they said, practising not only speaking but also listening at the same time. They mentioned that videos can be a bit intimidating and not everyone would like to do them, but could be beneficial.

To sum up, students discussed the success of the research project within the hosting organisation and stated that they would like to use them (mobile phones) in the future in class as it was something new and interesting.

6. DISCUSSION

The research project dealt with Intermediate students of English and at this level the students might feel the decrease in motivation and do not progress so fast, they need to focus on all language competences and still practice as much as possible. The research showed these students are really enthusiastic about using technology in class, they have the access to WIFI and already use their mobile devices to connect to each other. They already spend a lot of time online and this potential should be explored when implementing BYOD projects. The research showed also that the traditional pen and paper can be substituted by personalised mobile devices with no negative impact on the students. While the students were taught with the communicative method, the classroom enhancement did not impede on the interactions and grammar practice in the classroom.

As far as teachers are concerned, they would like to take part in future BYOD projects and felt as if they really involved the students in classes. The BYOD lesson plans were easy to follow but the research project findings showed that all instructions should have a reference to specific websites and a generic reference to the activities (for more technology advanced teachers). This finding is not in line with Device Neutral Application approach (Campo, 2013) in which students choose their own applications, websites according to their own preferences, learning styles. The lesson plans in this project were based on the DNA theory which was found to be not effective in the context of this research.

The project involved using technology that failed at times. Technical issues can always occur whenever we use devices so the teachers should anticipate the problems not only with connections but also with the capacity of the mobile devices students bring to school. This issue arose during the research project and resulted in time-consuming resolutions to the problem. Students had to check the compatibility of their mobile devices, then change pairs/ groups to successfully finish the activities assigned. Informing students of the prospects of using their devices prior to the class might have helped in classroom management, and in getting the best outcomes in a limited time.

While some of the problems can be eliminated, teachers should always try to prepare for the worst. One of the recommendations stemming from the study is that teachers involved in BYOD projects should be fully prepared and have a backup plan for their classes.

The students' perspective was really of importance in the study, and they seemed to enjoy the BYOD enhanced classes. They really liked social communicators and the idea of sharing things online and interacting with others.

7. CONCLUSIONS AND RECOMMENDATIONS

This research gives an insight into the changes that BYOD brought both for teachers and the students. Students felt really motivated while using technology in the class, it really personalised their learning experience as they were using their own devices with their own settings and preferences on them. Another extra value was the social aspect of the BYOD classes in which students had to share and collaborate. It is recommended to introduce technology in a gradual way, starting off with just one small parts of individual classes e.g. just the warm up or free practice. Then moving to more sophisticated enhancements in a form of project work or keeping a diary. Only when these two work fine, it is suggested to move to the syllabus enhancement. Teachers who do not feel confident using technology should not fear it with the BYOD classes, as there is no need for complicated and time consuming training or a complex school's infrastructure as students are using their own, fully configured devices. When implementing the changes, all staff members should be fully informed and prepared. All activities in lesson plans and syllabi should be device specific to avoid technical issues and BYOD lessons might include some short activities in the classroom, one-off projects or ongoing reflective diaries. It is advisable to check the Internet connections within the organisation and review the devices accessible to the students before embarking on a BYOD project.

REFERENCES

Alberta Education. (2012). Bring your own device: a guide for schools. Edmonton: Alberta Education.

Al-Okaily, R. (2013). Mobile learning and BYOD: Implementations in an Intensive English Program. Learning and Teaching in Higher Education. *Gulf Perspectives*, 10(2), 1-17.

Al-Okaily, Rasha. (2013). Device Neutral Assignemts for Mobile Learning in an English Language Classroom, QScience Procedings Vol 2013, *12th World Conference on Mobile and Contextual Learning* (mLearn2013).

Ballantyne, N. (2010). An APPettite for Learning. CALL Review Spring/Summer.

Beckett, P. (2014). BYOD - popular and problematic. *Network Security*, Volume 2014, Issue 9, 7–9.

Campo, S. (2013). Device Neutral Assignments: DNA for BYOD.

Council of Europe. (2011) The Common European Framework of Reference for Languages. Oxford, England: Oxford University Press.

Disterer, G. & Kleiner, C. (2013). Bring Your Own Device. *Procedia Technology 9*, 43 – 53.

Dudeney, G., Hockly, N., Pegrum, M. (2013). Digital Literacies: Research and Resources in Language Teaching. Harlow, UK..

EF EPI. (2014). Education First Limited.

El-Hussein, M. O. M., & Cronje, J.C. (2010). Defining Mobile Learning in the Higher Education Landscape. *Educational Technology & Society*, 13 (3), 12–21.

English Language Classroom QScience Proceedings: Vol. 2013, *12th World Conference on Mobile and Contextual Learning* (mLearn 2013).

Gartner, Inc. and/or its Affiliates (2012). *Gartner's Hype Cycle for Emerging Technologies*.

Hockly, N. & Clandfield, L. (2010). Teaching Online. Delta Publishing. UK.

Hockly, N. & Dudeney, G. (2010). How to Teach English with Technology. Pearson Publishing Ltd. UK.

Khristat, A. A. & Mahmoud, S.S. (2013). Integrating Mobile Phones into the EFL Foundation Year Classroom in King Abdulaziz University/KSA: Effects on Achievement in General English and Students' Attitudes, English Language Teaching. *Canadian Center of Science and Education* 6(8), 162-174.

Kolade, T. A. (2012). Imperatives of Information and Communication Technology (ICT) for Second Language Learners and Teachers. English Language Teaching. *Canadian Centre of Science and Education*. 5(1*), 44-48.*

Kukulska-Hulme, Agnes and Shield, Lesley (2008). An overview of mobile assisted language learning: From content delivery to supported collaboration and interaction. *ReCALL*, 20(3), 271–289.

Lewis, G. (2009). Bringing Technology into The Classroom. OUP, Oxford, UK.

M., & Whitelock, D. (2014). Innovating Pedagogy 2014: Open University Innovation Report 3.Milton Keynes: The Open University.

Mishra, P. and Koehler, M.J. (2006). Technological pedagogical content knowledge: A framework for teacher knowledge. *Teachers College Record*, 108 (6), 1017 - 54.

Palalas, A., & Anderson, T. (2013). Educational design research: Designing mobile learning interventions for language learners. In T. Plomp, & N. Nieveen (Eds.), *Educational design research – Part B: Illustrative cases* . Enschede, the Netherlands: SLO, 967-990

Piccioli, V. (2014). Becoming a modern Enterprise. Learning On The Go. Tips and Trends in m-Learning - a Report. Docebo: USA.

Puentendura, R.R. (2014). Integrating Technology and Teaching. Weblog Hoppasus.com.

Raths, D. (2013). Crossing the Device Divide. *The Journal*, 9-13.

Schmidt, D. A., Baran, E., Thompson, A. D., Mishra,P., Koehler, M. J., Shin, T.S. (2009) Technological Pedagogical Content Knowledge (TPACK). *Journal of Research on Technology in Education*, 42(2), 123-149.

Seliger, H. W. and Shohamy, E. (2011), Second Language Research Methods. OUP, Oxford, UK.

Sharma, P. (2013) The Woderful World of Apps. *IATEFL LT SIG Newsletter* Issue Spring, 19-25.

Strasser, T. (2012). Mind the App! Helbling Languages, Vienna, Austria.

Sweeney, J. (2012). BYOD in education: Nine Conversations for Successful BYOD Decision Making: Microsoft.

Vygotsky, L.S. (2002). Thought and Language (13th ed.). Massachusetts, USA, Massachusetts Institute of Technology.

Yang, J. (2013). Mobile Assisted Language Learning: Review of the Recent Applications of Emerging Mobile Technologies. English Language Teaching. *Canadian Center of Science and Education,* 6 (7), 19-25.

POST GRADUATIONS IN TECHNOLOGIES AND COMPUTING APPLIED TO EDUCATION: FROM F2F CLASSES TO MULTIMEDIA ONLINE OPEN COURSES

Bertil P. Marques, Piedade Carvalho, Paula Escudeiro, Ana Barata, Ana Silva and Sandra Queiros
GILT - ISEP
Rua Dr. António Bernardino de Almeida, 431 – 4200-072 Porto, Portugal

ABSTRACT

Promoted by the significant increase of large scale internet access, many audiences have turned to the web and to its resources for learning and inspiration, with diverse sets of skills and intents. In this context, Multimedia Online Open Courses (MOOC) consist in learning models supported on user-friendly web tools that allow anyone with minimum computer literacy to get involved. Although this model is popular abroad, it is not commonly used in the Portuguese Higher Education scenario. Therefore, this paper presents a proposal for structuring in a MOOC an already validated set of post-graduation courses in the field of Information and Communication Technologies applied to education in Portuguese. This paper also aims to establish a threshold for perfect MOOC framing in higher education contexts. The Quantitative Evaluation Framework (QEF) approach was selected for this evaluation to highlight the strengths and limitations of the Post-graduations in Technologies and Computing Applied to Education. With this project we intend to contribute for promoting education professionals' personal training at distance, in a stimulating, interactive and flexible environment, giving access to knowledge to innumerable amount of professionals who might not have access to these courses with adjustable schedules, and real life validation (and accreditation).

KEYWORDS

Education, MOOC, Online Courses, Post-Graduation

1. INTRODUCTION

When looking for specialized training, educators and other professionals in the area do not look only for face to face (F2F) opportunities. Online offers have been increasing in variety and quality, and some of the most recognized universities are following the trend (Harvard, n.d.). Although the Portuguese have also been participating in this model for quite some time, providing technical, specific courses in diverse training areas, only recently has higher education in Portugal began to bet on this teaching model (Aberta, 2013), including the MOOC. Autonomy is definitely the master word behind this trend (Henriques, 2014).

Within online learning, MOOCs promote autonomy, and learning at one's own rhythm. This is also one of the characteristics that have been distinguishing the face-to-face, blended model of the Post-graduations in Technologies and Computing Applied to Education (PGTIAE) at ISEP. These PGTIAE adopt a distinct and more flexible approach to course units' structure when compared to the regular post-graduations in Portugal as they do not follow the line of a traditional school year, and enable attendees to enrol in diverse course units or in a single one any time throughout the year (Marques and Escudeiro, 2016) (ESTAE, 2012). Taking this already innovative feature into account, next step is to apply this flexible and integrating post-graduation degree model to online learning and teaching using MOOCs. The Open University of Lisbon (Aberta,_2017) as well as the University of Porto (Porto, 2017) offer MOOC courses but as complementary training, not as complete accredited degrees such as this paper is presenting. The pedagogical insight of the courses and the transversal features of the considered subjects were decisive to carry out this proposal of having the PGTIAE course units massively available worldwide, targeting at being an additional contribution to widen post-graduation training certification prospects for education professionals in Portuguese Speaking countries all over the world.

Having that in mind, this paper presents the pedagogical model chosen for developing the PGTIAE MOOC, believing that this is an effective way to qualify and train those interested and active in education related subjects in Portuguese.

To cover the essential contents implied in this still in progress project, the paper is structured as follows: First, a general overview of the MOOC history and main features are introduced, followed by a brief reference to the most relevant technology related to MOOC development, and to some crucial aspects involved in their setting and preparation. Afterwards, the considered structure for the PGTIAE MOOC model is detailed, and then the evaluation framework QEF, which is being used to assess the MOOC, is described. Finally, few conclusions concerning the proposal are drawn.

2. STATE OF THE ART

In this section, a brief overview of the MOOC first steps and implications is included, followed by a short explanation concerning the most common technologies and platforms that make MOOCs useful and appealing learning online options.

2.1 Brief Overview of the History of MOOC

MOOC is a learning model based on the learning process (vs accreditation) that bets on interactive participation in large scale, using Web tools to allow anyone even with very limited computer skills to broaden and/or improve their knowledge on a topic, or to learn something new (Escudeiro, 2016). This can be defined as a model for teaching an online course that integrates knowledge and skills of professionals in various fields, social networks connections, and a diverse collection of online educational resources (Matta, 2013).

Based on the connectivity provided by the internet, where the number of possible participants is unlimited, it allows people from anywhere in the world, at any time of the day, to learn by the principles of the so-called "distance education" and "open education" (EADTU, 2015) (Openuped, 2015) (Sanchez-Gordon and Luján-Mora, 2014).

Since its emergence in 2008 in Canada, the MOOC concept has widespread, especially after 2012, the recognized "Year of the MOOC" (Estadão, 2013). Although the first experiment had already been conducted in 2007, by David Wilder at the Utah State University in 2007, only in 2008, during the development of an innovation process in the training field, was the first official MOOC course launched. It was titled "Connectivism and Connectivist knowledge". The credits for this first MOOC belong to George Siemens, Stephen Downes, and the technologist David Cormier. Twenty five hundred students enrolled in this course, including 2.300 graduates. The idea of connectivity to construct knowledge was there to stay, and in 2011 it had acquired even wider impact with the opening of a course on Artificial Intelligence, which was considered an educational revolution. The following year, the emphasis on dissemination among the major North American universities like Harvard, MIT, Yale and Stanford, led MOOC to be at the top of the discussion and analysis lists, regarding education (Estadão, 2013).

The leading aspect that has prompted Siemens to draw this kind of model courses, in which knowledge is acquired through the participation of all, was undoubtedly the leverage of internet potential (Henriques, 2014). It is worth mentioning that MOOCs may have various formats: they can be "free", requiring no payment, provided at "large scale", bearing a high number of participants, and "simple", requiring only a teacher to organize the information that will be available (Aberta, 2013).

In the following section, an overview of the fundamental technology that has been supporting this worldwide learning tool is provided for a better understanding of the implications of structuring a MOOC proposal.

2.2 Relevant Technology

Considering the rapid development of technology, more and more companies invest in innovation aiming to create solutions, and especially to meet the present society's needs and challenges in diverse areas, like culture, education, sciences, and economy. The development of the project proposed in this paper targets all those who wish to improve their professional skills, and knowledge. Distance learning overcomes, among other aspects, the incompatibility of timetables, travelling infrastructures, or health conditions. The integration of online content can thus promote quality learning and accessibility.

Looking back at the first developed MOOCs, any educational institution can be a MOOC supplier if they choose to develop a platform or use an existing open source solution. At present there are diverse kinds of MOOC providers. There are those aiming at making a profit, and others that do not intend to have any kind of financial return (Gonçalves, 2015). Coursera, Udacity and Udemy, the currently best known and recognized providers, are some examples of platforms with profit at sight, while edX is a non-profit MOOC supplier. Providing open source software, it is available for any education institution that wishes to develop or offer their own MOOCs. Besides these, there are other suppliers and platforms that enable creating and distributing MOOCs, such as Canvas Network, the Blackboard, P2PU (Peer-to-Peer University) CourseSites, and OpenClass. Furthermore, the Google Coursebuilder tool is to be mentioned as a platform specifically designed for the development of MOOC courses (Costa et al., 2015).

Udemy has been selected to be PGTIAE MOOC provider due to its versatility – it enables both paid and free courses to be offered to any registered user -, and to the fact of embracing an already large Portuguese from Brazil spoken audience (Adriano-Stoyke, 2016).

2.3 Pedagogical MOOCs: Brief Comparison

To understand the potential of the MOOC approach proposed in this paper a brief comparative analysis between the PGTIAE MOOC and other MOOC courses was performed, including one available at Udemy, the platform chosen to host the PGTIAE. This analysis has also considered two examples authored by the University of Porto, in Portugal (UP), one by the Open University in Lisbon (UA), and another by an independent author (Alexsandro Sunaga). As presented in Table 1, the PGTIAE MOOC is the only one enabling participants to get a certification corresponding to an academic degree, simultaneously granting them the possibility of getting independently certified training courses.

Table 1. Comparison analysis between four pedagogical MOOCs and the PGTIAE's proposal

Author	Platform	MOOC Title	Certificate of Participation/ Conclusion	Academic degree certification	Independently Certified course units
ISEP	Udemy	PGTIAE	✓	✓	✓
UP	Open edX MiriadaX	As alterações climáticas dos Média Escolares 1ª Edição	✓	x	x
	Open edX MiriadaX	Laboratório de Aprendizagem: Cenários e Histórias da Aprendizagem 2ª Edição	✓	x	x
UA	Eco	Necessidades Educativas Especiais	✓	x	x
Alexsandro Sunaga	Udemy	Tecnologias na Educação	✓	x	x

3. PROPOSED COURSE STRUCTURE

Within the scope of both PGTIAE (Supporting Technologies to Education; Computing in Education), each curricular unit (UC) is understood as a single training course (ESTAE, 2012). To guarantee the homogenization of all these courses, the model outlined in this paper considers a set of recommendations based on a pedagogical structure adapted to the online format. In this format, the production of any content must consider determining aspects, such as structure, effort, length, pedagogical design, content production, supporting material, and validation.

The course structure, and the structure of each class, as well as the pedagogical model chosen, and its background are described in the section that follows.

3.1 Proposed Structure of a Training Course within the PGTIAE MOOC

Each course consists of eight lessons that will be open in the same week. These lessons include prerequisites, and their respective recipients, learning objectives, the definition of the type of content supporting the course, ensuring the quality of all available materials, the description of the evaluation strategy (assessment methods, type of tasks and activities to be carried out), aligning that with the intended learning outcomes, the description of the interaction model to be adopted (it should be clear to the trainee if the course is entirely autonomous, with no tutoring, or if the trainer is present throughout the process and, if this is the case, a balance between the presence of the trainer, the interaction between the participants, and the individual cognitive process are clarified). Besides that, each lesson includes an introductory video at the beginning of each lesson, introducing the trainee.

A video introducing the course, providing a short overview of maximum 2 minutes, is included at the very beginning contextualizing and explaining the complete course structure. The elements that are part of a course are as follows: Topic; Learning objectives; Lesson description; Promotional video; Complementary material; Video lessons; Lesson Summary; Lesson title; Subtitle; Course promotional image (common to all lessons); Trainer's biography.

3.2 Structure of Each Lesson

At the beginning of each lesson, an introductory welcome video presenting the trainer(s) needs to be included (this should be the same for all PGTIAE lessons). Besides that, the following has to be considered to sustain the structure of each lesson:

- Definition of prerequisites and respective recipients;
- Definition of lesson structure;
- Definition of learning objectives (summary);
- Definition of the type of contents supporting the lesson;
- Title and subtitle;
- Lesson conclusions and next lesson theme;
- Last lesson presents the evaluation strategy (evaluation methods, type of tasks and activities to be carried out), aligning it with the defined learning outcomes;
- Continuous and active learning have to be enabled (bibliography to be used has to be included, contents have to be appealing, well distributed, and at least 2 questions need to be launched in each lesson so that the trainee may effectively apply and demonstrate the skills and knowledge acquired);
- The model of interaction to be adopted has to be defined (as pointed out at the beginning of section 3.1.);
- Bibliography to be used has to be included.

3.2.1 Effort

Trainers should consider that the materials used in face-to-face or face-to-face and online teaching must be redesigned to incorporate a MOOC.

3.2.2 Length

Each course will have from 35 to 50 minutes, which will correspond to 5 (4+1) lessons taking from 7 to 10 minutes each, so that the trainees do not consider the contents as excessively lengthy, and thus leading to a possible demotivation and early abandonment. The 5 (4+1) lessons must take place on the same week. The image of the trainer should be present about 60% of lesson time.

3.3 Pedagogical Design

From a methodological point of view, the course is organized asynchronously, based on a flexible combination of moments of independent learning and collaborative learning, the various stages being previously defined at the time of the course presentation. The course should be clear about what is expected from the participants, therefore it is essential to include: The course programme; The skills to be acquired/developed; The calendar of the activities, and the typology of the activities; The specifications of the activity(s) to be developed and their evaluation criteria; The objectives of each communication/ interaction session; The bibliography.

Participants who conclude the course will have a certificate from the service provider confirming the domain of the competences acquired. To ensure pedagogical consistency of all the lessons in the MOOC, both PGs have a baseline structure designed as presented in Table 2.

The MOOC structure is based on making content available weekly, and each week the eight lessons should follow sequential topics. For each of the topics it is important to clarify the learning objectives, which can be presented in the form of text or small videos, explaining to the learner not only the expected learning outcomes, but also the type of activities that will take place to evaluate the acquired skills. The expository videos for each lesson, as mentioned before, should be short and objective, taking no more than 7 to 10 minutes each. It is not recommended to produce and make available videos in which the content exposure exceeds 10 minutes.

The type of learning content to be used in each of the topics, like content matter videos (simple video, voice-over video, video with PPT, video whiteboard, etc.) can be complemented with other material, such as, text, images, links, among others.

Table 2. A Typical MOOC Structure

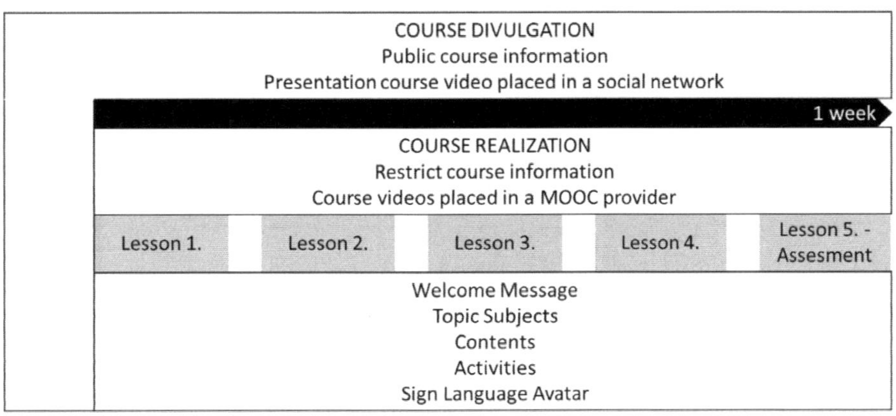

3.4 Background of the Training Course

Recordings are performed at ISEP facilities. It is necessary to make a plan of all the contents that are included in the course (texts, images, videos, among others). Knowing that most MOOCs rely on video production, it is essential to create a script so that the content producer understands the idea and resources that will be needed to affect that production.

Double validation: The Organization Committee of both PGTIAE ensures that the published courses comply with the rules of the MOOCs. The MOOC provider ensures that the courses meet the quality criteria. All courses published within these two post-graduations are the property of ISEP.

4. QEF APPROACH

The approach has been adapted so that the essential criteria are assessed in a pre-evaluation phase, covering the general usage requirements. This section presents the application of the Quantitative Evaluation Framework (QEF) approach to assess the PGTIAE MOOC, which has been applied in an operating teaching environment for the last 30 years.

The QEF approach has been developed to highlight the strengths and limitations of the pedagogical models. A set of requirements were chosen and validated by the teachers in order to evaluate the educational courses developed by a group of teachers from the Polytechnic Institute of Oporto, from different fields of knowledge, having in common the support on technology. Tables 3, 4 and 5 represent the Educational Requirements established by the group of teachers from educational technology. The dimensions from our quality space are: Pedagogical, Ergonomic, and Technician. Each dimension has a set of factors, and for each factor we have a group of requirements. The QEF framework is not restricted to measure the final quality, instead it allows for the evaluation of systems quality at any moment during their lifecycle.

Table 3. Pedagogical Dimension

Pedagogical	Learning	PL01 - The learning context is suited to the concept of post-graduate degrees
		PL02 - MOOC model can be integrated in different pedagogical methodologies
		PL03 - The learning context effectively addresses the learning objectives
		PL04 - MOOC model promotes to the forming is self-taught
	Evaluation	PA05 - There are steps that promote the assessment of learning acquired
		PA06 - Throughout the course the forming is evaluated with minor issues related to the topic dictated
		PA07 - Each form has access to your progress and status in relation to the content made to date

Table 4. Ergonomic Dimension

Ergonomic	Usability	EU08 - The conditions and the field of MOOC model are clear, precise and concise
		EU09 - The form whenever you want you can easily start and leave school
		EU10 - Interaction with MOOC model is intuitive
		EU11 - The communication between trainee is suitable
		EU12 - The content written/spoken is free of grammatical and syntactic errors
		EU13 - The trainee receives feedback whenever he ask questions on the forum
	Content Quality	EQC14 - MOOC model is inclusive
		EQC15 - The use of audio is critical to MOOC model
		EQC16 - The use of video is fundamental to the lessons of the template created
		EQC17 - Graphics and images make the lessons more appealing
		EQC18 - The overall objective of the curricular units are at the beginning of the course
		EQC19 - The trainee feels he is an asset to attend the course
		EQC20 - MOOC model features a format that surpasses the expectations of forming
	Socio-Cultural	ESC21 - MOOC model is exclusively produced in Portuguese
		ESC22 - MOOC model is suitable for the target audience
		ESC23 - MOOC model does not contain discriminatory aspects

Table 5. Technical dimension

Technical	Learning Objects	TOA24 - MOOC model has supported educational material
		TOA25 - MOOC model supports exercise throughout the course
		TOA26 - In the process of learning the trainees go through various stages (acquire new knowledge, new concepts, think where to apply what they're learning in practice, etc.)
	Content Management	TGC27 - The MOOC model offers a wide variety of contents
		TGC28 - MOOC model presents the organization in all content
		TGC29 - Is presented in a linear manner all content
		TGC30 - All are adapted to each course unit
		TGC31 - Use of short titles and topics
		TGC32 - All contents are developed by an expert team in the area that are tasked
	Video/Audio	TVA31 - Video capture in formal format
		TVA32 - Videos lasting 8 to 10 minutes for each lesson
		TVA33 - Each curricular unit has a brief introduction in video format
		TVA34 - Video capture in formal format
		TVA35 - Quality videos and audios
		TVA36 - All videos and audios are written in Portuguese Language
	Text	TT36 - The text is presented in a linear way and of course
		TT37 - The text presents only one language (Portuguese Language)
		TT38 - All text taught in class is drawn up with the new orthographic agreement

5. CONCLUSION

Trainers, instructors, teachers are expected to be effective in establishing a connection with their trainees/ course participants, so that the learning objectives are accomplished. It is therefore crucial to set appropriate means targeting at motivating and engaging learners in the content matter. This is what professionals also look for when searching for new and challenging ways of improving their skills, and developing their knowledge. In the digital age they look mainly for online offers for their continuous training, and it is here that well-structured, appealing, and quality controlled content MOOCs still have a role to play.

This paper has presented a proposal for structuring in a MOOC two face-to-face, and blended, Portuguese post-graduation courses that have already been validated in the field of Information and Communication Technologies applied to Education: "Supporting Technologies to Education," and "Computing in Education" post-graduations. The course contents and structure, each lesson requirements and specifications are defined, and all the recording infrastructures prepared at ISEP premises. The QEF approach is being used to evaluate the PGTIAE MOOC so that its strengths and limitations are identified. With this still in progress project a serious contribution for promoting education professionals' personal training at distance, in a stimulating, interactive and flexible environment, is being prepared.

We believe that the transversal features of the PGTIAE course units offered as MOOC consist in an added value within academic degree certification for education professionals in Portuguese Speaking countries all over the world.

ACKNOWLEDGEMENT

This work is being supported by ISEP (Instituto Superior de Engenharia do Porto), and GILT (Games, Interaction and Learning Technologies).

REFERENCES

Aberta, U. (2013). *O Primeiro MOOC em Língua Portuguesa*. Lisboa: Rita de Cássia da Silva Pedroso de Albuquerque.

Aberta, U. *Lista de MOOCs disponíveis na UP*. http://eco.imooc.uab.pt/elgg/ view on 01 June 2017.

Adriano-stoyke, (2016). *Escolha do Udemy*. Online Available at: http://adriano-ostoyke.com, Accessed February 2017.

EADTU, (2015). *Institutional MOOC strategies in Europe*. Status report. Darco Jansen, Robert Schuwer, February 2015 ISBN 978-90-79730-15-5.

Escudeiro, P. (2007). *Capítulo VII - Avaliação Da Qualidade Em Conteúdos Digitais.* In T. D. Minho, E - Conteúdos Para E - Formadores. Guimarães. Retrieved Fevereiro 25, 2017

Escudeiro, P. (2015). *Unidade Curricular-Camul.* Porto.

Estae, 2012. Official Website Of *Postgraduate Specializations In Technologies And Computer Applied To Education*, Url: Http://Www2.isep.ipp.pt/estaei/, view on 15 February 2017.

Costa, F. A., Moura Santos, A., Silva, A. G. and Viana, J. (2015). *Guiões para desenho de cursos MOOC.* In MEC. Experiências de Inovação Didática no Ensino Superior. Lisboa: MEC, pp. 327- 342.

Gonçalves, V.and Gonçalves. B. (2015). *Avaliação de plataformas para criação e distribuição de MOOC.* Bragança.

Harvard. *Harvard Online Learning.* http://online-learning.harvard.edu/

Henriques, A. M. (2014). *Mooc os cursos gratuitos online que democratizam o ensino.* p3.publico(http://.pt/actualidade/educacao/12052/).

Matta, C. E. (2013). *MOOC: Transformação das Práticas da Aprendizagem.* Belém, Pará.

Marques, B., Escudeiro, P. 2016. *Trainning portuguese teachers using blended learning - A different aproach*, Nunes, M. B., McPherson, M. (Vol. Ed.), Kommers, P, Isaías, P. - Computer Science and Information Systems Series Editors: fom ELearning 2016 Conference. Madeira, Portugal, 1 a 3 de Julho. ISBN 978-989-8533-51-7. , Pp. 185-190.

Minho, U. d. (2003). *Estado da Arte Parte II.* Universidade do Minho.

Montes, R., Gea, M., Bergaz, R., & Rojas, B. (2014). *Generating lifelong-learning communities and branding with Massive Open Online Courses.* Information Resources Management Journal, 27(2), 27–46. http://doi.org/10.4018/irmj.2014040103.

Openuped, (2015). *Definition Massive Open Online Courses (MOOCs)*, https://www.openuped.eu/images/docs/Definition_Massive_Open_Online_Courses.pdf, view on 07 February 2017.

Porto, U. *Lista de MOOCs disponíveis na UP.* https://www.mooc-list.com/university-entity/universidade-do-porto/ view on 01 June 2017.

Sanchez-Gordon S., Luján-Mora S.. (2014). *MOOCs gone wild.* Proceedings of the 8th International Technology, Education and Development Conference (INTED 2014), p. 1449-1458, Valencia (Spain), March 10-12 2014. ISBN: 978-84-616-8412-0. ISSN: 2340-1079.

TOWARDS ARCHITECTURE FOR PEDAGOGICAL AND GAME SCENARIOS ADAPTATION IN SERIOUS GAMES

Wassila Debabi[1] and Ronan Champagnat[2]
[1]*Badji Mokhtar University, Annaba, Algeria*
[2]*La Rochelle University, La Rochelle, France*

ABSTRACT

Serious games seem to be a promising alternative to traditional practices for learning. Recently, their use in computer science education and learning programming became more widespread. Actually, many students in programming courses have difficulties to master all required competencies and skills especially at introductory level and games have the potential to be an important teaching tool for their interactive, engaging and immersive activities. However, the critical point of a serious game remains the relation between the game and its pedagogical content. In fact, a serious game has to deal with two scenarios: the game scenario and the pedagogical scenario.

In this paper, we introduce a system that aims to improve algorithmic learning using serious games. We propose a method for managing both game and pedagogical scenarios along with a double adaptation: the first phase that adapts the pedagogical scenario and the second phase that adapts the game scenario. We propose a software architecture that ensures the interaction between the aforementioned two phases. The learning and the game scenarios are planned according to the student's profile, his pedagogical path, his progress in the game and also taking into account the collected traces in the observation phase.

KEYWORDS

Serious games, algorithmic, learning, adapting, motivation

1. INTRODUCTION

Data structures and algorithms are important foundation topics in computer science education. However, they are considered to be hard to teach and learn because they usually model complicated concepts, refer to abstract mathematical notions, or describe complex dynamic changes in data structures. Many students in programming courses have difficulties to master all required competencies and skill especially at introductory level. Several reasons are pointed out, and a number of researches have been carried out to recognize the characteristics of novice programmers. Mostly, the traditional learning methodologies usually based on lectures and specific programming language syntaxes, rendering learning difficult for beginners, and fail often to attract and motivate them to be implicated in programming activities (Lahtinen *et al.*, 2005; Schulte & Bennedsen, 2006). Also, programming languages typically used in programming classes are professional in nature (C, C++, C# and Java), and they have extensive and complex syntaxes, that makes learning difficult for beginners (Jenkins, 2002; Motil & Epstein, 1998). Another concern is the students' difficulties with abstract concepts: knowing how to design a solution to a problem, subdivide it into simpler sub problems, and conceive hypothetical error situations for testing and finding out mistakes (Esteves *et al.*, 2008); and difficulties in understanding even the most basic concepts (Lahtinen *et al.*, *op. cit.*; Miliszewska & Tan, 2007) such as variables, data types or memory addresses as these abstract concepts do not have direct analogies in real life (Lahtinen *et al.*, *op. cit.*; Miliszewska & Tan, *op. cit.*). Many technological solutions attempt to solve these problems by providing environments which give facility in tasks of execution and visualization mechanisms, while they failed in other aspects such as the lack of motivation and the inability to properly portray in a comprehensible way the complex computer programming concepts (Henriksen & Kölling, 2004). Recently, interest has turned to serious games as providing engaging ways of learning. Serious games technology offers tools that may have the potential to help computer-programming students become more engaged in their learning through a "learn while having fun" approach (Coelho *et al.*, 2011).

More importantly, games offer methods of learning that are highly consistent with modern theories of effective learning which recommend that learning activities should be active, situated, problem-based, interactive, and socially mediated (Boyle *et al.*, 2011).

As previously said, acquiring and developing knowledge about programming is a highly complex process, and algorithmic thinking is a term used very often as one of the most important competences that can be achieved by education in Informatics. Algorithmic thinking is somehow a pool of abilities that are connected to constructing and understanding algorithms (Futschek, 2006). Our principal attention carries on enhancing student's algorithmic thinking skill, where our goal is articulated according three aspects. The first one is to let students focusing on the resolution of the problem more than on the syntax of the programming language. The second one is to reduce their difficulties with abstract concepts: students apply human principles of thinking and acting to the computer. This includes understanding the way programs are executed, both in terms of internal variables and external files and I/O (Kaasboll, 1998). And the last one is to allow students knowing how to design a solution to a problem by dividing it into simpler sub-problems.

Another concern is the diversity of learners. This phenomenon can be met in all classrooms, where each learner is characterized by some diversity in results, abilities, interests, motivation and needs. Adaptation in serious games is an important feature and many researchers agreed that serious games and simulations have to become more challenging, unpredictable and player-centric, to be fully embraced as an effective way of knowledge transfer (Barnes *et al*, 2008; Bourse & Labat, 2012). It can also manage the players-learners' frustration while increasing their motivation.

Our goal is the contextualisation and the individualization of the gaming path, and therefore the learning path for each learner according to his/her own need. Thus, we provide the player-learner a unique game experience and effective learning experience. As a result, we are confronted to a double adaptation: the adaptation of the pedagogical scenario and the adaptation of the game scenario. To ensure this double adaptation, our game is integrated into "POLARIS" (Trillaud, 2013), a software platform that has functions to analyse users' actions and provide adaptation mechanisms. The adaptation process and the proposed architecture to ensure this feature are detailed in the following sections.

We present a brief study and discussion about existing educational games in Section 2. Section 3 introduces our proposed system. A case study is presented in Section 4. Finally, conclusions drawn from the work done so far are discussed in Section 5.

2. RELATED WORK

In order to help students and improve their learning, diverse games dedicated to learning programming were implemented. All these initiatives proposed a number of features that met the problems typically encountered in computer programming. We distinguish two categories of games, the first one aims to teach programming by asking the learner to develop his/her own game, as in **Robocode** (O'Kelly & Gibson, 2006), this game developed by IBM aspires to teach programming using Java language. The concepts taught by Robocode are the basic concepts of structured programming but also the main structures of object-oriented programming such as inheritance, polymorphism, etc. **M.U.P.P.E.T.S** (Phelps et al., 2003) "The Multi-User Programming Pedagogy for Enhancing Traditional Study" that aims to teach the basic concepts of object-oriented programming using exclusively the JAVA programming language. **EEClone** (Gestwicki & Sun, 2008), This game is an arcade-style computer game. Students analyse various design patterns within EEClone, and from this experiment, learn how to apply design patterns in their own game software. The second category includes games that ask learners to code so they can progress in the game, such as **GAME2LEARN project** (Barnes *et al.*, *op. cit*). This project gathers two games with two distinct scenarios: "**Saving Sera**", where player must perform various tasks involving programming concepts. When the player makes a mistake, the character must fight a script bug by answering various computer science questions. The second game is "**The Catacombs**", it aims to familiarize students with activities such as variables declaration and the usage of simple as well as nested if statements and loops. Another initiative is the well-known **Hour of Code** (Code Studio, 2015) designed to demystify code and show that anybody can learn the basis using Scratch. Also **Prog & Play** (Muratet et al., 2010) a real-time strategy game, where students write programs to control units in a battlefield. They can choose the programming language amongst Ada, C, Java, OCaml, Scratch and Compalgo. **Wu's Castle** (Eagle & Barnes, 2009) is a role playing game, where students program changes in loops and arrays in an interactive, visual way. The game provides immediate feedback and helps students visualize code execution in a safe environment. It uses the programming language C ++. **CoLoBot: Colonize with Bots** (CoLoBot, 2013) combines both a real time game of strategy and an initiation to programming. It aims to teach students Object Oriented programming style similar to C++ or Java. And **PlayLogo3D** (Paliokas *et al.*, 2011) a role playing game, especially designed for children aged 6-13 years in the early stages of programming education. PlayLogo3D aspires to introduce the very basic concepts of structured programming using LOGO programming language.

Some games listed before use macro-languages to support students' understanding the logic behind the programming elements, while others use a distinct programming language for teaching such as Pascal, JAVA, C / C ++. We believe it is a challenging situation for the learner. Dealing with the syntax of a particular programming language is an additional charge, especially for novice learners that may discourage them, leading them to withdraw the learning. Several common deficits in novices' understanding of specific programming language constructs were pointed out in many studies (Soloway & Spohrer, 1989; Jenkins, 2002) and inappropriate analogies may be drawn from natural language leading learners to serious confusion. Another concern is about actions that take place "behind the scene": the abstraction is a powerful programming concept but beginners face difficulties moving from the abstract toward the concrete (Soloway *et al. op. cit*).

Our work is based on these tools, we are inspired by the second approach but instead of asking learners to code in order to progress in the game, our approach is designed such that to bring them to take actions in the game and see the translation of their actions into algorithmic instructions, this way allows the learner to be free from the syntax complexity of programming languages, and focusing more on solving the problem. All the initiatives mentioned above propose a number of features that meet the problems typically encountered in computer programming. They introduce interesting notions such as attractive graphical interfaces, visual representation of the programming tasks, interactive and interesting scenarios that keep the learner immersed. However, these games do not take into account the learner's profile and his/her progression in the game. Adaptation in games that are either serious or not, is an important feature that allows to individualize and contextualize the gaming experience. It also allows managing the frustration of the players-learners while increasing their motivations (Hocine *et al*, 2011). Unlike video games, which are only concerned by the game aspects, adaptation in serious games must take into account the "serious" aspects related to learning goals, information or skills gaining. Therefore, adaptation must take into account not only the information collected about the player-learner during his/her interaction with the game (traces, scores achieved, progression in the game, etc.) but also the parameters related to the pedagogical goals and the goals he/she achieved by so far.

3. PROPOSED SYSTEM

The use of serious games in education is controversial. If their effects on motivation have been shown, their pedagogical potential remains questionable in the absence of a tutor's direction. (Conati *et al*, 2009) advanced as an explanation the lack of a sufficient adaptation of the program to the learner who would substitute the tutor by proposing personalized learning and activities. It should be taken into account that learners have different learning needs and styles that are difficult to define.

As a consequence, we decided to built a serious game scenario management based both on controlling the game experience and the learning progression. Our purpose is to show how to perform the interleaving decision of game and learning to progress in the game. We suggest starting from the game point of view (according to multicriteria decision algorithm as PROMETHEE II) and then to chose the best pedagogical activity (according to user profile, learning objectives and possible activities, using classification algorithm).

We propose to integrate our serious game in POLARIS platform, which ensures adaptive and dynamic execution of the learning scenario, and also the game scenario based on the user profile (who becomes a learner-player or player-learner), his/her pedagogical progression, his/her progression in the game, the score achieved in the game and the trace generated during the game session.

3.1 Constraints and Specifications

The critical point of a serious game is the relation between the game and its educational content. Several experiments have shown that serious games achieve their goals when they have a strong "game" component clearly highlighted. Thus, serious games have double script. Actually, there are two scenarios to design: a game scenario (explicit) along with another learning scenario (implicit). Our idea is that the game has n-different stages; each stage is dedicated (implicitly) to a learning goal. In each stage, the game simulates the algorithm's behavior.

Another fundamental point is how to maintain the player's motivation during the game. In fact, adaptation can significantly increase the effectiveness of the learning task by reinforcing the motivation and the learner's interest. Several approaches address this issue as (Hocine *et al*, *op.cit.*): The use of general principles and good game design practices in order to create immersion (flow); The use of appropriate and attractive human-machine interfaces in order to facilitate the player-learner's interaction and acceptance; Finally, allow a dynamic adaptation in order to individualize and contextualize the game experience for each player-learner.

In order to enhance the player's motivation and immersion, we take into account, for the development of our game, the game design specifications related in (Carron *et al.*, 2009). In addition, we focus on adaptation by proposing a system that ensures a dynamic adaptation in order to individualize and contextualize the game experience and consequently increase the satisfaction for each player-learner while improving the effectiveness of the learning.

3.2 Method

We propose in the rest of this paper a software architecture that ensures this process of adaptation and the interaction between the adaptation phases. Indeed, we proceed to a double adaptation planned in two phases: the former is "**the decision phase**" that determines the most appropriate concept to teach in the next step (adapting the pedagogical scenario). Once the concept is decided, we proceed to the second phase called "**the realization phase**" that chooses the most appropriate game mission to play (adapting the game scenario).

3.2.1 Learning Scenario

Our game is mainly dedicated to teach basic algorithmic concepts but also to improve the learner's competence with regards to algorithmic thinking and decomposition of the problem in hand. Therefore, *AlgoGame* is designed essentially for computer science students that are dealing for the first time with this area, because they have the most difficulties in understanding the theoretical concepts. Therefore, we classified the programming concepts in four categories as follows:

Fundamentals: group the very basic programming concepts such as Assignment, Instructions order, Boolean expressions, Inputs/ Outputs.

Control structures: group algorithm of Permutations, IF-THEN Statement, IF-THEN-ELSE Statement, and Loops.

Data structures: includes algorithm related to Arrays, Stacks, Queue, and Linked lists.

Further concepts: contains concepts that require the abovementioned categories to be assimilated as functions and record structures.

Some concept categories are prerequisite for learning concepts in other categories, e.g. it would be inappropriate to teach "IF-Then statement" from the Control Structures category before teaching "Boolean expressions" from the Fundamentals category. Therefore, concepts of different categories are interconnected by prerequisites. Only concepts from Fundamental category do not require any prior notion.

Our work considers the adaptation of the learning scenario (and consequently the game scenario) in an Interactive Adaptive System. We limit the interactions using contextualized blocs called situations (Pham et al. 2015). *A situation* in an interactive application is a component where actors interact using resources in a specific context to achieve the defined goals. The application execution consists in choosing, related to a given situation, the most appropriate following one (Hoang et al, 2015). In our case, a situation refers to a learning concept; there are two parameters to define: *A pre-condition*, which is a set of conditions that must be verified in order to begin a new situation (a new learning concept). *A post-condition* is the expected result after executing the situation. It represents the exit conditions from a situation.

3.2.2 The Game Scenario

AlgoGame is an exploratory game; it is designed as exploratory areas where the player must solve a mission to unlock access to new missions, which were before forbidden for access. Each mission ensures learning of one or more algorithmic concepts.

Like every game, *AlgoGame* has a set of rules that indicates how it is meant to be played by the players (the game mechanics) serving as a basis for the gameplay. The proposed core mechanics for our game are related in [4] and taking into consideration all the aforementioned constraints and specifications to meet the aimed academic goals.

3.2.3 Relation between Learning and Game Scenario

In the concern of having a coherent link between the game and its educational content, all the aforementioned learning concepts are related to one or more mission in the game. In other words, one mission in the game can be dedicated to one or more learning goals. In fact, we aim to provide an individualized gaming and learning experience to learners according to their needs. For that purpose, the learning path is planned according to **the student's profile** but also taking into account **the model of the student' scenario**, which indicates his/her progress in the game (and consequently his/her actual learning path), and the **model of learning scenarios**, which contains all the relations established between the concepts of the different categories. All these information combined to **the collected traces** in the observation phase are used in the decision phase. This phase uses a Trace-Based Subjective logic (Hoang *et al. op.cit*) to determine the most appropriate next concept to learn.

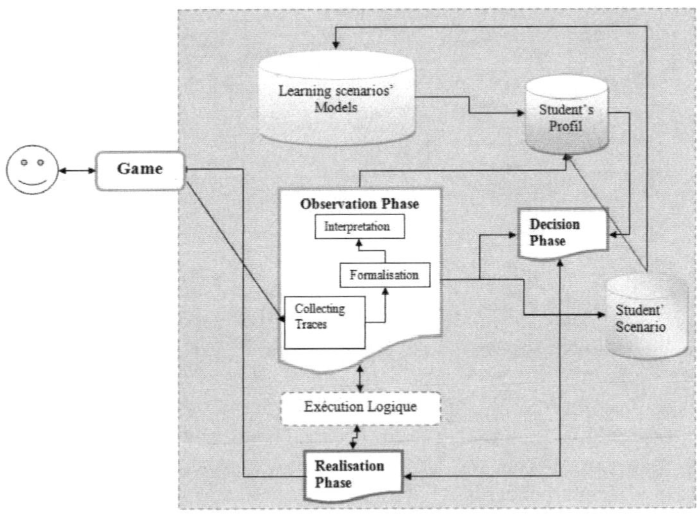

Figure 1. Software architecture

Once the learning concepts are defined, "TF-IDF" algorithm is used in the realization phase (Sawadogo, 2016) to determine the most appropriate next resource to deliver to learner and thus the next mission in the game. The figure 1 illustrates the system's architecture and the different models involved in the decision and realization phases.

4. CASE STUDY

AlgoGame aims to introduce students to algorithmic concepts, to help them get familiar with how the algorithms are structured and also enable them to understand the algorithmic thinking. The game has several levels; each one aspires to teach a programming concept from the four aforementioned categories (3.2.1), or to teach an algorithm that combines several concepts. This section will describe a case study, and we have chosen to present an illustrative example of the system functioning. This operating principle ensures an implicit adaptation of the pedagogical scenario and also of the game scenario by providing the learner-player by the most appropriate mission to play according to his/her own needs in the current situation. We will then describe the game mission selected in our example to illustrate the programming concepts involved.

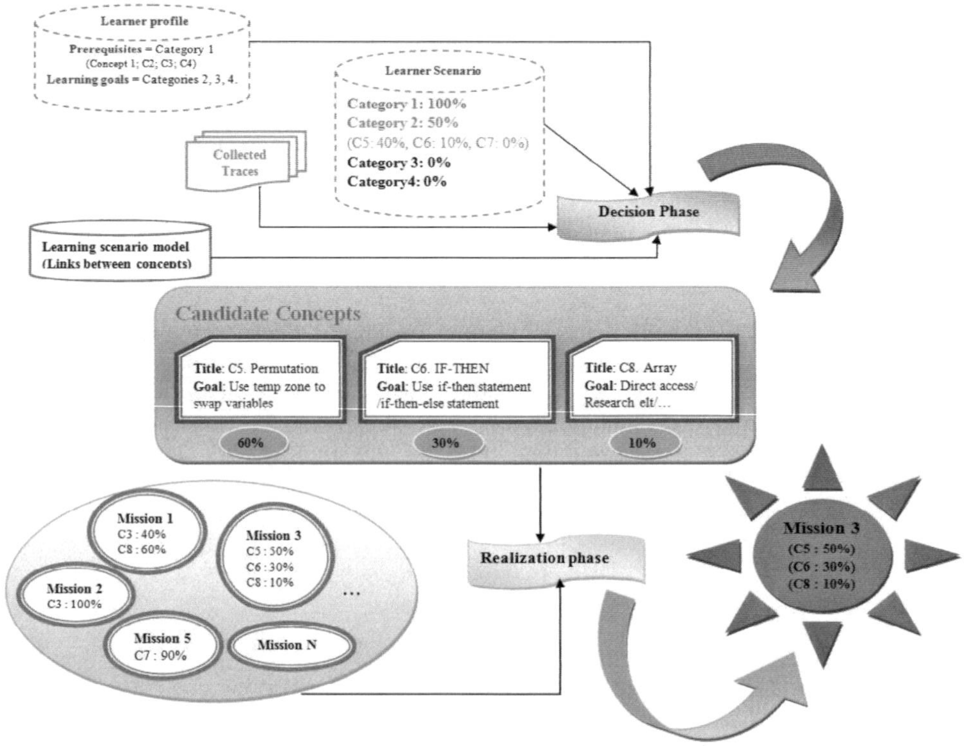

Figure 2. Case of the system's operating principles

The figure 2 represents a case of the system's operating principles. We consider a learner's profile that has the algorithmic concepts of **category1** as prerequisite and as learning goals the algorithmic concepts of the **categories 2, 3 and 4**.

Based on this learner's profile, his/her learning path (learner scenario), traces collected and the model of learning scenarios predefined in the system, the **decision phase** is launched. This phase ensures the adaptation of the pedagogical scenario. It allows deciding on the "next" most appropriate concepts to learn. We call them the "candidate concepts". Each candidate concept has a weight ranging from the most to the least relevant. In our example, the candidate concepts are: the concept **C5.Permutation** with 60%, the Concept **C6.IF-THEN statement** with 30% and the concept **C8.Array** with 10%.

Once the candidate concepts are defined, a second phase ensures the adaptation of the game scenario, it is the **realization phase**. This one is founded on the candidate concepts resulting from the decision phase as well as the game's missions predefined in the game scenario database. In our example, "Mission 3" is selected and presented to the learner as the most appropriate mission to play according to his/her evaluation in the game scenario as well as in the pedagogical scenario.

The game mission "Mission 3" introduces the selection sort algorithm, while focusing on the concept **C5.Permutation** (permutation of two variables). The concepts **C6.IF-THEN statement** and **C8.Array** are also introduced.

Gameplay: The player is placed in the Computer Science department parking; he/she has to sort, within a given time, the parked vehicles in the garages. This sorting will be done according to vehicle weight, from least heavy to heaviest. To achieve this, the learner must complete a series of specific tasks to establish the desired order before time limit; otherwise, the game ends.

The selection sort algorithm consists in sorting array elements in a given order. In order to concretize the abstract concepts related to this algorithm, we thought to materialize the array cells by garages and items by parked vehicles within these garages. Furthermore, the vehicle weight is not communicate to the player, we suggest to indicate (graphically) only, the number of the least heavy truck, so the player has no choice other than browse all the vehicles to determine the minimum, as this goes on in the algorithm. To swap two vehicles, the player must go through an intermediate zone because the road leading to the various garages passes one vehicle at a time. This operation makes the learner get aware of the "machine" constraints, i.e. the need to go through temporary variable when permuting array's elements.

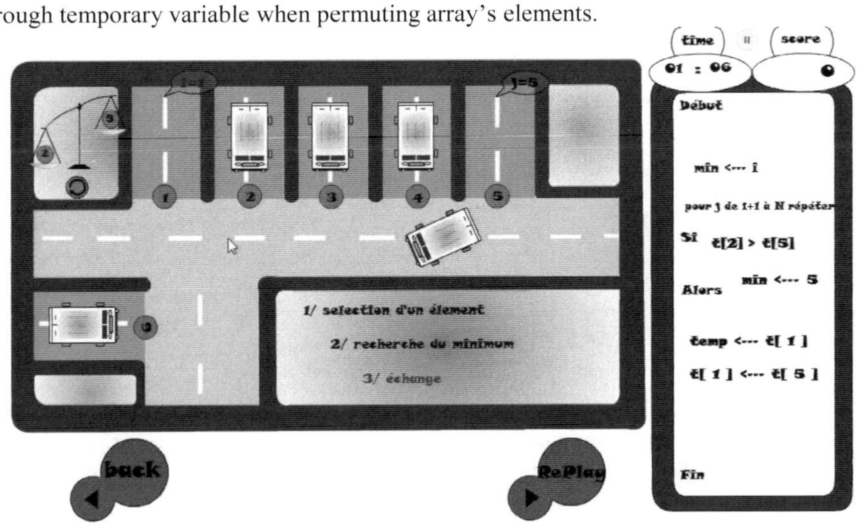

Figure 3. Mission 3 : selection sort algorithm

Every action made in the game generates an algorithmic command which appears at the right of the screen, until the whole algorithm is constructed. The game include explanatory messages that assist students in understanding the theory while playing, such as the hints with index (i) and (j). Besides, the selection sort algorithm goes by three phases: 1) Selecting an element. 2) Find the minimum or the maximum. 3) Swap the tow elements. In order to highlight these phases, the player is informed each time he/she goes through one of them.

5. CONCLUSION AND FUTURE WORKS

AlgoGame is a new solution for learning and teaching algorithmic bases that has been presented in this paper. Our principal concern was to reduce the abstraction and help students to make relation between their real world and the abstract algorithmic concepts. Also, bring them to realize that a problem can be divided into simpler sub problems by highlighting the algorithm's steps when the player goes through them. The game discharge student from syntax and debug errors, thus the algorithms are not constructed by typing text or arranging icons but by taking actions in the game.

Another important aspect is the diversity of learners, the adaptation of the learning scenario (and consequently the game scenario) according to learners needs was a main concern for us, thus we propose to integrate our game in the adaptive platform POLARIS. The proposed architecture uses different modules to ensure the adaptation of both pedagogical and game scenarios according to students needs. The particularity of serious games is the double point of view "*game*" and "*serious*". We have highlighted the need to have an adaptation for each one: adapting the progress of the game and adapting the pedagogical sequence. To do this we assume that it is better to decouple adaptation in two stages. Firstly, the adaptation of the pedagogical scenario and then the adaptation of the play activity, we then showed how to make the interaction in the piloting of each scenario.

So far, we chose to verify the usability and effectiveness of the game apart. We have analyzed the impact of introduction of gaming in the programming activity. The first evaluation results are encouraging and motivating. In a second step, we aim to integrate the game into POLARIS platform. This will involve another controlled experiment to study whether the use of this system has any impact of the student programming experience, and if so, whether these effects are positives or negatives.

REFERENCES

Barnes, T. et al. (2008). Game2Learn: improving the motivation of CS1 students. In *Proceedings of the 3rd international conference on Game development in computer science education* (pp. 1-5).

Bourse, Y., Labat, J.M. *Adaptation sur la progression de l'apprentissage dans les jeux sérieux*. Dans IREC Conference 2012.

Boyle, E. et al. 2011. The role of psychology in understanding the impact of computer games. *Entertainment Computing*, *2*(2), 69-74.

Carron, T. et al. 2009. How to bring immersion into Learning Games?. In *Advanced Learning Technologies, 2009. ICALT 2009. Ninth IEEE International Conference*, pp. 358-360.

Coelho, A. et al. 2011. Serious game for introductory programming. In *International Conference on Serious Games Development and Applications* (pp. 61-71). Springer Berlin Heidelberg.

Code Studio: https://studio.code.org/. Accessed: 28 August 2015.

CoLoBoT 2013: http ://www.ceebot.com/colobot/index-e.php. Accessed 18 September 2013.

Conati C., Manske M., 2009. Evaluating Adaptive Feedback in an Educational Computer Game, Proceedings of the 9th International Conference on Intelligent Virtual Agents, 2009, Amsterdam, The Netherlands.

Eagle, M., Barnes, T. 2009. Experimental evaluation of an educational game for improved learning in introductory computing. *ACM SIGCSE Bulletin* 41(1), 321-325.

Esteves, M, et al. 2008. Contextualization of programming learning: A virtual environment study. In *Frontiers in Education Conference, 2008. FIE 2008. 38th Annual* (pp. F2A-17). IEEE.

Futschek, G. 2006. Algorithmic thinking: the key for understanding computer science. In *International Conference on Informatics in Secondary Schools-Evolution and Perspectives* (pp. 159-168). Springer Berlin Heidelberg.

Gestwicki, P., Sun, F.S. 2008. Teaching Design Patterns through Computer Game Development. Journal on Educational Resources in Computing (JERIC), vol. 8(1), March 2008.

Henriksen, P., & Kölling, M. 2004. Greenfoot: combining object visualisation with interaction. In *Companion to the 19th annual ACM SIGPLAN conference on Object-oriented programming systems, languages, and applications*, pp 73-82.

Hoang, N.H. et al. 2015. Application of Trace-Based Subjective Logic to User Preferences Modeling. 20th International Conference on Logic Programming, Artificial Intelligence and Reasoning, EPiC Series, vol. 123, pp. 80 – 90.

Hocine, N. et al. 2011 *Techniques d'adaptation dans les jeux ludiques et sérieux*. Revue d'Intelligence Artificielle, Lavoisier (Hermes Science Publications), 2011, 25 (2), pp.253-280.

Jenkins, T. 2002. On the difficulty of learning to program. In *Proceedings of the 3rd Annual Conference of the LTSN Centre for Information and Computer Sciences*. Vol. 4, No. 2002, pp. 53-58.

Kaasbøll, J. J. 1998. *Exploring didactic models for programming*. In NIK 98– Norwegian Computer Science Conference. p.p. 195-203.

Lahtinen, E. et al, 2005. A study of the difficulties of novice programmers. In *ACM Sigcse Bulletin*, Vol. 37, No. 3, pp. 14-18.

Miliszewska, I., & Tan, G. 2007. Befriending computer programming: A proposed approach to teaching introductory programming. *Informing Science: International Journal of an Emerging Transdiscipline*, *4*(1), 277-289.

Motil, J., & Epstein, D. 1998. JJ: a language designed for beginners (less is more). *Available at http://www.publicstaticvoidmain.com.*

Muratet, M. et al. 2010. Experimental feedback on Prog&Play, a serious game for programming practice, *Eurographics, pp.1-8.*

O'Kelly, J. & Gibson, J. P. 2006, RoboCode & problem-based learning: a non prescriptive approach to teaching programming, *in: Proceedings of Conference on Innovation and Technology in Computer Science Education. 217–221.*

Paliokas, I. et al. 2011, *PlayLOGO 3D: A 3D interactive video game for early programming education, in:* Proceedings of 3rd International Conference on Games and Virtual Worlds for Serious Applications. 24-31.

Pham, P.T. et al. 2015. A Situation–Based Multi–Agent Architecture for Handling Misunderstandings in Interactions. International Journal of Applied Mathematics and Computer Science, De Gruyter, 2015, 25 (3), pp.439-454.

Phelps, A.M. et al. (2003), MUPPETS: multi-user programming pedagogy for enhancing traditional study, *in: Proceedings of 4th conference on Information technology education. 100-105.*

Schulte, C. & Bennedsen, J. (2006), *what do teachers teach in introductory programming? In*: Canterbury, UK, 2ed International Workshop on Computing Education Research. Pp 17–28.

Soloway, E. & Spohrer, J. 1989. *Studying the Novice Programmer*, Lawrence Erlbaum Associates, Hillsdale, New Jersey. p.497.

Sawadogo, D. 2016. Thesis : *Architectures logicielles et mécanismes pour la gestion adaptative et consolidée de ressources numériques dans une application interactive scénarisée.*

Trillaud, F. 2013. Thesis: *Architecture for interactions control and interactive and adaptive multiusers applications driving: application to e-learning*. Rochelle University. https://tel.archives-ouvertes.fr/tel-01140071

SEMANTIC MODELLING FOR LEARNING STYLES AND LEARNING MATERIAL IN AN E-LEARNING ENVIRONMENT

Khawla Alhasan, Liming Chen and Feng Chen
Software Technology Research Laboratory, De Montfort University, Leicester, UK

ABSTRACT

Various learners with various requirements have led to the raise of a crucial concern in the area of e-learning. A new technology for propagating learning to learners worldwide, has led to an evolution in the e-learning industry that takes into account all the requirements of the learning process. In spite of the wide growing, the e-learning technology is still lacking the ability to achieve the best personalised learning path for each learner resulting in performance dissatisfaction. Recent research indicates that each learner has a unique way of learning that leads to different preferences in the selection of the learning resources. Thus, the learning material must be tailored for the individual learners in order to meet their own personal needs. In this paper, we present a novel approach for designing a model for an adaptive e-learning course and learning styles based on ontology and semantic web technologies. In this approach, we build an adaptive student profile through analysing the pattern of the learner's behaviour while using the e-learning course in accordance to the Felder- Silverman learning style model (FSLSM).

KEYWORDS

E-learning; Semantic Web; Personalisation; Adaptive System; Learning Style; FSLSM

1. INTRODUCTION

E-learning industry has created vast and growing revolution due to many advantages such as scalability, simplicity and access flexibility. Technology enhanced learning currently trends to focus on the significant concern of learning in terms of cognitive processing. In addition, recent research endorses the necessity of the content relevance for each learner. Therefore, customising the content and context of the information has to be attained for each learner in an exciting, easy and creative way.

The main issue of e-learning courses is the scarcity of personalisation that can be defined as the ability of the learning process to get customised and tailored according to the learners' preferences and characteristics (Chen, Lee & Chen, 2005). The personalisation process covers the learning objectives, the content and the learning method. While demonstrating the significance and the effectiveness of adaptive systems, researchers regularly emphasise the importance of personalisation after taking into account the user performance, cognitive style, knowledge level, or learning style in order to determine the most suitable learning path (Montazer & Ghorbani, 2011). In a fully personalised e-learning environment, the learning objectives and content, as well as the method and pace, may vary (Keefe, 1991). The idea of an adaptive system is to provide contents to different users based on their individual learning preferences.

According to Brusilovsky (Brusilovsky, 1996), the system has to be able to determine different content paths for the same learners at different times according to their chosen preferences, goals, experiences and knowledge. It is significant that the course content is well customised according to the needs of the individual learners in order to personalise their learning experiences (elkherj & Freund, 2014).

Thus, our approach will focus on the personalisation by enhancing the performance of the personalising procedure in the learning process. This could be achieved by increasing the effectiveness both of monitoring the learner's behaviour to determine the accurate learning style, and filtering the content of the learning material according to a relevant recommendation. In addition, our approach provides recommendations for the appropriate type of knowledge resources by using semantic rules reasoning.

As such, we assume that our model will meet the expectations to achieve an effective personalised system. The aim of our approach is to present a novel semantic model for both the learning material and the learning style. Our model extends the model of previous work (Halimi & Seridi-Bouchelaghem, 2015) by integrating the learning material with comprehensive features, along with structuring the tendencies of the learning style in order to enhance the efficiency of the semantic inference mechanism.

This paper begins with an overview of the related work for both the learning style theories and the approaches for the automatic User Model. The proposed architecture of the ontology model is illustrated next, along with the elaboration of the semantic modelling, and the computational model. Then, an application scenario of learner interaction with the e-learning course is presented. The conclusion will be given in the last section.

2. RELATED WORK

2.1 Learning Style

Definitely, learning style is one of the main factors in personalisation as a cognitive perspective for the learner. According to Keefe, the learning style consists of the modality meter of learning (Keefe, 1991; Bansal, 2013). Coffield et al. (Kanninen, 2008) provide a comprehensive categorisation, shown in TABLE 1, for the existing learning style models, divided into five families according to the related concept of their structure which are learning style preferences, cognitive structure, personality type, steady learning preferences, and other learning strategies and orientations (Coffield, 2004).

Table 1. Coffield comprehensive categorisation of learning style models (Kanninen, 2008)

Author(s)	Assessment tool	Year
Genetic and other constitutionally based learning styles and preferences including the VAKT		
Gregorc	Gregorc Mind Styles Delineator (MSD)	1977
Cognitive structure		
Riding	Cognitive Styles Analysis (CSA)	1991
Stable personality type		
Apter	Motivational Style Profile (MSP)	1998
Myers-Briggs	Myers-Briggs Type Indicator (MBTI)	1962
Flexibility stable learning preferences		
Herrmann	Brain Dominance Instrument (HBDI)	1995
Honey and Mumford	Learning Styles Questionnaire (LSQ)	1982
Felder and Silverman	Index of Learning Styles (ILS)	1996
Kolb	Learning Style Inventory (LSI) LSI Version 3	1979 1999
Learning approaches and strategies		
Sternberg	Thinking Styles	1998

Some of these models were mentioned vastly in the literature (Graf, Kinshuk & Liu, 2008) due to their effectiveness. Like the Myers-Briggs Type indicator (MBTI) from the personality type family that refers to the Carl Jung's theory. This theory divides humans as introverts or extroverts, by sensing or intuition, thinking or feeling, and judging or perceiving.

In the family of learning style preferences, Kolb's experiential theory is displayed within a four stage learning cycle. The stages are: concrete experience, reflective observation, abstract conceptualisation, and active experimentation. Honey and Mumfords' model divides learning styles into activists, theorists, pragmatists, and reflectors. Another model is Pask's model of the Serialist/Holist/Versatilist learning styles (Graf, Kinshuk & Liu, 2008). The Herrmann Whole Brain Model, represents learning styles according to the quadrants of the brain along with their functionalities. From the same family, we have chosen the Felder and Silverman learning style Model (FSLSM) that will be explained in more detail in the following section.

2.1.1 Felder and Silverman Learning Style Model

As shown in Figure 1, our chosen model considers the cognitive science along with the principles of learning and personalisation.

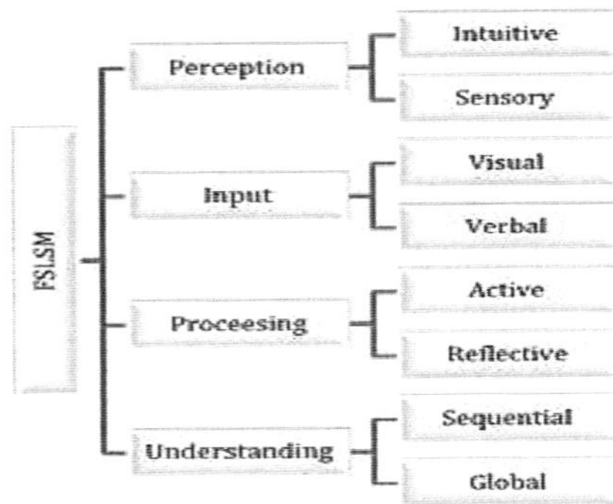

Figure 1. Learning styles of Felder and Silverman learning style model (Felder & Silverman, 1988)

According to the FSLSM, learning styles are classified into four dimensions (Nafea, Maglaras, Siewe, Smith & Janicke, 2016). These dimensions start with the perception, which is the kind of knowledge that the user desires to recognise. Learners may be intuitive when they prefer abstracts or theories. Other learners may be sensory when they prefer examples or practices. The second dimension is the input which is the method of learning the user favour to learn with. Learners may be visual when they prefer images, graphs and flowcharts. Other learners may be verbal when they prefer texts or spoken notations. The third dimension is the processing, which is the way the learner demonstrates learning. Learners may be active when they prefer working with other users. Other learners may be reflective when they prefer thinking and working by themselves. And the fourth dimension is the understanding, which shows the user knowledge development. Learners may be sequential when they prefer learning in continuous minor stages. Other learners may be global when they prefer viewing the end results and the whole picture.

2.1.2 Reasons for choosing FSLSM

We chose the FSLSM as a basis for the adaptive system because of many reasons. It has been approved by various specialists, since it is the most appropriate model for educational systems. It is capable of describing learning style in terms of tendencies and balanced preferences. It is user-friendly and the results are easy to interpret. Furthermore, the FSLSM is comprehensive for many major learning style models, and describes the learning style in more details than other models (Liyanage, Gunawardena & Hirakawa, 2014; Franzoni, Assar, Defude & Rojas, 2008; Darwesh, Rashad & Hamada, 2011).

2.2 Existing Learning Approaches for Automatic User Model

Recent researchers of automatic user modelling have been adopting the new concept of the knowledge-based approach, that is sometimes called literature-based by some researchers. Graf et al. (Graf, kinshuk & Liu, 2008; Graf, 2007) suggested a novel methodology built in LMS Moodle, to collect the appropriate hints related to the user preferences originally from the LMS. The system achieved good precision rate comparing to other approaches. Later, Graf et al.(Graf, kinshuk & Liu, 2009) suggested an automatic modelling with an innovative tool to support it. A similar implementation to the previous was the work of Simsek et al. (Simsek, Atman, lnceoglu & Arikan, 2010) in Moodle LMS, however, they focused on the dimension of processing (active- reflective) and the implementation was able to achieve a rate of accuracy of 79.6%.

Dung et al. (Dung & Florea, 2012) extended the work of Graf et al. (Graf, Kinshuk & Liu, 2008) in addition, they concentrated on the number of visits and their durations. The rate of accuracy was roughly the same as in Graf et al (Graf, Kinshuk & Liu, 2008). Pursuing developing applications, Atman et al. (Atman, Inceoglu & Aslan , 2009) suggested a web-based system that provided a specific label to the modules in order to correlate them to one of the learning styles, achieving 83.15% accuracy for the processing dimension with the use of the formula of Garcia et al. (Gregorc & Ward, 1977). Dung et el. (Dung & Florea, 2013) proposed POLCA in 2013 that focused on tracking the learners' behavior through their interactions with the labeled learning objects.

Recent studies focused on improving personalised learning environments based on describing knowledge using ontologies. Such approach was implemented by Halimi et al. (Halimi & Seridi-Bouchelaghem, 2015) in a social learning environment. It formulated a powerful method that can analyse the behaviour by semantic inferences, identify learning style, and provide better recommendation. The Didaskon Platform (Didaskon & Sound, 2013) was developed by semantic web technologies to automatically arrange a different learning path for each student according to his preferences and characteristics. Another application annotated the learning objects of the content automatically with the use of ontologies (Jovanovic, Gasevic & Devedzic, 2006; Gasevic, Jovanovic, Devedzic & Boskovic, 2005).

Gutierrez et al. (Gutierrez, Pardo & Kloos, 2004) developed an algorithm for monitoring the learner's activities during the learning process, and constantly adjusting his profile with the use of ontology. The study of Nafea et al. (Nafea, Maglaras, Siewe & Shehab, 2015;Nafea, Maglaras, Siewe, Smith & Janicke, 2016) is about an adaptive LMS that depended on the technology of semantic web and ontologies. Focusing on semantically modelling the user, the framework automatically reviewed the learners' behavior pattern based on the Myers-Briggs theory and the FSLSM using the Moodle.

3. CREATION OF SEMANTIC MODELLING

The created ontology for an e-learning system, provides a clear illustration of the distribution of the knowledge resources domain. The ontology structure divides the knowledge domain into definite resources like chapters, exercises, and forums. The knowledge resources are extended by behavior pattern substructure of stay, visit, and many trials. Furthermore, each resource is supported with multiple types of media representation such as text, image, and video. Another class, learning style, is constructed according to the FSLSM of four dimensions explained earlier, along with their opponent styles. Lastly, the ontology provides various users such as Tutor, and Student based on their usage and interaction with the system.

The use of ontology benefits the system in several aspects like supporting the knowledge resources with a detailed annotation that leads to sharing and reusing data. The ontology is capable of providing clear definitions for users, knowledge domain resources, and different learning styles. Also, the support of the based on demand knowledge can be efficiently achieved by the ontology, by the inference mechanism and the precise tracking and response of ontology among resources. In addition, the ontology enhances the system effectiveness in getting the proper resources since it minimises the terminology imprecision.

3.1 Proposed Architecture

Recent ontology-based systems for e-learning courses using the semantic web are ready to apprehend hidden semantic associations by exploring the knowledge and structure of the ontological model. By using linked data in the ontology, it becomes easier for the system to interpret data and make good detections or suggestions to users.

In this paper, the proposed architecture for e-learning courses based on Semantic Web, as shown in Figure 2, is to represent the course knowledge domain, and the user profile or the learning style model. It analyses the pattern of the learner's behavior to establish and update the learning style model, as well as to develop a personalised learning path most suitable for the individual needs. The significance of this system is that individual learners would get a unique learning experience according to their learning styles.

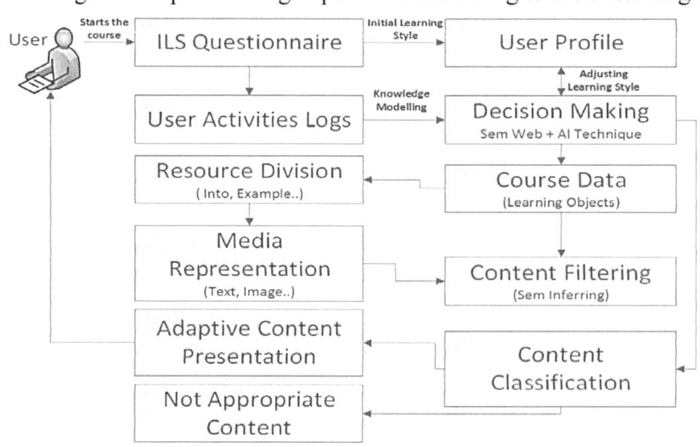

Figure 2. Architecture for personalising the learning material to learning style

The main components of the proposed architecture are:

3.1.1 ILS Questionnaire

It is FSLSM ILS Questionnaire. The answers will be gathered and used to initially model the learner's learning style. And the result will be used later in the evaluation process.

3.1.2 User Activities Logs

They are records of the learner's interactions with the learning material, which includes his behavior, tests results, visit timings and frequencies.

3.1.3 Decision Making

It is the process of analysing the learner's behaviour by the semantic web inference, and the classification of the learning style based on the FSLSM. An AI technique will be added in the future work to this component to support the accuracy of decision making. Consequently, it will be followed by the process of designing the recommended learning content for the learner.

3.1.4 Course Data

It is all the resources of the learning material with the different media presentations.

3.1.5 Content Filtration

It is the process of designing the recommended learning content for the learner.

3.1.6 Content Classification

It is the process of splitting the learning resources into appropriate and not appropriate resources.

3.1.7 Adaptive Content Presentation

It is all the suitable resources for the learning material that construct the adaptive learning path based on the learning style.

3.2 Conceptual Model

The conceptual model for the e-learning course ontology, shown in Figure 3, describes how the learner interaction is demonstrated by the semantic reasoning mechanism to model his learning style, and to recommend the learning material.

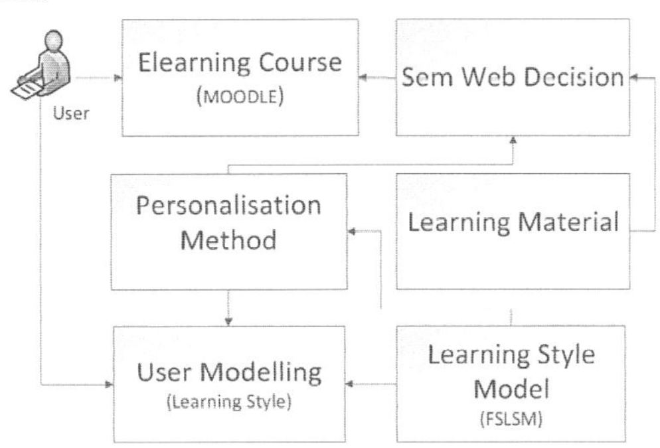

Figure 3. Conceptual model

3.2.1 Moodle platform

Moodle is the learning management system that is used to build the learning course, and allows the student to interact with the learning material.

3.2.2 Learning material

Since it is personalised learning it is crucial to support a variety of representation and media to the learning material in order to fit to the various learning styles. Also, the content is well organised into units to facilitate the path recommendation and distribution. At some level, the learning material will be under the filtration process by the semantic web inferring mechanism to segregate the appropriate resources from the not appropriate, in order to structure the suitable content to the learner.

3.2.3 User Model

The learner's model is the reflection of the information that emerges during the learner's interaction with the system (Nafea, Maglaras, Siewe & Shehab, 2015). The learner's profile will include his personal information, along with his model of learning style and preferences. Interactions history and recommendations are also helpful data that need to be stored.

3.2.4 Learning Style Model

The Felder and Silverman learning style model was chosen in our research to be our criteria to refer to when analysing the behavior and deciding the learning style.

3.2.5 Semantic Web Decision

The semantic web inferring mechanism gives the privilege of sharing and reusing the data which will enhance the efficiency. The Semantic Web is in charge of detecting the learner's behavior in order to infer his learning style. After updating the learner's model, the semantic web will decide how the learning material is filtered to get the useful resources. Moreover, there will be a semantic decision for the recommended path for the learner.

3.3 Computational Model

The e-learning material and the learning style ontologies were constructed in Protégé assistive technology to model various interlinking hierarchies. The schematic structure of the ontology based e-learning course is presented in Figure 4 and Figure 5. It starts when the user enters the e-learning course, and an initial learning style is determined by the results of ILS questionnaire and thus the learner's initial model is developed. The ontology is in charge of detecting and storing the result that indicates a preference of one of the 16 learning styles combinations of FSLSM.

In our approach, the critical features are the knowledge domain resources, the multiple representations for these resources, and the learning styles preferences that match these different resources. These features determine the key concepts of our ontology-based e-learning course.

The ontology describes the domain of knowledge by representing its objects and the relationships between these objects; it allows to formally defining different users and their roles (student, tutor, etc.), resources (courses, tutorials, videos, etc.), learning styles and preferences. It also provides various representations for several objects in the learning content, which means, once the learning style is determined, the nearest proposed type of media, which corresponds to his learning style is recommended. For example, if it is determined that a learner is visual, the video explanation will be provided to him instead of the text or spoken notation.

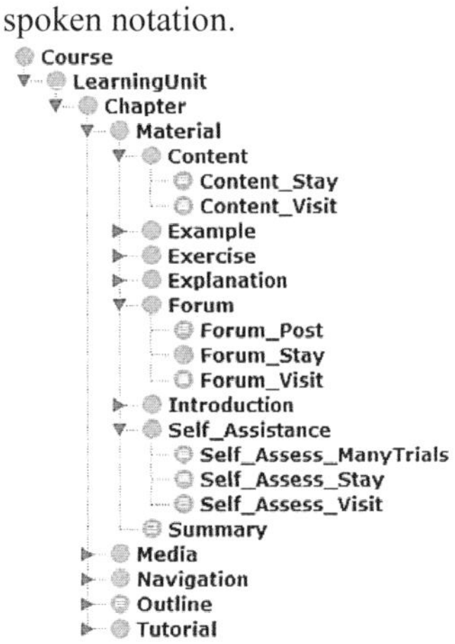

Figure 4. Part of the learning material ontology

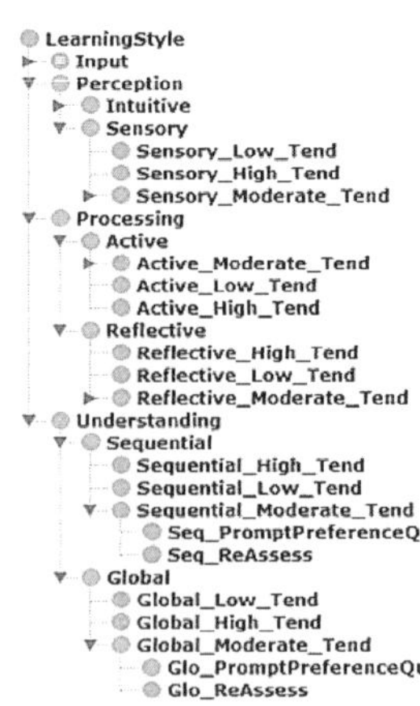

Figure 5. Part of learning style ontology

3.3.1 Basic heuristic of the Ontology Classes

The structured ontology contains many classes which are the course, the learning styles and the user. For the course class, there are subclasses and further divisions such as of the learning units, chapters and as the type of content media.

Moreover, each unit of the learning material is extended with some features that can help the content filtration and the reasoning process to be quicker, and more accurate. An example of a material unite is the forum. The forum unit is supported by several features like the Forum_Post, the Forum_Stay and the Forum_Visit. After monitoring the learner's behavior during a learning the course, these features assist the Semantic decision for the learning style modelling. When the learner is active in posting and asking in Forums, it is an indicator that the learner is of type Active. While if the learner rarely participates, or keeps watching and observing only, then it is an indicator that the learner has a reflective learning style.

The learning styles class is also divided according to the FSLSM. Further divisions describe the four dimensions learning styles into the different learning styles. In turn, each learning style is structured according to the learning preferences that result to the learning material.

For example, one of the learning style dimensions is perception, which is in turn divided into the intuitive and the sensory. The intuitive object is divided into preferences like theories and abstracts, while the sensory is extended with exercises and examples. Also, the learning styles are categorised into style tendencies to help the process measuring and deciding the exact learning style. However, once a style is trivial, or moderate, there are two options to deal with the case as shown in Figure 5, either to send a direct prompt question for the learner's preference for the next content or to focus on the reassessment process.

3.3.2 Phases of Content Personalisation

The personalisation process starts with the determination of the initial learning style of the learner via answering the ILS Questionnaire of FSLSM. Next phase is the semantic modelling decision of learning style that is established for the learner after the interaction with the system, along with the decision of the appropriate content resources from the knowledge domain. Then there is the refinement process by the inferring mechanism of the Semantic Web, which happens by studying the learner characteristics, to set the possible resources that better suit the learner's learning style model.

When two opponent Learning Styles have equal tendencies, the ontology provides some options. The first is to show a direct prompt question to ask the learner about his preference of the next content. Another option is to focus on the reassessment process through his interaction with the content in order to become more accurate in the next decision of his learning style. Both options can be applied for the learner in the same time. Considering, that in some cases the learner may have moderate tendency towards a learning style, the ontology can support him with these options many times to avoid errors. As mentioned above, a technique of artificial intelligence will be added in a later phase to model quantitative and qualitative information of the behavior pattern; however, it is not the focus of this paper.

Finally, after updating the learner model, a division process is conducted on the content material, to separate the needed appropriate from the not appropriate content resources. Learner characteristics are examined, to set the possible resources that better suit the learner's learning style model.

4. APPLICATION SCENARIO

In this section, we will elaborate on the scenario for the learning styles of the input dimension of the FSLSM. When a learner first enters the course, he will fill in the ILS Questionnaire to initially model his learning style. Assuming that the result of the questionnaire determines that he is verbal, which would mean he likes to receive the knowledge from texts, or spoken notations.

After interacting with the course content, his behavior including the number of visits for each item in the content, the time spent on each item and the frequencies will all be monitored. The ontology built for the learning course does the reasoning and evaluates the results. By the semantic referencing mechanism the learner will be assigned to the learning style. Below is an ontograf presentation for the Input learning style in Figure 6.

Once the evaluation resulted in reaching a threshold percentage of usage and interaction with a specific type of items, the ontology will infer his learning style. This learner could have answered the ILS

Questionnaire randomly, or he could have had a misconception about his preferences. When his behavior shows that he prefers focusing on videos, graphs, and images rather than the text and spoken notes, the semantic decision will model him as a visual learner, his profile will be updated, and the learning material will be filtered in order to be presented with the recommendation according to his learning style.

In case the learner is indifferent in learning from texts images or videos, that has a moderate tendency towards verbal or visual styles, a couple of direct prompt messages in the learning chapter will be shown to ask him "Would you Like the next section to be an article or video?", that will help in the behavior monitoring and the learning style modelling. With further collaboration and interaction with the learning course, the ontology keeps refining his learning style model and adjusting the recommended learning path for the learner.

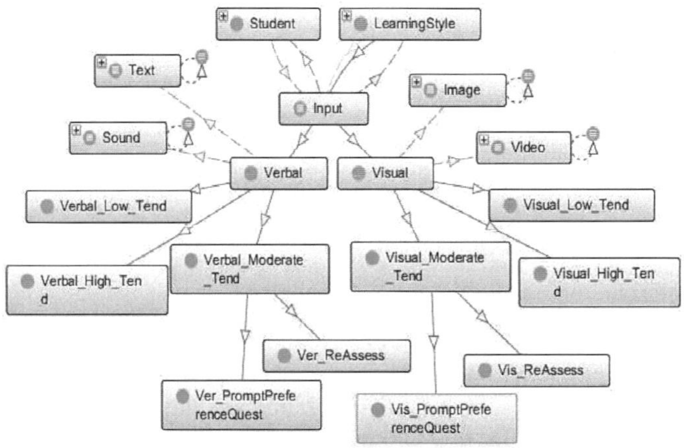

Figure 6. Ontograf presentation of the inputlearning style

5. CONCLUSION

A revolutionary change is emerging to enjoy the privileges of the technology and the Semantic Web to serve the creating of an operative e-learning courses system, capable of determining the learning style and providing the most appropriate learning path accordingly.

Our approach provides a model for an adaptive ontology-based e-learning environment that has the advantage of semantic inference mechanism to link the behavior of learners to their learning styles and, then, to the appropriate knowledge resources. This model is being implemented and will be used in the next piece of study. The approach is distinctive in embedding the personalised ontology of e-learning courses with many details of the different media representations of the existing knowledge resources that facilitate the selection amongst them in order to meet the needs of each learning style.

Furthermore, the structure of the learning material includes some new features such as visits and number of trials to induce higher levels of semantic reasoning mechanism, in less time, and definitely more accurate. Moreover, the learning style ontology structure includes some new features like the styles tendencies. The e-learning course ontology was constructed according to the criterion of the Felder and Silverman learning Style Model that provides eight different learning styles categorised into four dimensions, which are the perception, the input, the processing, and the understanding.

REFERENCES

Atman, N., Inceoglu, M., and Aslan, B., 2009. Learning Styles Diagnosis Based on Learner Behaviours in Web Based Learning. *in International Conf. on Computational Science and Its Applications,* pp. 900-909.

Bansal, N., 2013. *Adaptive recommendation system for MOOC*, PH.D thesis, Indian Institute of Technology, Bombay.

Brusilovsky, P., 1996. Methods and techniques of adaptive hypermedia. *User Modeling and User- adapted Interaction,* vol. 6, no. 2-3, pp. 87-129.

Chen, C., Lee, H., and Chen, Y., 2005. Personalised e-learning system using item response theory, *Computers & Education*, vol. 44, no. 3, pp. 237- 255.

Coffield, F., et al. 2004. Learning styles and pedagogy in post-16 learning: A systematic and critical review.

Darwesh, M., Rashad M., and Hamada, A., 2011. From Learning Style of Webpage Content to Learner's Learning Style. *International Journal of Computer Science and Information Technology*, vol. 3, no. 6, pp. 195- 205.

Didaskon and Sound, T., 2013. Didaskon, SourceForge, viewed 01 July 2017, http://didaskon.sourceforge.net/.

Dung, P., and Florea, A., 2012. An approach for detecting learning styles in learning management systems based on learners' behaviours. *in International Conf. on Education and Management Innovation, Kuala Lumpur, Malaysia*, pp. 171-177.

Dung, P., and Florea, A., 2013. A method for detection of learning styles in learning management systems, *UPB Scientific Bulletin, Series C: Electrical Engineering,* vol. 75, no. 4, pp. 3-12.

Elkherj, M., and Freund, Y., 2014. A system for sending the right hint at the right time. *in Proceedings of the 1st ACM Conf. on Learning @ scale Conf., ACM*, pp. 219-220.

Felder, R. M., and Silverman, L. K., 1988. Learning and teaching styles in engineering education. Engineering education. ISO 690 78(7), pp. 674-681.

Franzoni, A., Assar, S., Defude, B., and Rojas, J., 2008. Student learning styles adaptation method based on teaching strategies and electronic media. *in Eighth IEEE International Conf. on Advanced Learning Technologies*, pp. 778-782.

Gasevic, D., Jovanovic, J., Devedzic, V., and M. Boskovic, M., 2005. Ontologies for reusing learning object content. *in Advanced Learning Technologies ICALT '05. Fifth IEEE International Conf.*, pp. 944–945.

Graf, S., 2007. *Adaptivity in learning management systems focussing on learning styles*, PH.D thesis, Vienna University of Technology.

Graf, S., kinshuk and Liu, T., 2008. Identifying learning styles in learning management systems by using indications from students' behaviour. *in Advanced Learning Technologies, ICALT '08. 2008 Eighth IEEE International Conf*, pp. 482-486.

Graf, S., kinshuk and Liu, T., 2009. Supporting teachers in identifying students' learning styles in learning management systems: an automatic student modelling approach. *Journal of Educational Technology and Society*, vol. 12, no. 4, pp. 3-14.

Gregorc, A., and Ward, H., 1977. A New Definition for Individual. *NASSP Bulletin,* vol. 61, no. 406, pp. 20-26.

Gutierrez, S., Pardo, A., and Kloos, C., 2004. Beyond simple sequencing: Sequencing of learning activities using hierarchical graphs. *Web-Based Education*.

Halimi, K., and Seridi-Bouchelaghem, H., 2015. Semantic web based learning styles identification for social learning environments personalisation. *Web Intelligence*, vol. 13, no. 1, pp. 3-29.

Jovanovic, J., Gasevic, D., and Devedzic, V., 2006. Ontology-Based Automatic Annotation of Learning Content. *International Journal on Semantic Web and Information Systems*, vol. 2, no. 2, pp. 91-119.

Kanninen, E., 2008. *Learning styles and e-learning.* Master of Science thesis, Tampere University of Technology.

Keefe, J., 1991. Learning style: Cognitive and thinking skills. *Instructional leadership series.*

Liyanage, M., Gunawardena K., and Hirakawa, M., 2014. Using learning styles to enhance learning management systems. *International Journal on Advances in ICT for Emerging Regions (ICTer),* vol. 7, no. 2, p. 47.

Montazer G., and Ghorbani, F., 2011. Learners grouping in e-Leaming environment using evolutionary fuzzy clustering approach. *International Journal of Information and Communication Technology*, vol. 3, no. 1, pp. 9-19.

Nafea, S., Maglaras, L., Siewe, F., and Shehab, M., 2015. A novel adaptive learning management system using ontology. *in Intelligent Computing and Information Systems (ICICIS), 2015 IEEE 17th International Conference on*, pp. 328-335.

Nafea, S., Maglaras, L., Siewe, F., Smith, R., and Janicke, H., 2016. Personalised Students' Profile Based On Ontology and Rule-based Reasoning. *EAI Endorsed Transactions on e-Learning*, vol. 3, no. 12, p. 151720.

Simsek, O., Atman, N., Inceoglu, M., and Arikan, Y., 2010. Diagnosis of Learning Styles Based on Active/Reflective Dimension of Felder and Silverman's Learning Style Model in a Learning Management System. *in International Conf. on Computational Science and Its Applications,* pp. 544-555.

PHYSICAL INTERACTIVE GAME FOR ENHANCING LANGUAGE COGNITIVE DEVELOPMENT OF THAI PRE-SCHOOLER

Noppon Choosri and Chompoonut Pookao
College of Arts, Media and Technology, Chiang Mai University , 239 Huaykaew Rd., Suthep, Muang, Chiang Mai, Thailand 50200

ABSTRACT

The intervention for cognitive language development is required to conduct at the young ages. As children usually gain the skill through their plays, this study proposed a physical interactive game to help children improve their language skill in both Thai and English language for pre-schooler. The motivation of this research is to create a game that has a characteristic of a toy where children require bodily engagement to touch and move the objects to enhance their cognitive for gaining language skill using interactive and game technologies. The game is evaluated in three methods: paired t-test is used to determine the overall performance of the proposed game; the 90/90 standard evaluation is also applied to see whether if the game is used for formal education majority of the group (>90%) will achieve the objective of learning. Also, the feedbacks from expert validation are collected. All three evaluations method indicate the primary success of the game to assist Thai pre-schooler in improving their skill at the young age.

KEYWORDS

Physical User Interface, Interactive game, E-learning, Education, Language development, Pre-schooler

1. BACKGROUND

Child development test is a measurement conducted to evaluate a development of children in a certain age covered several aspects including language, fine motor, and adaptation, gross motor, personal and social aspects. Several studies indicated that the most occurred development delayed at all times to Thai children is the language development (Voramongkol and Wongdejakul, 2011, Jintana, 2015, Pongpol, 2014).

Developmental problems of children can associate with many problems in their future such as risk of academic failures, behavioural and psychiatric problems, unemployment and economic and social impairment (Bishop, 2014). However, the golden period of language development exists as the brain research indicated that Children would gain biological advantage to learn foreign languages in pre-primary or primary school (Hinton et al., 2008).

A child development in pre-school ages is usually progressed from their activities and parenting. Plays are primary activities of children contributing several aspects to child development such as the cognitive, physical, social, and emotional well-being of children and youth (Goldstein, 2012). Also, many studies have reported that knowledge can be created when children play (Plowman et al., 2010). In addition, a play is a mean to improve language in fun and supportive ways (Jackie M. Oddo et al., 2013).

Nowadays, children are grown up with the new era of Information Technology (IT) and new kind of media and toys. This is inevitably affected the way children are fostered and play. There are several studies showing evidence that interactive digital media can enhance language development skills such as boosting children's vocabulary skills and their acquisition of spelling and reading/writing skills as well as improving word recognition and word creation (Lieberman et al., 2009). The digital media presented as digital toys can both catalysts new form of child play and augment the content of traditional play to bring challenges as well as opportunities to early childhood education (Meyer, 2012). With a bodily engagement, abstraction learning of children can be improved (Resnick et al., 1998). This association with the Piagetian developmental theory on the manipulation of concrete physical objects in supporting and developing thinking, particularly in young children.

Currently, computer games are widespread plays for children. Education game is a genre of game that has a purpose of offering benefits of child learning development rather than fun. A kind of this games is considered as one of the effective channels that can enhance language learning as they can increase intrinsic motivation, and providing meaningful exposure to the target language (Meyer, 2012). This study is motivated by the study of Hengeveld et al. (2008) where physical interfaces are integrated into the computer game to amplify the advantages to intervene development of toddlers with multiple disabilities. The major benefits of that system to children compared to the familiar PC interface were that it was closer to the usual style of exploration of children and enhancing their concentration (Hengeveld et al., 2008). That system also offered the practical benefit to slowed down the interaction of children with computer interface and creating the human-to-human interventional environment between children and caregivers (Hengeveld et al., 2008).

Jamil et al. (2012) identified that majority of the current literature on the study of using digital objects for children intervention only based on the cases in Western countries, the little understanding on how children in another part of the globe who are living in different cultural settings interact with digital objects.

The motivation of this study is to implement and investigate the solution of a physical and interactive game that can improve language recognition skill in both Thai and English for Thai pre-schooler at the same time they feel enjoy to play but are not being forced to learn. The rest of the paper is Section 2 review the current research in this area, Section 3 explains the design and implementation detail. Section 4 discusses the method to verify and validate the proposed system and finally, Section 5 is a discussion.

2. RELATED WORKS

Computer games are common plays of children in digital ages. There are some games especially dedicated for language skill development of pre-schoolers. For instance, "My name is Haas" is a game that create a playful learning environment for children aged 3 to 7 having purposes to increase young children's vocabulary as well as story comprehension and problem solving skills (Schuurs, 2012). "weMakeWords" is a game that has an aim to make children learn to read through motivating stories (Demmel et al., 2011). For example, the mission to save the animal in the game, they are asked to combine alphabetical words or Chinese ideographs out of individual letters (Demmel et al., 2011). Agudo et al. (2007) developed a Web-based adaptive hypermedia system called SHAIEx focusing on the adaptive mechanism of the game that fit user background such as educational level and the psychomotor skills captured from mouse interaction.

Since currently there are several off-the-shelf embedded development platforms i.e. sensors, actuators, and microcontroller and their cost are competitive. They are utilized to generate tangible game interfaces to create toy-like feeling to users. Wang et al. (2014) proposed a StoryCube which is children 's storytelling tool in a 3D environment. The tool has a controller integrated several tangible inputs and sensors including button, joystick, RFID, and accelerometer. Another story telling tool called StoryTech offers children a mixed reality environment in which to tell imaginative stories using RFID tags attached to plush dolls (Kara et al., 2014). Hengeveld et al. (2008) explored a language development system for multiple disabilities toddlers aged between 1–4 years. The study demonstrates the evolution of developing three different of tangible interfaces.

3. DESIGN AND IMPLEMENTATION

The important challenge of this research involved designing and implementing a game system for the specific type of users. To be precise, children have limited ability and experience interacting with the computer system. Another challenge is that the game shall lead the user to achieve the aim of improving language recognition skills. The design of the system this are intended to meet these two requirements. In general, the UX/UI design for children follow the guideline of Hourcade (2008) as shown in Table 1.

Table 1. General principle of interactive design for children (Hourcade, 2008)

Interactive design principle
1. Minimize using Text and using Icon instead in particular for children who are pre-literate.
2. Minimize visual complexity of the user interfaces
3. Deploy direct manipulation which is: visibility of objects and actions of interest; rapid, reversible, incremental actions
4. Providing menu for actions
5. Avoid using text-based interaction i.e. typing
6. Choose the most appropriate pointing input device for children
7. If a mouse is used as pointing device, consider the following guideline a. be aware of inaccurate click; b. expect an unexpected click such as "machine gun style" click; c. compound action such drag-an-drop can be a challenge, d. the speed of the curser shall be slow down e. Use only one button or enabling only one button to control the system (the experiment left button is outperformed the right button)

The game developed for this research is entitled "Kid Society". It is functionally designed based on the Developmental Surveillance and Promotion Manual (DSPM). DSPM is one of the most recognized medical batteries for monitoring growth and development for Thai children (MOPH, 2016). The battery covers five areas of developmental monitoring including Gross Motor (GM), Fine Motor (FM), Receptive Language (RL), Expressive Language (EL), Personal and Social (PS) (MOPH, 2016). This research investigates the solution focusing on RL improvement for pre-schooler (children aged from 3-5 years old). DSPM suggests the protocol to practice to gain certain skill together with the guideline to operate them. The training activities of selected skill (RL) for 3-5 year children are indicated in Table 2. They are used to mapped to the game mechanical design of the system.

Table 2. DSPM guideline for receptive language skill evaluation (MOPH, 2016)

RL Skills	DSPM
Continuously perform 2 actions with 2 objects	1. Put 4 items in front of the children in a grabbable distance then asking children to perform 2 actions. 2. Shuffle the items. 3. If children ca not perform the action, change the command **Passed criteria**: child can perform successfully at least 1 out of 3 attempts
Able to differentiate between large and small items	1. Prepare set of items by making sure that all items are not located in the order of size 2. Select the item that has a middle size among the group, then asking a question "which item is larger/smaller than this one?" **Passed criteria**: children can perform successfully at least 2 out of 3 attempts

Able to differentiate between daytime and nighttime	1. Prepare one picture indicated daytime, and one picture indicated night time, then asking a question "which one is depicted a daytime picture?", and "which one is depicted a nighttime picture?" 2. Asking a child to choose 3 times, each time swap the pictures **Passed criteria**: child can perform successfully at least 2 out of 3 attempts
Able to differentiate 8 different colours	1. Prepare 10 coloured blocks, and asking a child to choose each colour of block. When each selection is finished, return that block to its position **Passed criteria**: child can select all colour of block correctly

Regarding there are four objectives to achieve, this research introduces four computer games mapped to each learning objectives of RL skills.

As it was indicated that the game for small children should immerse children to a toy play, one of the important focuses is to build a game interface that has a look and feel the same tone as a toy. A physical interface is tailored for this game by the support of Makey Makey (MakeyMakey) as shown in Figure 1. It has a specification turning everyday objects into touchpads.

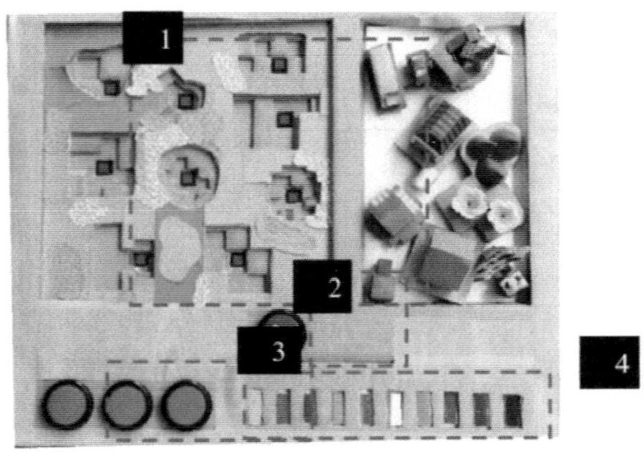

Figure 1. Controller of the game

The developed controller is tailored to operate the four mini games that are designed based on the DSPM guideline discussed in Table 1. There are four types of buttons which are 1) a group of buttons that are embedded to operate as switches to trigger the action when the shapes are located to the correct position, 2) a confirm/forward button,3) a group of buttons to represent the direction (i.e. for Left centre and Right), and 4) a group of buttons for colour section. All buttons are extended their functions from the Makey Makey. Regarding the proposed controller is identical, to make sure that a player can play the game. The tutorial on how to use the controller to play the game is also provided at the beginning of the game.

The game system contains four mini-games designed to associate with the developed controller. In general, the story of the game is progressed through a boy who is designed to have a similar age to players. The boy will challenge a player to perform certain tasks indicated in DSPM using voice instructions. During the play, when a player answers a question/perform the correct action. The applause will be given to a player as a small reward. Otherwise, the encouraging sound will response back to encourage a player to try again. When players can achieve the mission of that mini-game, the game will lead the player to the new game. The interfaces of the four mini-games are illustrated in Figure 2.

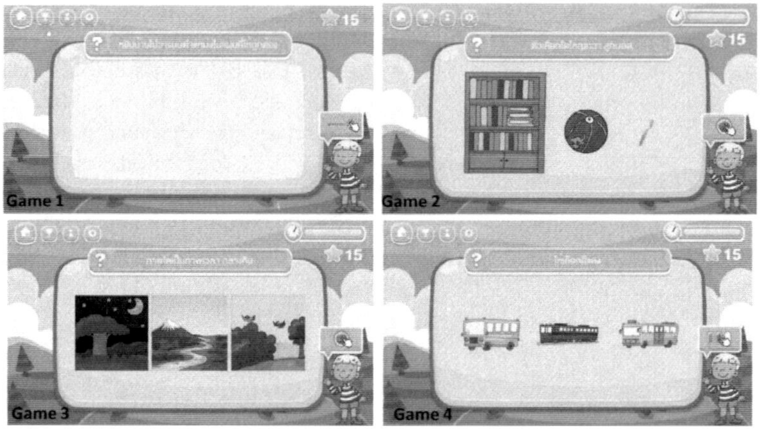

Figure 2. Game interfaces

The details of four minigame games are:

Game 1: A player is encouraged to build a town using jigsaw-liked 3D-items representing basic objects and places in everyday life such as car, tree, house, market and zoo. A player will ask one vocabulary at a time, and he/she requires to pick the item to locate in a block. Only correct item can be filled in the block. If a play selects the correct item, a switch located underneath the item will be activated to give a response back by commending players together with repeating the pronunciation of the word in both English and Thai. The physical interface of this game is demonstrated in Figure 3 when a user is asked to locate a bus into a block.

Figure 3. Demonstration of using physical interface in game 1

Game 2.: This game has an objective to encourage children to achieve the identified goal of DSPM in which he/she shall be able to differentiate between the item that has larger and smaller sizes. 3 choices of items are provided on the screen and asking a play which item is larger/smaller than another. The selection will be made by the controller type 3. From Figure 2, the question is asking that "Which item is larger than the ball?"

Game 3: This game has an objective to encourage children to achieve the identified goal of DSPM in which he/shall be able to differentiate between daytime and nighttime. The game will randomly show the picture indicating a nighttime or daytime, and asking children to use type 3 controller to answer the questions. Figure 2 is asking a question that 'which picture is showing a nighttime?'

Game 4: This game has an objective to encourage children to achieve the identified goal of DSPM in which he/shall be able to differentiate 8 colours. 3 picture of things having different colour is shown, a player is asked what colour of the specific item has. A player uses a controller type 4 to answer this kind of questions. Figure 2 is asking a question that "which one has the red colour?"

Another game components include a scoring system to evaluate the performance of players and to test that a child can pass DSPM test. The score can be viewed per mini-games, record a statistic to analyse the progress of learning, and can also share the results to the Facebook to motivate other children/parent and to build up society. The game also has administration menu for the flexibility to expand and adjust the content of the game. The software is designed to allow new vocabulary can be updated to associate with the new tangible items (i.e. in game 1). New pronunciations can also be re-recorded. New graphic can be added as well.

4. VERIFICATION AND VALIDATION

The implementation of this project is under the supervision of the two experts who have the strong experiences about child development. The background of the experts is listed in Table 3.

Table 3. Issue detection and action conducted to improve the system

Qualification	Expert I	Expert II
Position	Registered Nurse (Experienced level)	Registered Nurse (Operational level)
Academic degree	M.N.S. (Psychiatric and Mental Health Nursing)	B.N. S
Working experience	1) Working at Institute of Child Development 2) 20-year experiences 3) Child development trainer in several Thailand guidelines including TDSI DSPM TEDA 4I	1)Working at Institute of Child Development 2) Child development trainers in several Thailand guidelines including TDSI DSPM TEDA 4I

When the first version of the system was developed, it was then first evaluated by the experts. The comments received from the experts which were used to improve the implementation are:

- The icons in the games shall be larger.
- The pictures indicated nighttime and day time in the game should have more variation and indicate common activities or atmosphere of the famous festival.
- At the result page, it shall not indicate that the result either pass or fail. If the score is lower than the standard it shall indicate the message to encourage children to practice by playing more instead.
- The system shall provide more guideline on which controller shall be used for specific game i.e. showing the picture of the controller to use on the screen.

The verification is also conducted by trying the drafted prototype with the representative of Three to five year's old pre-schooler (1 representing each age). Then, the field observation is conducted to capture the User experience to detect the problems from the design to improve them. The results from the field investigation and the improvement actions are provided in Table 4.

Table 4. Issue detections and actions proceeded to improve the system

Issues	Actions
1. For the game 1, a player can select the item correctly, but confuse to locate the block where the selected item is fitted due to the boundary is unclear	1. Make a boundary of each block more obvious using space and colour
2. A child is over-enthusiastic about the game kit when he first saw it, he is distracted by the game items before the game can start	2. Modify the game package to have a cover sheet such that a caregiver control opening the box when a child is ready.
3. Sometimes a child cannot pick up words and cannot manage to repeat the word in time	3. Slow down the speed of the game especially the speech
4. A child has a difficulty to reach a far-end of the controller	4. Adjust position of buttons so that small children can reach them all

After the modification was made from the verification procedure, the evaluation was conducted at the kindergarten in Chiang Mai, Thailand. There are fifteen participants broken down into five of Kindergarten level 1 (3 year's old), five of kindergarten level 2 (4 year 's old), and five of kindergarten 3 (5 year 's old). They were invited to play the game then; the results were recorded for analysis by 3 evaluation method.

First, A paired-t-test was used to examine whether a child who plays with the game gain better receptive language skill. The Pre-test was conducted to measure the skill of the group before the intervention by playing the proposed game. The Mean of the Pre-test is 28.87 and the SD. is 3.29. Children are then asked to play the game and after the Post-test is conducted and the mean has risen to 31.60 with the SD =3.29. Both Pre-test and Post-test were tested for normality and they are normally distributed. The analysis results in Table 5 is shown that the P value < 0.01 which indicates the effectiveness of the intervention by the proposed game.

Table 5. Paired t-test result

Score	Mean	SD	T	P value
Pre-test	28.87	3.29	3.030	0.009
Post-test	31.60	2.06		

The second evaluation was analysed having a purpose to explore the feasibility to apply the proposed system for formal education in a school. One of the most recognized evaluation methods for instructional material and media in Thai academic society is the 90/90 Standard (Kumut, 1976).The main principle was underpinned by the Mastery Learning theory stating that everyone can learn if appropriate learning environment is arranged and adequate time is supplied (Yamkasikorn, 2007). The first 90 indicates the average score in the percentage of the group. The second 90 indicate the percentage of the learners who can achieve every objective of the lesson (Yamkasikorn, 2007) cited (Kumut, 1976).

The evaluation conducted by allocating the game to each player adequately (approximately 15-20 minutes). Players can explore the system freely under the observation of the research team who provided the guidance and assist the players in using the developed game system. Then, the players are evaluated their learning outcome again. The evaluation result found that the average score of the participant is 95.75%. Also, the number of the players who can pass the receptive language test is 14 out of 15 equivalents 93.33 % (to pass the test, the DSPM requires children achieve at least 3 out of 4 activities). The score 95.75% and 93.33% are both higher than 90/90. Therefore, it can be concluded that the developed game achieves 90/90 standard.

The final evaluation investigates the effectiveness from the experts point-of-view. The two experts who are the consultant of this project invite their colleague to join the evaluation. The evaluation measures the satisfaction of the system in several aspects using a Likert scale. The summary of the evaluation result is shown in Table 6.

Table 6. Result of expert satisfaction evaluation

Satisfactory criteria	Average score
Game mechanics and interactivity	3.52
Game administration system	3.83
The Proposed game controller	3.22
Look and feel	3.55
Total	**3.53**

The game can achieve relatively high satisfaction from the expert in Likert scale. The expert judge that the best part of the proposed game is the system administration part where the new set vocabulary can be added to provide flexibility for tweaking or amending the game content in the future. However, the evaluation result indicated the lowest score in the physical interactive controller which shall require further research to improve it.

Additionally, this game apparently contributes extra benefit to the child development apart from the primary goal to improve language skill as in the game 1 children are required to have a tangible interaction of grasping the objects and locating objects to the blocks, and this encourages children to practice and develop their fine-motor during the play.

5. CONCLUSION AND FUTURE WORK

The paper discusses the investigation of the game solution to improve the language skill of Thai pre-schooler. The game system is composed of 4 mini computer games designed to operate with the proposed game controller to enhance interactivity between children and the game. The process of the game implementation is under the supervision of the expert, and the game is evaluated in 3 methods including paired t-test, the 90/90 standard, and expert evaluation. The evaluation results, in general, show promise of the proposed system. The further research is to focus on the improvement of the design of the interface of the controller to be more effective. Even though the result of the expert evaluation indicated that the satisfaction to the system is high, the satisfaction to the proposed controller is relatively lower compared to the other aspects. Another direction is to expand the functionalities of the system to serve other skills necessary for child development and to apply proper measurement to the game.

REFERENCES

Agudo, J. E., Sánchez, H., Holguín, J. M. & Tello, D. Adaptive computer games for second language learning in early childhood. Proceedings of the 3rd International Online Conference on Second and Foreign Language Teaching and Research, 2007. 167-180.

Bishop, D. 2014. Ten questions about terminology for children with unexplained language problems. *International Journal of Language & Communication Disorders,* 49, 381-415.

Demmel, R. B., Köhler, B., Krusche, S. & Schubert, L. The serious game: wemakewords. Proceedings of the 10th SIGPLAN symposium on New ideas, new paradigms, and reflections on programming and software, 2011. ACM, 109-110.

Goldstein, J. 2012. Play in children's development, health and well-being. *Toy Industries of Europe. Brussels.*

Hengeveld, B., Voort, R., Hummels, C., De Moor, J., Van Balkom, H., Overbeeke, K. & Van Der Helm, A. 2008. The development of LinguaBytes: an interactive tangible play and learning system to stimulate the language development of toddlers with multiple disabilities. *Advances in Human-Computer Interaction,* 2008, 1.

Hinton, C., Miyamoto, K. & DellaChiesa, B. 2008. Brain Research, Learning and Emotions: implications for education research, policy and practice1. *European Journal of education,* 43, 87-103.

Hourcade, J. P. 2008. Interaction design and children. *Foundations and Trends in Human-Computer Interaction,* 1, 277-392.

Jackie M. Oddo, M.S., O. L. & Leigh, C. 2013. *The Importance of Play in the Development of Language Skills* [Online]. Atlanta Speech School. Available: https://www.atlantaspeechschool.org [Accessed].

Jamil, I., Perry, M., O'hara, K., Karnik, A., Marshall, M. T., Jha, S., Gupta, S. & Subramanian, S. Group interaction on interactive multi-touch tables by children in India. Proceedings of the 11th International Conference on Interaction Design and Children, 2012. ACM, 224-227.

Jintana, P. 2015. The study of Thai Early Child Development. *Silpakorn Educational Research Journal,* 7, 256-269.

Kara, N., Aydin, C. C. & Cagiltay, K. 2014. User study of a new smart toy for children's storytelling. *Interactive Learning Environments,* 22, 551-563.

Kumut, P. 1976. *Technic of instuctional program,* Faculty of education, Srinakharinwirot University

Lieberman, D. A., Bates, C. H. & So, J. 2009. Young children's learning with digital media. *Computers in the Schools,* 26, 271-283.

Makeymakey. *What 's Makey Makey?* [Online]. Makey Makey LLC. Available: http://makeymakey.com/ [Accessed 16 January 2017].

Meyer, B. Game-based language learning for pre-school children: a design perspective. Proceedings of the 6th European Conference on Games Based Learning: ECGBL, 2012. Academic Conferences Limited, 332.

Moph 2016. Developmental Surveillance and Promotion Manual (DSPM). Ministry of Public Health.

Plowman, L., Stephen, C. & Mcpake, J. 2010. Supporting young children's learning with technology at home and in preschool. *Research Papers in Education,* 25, 93-113.

Pongpol, V. 2014. The study of early childhood development screening in Kongkrailas, Sukhothai. *Rajanukul Journal* 29, 10-19.

Resnick, M., Martin, F., Berg, R., Borovoy, R., Colella, V., Kramer, K. & Silverman, B. Digital manipulatives: new toys to think with. Proceedings of the SIGCHI conference on Human factors in computing systems, 1998. ACM Press/Addison-Wesley Publishing Co., 281-287.

Schuurs, U. 2012. Serious gaming and vocabulary growth. *Serious Games: The Challenge.* Springer.

Voramongkol, N. & Wongdejakul, S. 2011. Early Childhood Growth And Development in Thailand, 2007. *J Health Res vol,* 25.

Wang, D., He, L. & Dou, K. 2014. StoryCube: supporting children's storytelling with a tangible tool. *The Journal of Supercomputing,* 70, 269-283.

Yamkasikorn, M. 2007. How to use efficiency criterion in media research and development : The Difference between 90/90 Standard and E1/E2. *Journal of Education,* Vol 19,.

FROM A CV TO AN EPORTFOLIO AN EXPLORATION OF ADULT LEARNER'S PERCEPTION OF THE EPORTFOLIO AS A JOBSEEKING TOOL

John Kilroy
Dublin Institute of Technology, 37 Northwood, Northwood Business Campus, Santry, Dublin 9, Ireland

ABSTRACT

ePortfolios are emerging as an alternative to the paper based CV in the employment recruitment process. This paper reports on the findings of research project that was designed to explore the perceptions of adult jobseekers on the use of an ePortfolio as a jobseeking tool. The research project utilised a qualitative exploratory case study to investigate the jobseekers perceptions over the course of a six week online ePortfolio development programme. The perceptions of jobseekers were investigated in the context of three questions; what was the learner's perception of the ePortfolio as a potential job seeking tool, what was the learner's perception of the ePortfolio development programme and what was the learner's perception of the ePortfolio system. Data was collected through structured online questionnaire, virtual focus groups and observations from the researcher during the programme. The research findings were discussed in the context of a number of themes that emerged from previous research including the importance of a programmatic approach to ePortfolio development, the challenges with institutional ePortfolio systems and the barriers to the use of an ePortfolio as a jobseeking tool. The research project built on a number of existing research themes while also positioning new concepts such as the role of eMentoring and gamification design principles in ePortfolio development.

KEYWORDS

ePortfolios, jobseeking support, ePortfolio development, ePortfolio systems, adult learning

1. INTRODUCTION

The emergence of new internet based jobseeking tools and specialised social networking sites such as LinkedIn indicates that the practice of preparing and submitting a paper-based CV in support of employment may become outdated (Garis, 2009). Recent research suggests that ePortfolios are also emerging as a contemporary approach to helping jobseekers present themselves to employers (Kersten, 2004; Yu, 2011; Wuetherick and Dickinson, 2015). Portfolios are generally regarded as compilations of personal and professional work used for describing skills, growth, or development over a period of time. Bollinger (2010) describes ePortfolios as essentially digitised, computer or web-based versions of traditional portfolios.

Bryant and Chittum's (2013) review of the current landscape of ePortfolio studies points to extensive research on the use of ePortfolios within Higher Education. The review however highlights relatively limited research on the use of ePortfolio in adult based learning or further education. Wuetherick et al. (2015) further supports this research gap while proposing that ePortfolios have been significantly underexplored in the context of non-traditional continuing education environments. ePortfolios have a potentially important role to play in supporting adult based learning in a wide variety of areas including work based learning, continuous professional development, career management and the job seeking process itself. This paper will focus on the potential use of an ePortfolio as a jobseeking tool.

This paper will examine and discuss the findings of a research project that was conducted with a group of adult jobseekers engaged in reskilling programmes with SOLAS eCollege in Ireland. eCollege provide a range of high quality interactive online learning courses in areas such as software development, accounting and project management for jobseekers looking to make a transition in their career. Learners who had completed a career development programme in 2014 were offered an opportunity to participate in an online ePortfolio Development Programme over a 6 week period from February to March 2015. The overall aim of the online programme was to help the learners develop an ePortfolio that could be ultimately used as a jobseeking tool following the programme itself. The learners had access to a dedicated ePortfolio system to assist them with this process. 15 learners registered for the programme with a mixed age profile and work experience background.

The aim of the research was to explore the learner's perception of the ePortfolio as a potential jobseeking tool over the course of the development programme. The research also explored the learner's perception of the ePortfolio system and the development programme itself. The research utilised a condensed exploratory case study to identify some key themes under these areas with a view to building on the existing research in the ePortfolio field and how it might transfer to adult based learning. The nature of themes explored in the research project included; the ePortfolio as a jobseeking tool, using a programmatic approach to ePortfolio development, the role of eMentoring in ePortfolio development, the connection between social networking sites and ePortfolios and the ideal ePortfolio system for adult based learners.

2. BODY OF PAPER

2.1 Literature Review

The literature review will initially set the context for the research project by positioning the potential importance of ePortfolios within the Further Education and Training Sector in Ireland. It will then examine the literature associated with the use of ePortfolios as a jobseeking tool both in terms of the type of content required and its actual application to the hiring process. The review will them move on to examine the literature associated with ePortfolio development particularly the use of a programmatic approach. This will facilitate the examination of some potential emerging trends in ePortfolio development such as gamification, eMentoring and social networking. The review will conclude with a look at the literature associated with ePortfolio systems and the potential ideal fit for adult learners.

2.1.1 The ePortfolio as a Jobseeking Tool

Gordan (2013) proposes that while there are numerous variations to the design and structure of ePortfolios, the majority of ePortfolios fall within one or more of the following types – Assessment Portfolios, Showcase Portfolios, Development Portfolios and Reflective Portfolios. There have been a number of studies completed which have examined the role of ePortfolios in the jobseeking process while highlighting the potential benefits to jobseekers (Hartwick et al. 2014; Whitworth, Deering, Hardy and Jones, 2011; Heinrich, Bhattacharya & Rayudu 2007; Jwaifell, 2013). It provides learners with an opportunity to reflect on how well their learning matches the requirements of employers, it can be helpful in searching for jobs and even in looking for employees. It can also provide opportunities for jobseekers to showcase their talents, creativity, and individuality by displaying information about an applicant well beyond what can be viewed on a paper based CV. The role of ePortfolios in helping adults manage a transition in their career has also been addressed to a certain degree in the literature. Herman and Kirku's (2008) research on the use of an ePortfolio by women at a transition point in their lives concludes that the process can be a life-changing experience that can enhance their employability. Furthermore, Koper and Verjans (2007) study on the use of ePortfolios in enhancing employability of older adults in the UK found that ePortfolios were effective tools in giving participants a better understanding of their skills and attributes, and may well enhance their self-confidence. Despite the proposed benefits of ePortfolios as a jobseeking tool, there is little evidence in the literature of their actual application in the hiring process. This may be due to a reluctance by the employer to use the ePortfolio in the recruitment process. A report by Precision Consultancy (2007) in Australia pointed out that there is very little literature on how employers use ePorfolios, except to suggest that it is not common. Furthermore, Woodley and Sims (2011) highlight the potential barriers to employers in using ePortfolios in the hiring process. This includes a lack of adequate technological skills to examine the ePortfolios effectively, a lack of time to review them and the potential lack of accuracy of ePortfolios given that applicants can self-select items.

2.1.2 A Programmatic Approach to ePortfolio Development

A number of studies have highlighted the challenge of gaining learner engagement and motivation in an ePortfolio development process (Ehiyazaryan-White, 2009; Heinrich, 2007; Yancey, 2009). Equally, engagement and motivation is generally perceived to be an ongoing challenge in field of eLearning (Admiral, Lockhorst, 2009; Cheng, Wang, Moormann, Olaniran, Chen 2011; Beetham, 2002). Laurillard (2002) proposes that effective eLearning delivery requires an underlying pedagogical approach, which is ideally learner-centered and allows for a continuous dialogue to evolve between the learner and tutor. This learner-centered approach has emerged from social constructivist pedagogy, articulated by Vygotsky (1978) as the idea that dialogue, guidance, feedback, and social interactions are drivers for transforming potential development into actual ability. Brown (2010) proposes that the ePortfolio has an important role to play in facilitating this learned centred or personalised learning environment in online learning. However, it is also important important to consider how this type of online environment can be created in the context of an ePortfolio development programme. Koper et al. (2007) propose that a successful ePortfolio development programme is dependent on a programmatic approach. This programmatic approach includes four core factors: access to portfolio technology, an explicit process of content development, mentor support and group collaboration.

2.1.3 The ePortfolio System – Learner Owned or Institutional Specific

Garrett (2011) points to a number of key factors associated with implementation and selection of ePortfolio technology including ownership, ease of use and portability. Heinrich et al. (2007) discuss two directions that can be taken in setting up an ePortfolio system. One is to go for an institutional portfolio setup with a centrally controlled ePortfolio system. The other direction stems from a social networking paradigm where learners have full ownership of their portfolios that reside in systems outside the control of the institution. Herman et al. (2008) feel that adults who are life-long learners have different needs which include learner-owned rather than institution-specific ePortfolios. A successful ePortfolio system for an adult learner should be portable, serviceable throughout a working life and provide flexibility to the end user whose needs and circumstances change over time. Wuetherick et al. (2015) also highlight the importance that adult learners place on the transportability of their portfolio upon the completion of their courses or programme.

2.2 Research Design and Methodology

The aim of this research project was to explore adult learner's perceptions of the ePortfolio as a potential jobseeking tool. This research aim will also be underpinned by an exploration of the learner's perception of the ePortfolio development programme and the ePortfolio system. Based on this the research design was framed in terms of the following research questions.

Core research question

- What was the learner's perception of the ePortfolio as a potential job seeking tool?

Sub research questions

- What was the learner's perception of the ePortfolio development programme?
- What was the learner's perception of the ePortfolio system?

An exploratory case study was chosen as the research methodology for this project due to the investigative nature of the research, the requirement to explore interventions and the need for flexibility. The ePortfolio development programme was delivered online over a 6 week period. The programme included a wide variety of interventions including access to a dedicated virtual learning environment, weekly live virtual classroom sessions, weekly discussion forums, access to an ePortfolio system, pre-recorded ePortfolio demonstrations and access to additional online resources. The programme utilised a Moodle based learning management system to host the various interventions. Participants were given an option of using a Moodle hosted ePortfolio system called Exabis or developing a personalised ePortfolio using a website development such WordPress. Participants were made aware at the start of the programme that support would only be available for the Exabis system. They were equally made aware of the limitations of the Exabis system in terms of portability following the programme.

15 learners initially registered for the programme. All of the participants had previous work experience. 11 of the participants (73%) came from administration roles and were completing reskilling courses in areas such as Accountancy Technician, ECDL and Project Management. 4 of the students came from an IT background i.e. software or website development and were completing software development courses with a view to furthering their careers in this area. There was a mixed age profile between the participant group with 15% between the age of 20 to 30, 40% between the age of 30 to 40, 14% between the ages of 40 to 50 and 30% between the ages of 50 to 60. Overall, 10 of the 15 participants engaged with the programme in terms of participating in the learning interventions and creating an ePortfolio. 80% of this participant group had never created an ePortfolio before while 20% had created personal websites that were used for blogging and showcasing work. 80% of the participant utilised some form of social networking platform such as Linkedin, Twitter or Facebook. Prior to the programme, the majority of participants from a non IT background rated their levels of comfort with technology as moderate to low.

2.3 Findings

2.3.1 Learner Perceptions of the ePortfolio Development Programme

The majority of participants rated the various learning interventions on the programme from good to excellent with the live virtual classroom (VC) sessions rated as the most beneficial support intervention on the programme. The participants indicated that the virtual classrooms provided them with structure, guidance on content and it also provided them with an opportunity to interact with other participants on the programme. There was a marked increase in engagement levels following the receipt of personalised feedback. Overall, the structure and format of the programme with the blend of support structures played an important role in the high levels of engagement in the online programme.

2.3.2 Learner Perceptions of the ePortfolio System

All of the participants opted to use the Exabis system during the programme given the support structures that were available. At the initial stages of the programme, the majority of participants rated the following aspects of the system from good to excellent; navigation, security, accessibility and ease of use. In light of this, the structure and format of the Exabis system was beneficial for participants engaging in ePortfolio development for the first time. As the programme progressed and the participants started to get comfortable with the technology, their perception of the exabis system started to change. The limitations of an LMS hosted system became more apparent particularly in terms of functionality and ease of use. Towards the end of the programme, participants started to question how they would be able to export the ePortfolio outside of the learning management system. In light of this, eMentor support and guidance was provided to participants on making the transition from an LMS hosted ePortfolio to a personalised ePortfolio. This support was greatly appreciated by the participants and it provided them with comfort on the long term use of the ePortfolio.

2.3.3 Learner Perceptions of the ePortfolio as a Jobseeking Tool

At the start of programme, participants were asked to express their understanding of the concept of an ePortfolio. They majority felt that it was an online or virtual CV that could provide more information. When asked what they felt an employer would like to see in an ePortfolio, the participants articulated the following pieces of content; video / audio introductions, blogs, samples of projects, profile picture, soft copy of CV, website links of courses, online certs, personal interests and a personal profile. At the start of the programme, participants indicated that were attending the programme with a view to developing an ePortfolio that could be used as an additional jobseeking tool to help them secure employment. Equally participants felt that the process of developing an ePortfolio would help them develop new skills in areas such as IT, research, selling and self-reflection. Following the programme, 90% of the participant's stated that they were planning to use an ePortfolio as a job seeking tool in the future. The participants outlined a wide range of potential benefits to using an ePortfolio as a jobseeking tool including; scope to showcase a wider range of skills and competencies by providing example of work with reflections, opportunity to stand out from the crowd and it provided more flexibility than the paper based CV. Furthermore, a number of participants indicated that the process of doing the ePortfolio may be more beneficial than the results particularly in terms of career planning and job interview preparation. The participants outlined a number of potential challenges to the concept of an ePortfolio as a jobseeking tool. The majority of participants felt that employers were not using ePortfolios as a recruitment tool. Based on the above, the participants found it difficult to identify opportunities to showcase their ePortfolio to employers.

2.4 Discussion

The main findings will be discussed under each of the research questions but equally in the context of patterns and themes that emerged from the literature review.

2.4.1 Learner Perceptions of the ePortfolio Development Programme

The challenges with ePortfolio engagement and motivation were discussed in the literature review (Ehiyazaryan-White, 2009; Heinrich, 2007; Yancey, 2009). To overcome this challenge, Koper et al. (2007) propose a programmatic approach to ePortfolio development. This programmatic approach is dependent on four core areas: access to portfolio technology, an explicit process of content development, mentor support and group collaboration. There was strong evidence of all of these factors during this research project. The high levels of engagement in both the learning interventions and the ePortfolio development process potentially validate the ingredients of this programmatic approach. Furthermore, the application of gamification design principles as part of the content development process may also have facilitated the high levels of engagement during the programme.

2.4.2 Learner Perceptions of the ePortfolio System

The literature discussed the importance of providing adult learners with a non-institutional or personalised ePortfolio system that is portable and serviceable throughout their working lives (Heinrich et al. 2007; Herman et al. 2008). The findings from this research project validate the challenges with an institutional ePortfolio and also the importance of a personalised ePortfolio for adult learners. However, the institutional system also played a potentially important role in introducing the concept of an ePortfolio particularly for participants with low levels of IT competence who were completely new to ePortfolio development. The embedded structure and format of an institutional ePortfolio played an important guidance role during the design process. This research has highlighted the potential of transitioning participants from an institutional to personalised ePortfolio system as part of an overall development programme.

2.4.3 Learner Perceptions of the ePortfolio as a Jobseeking Tool

The feedback from participants on the benefits of ePortfolios in the jobseeking process has validated a number of points referenced in the literature such as; enhanced scope to showcase skills, improved interview preparation, an opportunity to stand out from the crowd and the scope to develop new employability skills. The biggest barrier identified by participants was the lack of use of ePortfolios by employers in the hiring process which is also in line with findings from previous studies. Furthermore, the participants initially struggled with the role of the ePortfolio in the hiring process. However, the benefits of the ePortfolio emerged when it was positioned as a supporting resource to the CV and as a platform to showcase social networking sites.

3. CONCLUSION

This research project aimed to explore learner perceptions of the ePortfolio as a jobseeking tool while also exploring their perception of the development programme and the ePortfolio system itself. The research data was analysed in the context of a number of themes that emerged from the literature. The findings from this research project have validated a number of these themes while also potentially identifying topics for further research in the future. The following is a summary of the main conclusions from this research project.

3.1 Gamification and ePortfolio Development

This research project provided further insight into the potentially important role of a structured, programmatic approach to an ePortfolio development initiative. However, the delivery of the programmatic approach inevitable becomes more challenging in an online or virtual learning environment. The utilisation of gamification design principles in this research project and the subsequent positive results in terms of engagement and motivation highlight the potential future role of game based learning in the context of ePortfolio development. The personalised nature of ePortfolio development and the associated content development process potentially fit quite well with a number of the principles associated with gamification. Research in the field of gamification is at early stage and there may be scope in the future to investigate its application to ePortfolio development.

3.2 Transitioning from an Institutional to a Learned Centred ePortfolio System

Previous research has pointed to the fact that there are generally two choices in terms of ePortfolio systems – an institutional system or a personalised learner centred system. The use of a personalised system has been advocated for adult learners developing a showcase ePortfolio due the need for portability and flexibility. This research project has highlighted that the two systems don't necessarily need to be mutually exclusive during a development programme. The institutional ePortfolio can be very useful for learners getting started on their ePortfolio journey particularly if they have low levels of technical competence. The transition to the personalised system can then add significant value at a later stage in the journey. The management of this transition may need further consideration and research. The transition would need to be positioned clearly with the learners at the start of the programme and a number of factors need to be considered in the transition process including technical support, IT skills support, privacy, ownership and accountability.

3.3 Role of the ePortfolio in the Hiring Process

There are undoubted potential benefits in using ePortfolios during the hiring process. This is well documented in the literature and there has been extensive research undertaken on the perceptions of ePortfolio amongst employers and jobseekers. These perceptions have again been validated in this research project. There may now be a need to shift the research from perception analysis to application analysis. This could involve an investigation on the actual impact of ePortfolios on helping jobseekers secure employment. Equally, an investigation may look at the actual use of ePortfolios amongst employers to identify where they may fit into the hiring process. Are they a replacement to the CV? Could they assist the interview process? Are they more suited to recruitment or selection? In the interim, the Further Education Sector has an important role to play in generating awareness of ePortfolios amongst employers and jobseekers by promoting its benefits as a showcase tool.

ACKNOWLEDGEMENT

The researcher would like to thank Michael Mooney and Solas eCollege for facilitating the delivery of this exploratory case study with their learners. The research would equally like to thank the learners themselves for their input into the research project. Finally, the researcher would like to thank Dr. Jen Harvey in DIT for her support and guidance during the journey.

REFERENCES

Action Plan for Jobs. (2014). Published by the Department of Enterprise Trade and Employment. Retrieved from http://www.actionplanforjobs.ie/?gclid=CJy7ztqsq8YCFSau2wodUyUMqw on the 10th of April 2015.

Admiral, W., & Lockhorst, D. (2009). E-learning in small and medium-sized enterprises across Europe. International Small Business Journal, 27(6), 743–767.

Beetham, H. (2002). Understanding e-learning. University of Bristol: Skills for e-learning, Ulster, 29 July 2002.

Bolliger, D (2010). Student perceptions of ePortfolio Integration in Online Courses. Distance Education Vol. 31, No. 3, November 2010, 295–314.

Brown, S. (2010). From VLEs to learning webs: The implications of web 2.0 for learning and teaching. Interactive Learning Environments, 18(1), 1-11.doi:10.1080/10494820802158983.

Bryant, L. Chittum, J. (2010). ePortfolio Effectiveness: A(n Ill-Fated) Search for Empirical Support. International Journal of ePortfolio, 2013, Volume 3, Number 2, 189-198.

Cheng, B. Wang, M. Moormann, J. Olaniran, B. Chen, N. (2011). The effects of organizational learning environment factors on e-learning Acceptance. Computers & Education 58 (2012) 885–899.

Ehiyazaryan-White, E. (2012). The Dialogic Potential of ePortfolios: Formative Feedback and Communities of Learning Within a Personal Learning Environment. International Journal of ePortfolio. 2012, Volume 2, Number 2, 173-185.

Further Education 2014 – 2019 and Training. Published by SOLAS. Retrieved from http://solas.ie/ on the 10th of April 2015.

Garis, J. (2009). ePortfolios: Concepts, Designs, and Integration within Student Affairs. New Direction for Student Services, no. 119, Fall 2007 © Wiley Periodicals.

Garrett, N. (2011). An Eportfolio Design Supporting Ownership, Social Learning, and Ease of Use. Educational Technology & Society, 14 (1), 187–202.

Gordan, J. (2013). The role of ePortfolios in supporting continuing professional development in practice. The Medical Teacher, Volume 35, 2013.

Hartwick, J. Mason, R. (2014). Using Introductory Videos to Enhance ePortfolios and to Make Them Useful in the Hiring Process. International Journal of ePortfolio. 2014, Volume 4, Number 2, 169-184.

Heinrich, E. Bhattacharya, M. Rayudu, R. (2007). Preparation for lifelong learning using ePortfolios. European Journal of Engineering Education, Vol. 32, No. 6, December 2007, 653–663.

Herman, C. Kirkup, G. (2008). Learners in transition: the use of ePortfolios for women returners to science, engineering and technology. Innovations in Education and Teaching International Vol. 45, No. 1, February 2008, 67–76.

Jwaifell, M. (2013). A proposed Model for Electronic Portfolio to Increase Both Validating Skills and Employability. Procedia - Social and Behavioral Sciences 103 (2013) 356 – 364

Kersten, F. (2004). E-portfolios for the internet job hunt. Teaching Music, 11(4), 40-44.

Koch, A. (2010). The e-Portfolio as an Enabler for Work-integrated Learning in Universities of Technology, Informing Science + Information Technology Education (InSITE) Conference Southern Italy June 19-24, 2010. Pp. 719-729. Access at: http://proceedings.informingscience.org/InSITE2010/InSITE10p719-729Koch822.pdf on the 18th of April 2015.

Koper, R. Verjans, S. (2007). Employability and Lifelong Learning in the Knowledge Society. Proceedings from the ePortfolio2007 conference in Maastricht in October 2007.

Kuilpers, M. Meijers, F. Gundy, C. (2013). The relationship between career competencies, career identity, motivation and quality of choice. International Journal of Education Vocational Guidance (2013) 13:47–66.

Precision Consultancy (2007). Graduate Employability Skills, Business, Industry & Higher Education Collaboration Council, DEST, Canberrra. Accessed at: www.precisionconsultancy.com.au on the 15th of March 2015.

Rennie, F. Morrison, T. (2013). e-Learning and Social Networking Handbook – Resources for High Education. Published by Routledge. 711 Third Avenue, New York, NY 10017.

Salmon, G. (2011). E-moderating: The key to teaching and learning online (3rd ed.). London, England: Kogan.

Trochim, W. Outcome Pattern Matching and Programme Theory. Evaluation and Programme Planning, Vol 12. pp 355 – 366. Peragon Press Plc. (1989).

Wuetherick, B. Dickinson, J. (2015). Why ePortfolios? Student Perceptions of ePortfolio Use in Continuing Education Learning Environments. International Journal of ePortfolio, Volume 5, Number 1, 39-53.

Yu, T. (2011). E-portfolio, a valuable job search tool for college students. Campus-Wide Information Systems, 29(1), 70-76. doi: 10.1108/10650741211192064

Van Wesel, M. & Prop, A. (2008). Comparing students' perceptions of paper-based and electronic portfolios. Canadian Journal of Learning and Technology, 34(3). Accessed at http://www.cjlt.ca/index.php/cjlt/article/view/505/236 15th of April 2015.

Vygotsky, L. S. (1978). Mind in society: The development of higher psychological processes (M. Cole, M. Lopez-Morillas, A. R. Luria, & J. Wertsch, Trans.). Cambridge, MA: Harvard University Press.

Wang, C. (2009). Comprehensive Assessment of Student Collaboration in Electronic Portfolio Construction: An Evaluation Research. TechTrends, February 2009. Volume 53, Number 1

William O. Walker, D. Kelly, Hume, R. (1998). Career Mentoring Handbook. University of California, Davis School of Medicine. Access at at: http://som.ucdavis.edu/fs/facultydevelopment on the 18th of April 2015.

Whitworth, J. Deering, T. Hardy, S. Jones, S. (2011). Perceptions Regarding the Efficacy and Use of Professional Portfolios in the Employment of Teachers. International Journal of ePortfolio, 2011, Volume 1, Number 1, 95-106

Woodley, C. Sims, R. (2011). EPortfolios, professional development and employability: some student perceptions. Campus-Wide Information Systems Vol. 28 No. 3, 2011 pp. 164-174. Emerald Group Publishing Limited.

Yancey, K. (2009). Electronic Portfolios a Decade into the Twenty-first Century: What We Know, What We Need to Know. Association of American Colleges and Universities, Peer Review, Winter 2009.

Yin, R. K. (2003). Case study research: Design and methods (3rd ed.). Thousand Oaks, CA: Sage.

Zubizarreta, J. (2006). The Learning Portfolio: Reflective Practice for Improving Student Learning, Boston, MA: Anker.

THE EMOTIONAL GEOGRAPHIES OF PARENT PARTICIPATION IN SCHOOLING: HEADTEACHERS' PERCEPTIONS IN TAIWAN

Hsin-Jen Chen and Ya-Hsuan Wang
National Chung Cheng University, Taiwan

ABSTRACT

Based on Andy Hargreaves' theoretical framework of emotional geographies, this article attempts to analyze headteachers' perceptions of their interactions with parents in Taiwan. By using qualitative interviews with primary headteachers, the research findings show that headteachers' emotional distances from parents were intertwined with parents' sociocultural status, headteachers' moral purposes, headteachers' notions of professionalism, headteachers' political pretense, and the frequency to contact with parents.

KEYWORDS

Emotional geographies, professionalism, emotional masking, headteacher-parent relations

1. INTRODUCTION

Recently, the issue of parent participation in education has become a heated agenda. Specifically, schools and families should build strong partnerships for children's education (Sanders & Epstein, 1998). In spite of recent educational reform empowering parents to be active partners with influence over school decision making and participation in school activities and governance (Goldring & Sullivan, 1996), Ogawa (1998) stated, 'The assumption that more parent involvement of all types is always better has gone largely unexamined and unchallenged' (p. 8). Parent empowerment is deemed to introduce uncertainty into teachers' work and to raise questions concerning their control over their professional discretion.

However, there is also a significant body of work on school-family relations that teachers and headteachers still possess 'classical' beliefs of professionalism (Hargreaves & Goodson, 1996; Lasky, 2000). In other words, educational practitioners hold beliefs in 'teacher-as-expert' can create a hierarchy of knowledge, value, and status that affects teachers' willingness to collaborate with parents as equals.

Few empirical studies have paid attention to the investigation of emotional responses to headteacher-parent interactions, particularly when educational policies are emphasized on new standards (e.g. accountability practices) and expectations for schooling. The importance of studying headteacher's emotions in relation to parent participation resides in the aim of educational reform to improve student achievement. For headteachers, they may feel respected when some parents appreciate their leadership for the school and their children; but they may feel frustrated while some bothersome parents yell unreasonable demands.

2. EMOTIONAL GEOGRAPHIES OF PARENT PARTICIPATION IN SCHOOLING

In order to better understand headteachers' culturally embedded and politically contested emotions with regard to parent participation in schooling, the theoretical framework of the article mainly based on Andy Hargreaves' (2001) idea of the emotional geographies of schooling and human interaction. These consist of the spatial and experiential patterns of closeness and distance in human relationships that help create, configure and color the feelings and emotions we experience about ourselves, our world and each other.

This theoretical framework could provide a means of identifying the supports for and threats to the basic emotional bonds and understandings of headteacher-parent relationships that are constructed by the forms of closeness or distance in headteacher-parent interactions. In other words, we can ask what helps to create, configure and color the 'negative' emotions from my headteacher informants towards headteacher-parent relations, but also creates and configures 'positive' emotions? According to Hargreaves, the five dimensions of emotional geographies of human interactions are not merely physical aspects, but also interconnected with sociocultural, professional, political dimensions and headteachers' moral purposes.

Firstly, *sociocultural geographies:* Teachers and headteachers often assume that two-parent, middle-class nuclear family structures provide the 'best' environments for children's education. Hargreaves (2001) remarks differences of ethno-culture, gender and class between teachers or headteachers and parents can create sociocultural distance and usually lead them to be treated as stereotypes. Such social stereotypes produce a sense of 'otherness' or 'difference' (Parr, 2005; Sibley, 1995) which could further distance headteachers themselves from specific 'other' parents. In short, sociocultural geographies refer to the closeness or distance between headteachers and parents mainly based on parents' sociocultural backgrounds.

Secondly, *moral geographies:* Emotions are closely bound up with and triggered by our purposes, say, being a teacher or a headteacher. Positive emotions may occur when teachers and headteachers receive gratitude, appreciation, agreement and support from parents. By contrast, negative emotions may occur when teachers and headteachers feel their purposes as educational practitioners being threatened by parents' misunderstanding, disagreement or criticism. In short, moral geographies concern the closeness or distance between the headteachers' moral purposes (for example, their pedagogical and ideological philosophies) and those of parents in relation to children' education.

Thirdly, *professional geographies:* Teachers and headteachers often regard themselves as professional people, viewing themselves as experts in teaching and school management. In this respect, the notion of professionalism is defined as a 'classical' model based on the traditionally male preserves of being professionals who should avoid emotional entanglements with their clients' (or parents') problems and maintain professional distance from them (Hargreaves & Goodson, 1996; Sachs, 1997). On the contrary, the issue of social accountability has an inevitable bearing on the question of professional autonomy (Locke, 2001) which is the central standpoint of 'classical' model of professionalism. Much discussion of the new model of professionalism, or so called 'new professionalism' coined by David Hargreaves (1994), should be accountable to the wider community (mainly referring to parents) which is derived from the client-focused discourse. In short, professional geographies are concerned with the ideological conflict between competing forms of professionalism (i.e. classical or new model).

Fourthly, *political geographies:* Power relations between headteachers and parents are embedded in hierarchized forms of surveillance is integrated into institutional settings. Particularly, with the increase of 'parent power' during the latest decade (Hargreaves, 2000), headteachers feel more pressures from parent demands, and this seems to enlarge political distance between headteachers and parents. In addition, headteachers sometimes want to manage or even mask their emotions while interacting with parents. To paraphrase Hochschild (1983), through emotional masking headteachers present the 'right' emotional appearance to parents who can 'buy' the hearts of parents (Bryson, 2008, p. 344). Although Goleman (1995) argues that emotional management can be seen as emotional competence or intelligence, Hargreaves (2000) remarks that such emotional masking could enlarge political distance between stakeholders. In short, political geographies concern the stakeholders' relations in the hierarchical power structures.

Finally, *physical geographies:* The emotional distance may come from infrequent and non-face-to-face communication that can make emotional understanding and good partnerships between headteachers and parents more difficult to establish. Thus, the establishment of emotional bonds with headteachers and parents are based on intensity, frequency and continuity in interaction. Communication between headteachers and parents take place either formal or informal mechanisms. Formal mechanisms include staged meetings (e.g. parents' days or parents' nights in United Kingdom) or conferences. Informal ones may take place in strings of infrequent, fragmented, episodic and disconnected interactions. Concretely, we cannot understand people we rarely talk with, nor can we be understood by them in return. In short, physical geographies refer to the physical spaces which can bring and keep people over long periods so that relationships might develop, or which can reduce these relationships due to strings of episodic interactions.

3. THE STUDY

The sample was distributed across three varied schools of different sizes and serving different kinds of communities (i.e. urban, suburban and rural areas). The informants in this article are one female and two male headteacher, whose ages range from 45 to 60 years. All three headteachers, Adam, Ben and Eva (all anonym), in three varied schools were chosen as research participants. Due to their high positions, they have more frequent and significant interactions with parents than teachers. The study, then, focuses on a particular, homogenous, and highly educated group of headteachers. By focusing on this extraordinary sample, we can highlight headteacher-parent relations as perceived by headteachers who both are professional and have some interactions with parents. They all believed that teachers and headteachers are professionals with expert knowledge in children education. Additionally, in spite of empathy towards some minority parents, e.g. aboriginal parents or parents with low-income living, they admitted that they possessed some stereotypes on these minority parents. They regarded some parents as 'normality' while others as 'problematic'.

Interviews may serve as most efficient method of data collection in qualitative social research. Interviews with headteachers were semi-structured and iterative. Interviews with three headteachers were semi-structured and each interview lasted for around 1.5 hours and particularly concentrated on eliciting headteachers' reports of their emotional relationships with parent participation in children learning. All three headteachers were each interviewed three times, approximately over 10 hours. The first interview for three headteachers was undertaken based on Hargreaves' theoretical framework to obtain initial pictures of three headteachers' emotional reflections on headteacher-parent interactions. Then, the summary of the first interview was sent to the headteachers for validation. The second and third interviews took place in the following months when an early version of qualitative accounts was discussed in detail with three headteachers respectively. Specifically, the purpose of the second and the third interviews was to make up some important information which did not emerge at the first interview. Each interview was taped and then transcribed verbatim.

The interview protocol was designed to understand how headteacher perceived parent participation in education. This study borrowed Hochschild's (1983) methodological procedures whereby headteachers were asked to reflect on critical incidents regarding headteacher-parent interactions. Questions asked included: (a) Tell us a bit about what kinds of parent backgrounds in your school? How do you perceive parent backgrounds in relation to parent participation in schooling? (b) What is your primary responsibility as a headteacher? Does recent educational reform regarding parent participation in education affect your purpose as a headteacher? (c) What do you think of the word, professionalism, and what comes to your mind particularly related to parent participation? (d) How often do you contact with parents? Do you meet some parents on Parents' Day or during the meeting of Parents' Association? Whether are all parents willing to communicate with you? And why do some parents participate in headteacher-parent meetings? (e) In what circumstances do you hear parent criticism or obtain parent recognition in your headship?

4. EMOTIONAL GEOGRAPHIES OF PARENT PARTICIPATION IN SCHOOLING

4.1 Sociocultural Geographies and Parent Participation

Headteacher informants in the article often had assumptions about parent backgrounds that are socioculturally biased, delivering their comments on pupils' family backgrounds which had a significant impact on children's performances. As Headteacher Ben exclaimed:

At the community some parents are classified as 'the working class'. This rural community does not provide many job opportunities so they look for jobs away from this rural area to the city. Owing to living in the poor environment, parents unable to provide the better environment for their children. Usually, their children's academic performance is not good enough. Even worse, some children from the working class can not catch up with those who from the middle class since their parents do not support their children in schooling. (Headteacher Ben).

Headteacher Adam delivered similar comments on her experiences about parent participation in schooling which represented traditional norms of 'disadvantaged' families failing to support their children's education.

On Parents' Day, I was looking forward to all parents from this community who could visit the school exchange some experiences in children's education. It was a little pity that some parents, especially from low-incoming families, were unable to visit the school and have a chance to discuss with their children's learning and performance (Headteacher Adam).

Headteacher informants' responses of parent participation in schooling seemed to be consistent with the ways parent backgrounds have taken for granted that parents with middle to high socio-economic positions are primarily active participation in formal and informal activities in schools (Driessen, Smit, & Sleegers, 2005). From Headteacher Adam's judgment, parents' failure to attend meetings or officially organized events was regarded as failure to support their children's. There was a sense of 'otherness' towards those parents from the working class or low-incoming households which was seen to enlarge sociocultural distance between headteachers and parents.

Furthermore, the literature indicates a tendency to judge and to classify parents according to a range of normality, including parents' ethnic or racial status which is likely to be labeled as 'good' or 'bad' related to home-school interactions. For example, some studies have reported 'black' parents having unrealistic expectations of their children or not interested in their children's education (Charles, Roscigno & Torres, 2007; Jencks & Phillips, 1998). In this study, Eva delivered her opinions about some aboriginal parents whose attitudes towards their children's education. As she indicates:

Some parents are aborigines in our community whose seem not to take children's education seriously. One teacher told me that one of his pupils was absent for several days… Later I phoned his aboriginal mother but she did not say anything… I tried to urge she should bring her child to school according to the law, but she failed to do so. I really felt disappointed (Headteacher Eva).

Another aspect of parent backgrounds is concerned with parent marital status. The research findings are consistent with related literatures which present that single-parent families can be problematic in children's education (Lasky, 2000). Adam's statement illustrated that the single-parent family is usually failure to build up a warm and supportive family environment for children's education. For example,

I have a boy called Willy, who lives with his father only. Several years ago his mother died in a traffic accident. His father is unemployed and beats Willy quite often. … Later the social worker helped Willy away from his father bully. I am empathy with Willy's situation. (Headteacher Adam)

Headteachers' responses to teacher-parent relations illustrate their social distance from parents or social closeness to parents particularly in terms of parents' sociocultural status. Headteachers seem to be inevitable to see some parents as 'the others' by the presence of definite stereotypes. Under these circumstances, the gap of their emotional understanding between headteachers and 'other' parents may be formed, and the emotional closeness between the two parties could be difficult to achieve.

4.2 Moral Geographies and Parent Participation

Moral issues are concerned with value judgment and beliefs. People may achieve the moral agreement and support when their value judgment or beliefs are similar. This will bring about the emotional closeness among people involved. Three headteacher participants in this study indicated that the paramount purpose of teaching is the motto, 'no child left behind'. These headteachers expressed the importance of caring, with which they also emphasized that parents should be concerned.

Some parents recognize that I have a significant influence in leadership to encourage teachers who should spend time on children's behaviour in discipline… I feel that I obtain parents' support in leadership. Most teachers also convey their positive comments on my leadership and example in children's discipline. (Headteacher Ben)

Indeed, caring for children was one of moral purposes for headteachers. When headteachers' moral purposes are achieved, happiness, gratification, self-fulfillment, and other positive emotions are the consequence (Oatley & Jenkins, 1996). On the contrary, headteachers' negative emotions can occur when they feel their moral purposes in children's learning are being ignored.

Another moral purpose of being a headteacher is concerned with the caring purpose of schooling. Yet, when headteachers' purposes are at odds with those around them, particularly for parents, frustration, helplessness, anger, and even disgust may occur. Such negative emotions can be affect headteachers' moral purposes, leading them to reduce their efforts and enthusiasm for their work (Hargreaves, 2001). Headteachers in this study reported feeling helpless and powerless when parents did not value the significance of caring and support in children's education:

Some parents, as far as I know, seem to assume that children's education is not their responsibilities. They often expressed that they were not good at children learning. But I do believe if parents spend more time on caring for their children, children may try to improve their learning performance for their parents in turn. (Headteacher Ben)

Adam and Ben expressed similar comments on parents' indifferent attitudes towards children's learning:

Some pupils are chronically late in learning or they have some behavior problems and for me, this is not a really big problem. The real problem is when I phone pupils' home and I can tell by the uncaring responses from their parents, indicating that parents are disinterested in all efforts to find solutions for their children's learning. They have already given up their children. I cannot figure out why these parents do not care about their children .... (Headteacher Adam)

Caring is one of the most important elements in children's education. But I find that some parents in this community have already given up their children. I cannot understand why these parents do not care about their children... I feel very frustrated (Headteacher Ben).

Educators frequently identify that inconsistency in parents' and headteachers' moral purposes provokes negative emotions. Teachers feel responsible for children, and as Nias (1999) remarks, teachers feel that their moral 'answerability' to pupils puts on them an obligation to 'care' for them. She and her colleagues also comments that teachers may lose their sense of moral purpose and become 'demoralized' (Nias, Southworth, & Yeomans, 1989), particularly when their efforts to work with children were impeded due to lack of support from parents.

4.3 Professional Geographies and Parent Participation

Headteachers in this study perceived positive emotions when parents conveyed their respect and agreement with headteachers' professional judgment, regarding headteachers and teachers as experts on pupils' learning and curriculum planning. When headteachers received parents' positive acknowledgement related to their headship, they reinforced their authority and power over parents due to their professional status.

As a head, I need to focus on children's learning and behaviour.... I explained how to enhance children's academic performance ... and parents were impressed by my efforts of doing this. I am so glad that parents recognized what I had done for those children.... Some parents really appreciated my professional performance in helping students. (Headteacher Adam)

Eva delivered her opinion about how parents express their gratitude to teachers' help for children's learning.

As far as I know, most parents do appreciate teachers' professional performance in helping their children. Particularly in Chinese societies, there is an old saying, 'Even if someone is your teacher for only one day, you should regard him as your father for the rest of your life.' In other words, teachers are still regarded as respected people nowadays, even though teachers face more and more pressures from the general public. (Headteacher Eva)

However, headteachers and teachers may suffer professional vulnerability due to parents' disagreement with their professional judgment. Sometimes, parents demand 'unreasonable' questions or 'demanding' requirements. The following is an example, describing Adam who acknowledged that he felt defensive when the parent commented on his headship.

My school is located in the centre of the city. Some parents are doctors, university professors or working as managers, and sometimes they complained about how I paid little attention to their children's learning.... Actually these parents want 'more extra curricular activities' arranged for their kids but I need to take care of the whole school children's needs. It is difficult to satisfy these parents' expectations. (Headteacher Adam)

Respondents accounts indicated that their notion of headteacher professionalism was significantly influenced by parents' needs or viewpoints to define or redefine her professional identity. Headteacher interviewees seemed to possess the 'classical professionalism', revealing that they are experts in education, enjoying parents' gratitude and support for their profession and leadership (Lasky, 2000). However, 'flexible' professionalism possessed by parents ask headteachers to arrange some curriculum and activities for their children, which may challenge headteachers' profession and leadership. Headteachers' sense of emotional closeness or distance that headteachers perceptions of their relationships with parents is affected by their definition or redefinition of professionalism.

4.4 Political Geographies and Parent Participation

In Taiwan, the act, Education Basic Law, has empowered parents the rights to participate in schooling and to choose what sort of school or educational system would be appropriate for their children's learning. Lasky (2005) argues that with the emergence of parent power in education, headteachers and teachers face more requirements and pressures from parents.

One day a student's parent walked into my office, complaining about his son bullied by other pupils. Most important, he accused of the teacher lacking of care about his son's situation. ... after that I asked the teacher. She told me that she had dealt with his son's situation.... Lastly, I found this student lied to his father owing to his absence of attendance. (Headteacher Ben)

When educational practitioners interact with parents, they normally 'pretend' their authentic emotions (often referring to negative emotions, such as anger, frustration, helplessness) to avoid possible conflict with parents, particularly while facing parents' criticism (Hargreaves, 2001). Such an emotional response for educational practitioners can be in line with what Goleman (1995) coins the term, emotional masking. The following is an example when Headteacher Adam once encountered a parent angrily accusing of his child's teacher 'bad' instruction:

One day there was a parent angrily running into my office, accusing his child's homeroom teacher who used inappropriate teaching methods to his child. I tried to appease his emotions and patiently listened to his complaints.... Finally, he realized what he heard was not true. But you know, at that time I needed to 'manage' my emotions, patiently communicating with this parent (Headteacher Adam)

Emotional management above used by Adam could be a useful way to minimize possibly anxious, uneasy or even conflicting interactions. In spite of the use of emotional management avoiding conflicting interactions with each another, educational practitioners often manage their authentic emotions especially when they face parents' criticism. Although Goleman (1998) argues that the importance of managing one's emotions has been most widely highlighted in organizational operation, Boler (1999) criticize Goleman's view of emotional management, arguing that it involves 'selling out' the emotional self to the purposes and profits of the organization, for instance, a smile for a sale, or to the 'nice' relations with the clients (or parents in the study). Eva said that being an educational practitioner is laborious work and needs to be aware of the importance of 'professional image'. For example:

In oriental countries educational practitioners are regarded as intellectuals who are knowledgeable and have higher social status in the society. Whether being a headteacher or a teacher, we are expected not to fight with parents even though they lose their temper, accusing of something against you.... Over time we are getting used to pretend our real feelings, i.e. making our authentic emotions to ease up parents' anger or resentment. In doing so we could be viewed as 'qualified' educational practitioners. (Headteacher Eva)

As far as the pretence of emotions is concerned, headteachers or teachers usually adopt the strategy of emotional masking to encounter parents' criticism or unreasonable requirements. Ashforth & Humphrey (1993) argue that masking emotions can identify with the expectations of the role. Emotional masking and management can reduce the tensions between educational practitioners (including headteachers and teachers) and parents; however, it is used to protect educational practitioners themselves against parents' criticism and hostility (Hargreaves, 2000). In the long term, educational practitioners gradually keep political distance from parents owing to 'hiding' authentic emotions which may impede the authentic relations.

4.5 Physical Geographies and Parent Participation

Physical geographies are one aspect of emotional geographies which focuses upon physical phenomena. We may feel distance from people who are right next to us whereas we feel very close to ones who live miles away. In this respect, emotions have imaginary geographies (Shields, 1991). Headteachers-parents interactions can be involved by face-to-face, by meetings, by telephones, by notes, by e-mails and so forth. One of affecting the quality of Headteachers-parents relationships is frequency. For example:

Some parents are working as volunteers in my school. Some of them tell stories in the morning when homeroom teachers attend the staff meeting. Some work as lollipop men who temporarily stop the flow of traffic so children can cross an intersection. Some do other things, such as working as clerks in the school library, or working as cleaners who help first/second graders to clean their classrooms. (Headteacher Eva)

Headteacher Eva continued to express her positive emotions because of parents as volunteers for school children education:

I find that most parents working as volunteers in my school are housekeepers. They have lots of free time so that they come to the school as volunteers. …At the end of the year I usually give a letter to these volunteering parents, delivering my gratitude to them. (Headteacher Eva)

Parents' willingness and abilities to participate in and around the school can draw up physical closeness with headteachers. Working as voluntary parents would be a good example of building up physical closeness between headteachers and parents. Headteachers and parents meet each another frequently, positive emotions reported by headteachers occurred.

By contrast, related literatures reveal that communications between educational practitioners and parents in secondary schools are overwhelmingly episodic and infrequent (e.g. Lasky, 2000). Compared with the difficulties of physical closeness for secondary headteachers and teachers to develop better relationships with parents (Walker, 1998), primary school headteachers and teachers and parents engage more frequent interactions which seems to be positive influence on the quality of teacher-parent interactions. Similarly, Hargreaves (2001) found that half of the teachers selected reported positive emotions with parents involved informal discussions.

5. CONCLUSIONS

The primary purpose of this article has been to explore how headteachers' emotions can be influenced by their interactions with parents based on Hargreaves' five dimensions of emotional geographies. To achieve this goal, emotional geographies of headteacher-parent relations were analyzed by parents' sociocultural backgrounds, inseparable from headteachers' sense of moral purposes and professionalism, related to headteachers' emotional masking, and headteachers' physical connection with parents.

There are five dimensions of emotional geographies in relation to headteacher-parent interactions, and the research findings revealed headteacher-parent relationships were interconnected with conceptions of culture, status and power. First, research data illustrate that the emotions headteachers experienced in their interactions with parents were largely affected by parents' socioeconomic status, ethnic identity, or marital status. The respondent headteachers in this study seemed to be inescapable to regard some parents as 'the others' by the presence of definite stereotypes. Second, consistency in parents' and headteachers' moral purposes provokes positive emotions and vice versa. Headteachers' sense of emotional closeness could be achieved when headteachers and parents recognized each other particularly in educational beliefs. Third, a sense of 'classical professionalism' was still implanted in headteachers' minds, and this is difficult to see parents as partners in children's education. Fourth, emotional masking or management was usually used for headteachers to soften possibly conflicting situations between headteachers and parents. Finally, physical distance or closeness depended upon the frequency of headteacher-parent interactions, and parents' willingness to be volunteers in and around the school.

To sum up, this article tries to figure out their similarities and differences between the headteachers related to their perceptions of each aspect of the emotional geographies. The headteacher respondents regarded some parents as 'normality' while others as 'problematic'. The research findings, perhaps, merely from headteachers' accounts of headteacher-parent relations, reveal their similarities rather than differences. Why did the headteachers' in this research have similar viewpoints of five aspects of emotional geographies? The article agrees with Lasky's viewpoints (2000) that the headteachers delivered their personal and cultural beliefs in their interactions with parents, largely shaped by the professional norm-based discourses and values they possessed within the culture of schooling.

REFERENCES

Ashforth, B. E., & Humphrey, R. H. (1993). Emotional labour in service roles: The influence of identity. *Academy and Management Journal, 18*(1), 88-115.

Boler, M. (1999). *Feeling power: Emotions and education*. New York: Routledge.

Bryson, J. R. (2008). Service economics, spatial divisions of expertise and the second global shift. In P. Daniels, M. Bradshaw, D. Shaw & J. Sidaway (Eds.), *An introduction to human geographies* (3rd ed.) (pp. 339-357). Harlow, Essex: Pearson Education.

Charles, C. Z., Roscigno, V. J., & Torres, K. C. (2007). Racial inequality and college attendance: The mediating role of parental investments. *Social Science Research, 36*(1), 329-352.

Denzin, N. (1984). *On understanding emotion*. San Francisco: Jossey-Bass.

Driessen, G, Smit, F., & Sleegers, P. (2005). Parental involvement and educational achievement. *British Educational Research Journal, 31*(4), 509-532.

Goldring, E. B., & Sullivan, A. V. (1996). Beyond the boundaries: Principals, parents and communities shaping the school environment. In K. Leithwood, J. Chapman, D. Corson, P. Hallinger, & A. Hart (Eds.), *International handbook of educational leadership and administration* (pp. 195-218). Amsterdam: Kluwer.

Goleman, D. (1995). *Emotional intelligence*. New York: Bantam Books.

Goleman, D. (1998). *Working with emotional intelligence*. New York: Bantam.

Hargreaves, A. (1998). The emotional politics of teaching and teacher development: With implications for leadership. *International Journal of Leadership in Education, 1*(4), 811-826.

Hargreaves, A. (2000). Mixed emotional: Teachers' perceptions of their interactions with students. *Teaching and Teacher Education, 16*, 811-826.

Hargreaves, A. (2001). Emotional geographies of teaching. *Teachers College Record, 103*(6), 1056-1080.

Hargreaves, A., & Goodson, I. (1996). Teachers' professional lives: Aspirations and actualities. In I. Goodson & A. Hargreaves (Eds.), *Teachers' professional lives* (pp. 1-28). London: Falmer Press.

Hargreaves, D. H. (1994). The new professionalism: The synthesis of professional and institutional development, *Teaching and Teacher Education, 10* (4), 423-438.

Hochschild, A. (1983). *The managed heart commercialization of human feeling*. Berkeley, CA: University of California Press.

Jencks, C., & Phillips, M. (1998). The black-white test score gap. *Brookings Review, 16*(2), 24-27.

Lasky, S. (2000). The cultural and emotional politics of teacher-parent interactions. *Teaching and Teacher Education, 16*, 843-860.

Lasky, S. (2005). A sociocultural approach to understanding teacher identity, agency and professional vulnerability in a context of secondary school reform. *Teaching and Teacher Education, 21*, 899-916.

Locke, T. (2001). Question of professionalism: Erosion and reclamation. *Change: Transformations in Education, 4*(2), 30-50.

Nias, J. (1999). Teachers' moral purpose: Stress, vulnerability, and strength. In R. Vandenberghe, & A. M. Huberman (Eds.), *Understanding and preventing teacher burnout: A sourcebook of international research and practice* (pp. 223-237). New York: Cambridge University Press.

Nias, J., Southworth, G, & Yeomans, R. (1989). *Staff relationships in the primary school: A study of organizational cultures*. London: Cassell.

Oatley, K., & Jenkins, J. (1996). *Understanding emotions*. Cambridge, MA: Blackwell.

Ogawa, R. T. (1998). Organizing parent-teacher relations around the work of teaching. *Peabody Journal of Education, 73*(1), 6-14.

Parr, H. (2005). Emotional geographies. In P. Cloke, P. Crang & M. Goodwin (Eds.) Introducing human geographies (2nd ed.) (pp. 472-484). London: Hodder Arnold.

Sachs, J. (1997). Reclaiming the agenda of professionalism: An Australian experience. *Journal of Education for Teaching, 23*(3), 263-275.

Sanders, M., & Epstein, J. (1998). School-family-community partnerships and educational change: International perspectives. In A. Hargreaves, A. Lieberman, M. Fullan, & D. Hopkins (Eds.), *International handbook of educational change* (pp. 482-502). Norwell, MA: Kluwer Academic.

Shields, R. (1991). *Place on the margin: Alternative geographies of modernity*. London: Routledge.

Sibley, D. (1995). Geographies of exclusion: Society and difference in the West. London: Routledge.

Tripp, D. (1993). *Critical incidents in teaching: Developing professional judgment*. London: Routledge.

Walker, B. M. (1998). Meeting without communication: A study of parents' evening in secondary schools. *British Educational Research Journal, 24*(2), 163-178.

GEOPOLITICAL E-ANALYSIS BASED ON E-LEARNING CONTENT

Anca Dinicu and Romana Oancea
"Nicolae Bălcescu" Land Forces Academy, 3-5 Revoluției Street, Sibiu, Romania

ABSTRACT

In a world of great complexity, understanding the manner states act and react becomes more and more an intriguing quest due to the multiple relations of dependence and interdependence that characterize "the global puzzle". Within this context, an analysis based on a geopolitical approach becomes a very useful means used to determine not only the rank of some states from a region that is under observation, but also to identify the type of relation established between them according to the power potential they have. As an academic discipline, Geopolitics is meant not only to develop students' critical and creative thinking, but also to connect the most diverse fields of research and knowledge in order to get "the whole picture". Under this circumstance, given the need of simulation during the seminars, the paper proposes developing a geopolitical lesson, allowing students to analyze factors influencing the ranking of countries in terms of three criteria: economic, military and territorial. The geopolitical lesson, designed in Java, allows students to first establish the importance of a criterion in relation to the other and establish relative weights. Each criterion contains a variable number of sub-criteria that can be selected or disposed in the hierarchy made in order to determine the possible degree of influence of the region. To determine the weights associated with the three criteria, after selecting the importance for each criterion, Analytic Hierarchy Process algorithm was used and in order to establish the influence "ability" of the states in the region, Electre Method was implemented, which allowed a hierarchy of countries considered. Moreover, this paper demonstrates that a complex situation related with the international security environment can be analyzed in order to be understood and/or solved by using not only empirical case study, but also simulation.

KEYWORDS

Simulation based-learning, geopolitical lesson, java application

1. INTRODUCTION

Approaching the subject of analysis with the help of game-based learning, gamification or simulation-based eLearning is a new trend in providing knowledge. This suggests that information, knowledge is put in a context or scenario as real as possible to meet the student's needs in the learning process. Each of the learning methods can be applied to all levels of knowledge if they are adapted and designed according to the target groups. In game based learning and gamification, the core element is the game or game-specific mechanisms in order to encourage an appropriate learning behavior, competition or exceeding their own progress (Perrotta, C. et al., 2013). In simulation-based learning it is very important that visual instruments are in accordance with the designed pedagogical objectives and the student can test and check lab or seminar homework in agreement with the themes discussed. In terms of teaching, presentation accompanied by explanations and demonstrations may lead to achieving the designed objectives. Moreover, if phenomena described are accompanied by some practical-applied approach that is able to simulate the results by changing the input parameters, understanding and learning could be visibly improved. In a blended learning, and not only, simulation has beneficial effects both during face-to-face courses and online and can be successfully applied especially in seminar sessions if allowed. Although in terms of teacher, the effort to generate simulations may be higher. Lately it is considered that text-based learning is over and the focus is on simulation-based learning, especially in areas where the laboratories equipped to meet the latest requirements involves a considerable financial effort (Moreno-Ger P. et al., 2010). On the other hand, the simulation creates a certain level of interaction and is intended to transfer knowledge from a mentor to the student in a way different from the traditional course and at the same time a level of complexity in a controlled environment can be introduced (Deegan M. et al., 2014).

Given the need for simulation, no matter where it is applied, creating an eLearning object is aimed, which, from geopolitical perspective, allows students to become familiar with the factors that contribute to the analysis of the geopolitical framework and how these factors lead to a hierarchy of states' power in a given region. Initially, for testing the effects on groups of students, geopolitical lesson was designed in Java and used in the seminars for half of the students' groups, and then loaded on the institution's e-learning platform.

The rest of the paper is organized as follows: Section 2 provides the theoretical background related to the geopolitical context and methodology used and Section 3 focuses on the presentation of the Java-designed application and discussions on the observed impact among students.

2. APPROACHES USED IN CREATING THE LEARNING OBJECTIVE

The simulation-based Geopolitics lesson aims at understanding and analyzing the factors that contribute to national power, both in terms of national performances, and performance of other countries in a region. In literature, for measuring national power, various models were developed (Liao H. et al, 2015; Schwab K., 2016), but it was noted that national power is difficult to be measured (Chang C.L., 2004). In fact, power always depends on context and the context is given by the structure of the international system. This does not mean that evaluating the national power and understanding its projection at the international level are a lost cause.

In each of the models developed considered criteria's weights are equal, and for the determination of the country's power, world average energy consumption is taken into account. Because regional power hierarchy was wanted, we thought it would be more appropriate to assess countries economically, militarily and territorially based on national parameters, parameters dependent on the domestic policy of each country. Therefore, the model was carried out in the following steps:

- Criteria and sub-criteria that can influence regional hierarchy were determined;
- For each sub-criterion, values related to internal politics of each country of the ones considered were assigned;
- Criteria weights were determined, according to the degree of importance, and for the sub-criteria's weights within the criterion was considered equal;
- Based on the determined weights and the sub-criteria entering the model, the regional hierarchy was established.

2.1 Elements influencing Power of States

In the lesson designed, students can make a hierarchy based on three main pillars (criteria): economic and future development, military capability and territorial factors that contribute in different ways, depending on the weight associated with the hierarchy of states.

The economic dimension of the national security is very important not only due to the globalization process. Economy is the engine of a nation survival and the source of development for other fields of activity especially nowadays when the military power is no longer enough for a state to get a good ranking regarding its power of projecting the national interest abroad. From the economic point of view, the following criteria were chosen to contribute to the ranking of states:

- Gross Domestic Product per capita (GDP/C);
- Expenditure on research and development - a country where budget allocations for research and development are supported by the government can reach technological innovations beneficial for the economy and for the military development (Liao H. et al, 2015);
- Expenditure on education - a young educated person can be absorbed by the labor market and bring benefits in terms of economics. If absorption of the labor market due to low level of education is poor, not only will it lead to pressure on the state's social spending, but also to a large number of potential immigrants.

After the end of the Cold War, military has lost its supremacy in establishing "the global map of power and interest" which does not mean that it has not remain and important tool applied in foreign affairs. The military aspect of the national power can be quantified through factors related to:

- Military expenditure allocated from the state budget - this type of expenditure being directly related with the level of economic growth and development. But there are also exceptions, when the military budget is tailored rather according to the international ambition of a state than to its national output.

- The number of military personnel - a figure that in order to be relevant for a state's power must be analyzed together with other military or even economic criteria.

When talking about Geopolitics, territory becomes an indispensable element of the analysis. States get themselves into a competition that aims to control territory by using political, economic and military tools. Territorially speaking, elements that may influence the power of a state refer to:

- Land surface - it is generally considered that the size of a country is directly proportional to the reserves of natural resources. The higher the reserves are, the lower the dependency from other states is. There are also exceptions to this rule, very important being the geography itself and the strategic importance of the natural resources;

- Population - a sustainable economy cannot be sustained with labor shortages. In general, the higher the active population is, the cheaper the labor force becomes. And a cheap labor force can become a great attraction both for the national entrepreneur and the direct foreign investment;

- Sea outlet - the existence of the sea outlet may indicate a commercial and/or shipping and/or battle fleet, (access to) natural resources and tourist attraction. At worst it is seen as a challenge and at best, as an opportunity for fulfilling the national interest;

- Military alliances between states - meaning that the territories of such states are safely included under a common umbrella meant to provide security not only from military perspective, but also from an economic, political, cultural and societal point of view.

The research has taken into consideration 8 states belonging to the same geopolitical region. In the first stage, to every single state values for each sub-criterion within the three pillars (economic, military and territorial) were attributed.

Table 1. Values of sub-criteria associated for each country

	Economic and perspectives			*Military capabilities*		*Territorial*			
	GDP per capita	Government expenditure on education	Research and development expenditure	Military budget	Military personnel	Population (millions)	Sea/ ocean access	Allia nce	Area
Country1	7091.32	1775699158	398523407	660842590.3	47300	7114	1	1	108560
Country2	18325.89	8263944702	3851346741	1857935944	24800	10561	0	1	77210
Country3	11902.79	5420109863	1603790588	983346023.6	38500	9835	0	1	90530
Country4	1871.5	554610023.5	24605000.02	23940000.53	7750	3553	0	0	32870
Country5	12309.30	22479536133	4393089905	10234965210	172700	37967	0	0	306190
Country6	9438.99	5483511963	708753204.3	2592544556	151300	19760	1	1	230080
Country7	16648.06	3538309631	794314422.6	1001919327	15850	5422	0	0	48086
Country8	2051.64	5833546143	566786956.8	3479200134	204000	42501	1	0	579290

At first glance, the 8 countries cannot be ranked, on the one hand due to the high number of sub-criteria for which the hierarchy is desired, on the other hand, due to the varying weights associated with each criterion. Initially, in establishing the hierarchy, students can choose the degree of importance of a criterion in relation to the other considered, and within each criterion it will be considered that the weights for each sub-criterion are equal. In other words, countries' hierarchy or ordering according to the criteria considered is determined based on

$$\textit{Countries hierarchy}: \max(w_1 \cdot E\,\&\,P), \max(w_2 \cdot M), \max(w_3 \cdot T) \qquad (1)$$

where:

- *E&P – values associated with the sub-criteria from the economic and perspective pillar;*
- *M- military capability pillar;*
- *T – territorial pillar;*
- w_1, w_2, w_3 *– weights associated to the corresponding criterion, based on AHP algorithm.*

The three considered pillars contribute to varying degrees to the countries' hierarchy, based on the influence in the region and the weights associated to criteria will be stable with AHP algorithm. Thus, to determine weights associated with each criterion AHP algorithm (Analytic Hierarchy Process) was used, and then, Electre method was used as an outranking.

2.2 The Analytic Hierarchy Process

The AHP algorithm (Analytic Hierarchy Process) (Saaty Thomas L., 2008) allows determining the weights of each criterion according to the scale of importance of each criterion in relation to other criteria considered. The scale of importance was quantified by values between the range 1-9 and then the algorithm for calculating the weight was applied.

Table 2. Scale of pair wise comparison - The Saaty Rating Scale (Saaty Thomas L., 2008).

Intensity of importance (Saaty scale)	Definition
1	Equally importance
3	Somewhat more important
5	Much more important importance
7	Very much more important importance
9	Absolutely more important
2,4,6,8	Intermediate values

If we consider the criteria C_1, C_2, ... C_m, after selecting the importance of each criterion based on the scale, the associated weights can be determined.

Table 3. AHP algorithm for weight determination

	C_1	C_2	...	C_m		weight
C_1	a_{11}	a_{12}		a_{1m}		$w_1 = \frac{1}{m}\sum_i \frac{a_{1i}}{S_1}$
C_2	a_{21}	a_{22}		a_{2m}	=>	$w_2 = \frac{1}{m}\sum_i \frac{a_{2i}}{S_2}$
...	...	...	...	...		...
C_m	a_{m1}	a_{m2}		a_{mm}		$w_m = \frac{1}{m}\sum_i \frac{a_{mi}}{S_1}$
Σ	$S_1 = \sum_i a_{i1}$	$S_2 = \sum_i a_{i2}$	...	$S_m = \sum_i a_{im}$		$\sum_i w_i = 1$

Obtained vector $W = [w_1, w_2, ..., w_m]$ represents the importance of a criterion in relation with other criteria.

2.3 Electre Method

Electre method, based on concordance and discordance matrices, is a multi-criteria decision algorithm and allows the selection of the best option after a complete hierarchy of the variants considered. For a problem with n variants and m criteria, the steps in view of hierarchy are the following:

- Elements of the concordance coefficients' matrix are determined;

For each set of decision variants (V_k, V_l) concordance is calculated according to the formula (Figuera, J., Greco, S., Ehrgott, M., 2005):

$$c_{jk} = c(V_j, V_k) = \sum_{i|r_{ij} \geq r_{ik}}^{m} w_i, \mathrm{j,k} = \overline{1,n}, \mathrm{j} \neq \mathrm{k} \tag{2}$$

In other words, the concordance index c_{jk} is determined as the sum of the weights corresponding to the criteria according to which V_j is better than variant V_k. Variance matrix $C \in M_{nxn}$ is quadratic and it expresses the superiority of variant „*k*" in relation to variant „*j*"

- discordance coefficients are calculated for each pair of variants

Discordance coefficients for each pair of variants are calculated:

$$d_{jk} = \begin{cases} d(V_j, V_k) = 0, if \quad r_{ij} \geq r_{ik} \quad \forall i = \overline{1,n} \\ \max\left\{ \dfrac{r_{ki} - r_{ji}}{\max\limits_{1<=l<=n}(r_{li}) - \min\limits_{1<=l<=n}(r_{li})} \right\} \quad if\ r_{ij} < r_{ik} \end{cases} \tag{3}$$

where: $r_{ij,}$ are the normalized values of the variant "*i*" for criterion "*j*".

Discordance matrix $D \in M_{nxn}$ is quadratic and it expresses the superiority of variant *"j"* in relation to variant *"k"*.

- outranking. For outranking, modified Electre method was used (Căruţaşu V., 2014). Therefore, initially, three matrices were determined *F*, *G* and *E*

$$F = \begin{cases} 1, \text{if } c_{kl} \geq \alpha \\ 0, \text{if } c_{kl} < \alpha \end{cases}, \quad G = \begin{cases} 1, \text{if } d_{kl} \leq \beta \\ 0, \text{if } d_{kl} > \beta \end{cases}, \tag{4}$$

where:

$$\alpha = \frac{1}{n(n-1)} \sum_{k=1}^{n} \sum_{\substack{l=1 \\ l \neq k}}^{n} c_{kl} \tag{5}$$

$$\beta = \frac{1}{n(n-1)} \sum_{k=1}^{n} \sum_{\substack{l=1 \\ l \neq k}}^{n} d_{kl}$$

and the matrix

$$E = (e_{kl})_{k \in \overline{1,m}, l \in \overline{1,m}}, \; e_{kl} = f_{kl} \cdot g_{kl} \tag{6}$$

In matrix E, the sum of elements is calculated in line, and alternatives are arranged in descending order of the obtained values. However, symmetrical elements can exist in matrix E, $e_{ij} = e_{ji} = 0$, where variants V_i and V_j cannot be compared. In order to avoid situations of impossibility of comparison, matrices $\widetilde{D}$ and $\widetilde{F}$ were determined as follows:

$$\widetilde{D} = (\widetilde{d}_{kl})_{\substack{k=\overline{1,m} \\ l=\overline{1,m}}}, \; \widetilde{d}_{kl} = c_{kl} - d_{kl} \tag{7}$$

where:

c_{kl}, d_{kl} – are the elements of concordance and discordance matrices

$$\widetilde{F} = (\widetilde{f}_{kl})_{k,l=\overline{1,m}}, \; \widetilde{f}_{kl} = \begin{cases} -, k = l \\ 1, \; \widetilde{d}_{kl} > \widetilde{d}_{lk} \\ 0, \; \widetilde{d}_{kl} < \widetilde{d}_{lk} \\ 1/2, \; \widetilde{d}_{kl} = \widetilde{d}_{lk} \end{cases} \tag{8}$$

Matrix $E+\widetilde{F}$ is calculated and the sums for each line are also calculated. To make the hierarchy, the sums obtained are also are ordered descending.

3. SIMULATION DEVELOPMENT

Geopolitical lesson, developed in Java, contains two classes for determining the weights of the criteria chosen using AHP algorithm (*public class extends AHP_formjavax.swing.JFrame*) and the countries' hierarchy based on the criteria's weights and values entered for each sub-criterion considered (*public class Hierchy extends javax.swing.JFrame*).

Determination of weights is done after the student has assessed the relative importance of a criterion compared to other criteria considered. Thus, based on the values selected from the sites the combo boxes, a two-dimensional matrix is defined, whose elements can take values between the range 1-9 and reverse subunitary values. For example, if the economic criterion is more important than the military criterion in a moderate extent, option that is assigned a value of 4, then A(1,2) = 4 and A (2,1) = 1/4 (where A is a double type elements matrix of 3x3 size). After the construction of the matrix A, weights for each criterion are determined with AHP algorithm, weights which will be used in carrying out the countries' hierarchy. A variable number of sub-criteria were considered for each criterion, all sub-criteria have equal shares in the criteria they belong to:

$$\sum_{i=1}^{3} w_i^{\,e} + \sum_{i=1}^{2} w_i^m + \sum_{i=1}^{4} w_i^t = 3\cdot\frac{w^e}{3} + 2\cdot\frac{w^m}{2} + 4\cdot\frac{w^t}{4} = 1 \tag{9}$$

where:
w^e–weight of the economic criterion
w^m–weight of the military criterion
w^t–weight of the territorial criterion

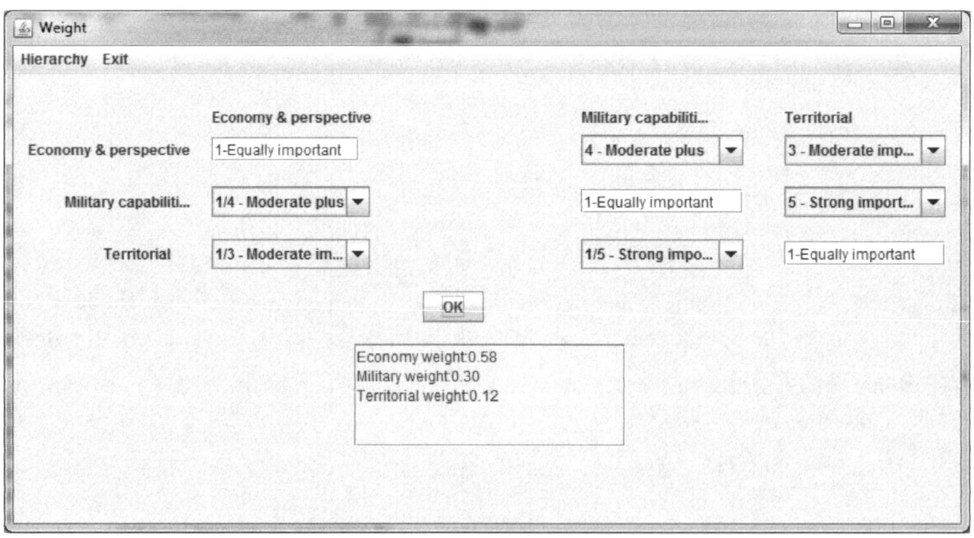

Figure 1. Significance of a criterion based on other criteria considered

On a first examination of the values entered for each sub-criterion (Figure 2), *Country5* reigns in terms of associated economic and military sub-criteria, but for the sub-criteria considered for the territorial criterion, *Country8* has the highest values for three out of four sub-criteria.

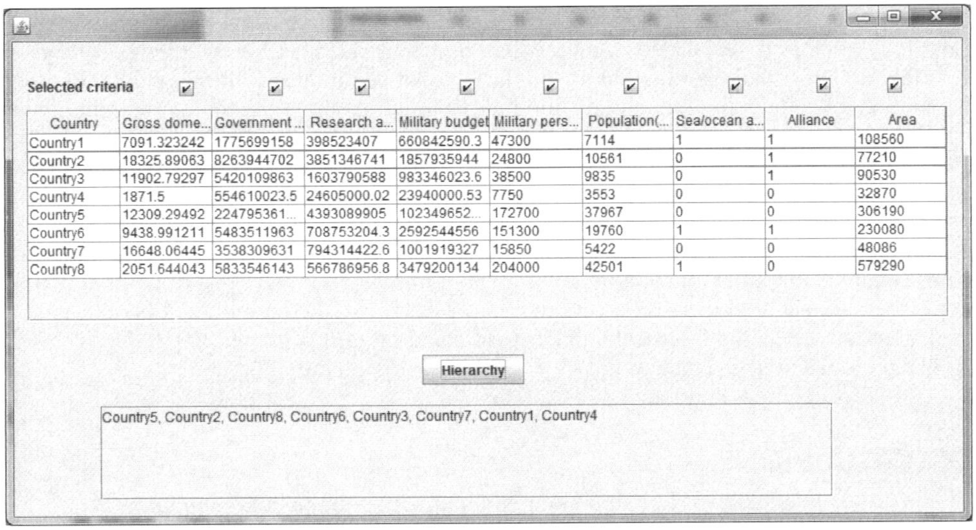

Country	Gross dome...	Government ...	Research a...	Military budget	Military pers...	Population(...	Sea/ocean a...	Alliance	Area
Country1	7091.323242	1775699158	398523407	660842590.3	47300	7114	1	1	108560
Country2	18325.89063	8263944702	3851346741	1857935944	24800	10561	0	1	77210
Country3	11902.79297	5420109863	1603790588	983346023.6	38500	9835	0	1	90530
Country4	1871.5	554610023.5	24605000.02	23940000.53	7750	3553	0	0	32870
Country5	12309.29492	224795361...	4393089905	102349652...	172700	37967	0	0	306190
Country6	9438.991211	5483511963	708753204.3	2592544556	151300	19760	1	1	230080
Country7	16648.06445	3538309631	794314422.6	1001919327	15850	5422	0	0	48086
Country8	2051.644043	5833546143	566786956.8	3479200134	204000	42501	1	0	579290

Figure 2. Countries' hierarchy

The obtained classification when weights 0.58, 0.30, 0.12 were considered for the economic, military or territorial criteria is illustrated in Figure 2, and is obtained from the implementation of the modified Electre method which allows the outranking of variants in the conditions under which each sub-criterion was associated the weight obtained with AHP, after selecting the button Hierarchy.

If territorial criteria are more important than economic and/or military criteria, hierarchy changes (Figure 3) and the first positions will be held by countries which, for the sub-criteria corresponding to the territorial criterion are larger.

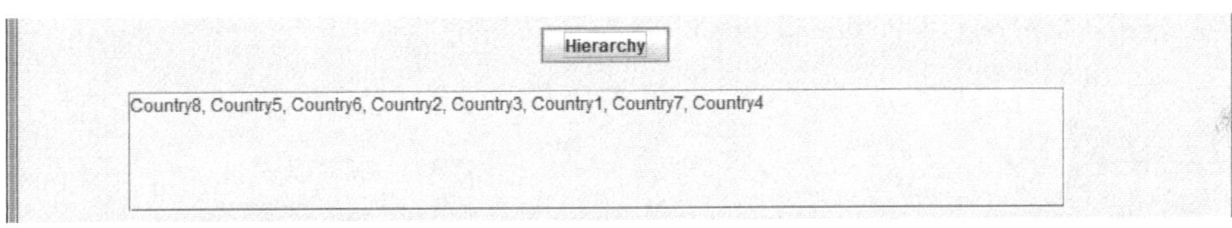

Figure 3. Hierarchy obtained if the weight of the territorial criterion is greater

3.1 Analysis of the Impact

The impact of blended learning on students can be appreciated, in the short term, from their results in evaluations (Barsan, G., et al., 2009), and in the long terms, through student preferences towards the field of study. In both traditional and blending or online education, the level of knowledge acquired by each student is assessed on the basis of final course checks or intermediate checks. The advantage of using e-learning platforms is that learning or progression of learning can be evaluated by the tutor and, moreover, he can intervene with explanations or additional materials to correct the gaps without waiting for it to be too late for the student (Serrano A. et al., 2012). With the help of Lesson reports provided by LMS, which allows viewing the time spent by each student, test scores or questions that have raised difficulty, etc., the teacher can adopt other teaching strategies or, as the case may be, can discuss with the students who go out of the "box".

Students, who chose to study Geopolitics, from the third year of undergraduate bachelor studies, were divided into two groups. Each group consisting of 75 students - 5 girls and 70 boys aged between 21 and 26 is relatively homogeneous, meaning that the environmental, technological and contextual variables were the same (Attwell G., 2006). In addition, the interest of each student, regardless of the group to whom he was assigned, was the same - to get the highest score in the Geopolitics course. One group had access within seminar hours at the lesson designed in Java, and the others held classical seminar classes. At the end of the course, all students took an evaluation on eFront e-learning platform, and questions of various types -

multiple choices, fill in the blank, matching have been designed in accordance with the materials studied. The geopolitical lesson was associated with random questions such as: What are the factors influencing geopolitical analysis? Make a hierarchy of the factors that can influence the geopolitical context? Do you think that a large budget allocated to education could influence the hierarchy of regional powers? Explain your answer, so on.

The last question that all students had to answer was: How attractive was the Geopolitics lesson that determines a hierarchy of regional powers? At this question all students who had access to the platform replied that the lesson was attractive and that simulation helped them understand elements related to this issue, while only some of the students who had a classical seminar hour found the Geopolitics lesson interesting and to some extent attractive.

As the evaluation results, based on the reports on the eFront platform, it has been found that the first group understood better the theoretical notions and could operate with concepts studied, while the second group had problems of interpretation.

4. CONCLUSIONS

Designing a simulation tool that allows students to explore various scenarios is suitable for any field. Modifying options and viewing the results lead to a better understanding particularly of the lessons that require significant financial resources or for phenomena more difficult to explain. It was chosen that the Geopolitics lesson is loaded as .jar file on the platform and not applet, due to the browser limitations. An applet requires that on the client machine Java Runtime Environment (JRE) is installed and the browsers are not able to run the Java plug-in.

As a further development of the simulation-based lesson it is intended to add a higher level of generality to allow several students to add more options (Countries), criteria or sub-criteria. On the other hand, one wants to add elements of gamification to make the lesson more attractive and students more motivated and to create an e-learning object directly integrated into the lesson, allowing analyzes available within the platform, such as time spent in class or progress of each student.

REFERENCES

Attwell G., 2006, *Evaluating E-learning: A Guide to the Evaluation of E-learning.* Evaluate Europe Handbook Series, Vol. 2, 1610-0875.

Barsan, G., et al., 2009, E-Plasticity: an Asynchronous e-Learning Solution for Artillery Barrels Autofrettage Process. *in Proceedings of the 8th European Conference on e-Learning: ECEL.* Bari, Italy, pp. 52- 59.

Căruțașu V., 2014, *Cercetări operaționale şi teoria deciziei*, Sibiu, Academia Forțelor Terestre Publishing House.

Chang C.L., 2004, A measure of national power. *Proceedings of the 2004 International Seminar at the National University of Malaysia*, Bangi, Malaysia, pp. 16–17.

Deegan M. et al., 2014, Simulation-Based Learning Environments to Teach Complexity: The Missing Link in Teaching Sustainable Public Management, in Systems, 2(2), pp. 217–236.

Figuera, J., Greco, S., Ehrgott, M., 2005, *Multiple criteria decision analysis: State of the Art Surveys*, New York, Springer.

Liao H. et al, 2015, Towards Measuring and Visualizing Sustainable National Power—A Case Study of China and Neighboring Countries. In *ISPRS International Journal of Geo-Information,* Vol. 4, 1672-1692

Moreno-Ger P. et al., 2010, Application of a low-cost web-based simulation to improve students' practical skills in medical education. *in Int. J. Med. Inform*, Vol. 79, pp. 459 -467

Perrotta, C. et al., 2013, *Game-based Learning: Latest Evidence and Future Directions* (NFER Research Programme: Innovation in Education). Slough: NFER.

Saaty Thomas L., 2008, Decision making with the analytic hierarchy process. in *Int. J. Services Sciences*, Vol. 1, No. 1, 2008, p. 83-98

Serrano A. et al., 2012, A framework to improve evaluation in educational games. *in Proceedings of the IEEE Engineering Education Conference (EDUCON),* Marrakesh, Morocco, April.

Schwab K., 2016. *The Global Competitiveness Report 2016 – 2017*, World Economic Forum Geneva.

PREDICTORS OF STUDENT PERFORMANCE IN A BLENDED-LEARNING ENVIRONMENT: AN EMPIRICAL INVESTIGATION

Lan Umek, Nina Tomaževič, Aleksander Aristovnik and Damijana Keržič
Faculty of Administration University of Ljubljana , Gosarjeva ul. 005, 1000 Ljubljana, Slovenia

ABSTRACT

Modern technologies radically simplify the availability of the latest scientific literature and offer new possibilities for sharing knowledge. Yet, most higher education institutions still rely on traditional face-to-face teaching and use e-courses 'only' to supplement it. Such a combination of teaching methods is known as blended learning and is also used at the Faculty of Administration (FA), a member of the University of Ljubljana. The paper presents the results of a survey among FA students. The study's aim was to identify which aspects of blended learning increase students' knowledge level. Students evaluated 23 different aspects of blended learning on a 7-level scale. As a measure of the level of students' knowledge gained from each course, we used their final grades. Applying principal component analysis, we extracted six dimensions of blended learning which represented predictor components in a multiple linear regression with final grade as the dependent variable. Since courses at FA vary in many aspects, we performed the regression analysis for each obligatory course individually. Our analysis revealed for which courses the final grade can be reliably predicted from the aspects of blended learning. The study also showed that the aspects of traditional face-to-face learning are more strongly linked to better grades than the aspects of e-courses. However, for some courses certain characteristics of e-courses play a significant role in the final grade received.

KEYWORDS

Blended learning, Moodle, Higher Education, Student Satisfaction, Student Performance, Public Administration Programmes

1. INTRODUCTION

The Bologna Process required European universities to adapt their programmes as part of building the Higher European Education Area (EHEA) with aspects of harmonization, compatibility and comparability, such as two-cycle degree study (3 year: bachelor; 2 year: master), a comparable system of measuring student achievement (ECTS, competencies), student and teacher mobility, and the teaching–research relationship. Universities and their teachers were forced to make major changes to the pedagogical process concerning how to design the programmes, and the methods deployed to comply with the new requirements. A major novelty was the shift from a teacher-based learning style to the student-based approach whereby students become active participants in their own learning process, interact with the learning context and are committed to the learning process through which they acquire new responsibilities. Thus, the student-based style emphasizes the individual student and their interests, abilities, and learning styles. The teacher becomes a consultant of learning for individuals, helping and supporting students in achieving and building knowledge (Alducin-Ochoa & Vazquez-Martinez, 2016).

Technological developments, especially in the field of information and communication, have enabled many innovative approaches in educational environments by introducing technology to the pedagogical process and by enriching the learning experience. Education via the Internet using computers or mobile devices using new multimedia technology is nowadays known as e-learning. E-learning is unlike the prevailing forms of teaching in that it is unlimited by time or space. Learning management systems (LMSs) provide supportive services not only for effective and efficient learning, but also to manage, guidance and control the e-learning process. An LMS must not only be a system that supports the sending of messages, keeping an online gradebook or providing handouts and learning material, but should also allow one to be an active participant in e-learning, both teachers and learners, e.g. by problem-solving teamwork, question and answer sessions or online simulations (Campanella et al. 2008; Kim & Lee, 2008).

Around the start of the new millennium, blended learning emerged as a new trend in teaching models and learning styles (Vo et al., 2017). Initially, blended learning was defined as 'the mixture of e-learning and classroom learning' (Masie, 2006) by the training field, as a promising alternative to e-learning because of the limitations in fostering 'interaction, context, and remediation' (Masie, 2006) of the latter. Subsequently, Graham (2006) elaborates blended learning as a combination of face-to-face instruction and computer-mediated instruction. Bernard et al. (2014) recommend that the proportion of blended course content delivered online range between 30 and 79 percent. The lower end of the range is sufficient to eliminate studies 'of incidental uses of Internet, such as downloading references and turning in assignments' (Means et al., 2013) and to differentiate blended learning from pure online learning (Allen & Seaman, 2009).

Graham (2006) posits that, as an interweaving of traditional face-to-face instruction and online learning, blended learning allows for more interactive and reflective knowledge construction. Multi-format resources, archived discussions, teachers' changing role as facilitators, and more time for discussion and reflection in this learning mode have been augmented by technologies (Mebane et al., 2008).

We are encountering the rise of e-learning in the higher education area. Allen and Seaman (2013) observed that e-learning courses in colleges and universities in the USA are showing greater growth in their number than traditional courses. In a survey conducted among European higher institutions, Gaebel et al. (2014) reported that almost all higher education institutions selected in the study had started to embrace e-learning, with most using blended learning (91%) and 82% offering online learning courses. They also found out that three-quarters of the institutions recognize that e-learning can change the approach to learning and teaching methods.

The recent boom in the blended learning industry has triggered an increase in the number of studies on blended learning. Considered as the 'new normal' mode of training (Norberg et al., 2011), the effect of blended learning on student performance has been researched in different contexts, e.g. in higher education, adult education, workplace training. There is a considerable volume of research on the benefits of satisfaction in higher education, especially linked to student performance (Martinez-Caro, 2011), retention (DeShields et al., 2005), class attendance or student engagement (Coates, 2005). Wu et al. (2012) observe that many e-learning studies conduct surveys to gauge learners' satisfaction with various items of blended learning, and a variety of methods is applied to assess the impact of these items on overall learning performance to provide a reference for improvements. Hung and Zhang (2012) point out that many researchers concentrate on evaluating the effectiveness of blended learning. Several models are available to measure student satisfaction, each with its own advantages and disadvantages (Chen, 2009).

In many studies, the results have shown blended learning has a positive impact on student performance (Larson & Sung, 2009; Lopez-Perez et al., 2011; Umek et al., 2015). On the other side, Brown and Liedholm (2002) compared three modes of instruction and discovered that face-to-face students did significantly better than online students and better than blended learning students for the most complex material. Results of a study by Kwak et al. (2014) strongly suggest that blended learning has no impact on student performance whatsoever. Moreover, student performance is not affected by the introduction of blended learning regardless of students' age, nationality, primary language or achievement level. But they found that introducing blended learning had a negative impact on male students but a positive one for female students.

The Faculty of Administration (FA) implemented blended learning in the 2010/11 academic year, using LMS Moodle. It was introduced progressively over three years, with some modifications, which have proved to be meaningful (for more, see Umek et al., 2015). Currently, 80% of every obligatory course is held in the traditional way while for the remaining 20% students gain knowledge from their activities in online courses. Each subject has its own e-course where an e-lecture is supported by e-content followed by a quiz in order to check understanding of the prepared content and the three extensive assignments intended for the tutorial are prepared during the semester. The teachers are obliged to give feedback on the correctness of the solutions in those assignments

In the study presented in this paper, we analysed 23 factors which we assumed influence students' perceptions of blended learning. They relate to the characteristics of an e-course (goals, materials, and assignments), lecturers' activities (assessments, responses), students' preferences regarding learning online or learning in the classroom, face-to-face learning and technical details about Moodle LMS (stability, administrative support). In the empirical study, we performed principal component analysis in order to extract components that describe dimensions of blended learning. We then used these components to predict the students' grades. Since courses at the FA vary in many aspects (teachers, content, required computer skills, etc.), we analysed these impacts on each course separately. We believe the study presented below contributes some important findings to both theory and practice in the field of blended learning.

2. EMPIRICAL RESEARCH

2.1 Methodology and Data

In our study, we investigated the impact of different aspects of blended learning on students' performance. For this reason, we used a questionnaire based on our own recent survey (Aristovnik et al., 2016), where students' attitudes to e-learning were measured (Table 1, statements EC1–EC6, GI1–GI7), extended with three questions regarding face-to-face learning (Table 1, statements FF1–FF3) and seven questions on general attitudes to e-learning (Table 1, statements GE1–GE7), meaning that we examined a total of 23 aspects of blended learning. The students expressed their level of agreement with the statements on an ordinal scale from 1 ("totally disagree") to 7 ("totally agree").

Table 1. Aspects of Blended Learning

Abb.	Aspect of blended learning
GE1	Working with computers for study purposes suits me.
GE2	The Moodle e-learning system is easy to use.
GE3	The Moodle system is reliable and stable (it does not crash, submitted tasks are not lost).
GE4	I am satisfied with the support and assistance in the event of technical problems.
GE5	Working with computers for study purposes is not difficult for me.
GE6	E-learning contributes to higher student academic performance.
GE7	E-learning is a quality replacement for traditional learning in the classroom.
FF1	The content of the course interests me.
FF2	Course lectures are interesting for me and I like to attend them.
FF3	I find the face-to-face tutorial attractive and useful.
EC1	The virtual classroom of the course is organized transparently.
EC2	The goals (workload demands, grading) of this e-course were clearly stated at the start of the semester.
EC3	This e-course offers a variety of ways of assessing my learning (quizzes, written work, forums, files…).
EC4	I receive the teacher's comment/feedback on an assignment within less than 7 days.
EC5	I prefer fewer lectures in the traditional way (face-to-face) and more learning material processed in the e-course.
EC6	More course exercises could be carried out in the e-course instead of in the classroom.
GI1	The general impression of the e-course is good.
GI2	Study material and tasks of the e-course are presented in a clear and understandable way.
GI3	Finding certain activities in the e-course is simple.
GI4	The prepared learning material and tasks are consistent with the lectures in the classroom and supplement them.
GI5	The prepared material and assignments supplement the tutorial in the classroom.
GI6	Learning materials and activities in the e-course helped me to effectively study this subject matter.
GI7	The teacher gives me feedback/a response on my submissions (assignment, forum posts).

Source: Surveys, 2015 and 2016

The questionnaire-based survey was held in two consecutive academic years (2014/15 and 2015/16) and was carried out online. Students voluntarily participated in the survey, without any coercion or undue influence. We asked them to insert their student ID number to help us link the results obtained with their grades. We obtained the opinions of 639 students. They evaluated 46 undergraduate obligatory courses; on average, each student evaluated 5.2 e-courses. We collected 3,334 evaluations of e-courses. In addition, we collected the students' grades from our student information system – the exam database for all courses included in the survey.

In order to reduce the high dimensionality of our data set and make the results more comprehensive, we performed principal component analysis on the questionnaire data. We used the Kaiser criterion to determine the number of components. A varimax rotation was used to increase the interpretability of the extracted components. New variables (components) were determined as arithmetic means of the variables with high factor loadings (above 0.5). We evaluated the new components using Cronbach's alpha. Components with Cronbach's alpha above 0.7 were kept in our data set.

Completing the described transformation of the original datasets split the dataset (consisting of extracted components) into 46 subsets, each corresponding to an individual course. We added a student's final grade to each dataset as the dependent variable and, since participation in the survey among higher years of the study was poor, certain courses received very few evaluations. Therefore, we retained only 24 courses (subsets) that each had more than 50 evaluations for further analysis. For each course, we performed linear regression analysis with extracted components as independent variables and final grade as the dependent variable. In the paper, we report regression models with R^2 above 0.13 and present components with a significant influence on the final grade.

2.2 Empirical Results

Principal component analysis reduced our 23 aspects of blended learning to six components, which explain 67% of total variance (TVE). We computed Cronbach's alpha for each of them. Since components 4 and 5 resulted in a poor Cronbach alpha, we skipped them from further analysis and therefore provided no names for them. We named the four other components based on the meaning of the aspects with the highest loadings. The factor loadings, naming of the components with the % of total variance explained (TVE) and Cronbach's alpha (factor loadings above 0.5) are shown in Table 2.

Table 2. Component loadings for aspects of blended learning

	Component					
	1	2	3	4	5	6
	aspect on e-course	technical aspect	aspect on F2F learning	/	/	teacher's feedback
% of TVE	24.8	10.8	9.8	8.9	7.0	5.7
Cronbach's alpha	0.914	0.721	0.838	0.325	0.405	0.741
GE1		0.512				
GE2		0.722				
GE3		0.788				
GE4		0.819				
GE5					0.76	
GE6		0.499				
GE7					0.736	
FF1			0.831			
FF2			0.808			
FF3			0.627			
EC1	0.797					
EC2	0.815					
EC3	0.769					
EC4	0.536					0.648
EC5				0.904		
EC6				0.916		

GI1	0.791			
GI2	0.763			
GI3			-0.524	
GI4	0.712			
GI5	0.713			
GI6	0.637			
GI7	0.572			0.62

Principal component analysis revealed four blended learning dimensions, namely aspects on e-course, technical properties and support, face-to-face (F2F) learning, and teachers' feedback. These four latent variables were later used in the regression analysis as predictors (independent variables). On the whole data set, we failed to detect any significant relationship between these four blended learning dimensions and the final grade. For this reason, we further investigated such relationships for individual courses. This approach has several advantages over a global analysis: it takes the courses' specific properties into account; the final grades within a course are more comparable than grades overall; and, most importantly – it provides a list of courses in which blended learning helps to achieve better grades.

The analysis was carried out on each individual course (with more than 50 students' evaluations) with the final grade as the dependent variable. Table 3 summarizes the results of the regression analysis for six courses where the linear regression model sufficiently explained the variability of the final grade, i.e. with R^2 above 0.13 (Cohen, 1992). In the table, we show unstandardized regression coefficients (B) with the corresponding significances (Sig.), R^2 and number of responses (n).

Due to personally identifiable information, we anonymized the course names as "course 1", "course 2" through to "course 6". Instead of providing each course's name, we reveal information about the chair to which the course belongs, the year of study and the study programme Courses at the FA are run by the teaching staff from three chairs (EPSM: Chair of Economics and Public Sector Management, ALA: Chair of the Administrative-Legal Area and OI: Chair of Organisation and Informatics). The undergraduate study lasts three years – there are two undergraduate study programmes (UN: university study programme, PS: professional study programme).

Table 3. Results of regression analysis on six courses. Regression coefficient is significant at the levels 0.1 - *, 0.05 - **, 0.01 - ***

course	1		2		3		4		5		6	
chair	EPSM		ALA		EPSM		EPSM		EPSM		EPSM	
year	1		1		2		1		1		2	
study programme	PS		PS		UN		PS		UN		UN	
R^2	0.18		0.16		0.15		0.14		0.14		0.13	
N	97		177		65		77		139		113	
	B	Sig.	B	Sig.	B	Sig.	B	Sig.	B	Sig.	B	Sig.
intercept	1.96	0.144	5.42	0.000 ***	5.89	0.000 ***	3.29	0.058	4.79	0.000 ***	5.49	0.000 ***
aspect on e-course	0.31	0.504	0.33	0.016 **	-0.36	0.306	0.94	0.054*	0.57	0.008 ***	-0.19	0.374
technical aspect and support	0.16	0.355	-0.05	0.674	-0.14	0.447	-0.03	0.856	-0.13	0.300	0.07	0.612
aspect on face-to-face learning	0.39	0.012 **	0.31	0.002 ***	0.59	0.004 ***	0.24	0.202	0.03	0.823	0.02	0.838
teacher's feedback	-0.04	0.900	-0.38	0.000 ***	0.02	0.921	-0.48	0.021 **	-0.02	0.908	0.28	0.006 ***

Table 3 reveals that almost all significant relationships between aspects of blended learning and the final grade are found in courses from the Chair of Economics and Public Sector Management, with one exception (course 2) from the Chair of the Administrative-Legal Area. It is interesting that none of the resulting courses belongs to the Chair of Organisation and Informatics where more computer-based skills are used in the teaching and learning process. Since we restricted our analysis to courses that received more than 50 evaluations, it is no surprise that we discovered relationships only for the courses in the first two years of study (due to the third-year students' unresponsiveness).

The aspect on e-course had a significant positive influence on the final grade in three courses (courses 2, 4, and 5) from both chairs, but only from the first year of study. The results therefore suggest that characteristics related to an e-course (organization, general impression etc.) are linked to the final grade only in the first year of study. We suspect that students in higher years of study become used to the Moodle environment and all their e-course obligations (quizzes, assignments, etc.). Therefore, the organization of an e-course in higher years of study plays a less important role than in the first year.

On the contrary, the technical aspect and administrative support do not have a significant impact on students' grade for any course. Since this component is the only one not related to a specific course, we computed the correlation between its values and the final grade with all courses together. Additional empirical findings revealed no significant correlation ($r=0.007$, $p=0.681$) for the entire data set. We can therefore conclude that the technical aspect and administrative support exert no influence on students' grades at the levels we analysed.

Face-to-face learning has a significant positive impact on three courses (courses with the highest R^2, i.e. courses 1, 2, and 3), from both chairs, years of study and study programme. The results suggest that the influence of this component is strongest especially for the course from the Chair of the Administrative-Legal Area. This is no surprise since courses from the ALA chair focus their teaching process on traditional classroom discussions. The regression coefficient of the aspect on face-to-face learning for course 2 is highly significant ($B=0.31$, $p=0.002$). This means that by increasing students' attitude to the content, the quality of lectures and tutorials by 1 point (on a 7-level scale), we would on average expect an increase in the final grade of 0.31 (on a scale of 1 to 10). For the other two courses (courses 1 and 3), the increase would even be higher – for course 3, we expect an increase in the average grade by more than 0.5.

The last component we analysed was the teacher's feedback. Although we discovered it had a significant impact on the final grade for three courses (courses 2, 4, and 6), the empirical findings are only promising for course 6. The regression coefficients of teacher's feedback are negative for courses 2 and 4 (-0.38 and -0.48, respectively). In the future, this surprising finding will be investigated in detail. The empirical findings suggest that students with higher grades expected richer and more useful feedback from the teacher whereas the feedback was more useful for students with lower grades.

3. CONCLUSION

At the Faculty of Administration, we are currently in the third year of measuring students' satisfaction with blended learning. Our previous studies (Aristovnik et al., 2016; Umek et al., 2015) revealed that the satisfaction level with e-courses in Moodle LMS is high. In the previous analyses, we also identified which factors influence students' perceptions of the usefulness of e-learning. The study presented in this paper represents an upgrade of our previous work. We investigated which aspects of blended learning increase students' performance. From previous experience, we deduced that there is no general rule and therefore performed an analysis for all obligatory undergraduate courses.

We employed principal component analysis to determine four dimensions of blended learning, namely aspects of e-course, technical aspect and administrative support, face-to-face learning, and teacher's feedback. We failed to detect an overall (global) significant relationship between aspects of blended learning and the final grade. Therefore, we looked for such a relationship within each individual course. We identified six courses where the students' final grade is significantly linked to components of blended learning. We found that e-course aspects play a significant role in the first year of study, while the face-to-face approach still has the strongest influence. We failed to link attitudes to the technical aspect and satisfaction with administrative support with final grades. The most surprising finding in our study was the identification of two courses where the teacher's feedback is significantly negatively linked to the students' final grade. We suspect that the teachers of these two courses did not fulfil the expectations of students with better grades while students with lower grades were satisfied with their feedback.

Our study revealed in detail that connecting satisfaction with blended learning and students' performance is a challenging task. We believe that the identification of courses which reflect this relationship is an important achievement – both for the course teachers and managers of the Faculty. On the contrary, for the teachers of other courses our study suggests they should focus on other pedagogical aspects such as motivation for study, more interactive lectures and tutorials, and the use of recent technology as complementary technique in the traditional classroom. This focus will increase students' grades and therefore "produce" more competent graduates.

Our study has several limitations: we did not investigate the teachers' role and did not ask the teachers to express their opinions on blended learning. Another future challenge is to increase the participation rate of students in the 3rd year of study. They have much greater experience with various e-courses, overcame technical challenges in the first year and hold different expectations regarding the e-course quality. Differences among years of study suggest we should extend our questionnaire with other aspects. Some of the new aspects will be more suitable for the first year of study, while others will be more relevant for more experienced students.

REFERENCES

Alducin-Ochoa, J.M. & Vázquez-Martínez, A.I., 2016. Academic performance in blended-learning and face-to-face university teaching. *Asian Social Science*, Vol. 12, No. 3, pp. 207–221.

Allen, I.E. & Seaman, J., 2013. Changing Course: Ten Years of Tracking Online Education in the United States. Babson Survey Research Group and Quahog Research Group, LLC.

Aristovnik, A. et al., 2016. Demographic determinants of usefulness of e-learning tools among students of public administration. *Interactive Technology and Smart Education*, Vol. 13, No. 4, pp. 289–304.

Bernard, R.M. et al., 2014. An exploration of bias in meta-analysis: The case of technology integration research in higher education. *Journal of Computing in Higher Education*, Vol. 26, No. 3, pp. 183–209.

Brown, B.W. & Liedholm, C.E., 2002. Can Web courses replace the classroom in principles of microeconomics? *American Economic Review*, Vol. 92, No. 2, pp. 444–448.

Campanella, S. et al. (2008). E-learning platforms in the Italian universities: the technological solutions at the University of Bari. *WSEAS Transactions on Advances in Engineering Education*, Vol. 1, No. 5, pp. 12–19.

Chen, S.H., 2009. Establishment of a performance-evaluation model for service quality in the banking industry. *The Services Industries Journal,* Vol. 29, No. 2, pp. 235–247.

Coates, H., 2005. The value of student engagement for higher education quality assurance. *Quality in Higher Education*, Vol. 11, No. 1, pp. 25–36.

Cohen, J., 1992. A power primer. *Psychological Bulletin*, Vol. 112, pp. 155–159.

DeShields, O.W. et al., 2005. Determinants of business student satisfaction and retention in higher education: Applying Herzberg's two-factor theory. *International Journal of Educational Management*, Vol. 19, No. 2, pp. 128–139.

Gaebel, M. et al., 2014, *E-learning in European higher education institutions: results of a mapping survey conducted in October-December 2013*, EUA publications 2014, European University Association, Brussels. Retrieved Apr 2017, http://www.eua.be/Libraries/Publication/e-learning_survey.sflb.ashx

Graham, C.R., 2006. Blended learning systems. Definition, current trends, and future directions. In Bonk, C. J. & Graham, C. R. (Eds.), *Handbook of blended learning: Global perspectives, local designs*. Pfeiffer Publishing, San Francisco, CA, pp. 3–21.

Hung, J. L. & Zhang, K., 2012. Examining mobile learning trends 2003-2008: A categorical metatrend analysis using text mining techniques. *Journal of Computer in Higher Education*, Vol. 24, No. 1, pp. 1–17.

Kim, S.W., & Lee, M.G., 2008. Validation of an evaluation model for learning management systems. *Journal of Computer Assisted Learning*, Vol. 24, No. 4, pp. 284–294.

Kwak, D.W. et al., 2014. Assessing the Impact of Blended Learning on Student Performance. *Economic Record*, Vol. 91, No. 292, 91–106.

Larson, D. & Sung, C., 2009. Comparing student performance: Online versus blended versus face-to-face. *Journal of Asynchronous Learning Networks*, Vol. 13, No. 1, pp. 31–42.

Lopez-Perez, M.V. et al., 2011. Blended Learning in Higher Education: Students' Perceptions and Their Relation to Outcomes. *Computers & Education,* Vol. 56, No. 3, pp. 818–826.

Martinez-Caro, E., 2011. Factors affecting effectiveness in e-learning: An analysis in production management courses. *Computer Applications in Engineering Education*, Vol. 19, No. 3, pp. 572–581.

Masie, E., 2006. The blended learning imperative. In Bonk, C. J. & Graham, C. R. (Eds.), *Handbook of blended learning: Global perspectives, local designs*. Pfeiffer Publishing, San Francisco, CA, pp. 22–26.

Means, B. et al., 2013. The effectiveness of online and blended learning: A meta-analysis of the empirical literature. *Teachers College Record,* Vol. 115, No. 3, pp. 1–47.

Mebane, M. et al., 2008. Evaluation of the efficacy of affective education online training in promoting academic and professional learning and social capital. *International Journal of Human-Computer Interaction,* Vol. 24, No. 1, pp. 68–86.

Norberg, A. et al., 2011. A time-based blended learning model. *On the Horizon*, Vol. 19, No. 3, pp. 207–216.

Porter, W. et al., 2016. A qualitative analysis of institutional drivers and barriers to blended learning adoption in higher education. *Internet and Higher Education*, Vol. 28, pp. 17–27.

Umek, L. et al., 2015. Analysis of selected aspects of students` performance and satisfaction in a Moodle-based e-learning system environment. *Eurasia*, Vol. 11, No. 6, pp. 1495–1505.

Vo, H.M. et al., 2017. The effect of blended learning on student performance at course-level in higher education: A meta-analysis. *Studies in Educational Evaluation,* Vol. 53, pp. 17–28.

Wu, W.H. et al., 2012. Review of trends from mobile learning studies: A meta-analysis. *Computers & Education*, Vol. 59, No. 2, 817–827.

PRACTICE OF ORGANISATIONAL STRATEGIES OF IMPROVING COMPUTER ROOMS FOR PROMOTING SMART EDUCATION USING ICT EQUIPMENT

Nobuyuki Ogawa[1] and Akira Shimizu[2]
[1]*Department of Architecture, National Institute of Technology, Gifu College*
[2]*General Education, National Institute of Technology, Gifu College*
2236-2 Kamimakuwa, Motosu-city, Gifu 501-0495, Japan

ABSTRACT

This paper describes our concrete efforts to improve the functions of the computer rooms in the Information Processing Center from among several organisational strategies which can assume a large role in the next-generation education, while examining the practice of active learning by the faculty in all classes using ICT equipment. We implemented the strategies to rapidly introduce smart education including e-Learning into all subjects of our college by improving the functions of the computer rooms, increasing the number of the computer rooms, and linking with the "Acceleration Program for University Education Rebuilding (AP)" which is being promoted as a collegewide project. Also, based on the circumstances leading to the increase in the number of the computer rooms, we conducted an aggregate analysis of use of the increased computer rooms and utilized the results for promoting smart education.

KEYWORDS

Organisational strategy, Educational management, e-Learning, Active learning

1. INTRODUCTION

National Institute of Technology (NIT), Gifu College is making efforts geared toward the creation of ICT-driven, advanced and diverse educational environment mainly in the computer rooms of the Information Processing Center. For the purpose of managing this kind of advanced educational environment with limited manpower and time, we have provided users with a stable system operation so far, while increasing efficiency of management and operation in a network boot system. The computer rooms are widely used as terminals for ICT-driven education and e-Learning as well as for practices of programming and CAD.

Our e-Learning and ICT-driven education practiced for more than 15 years being highly evaluated, and as a result, funded by the Ministry of Education, Culture, Sports, Science and Technology (MEXT) through the "Acceleration Program for University Education Rebuilding (AP)" from 2014, our college has been practicing smart education at a collegewide level. (Ogawa, N. et al, 2015, Ogawa, N., Shimizu, A., 2015) The AP project will be financially supported until 2020. So far, we have created an environment to practice smart education by introducing various kinds of equipment, such as an electronic blackboard system (all 25 classrooms of all the years from the first to the fifth year of all the five departments), wireless LAN (all 25 classrooms), tablet personal computers (more than 160), notebook personal computers (enough units for simultaneous utilization of two classes), LMS and software for creating teaching materials. The details are described in our papers. Also, we have been holding collegewide FD sessions to promote the faculty to practice smart education shown in our papers. (Ogawa, N., Shimizu, A., 2016)

The budget of our AP project was not used for the latest replacement of an educational electronic computer system. Using college expenses we replaced PC terminals which were introduced five years ago with the latest, highly-specified ones, and determined to maintain management and operation with a network-boot system. Moreover, we augmented students' opportunities to use ICT equipment freely by increasing the number of the computer rooms from 3 to 5 and also by closely coordinating with the AP project. An educational electronic computer system was introduced into the 1st, 2nd, 3rd and 4th computer rooms of the Information Processing Center and also into the 5th computer room on the third floor of Main Building I.

In this article, we describe the improvement of the computer rooms from 3 to 5 conducted as an organisational strategy with an aim to promote active learning (Bergmann, J. & Sams, A., 2012, Bonwell, C.C. & Eison, J.A., 1991, Hake, R. R., 1998, Michael, J., 2006, Prince, M., 2004, Renkl, A. et al, 2002) and smart education (Brant, G. et al, 1991, Hoellwarth, C., & Moelter, M. J., 2011, Westermann, K., & Rummel, N., 2012) or ICT-driven education and e-Learning at a collegewide level.

2. INTRODUCTION OF A NEW ELECTRONIC COMPUTER SYSTEM FOR EDUCATION

A new electronic computer system for education has equipment and technological functions shown below:

(Details of equipment)

1. A network boot server
2. Client terminals (desktop PCs)
3. A monochrome laser printer
4. Document cameras
5. Networking equipment
6. An uninterruptible power system
7. An education support system
8. Floor wiring at the 4th and 5th computer rooms

(Technological functions)

1. It became possible to provide education of all subjects in the computer rooms in the Information Processing Center and in the 5th computer room on the third floor of Main Building I.
2. A system booted via a network (network boot system) was introduced into the computer rooms in the Information Processing Center and in the 5th computer room on the third floor of Main Building I.
3. A function was introduced which administers OS and application of respective terminals by using virtual disk images.
4. A function which boots the terminals changing over plural virtual disk images was introduced into the terminals installed in the computer rooms in the Information Processing Center and in the 5th computer room on the third floor of Main Building I.
5. Software which makes it possible to display teaching materials displayed on the teacher's monitor on respective students' monitors was introduced into the terminals installed in the computer rooms in the Information Processing Center and in the 5th computer room on the third floor of Main Building I.
6. A redundant configuration was adopted for the network boot system in consideration of administrative operations.
7. A function which makes it possible to view educational information through the Internet under the control of the Information Processing Center was installed in the introduced system.
8. The entire system was designed to effectively and efficiently operate each function with consideration for linkages with the existing campus-wide network as well as the related systems which are expected to be introduced in the near future.
9. A system was introduced which makes it possible to automatically perform environmental restoration via a network or when booting terminals so that the same system would be kept after notebook personal computers are added to the system.
10. The boot-up time, from pressing the power button to displaying a login screen, was set within 120 seconds under the condition that the introduced 45 terminals were booted at a time in the Information Processing Center.
11. The communication speed of the server and switches inside a server rack was set more than 2 Gbps at all times. Windows 8.1 Enterprise (64 bit) was adopted for OS of a client terminal to be booted via the network by a server.

3. NEW COMPUTER ROOMS IN THE INFORMATION PROCESSING CENTER AND AN INTRODUCED SYSTEM

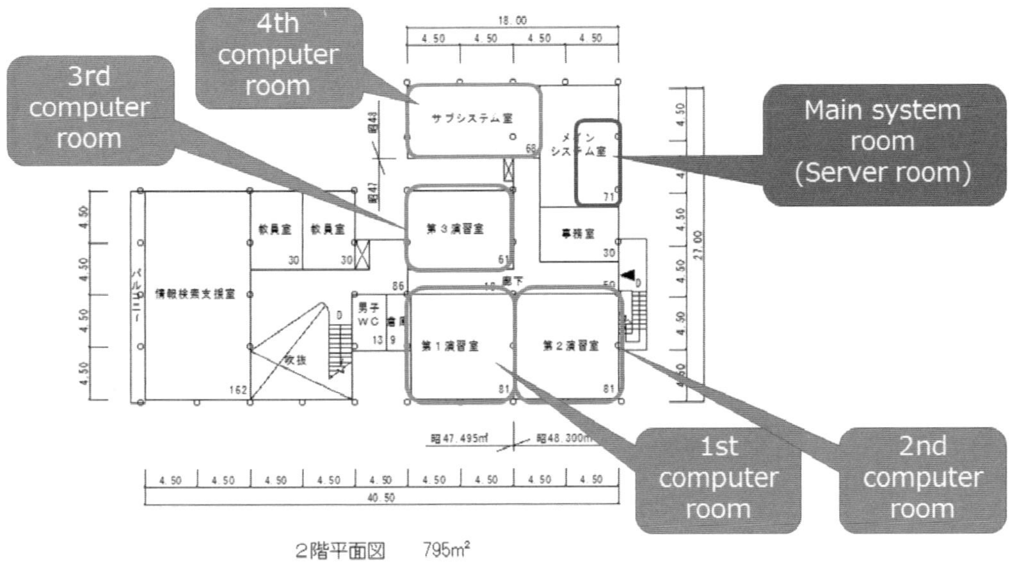

Figure 1. The arrangement of the computer rooms and others on the third floor of the library

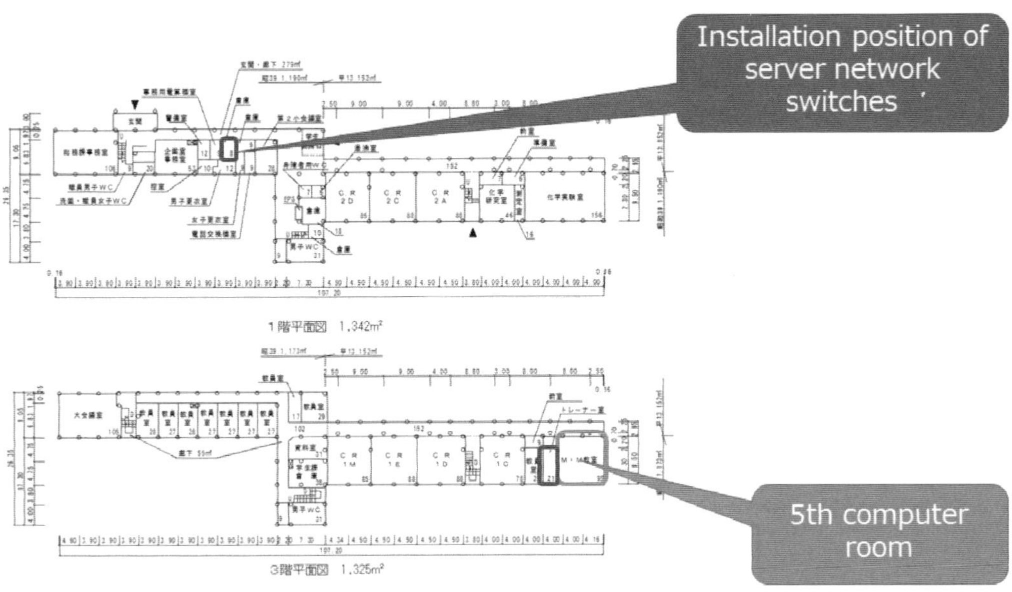

Figure 2. The arrangement of a computer room and others on the first and third floors of Main Building I

The number of the computer rooms was increased from 3 to 5, and as shown in Figures 1 and 2, the 1st, 2nd, 3rd and 4th computer rooms were arranged on the second floor of the library, and the 5th one was arranged on the third floor of Main Building I. Server equipment was installed in the main system room in the library, and the server network switches were used as the ones for the 5th computer room. The system was configured as shown in Figure 3, and it was linked with the equipment introduced through the AP project.

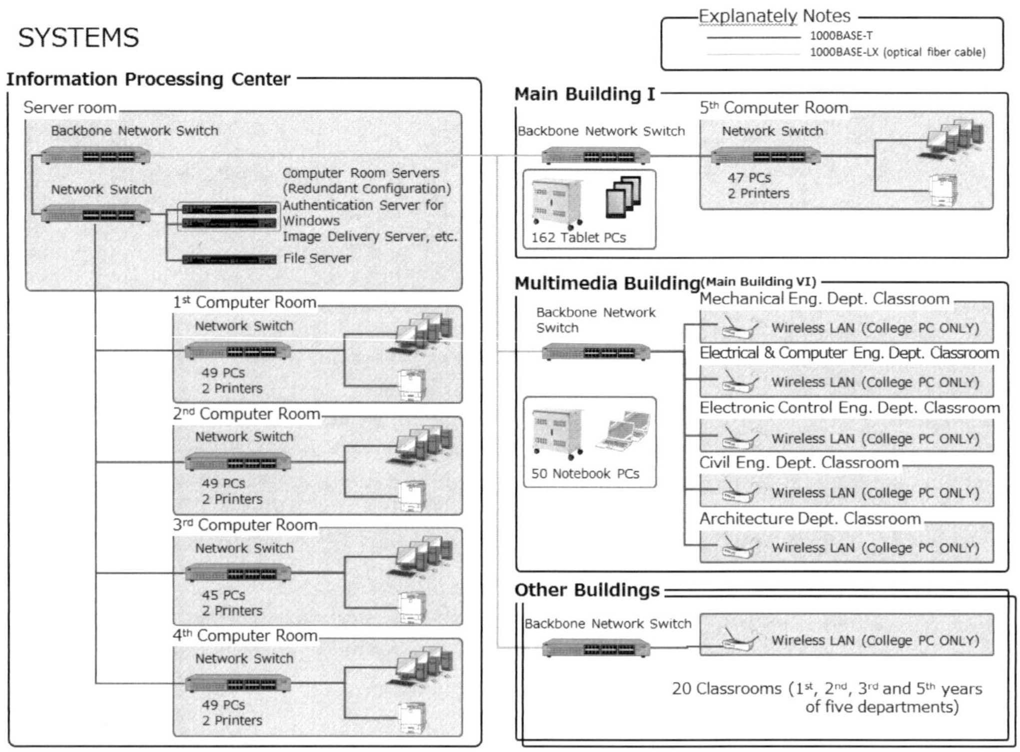

Figure 3. A configuration diagram of a new electronic computer system for education

4. USE OF NEW COMPUTER ROOMS

The new system made it possible to record the number of sheets printed by each student using a printer placed in a computer room of the Information Processing Center. Though wasteful printing by some students had been a problem, the new system enabled us to identify such students. Table 1 shows the monthly ranking of the number of sheets printed using the printers in the computer rooms of the Information Processing Center. Table 1 gives information only on the number of printed sheets to prevent identification of an individual. In fact, however, the system gives us data on student name, date and place. The high-ranking students are wastefully printing every month, and it was made clear that shared resources are largely occupied by some specific students. We are giving an educational admonishment to those students who are undoubtedly wastefully printing after confirming the necessity of their printed materials.

Moreover, we are also monitoring wireless LAN network load as an item related to an attempt of an educational admonishment on students' use of shared resources. On the basis of our information network security policy, we are restricting access to college wireless LAN by using MAC address in order to prevent access by unregistered devices. Our college regulations don't allow students' devices to get connected to college wireless LAN at present. However, we are considering a switch to recommend "Bring your own device (BYOD)" in the near future. We have an idea that BYOD will be useful for further promoting active learning and smart education in our college. For this reason, in this academic year, we have eased regulations on network access on a trial basis exclusively for the students at the Department of Electrical and Computer Engineering, and permitted those students who submitted a statement of reason and a special application with information including MAC address to use wireless LAN, while monitoring MAC address of a wireless LAN-connected device. While continuously analyzing the possibility that some specific students will largely occupy shared network resources, with the promotion of BYOD we intend to use the analysis results for designing a system to connect students' devices to wireless LAN and considering a threshold value to limit network communication band.

Table 1. The monthly ranking of the number of sheets printed using the printers in the computer rooms of the Information Processing Center

Ranking	Sheets printed in April	Sheets printed in May	Sheets printed in June	Sheets printed in July	Sheets printed in August	Sheets printed in September	Sheets printed in October	Sheets printed in November
1	271	357	358	260	277	160	152	297
2	246	221	344	176	88	142	97	249
3	172	211	336	169	55	119	83	101
4	172	161	234	169	53	113	81	79
5	171	146	187	150	50	103	80	74
6	165	137	164	135	40	103	68	72
7	147	132	129	132	24	96	56	69
8	126	125	126	126	18	90	56	69
9	114	116	121	120	18	89	56	69
10	90	107	109	110	16	83	56	64
11	90	107	106	108	15	82	56	61
12	82	94	100	83	15	78	54	60
13	81	93	100	75	15	69	51	60
14	80	93	95	75	13	66	50	55
15	79	92	86	74	13	58	47	54
16	74	90	84	72	12	58	47	54
17	71	88	83	70	9	57	46	53
18	61	87	83	67	9	56	45	52
19	61	80	79	66	8	55	42	52
20	60	78	77	65	6	55	41	49

Changing the number of computer rooms in the Information Processing Center from three to five, we decided not to keep about 150 PC terminals which had been installed in students' desks of the fourth-year classrooms of the five departments in Main Building VI (Multimedia Building) for more than 15 years. As shown in Figure 3, as part of "Acceleration Program for University Education Rebuilding (AP)", we installed wireless LAN in each of the 25 classrooms of all the years (from the first to the fifth year) of all the five departments and introduced more than 160 tablet PCs which match wireless LAN, as well as many notebook PCs which match wireless LAN enough to use in two classrooms at the same time, which became one of the major reasons why we decided not to keep PC terminals in Main Building VI.

In the fourth-year classrooms, where every student could use a desktop personal computer for exclusive use for more than 15 years, classes using high-spec computers such as programming and CAD could be practiced. Also, with the spread of active learning classes using ICT equipment in our college, needs for the computer rooms in the Information Processing Center began to increase, which brought too difficult a situation to maintain education under ICT environment. Though not all the computer rooms were entirely occupied by the classes in terms of a time schedule, some kinds of restrictions for making a time schedule invited a situation where we needed more than three computer rooms in a specific period of a specific day. Tables 2 and 3 showing the usage situation of the computer rooms for classes in the academic year 2016 revealed that changing the number from three to five would meet the needs of the faculty. As shown in Tables 2 and 3, in "Period I" (Friday, the first semester), "Period II" (Friday, the first semester) and "Period I" (Thursday, the second semester), four computer rooms were used at the same time. The new computer rooms are the fourth and fifth ones.

The fifth computer room, built not on the second floor of the library but in Main Building I, is situated closer to the classrooms of all years of all departments than the library. For this reason, it was frequently used. On the other hand, the fourth computer room was not well used because of inconvenience. However, it is expected that more and more active learning classes using ICT equipment will be practiced in future with the progress of our AP project and that the situation will increase the number of classes conducted in the computer rooms year by year. Considering the necessity of covering usage for the next five years by the latest replacement, it was appropriate to increase the computer rooms.

In addition to use in classes, students are allowed to use any of the five computer rooms after school for self-learning as well as some kinds of students' activities related to active learning such as group work. Table 4 shows the students' usage situation in the period spanning April through November, including their usage after school. Though the number of classes conducted in the 4th computer room is less than those conducted in the 5th computer room, more students, as shown in Table 4, used the 4th computer room than the 5th computer room in several months. This doesn't mean students are likely to avoid using the 4th computer room.

Table 2. Use of the Information Processing Center in the first semester of the academic year 2016

Day	Period	1st computer room	2nd computer room	3rd computer room	4th computer room	5th computer room
Mon	I			Advanced English B (2SK)		
	II		Soil Mechanics II (4C)			English A (3M)
	III	English C (1C)				English A (3E)
	IV					
Tue	I	Urban and Regional Planning (5C)				English A (4E)
	II					English A (4D)
	III	Design and Drawing (4C)				English Practice I (1Y)
	IV		Computer Literacy (2M)			
Wed	I	English C (1M)	Information Processing I (2D)			English A (3D)
	II	English C (1A)	Environment Design I (5A)			English A (3A)
	III					
Thu	I	English C (1E)	Instrumentation Engineering (4D)			
	II	English C (1D)	Information Processing III (4D)	Information Processing II (3D)		
	III	Design Drafting (1E)	Traffic Engineering (5C)			Introduction to Electronic Control Engineering (1D)

	IV	Electronic Control Circuits (4D)	Spatial Information Engineering (5C)			
Fri	I	English A (4 A)	Urban Engineering (4C)	Computer Literacy (1C)		English A (3C)
	II	Environmental Sociology (5A)	Surveying III (4C)	Design and Drafting I (2D)		Advanced English B (2SK)
	III	English A (4C)				
	IV			Numerical Analysis (4C)		

Note: Regarding the symbols used in Table 2, each of the digits represents a year (grade), and the alphabetical letters, M, E, D, C, K, S, K and Y respectively represent the Department of Mechanical Engineering, the Department of Electrical and Computer Engineering, the Department of Electronic Control Engineering, the Department of Civil Engineering, the Department of Architecture, the Course of Electronic System Engineering, the Course of Architecture and Civil Engineering and the Course of Interdisciplinary Technology Development.

Table 3. Use of the Information Processing Center in the second semester of the academic year 2016

Day	Period	1st computer room	2nd computer room	3rd computer room	4th computer room	5th computer room
Mon	I	English B (2A)				
	II					English A (3D)
	III	Building Equipment II (5A)	Numerical Calulation II (5M)			English A (4D)
	IV					
Tue	I	Information Processing II (4A)				
	II	Design and Drafting II (3D)				
	III		Information Processing I (2D)			
	IV			Design and Drawing (4C)		
Wed	I	English B (2E)		Advanced Experiment (1Y)		
	II	English B (2C)	Wood Structure (3A)	Advanced Experiment (1Y)		
	III			Advanced Experiment (1Y)		English A (3A)
Thu	I	English B (2D)	Surveying III (4C)	Infrastructure Planning (1Y)		English A (3M)

	II		Design and Drafting I (2D)	Information Processing II (3D)		English A (4E)
	III	English A (4C)	Information Processing III (4D)		A la Carte of Experiments (2SK)	
	IV	Numerical Analysis (4C)	Fundamental Drawing (2C)			
Fri	I	English B (2M)	Soil Mechanics II (4C)			English A (3C)
	II	Instrumentation Engineering (4D)				
	III	Design Drafting (1E)	English A (4A)		Exercises in Civil Engineering II (5C)	
	IV	Design Drafting (1E)	Information Processing I (3A)			English A (3E)

Table 4. Monthly number of users of the computer rooms in the Information Processing Center

Month	Number of users (Total of the five computer rooms)	Number of users (1st computer room)	Number of users (2nd computer room)	Number of users (3rd computer room)	Number of users (4th computer room)	Number of users (5th computer room)
April	9520	2906	2452	1672	1302	1188
May	8622	2403	2297	1485	676	1761
June	7371	1793	2504	1386	397	1291
July	6121	1589	1979	1117	568	868
August	1191	201	379	190	229	192
September	3750	911	1133	639	598	469
October	7595	2613	2753	1267	664	298
November	6635	2363	2576	850	512	334

5. CONCLUSION

In our efforts of promoting smart education by all the faculty members using some effective teaching methods such as e-Learning, our college has consolidated a particularly established curriculum called "Model Core Curriculum" by introducing its targets into our syllabuses. The advance in science and technology has increased the contents of what students should learn and also brought the sophistication and subdivision of specialty. Based on these backgrounds, our college has developed a wide variety of educational curriculum, carefully selecting essential learning content. Moreover, we are trying to have all the faculty members familiarized with new teaching methods including active learning using ICT equipment through FD sessions.

In order to realize our organisational strategies where all the faculty members practice next-generation education such as ICT-driven active learning along with the above-mentioned curriculum, it is necessary to improve the campus-wide educational environment by installing some useful equipment and systems. Especially, it is a must to create classroom ICT environment. The computer rooms in the Information Processing Center of our college is operated under the system that in addition to being used as classrooms, students have access to them after school. The system has created an environment where various types of learning activities such as group discussions and individual learning can be practiced. While promoting the current efforts through linkages with the above-mentioned AP project which our college is promoting and in a mutually complementary framework with the AP project, we are considering promoting BYOD for all students and planning to make flexible responses to operations.

REFERENCES

Book

Bergmann, J. & Sams, A., 2012, Flip Your Classroom: Reach Every Student in Every Class Every Day. International Society for Technology in Education. ISBN 1564843157.

Bonwell, C.C. & Eison, J.A., 1991, Active learning: Creating excitement in the classroom. Washington, DC: School of Education and Human Development, George Washington University.

Journal

Brant, G. et al, 1991, Which comes first: The simulation or the lecture? Journal of Educational Computing Research, 7(4), 469-481.

Hake, R. R., 1998, Interactive-engagement versus traditional methods: A six-thousand-student survey of mechanics test data for introductory physics courses. American journal of Physics, 66, 64.

Hoellwarth, C., & Moelter, M. J., 2011, The implications of a robust curriculum in introductory mechanics. American Journal of Physics, 79, 540.

Kapur, M., & Bielaczyc, K., 2012, Designing for productive failure. Journal of the Learning Sciences, 21(1) , 45-83.

Lage, M. et al, 2000, Inverting the classroom: A gateway to creating an inclusive learning environment. The Journal of Economic Education. , vol. 31, no. 1, pp. 30-43.

Michael, J., 2006, Where's the evidence that active learning works?. Advances in Physiology Education, 30(4), 159-167.

Ogawa, N. et al, 2015, Creation of an Environment for Active Learning and its Practices in NIT, GIFU College, *Transactions of ISATE, The 9th Interna-tional Symposium on Advances in Technology Education*, pp.213-217.

Ogawa, N., Shimizu, A., 2015, Promotion of Active Learning at National Institute of Technology, Gifu College. *Procedia Computer Science*, 60: pp. 1186-1194.

Ogawa, N., Shimizu, A., 2016, Collegewide promotion of e-Learning/active learning and faculty development, Proceedings of the international conference e-Learning, Organised by IADIS International Association for Development of the Information Society, pp.179-184, ISBN: 978-989-8533-51-7

Prince, M., 2004, Does active learning work? A review of the research. Journal of engineering education, 93(3), 223-231.

Renkl, A. et al, 2002, From example study to problem solving: Smooth transitions help learning. Journal of Experimental Education, 70 (4), 293–315.

Westermann, K., & Rummel, N., 2012, Delaying instruction: evidence from a study in a university relearning setting. Instructional Science, 40(4), 673-689.

WHY DO LEARNERS CHOOSE ONLINE LEARNING: THE LEARNERS' VOICES

Hale Ilgaz and Yasemin Gulbahar
Ankara University, Distance Education Center, 06830 Golbasi, Ankara, Turkey

ABSTRACT

Offering many advantages to adult learners, e-Learning is now being recognized - and preferred - by more and more people, resulting in an increased number of distance learners in recent years. Numerous research studies focus on learner preferences for online learning, with most converging around the individual characteristics and differences, if not the features of the technology and pedagogy used. For Turkey, the situation is also similar, with the number of adult learners who prefer online learning increasing each year due to several reasons. The result of this is an increase in the number of online programs offered by many universities. Hence, this research study has been conducted to reveal the prevailing factors causing learners to choose online learning. Through this qualitative research regarding online learners in a state university, it is found that having a full time job, accessibility and flexibility, individual responsibility, effective time management, physical distance, institutional prestige, disability are the common factors for under graduate and graduate learners in their preference for online learning. Awareness of these factors can support the stakeholders while designing e-Learning from both technological and pedagogical points of view.

KEYWORDS

Online learning, preferences, expectations

1. INTRODUCTION

Offering many advantages to adult learners, e-Learning is now being recognized - and preferred - by more and more people, resulting in an increased number of distance learners in recent years. Emphasizing that distance education has a bright and promising future, Zawacki-Richter and Naidu (2016) stress that, "In fact, there has never been a better time to be in the field of open, flexible, distance and online education than now!" (p. 20).

The commonly discussed factors that make online learning attractive for adults are: independence from time and place; accessibility, and; economic reasons. With the MOOC movement, extremely high quality online courses are now being delivered to learners by many well-known universities. Moreover, many universities are either providing online programs or courses as a support to traditional instruction, in the form of blended learning, flipped classes, etc. Indeed, there are almost no universities left who don't benefit from these advantages of technology usage and its support in teaching-learning processes.

A variety of reasons might account for these learning preferences. Çağlar and Turgut (2014) attempted to identify the effective factors for the e-learning preferences of university students; they concluded that, "Efficient usage of time and reduced educational expenses were found to be on top of the list as the most valued advantages of e-learning" (p. 46). Moreover, having responsibilities, a full-time job and no access to a nearby university may also cause learners to prefer online learning.

Among the factors that affect learners' attitudes toward e-learning, a positive attitude toward technology, ease of access and use of internet, computer literacy, perceived usefulness, self-efficacy, motivation, patience, self-discipline, and self-regulation seem to be widespread and the most commonly reported (Liaw, Huang & Chen, 2007; Nogueira & Machado, 2008; Sun, Tsai, Finger, Chen & Yeh, 2008; Bertea, 2009). On the other hand, Lim and Morris (2009) examined the influence of instructional and learner variables on learning outcomes for a blended instruction course and stated that "... age, prior experiences with distance learning opportunities, preference in delivery format, and average study time are those learner antecedents differentiating learning outcomes among groups of college students" (p. 282).

Regardless of learners' attitudes toward e-learning, instructional design plays an all important role during an efficient online learning process. From the literature, it can be seen that the most common instructional design models – such as ADDIE, ASSURE, Dick & Carrey, Smith & Ragan - start with the analysis step. This step can be broken down into analysis of the learner, content, media and aim. Nevertheless, the question is: after analysis, are designers really reflecting the possible applications in their instructional design process?

In many online learning programs learner analysis was carried out collecting learners' general demographic data. Even if the target group of learners have similar academic backgrounds, these learners tend to have very different individual properties (Navarro & Shoemaker, 2000; Conrad & Donaldson, 2010), expectations (Dabbagh, 2007; Moskal & Dziuban, 2001) and motivation (Keller & Suzuki, 2004; Kearsley, 2002) levels. Therefore, after enrollment, institutions or practitioners should conduct a deep learner analysis; this also influences the quality of instructional design in a holistic way. Thus, institutions can aim to decrease the drop-out rates (Park & Choi, 2009; Chyung, 2001), increase the attendance (Yudko, Hirokawa & Chi, 2008; Rovai, 2003) and, in general terms, maintain a more efficient learning process.

Numerous research studies have focused on learner preferences for online learning, with most converging around the individual characteristics and differences, if not the features of the technology and pedagogy used. A similar situation is seen in Turkey, with the number of adult learners who prefer online learning increasing each year due to several reasons. The result of this is an increase in the number of online programs offered by many universities. For this reason, the current research study has been conducted to reveal the prevailing factors causing learners to choose online learning. Thus, this research seeks answers to the following research questions:

1. What are the factors that affect students' preferences for online learning?
2. Are there any differences between program types in terms of student preferences?

2. METHODOLOGY

2.1 Research Design

This research is designed as a qualitative study. Participants were requested to answer two online open-ended questions at the beginning of fall semester, and asked underlying reasons for their choice of online learning method, and their expectations about online learning.

2.2 Participants

Participants of this study were the online learners of a state university who were enrolled in various e-learning programs. These programs were composed of six undergraduate degree and four graduate degree programs. Most of the online learners were females (55%), married (59%) and aged 18-25 (41%). Detailed demographics for the participants are presented in Table 1.

Table 1. Participant demographic data

		Undergraduate		**Graduate**	
		f	**%**	**f**	**%**
Gender	Female	1278	59,92	184	55,93
	Male	855	40,08	145	44,07
Marital Status	Single	1032	48,38	133	40,43
	Married	1101	51,62	196	59,57
Age	18-25	29	9	860	41
	26-33	136	41	761	36
	34-41	112	34	398	19
	42-49	45	14	80	4
	50 and up	7	2	18	1
Total		2133	100	329	100

2.3 Data Analysis

After checking all of the responses, it was found that 944 participants from undergraduate level and 178 participants from graduate level were suitable for data analysis. The collected data was coded separately by the researchers. None of the qualitative data analysis software has been used, because of not missing any statement. In this research, coding was conducted according to the participants' comments, and the codes and themes were generated by the researchers.

A member checking validation strategy was used in this research for validity (Creswell, 2007), and also an intercoder agreement strategy was used for reliability. Two different coders - apart from the researchers - analyzed the codes and themes for a second time. For this dataset, Cohen's Kappa coefficient was calculated and found to be 0.90, which is within the range of acceptability (Krippendorff, 2004; Landis & Koch, 1977). In terms of member checking, researchers called (via phone) 10 randomly selected participants, and talked about their online learning experiences and reasons for their preferences. During meetings they emphasized the similar preferences for online learning.

3. RESULTS

3.1 Undergraduate Students

After the qualitative analysis, researchers identified 12 themes within the undergraduate students' data. The themes for undergraduate level are presented in Table 2.

Table 2. Themes for undergraduate students

Themes	**f**	**%**
Having a full time job	441	38,31
Accessibility and flexibility	218	18,94
Individual responsibility	113	9,82
Effective time management	106	9,21
Individual difficulties	83	7,21
Features of learning environment	82	7,12
Physical distance	43	3,74
Academic preference	23	2,00
Having a second degree	16	1,39
Institutional prestige	10	0,87
Aging	8	0,70
Disability	8	0,70
Total	1151	100

According to the data analysis, having a full time job is the most significant theme regarding the student's reasons for their preferences. They stated that the desire to run their work life and education together, and also the high tempo of work life forcing them to choose distance education programs. The majority of students were between 26 and 41 years of age, this data also proves that these students can be active workers in life. The students stated their situation, as is seen in the example below:

> *"I am working, and my age is 35. Still, I can complete my education into my area of interest, and have a diploma via distance education."* [P-722]. "*I am working, and I don't have any time for traditional learning programs. I choose this program, because it was the only way for me to learn.*" [P-715].

The other emerging theme was that of accessibility and flexibility. The nature of distance education is that it is independent from location and time, which are also important criteria in terms of students' preferences.

> *"Distance education gives me a large choice of time and location, so I don't need to be at an exact place and time. Also, I can continue to my other diploma program which I enrolled in before."* [P-23]. *"It's very easy to access and the practical, discretionary participation feature to the synchronized sessions is very important for me. Also, the opportunity of listening to sessions from records, and from different lecturers makes me choose distance education."* [P-92]. *"I choose distance education, because I can study whenever I want. I can listen to session recordings and there isn't an obligation about attending synchronized sessions."* [P-373].

Another characteristic of distance education students is that, generally, they couldn't complete, or even start, their education because of their individual responsibilities. This situation can be seen from the codes and themes emerging from the data. Most of the students stated that they have to take care of their family and children, or even a relative such as a nephew, or their grandparents.

> *"I had to choose distance education, because there is no one to take care of my nephew."* [P-53]. *"I am married, and have 3 kids. I really appreciate that this opportunity is provided to us."* [P-491]. *"I choose distance education because I am married and have 2 kids. My kids are going to elementary school, so they need me at home."* [P-592].

According to the analysis, a point will soon be reached where the large majority of students are likely to enroll on a distance education program, as this enables them to manage their time very efficiently, and also handle with family and work responsibilities as well.

Financial problems and being in a prison are addressed in the individual difficulties theme. Students stated that living far away from the university can cause a high level of transportation, accommodation and educational expenses for them. As a solution to such potential financial issues, they prefer distance education. In addition to this, students who have been in prison stated that continuing their education through distance education is a huge disadvantage for them even if in their circumstances.

After analyzing the students' data, researchers found that students consider distance education as systematic, coordinated, repeatable, offering good interaction with teachers, enabling participation from home, creating the chance for individual work, containing visual-audio presentation techniques, and offering virtual classroom activities. All of these specifications are considered in the features of the learning environment theme. Physical distance, having a second degree, institutional prestige, aging and disability themes also emerged from the qualitative data. Students stated their reasons as follows:

> *"I have a physical disability; as a result of this, transportation is a problem for me. So, I choose distance education"* [P-522]. *"I am a congenitally hearing disabled person; with distance education I can listen to my courses over and over"* [P-840]. *"The city I lived in doesn't have my program's formal version"* [P-121]. *"I am travelling a lot because of my job, so I have to be in different cities most of the time"* [P-327]. *"The appealing factor for me was the university's prestige. Having a diploma from such big university is very important for me"* [P-878]. *"I lost the chance to go to university years ago. I believe that learning should be from birth to death. Now I am at the age of 35, and continuing my education at this age makes me happy"* [P-911].

3.2 Graduate Students

After analyzing the graduate students' data, 8 themes arose. Compared with the under graduate students' themes, it was found that there were 7 common themes, and only 1 of these was different from the others. These themes are presented in Table 3.

Table 3. Themes for graduate students

Themes	f	%
Having a full time job	90	44,12
Effective time management	42	20,59
Accessibility and flexibility	26	12,75
Lifelong learning	24	11,76
Physical distance	13	6,37
Individual responsibility	7	3,43
Institutional prestige	1	0,49
Disability	1	0,49
Total	204	100

The lifelong learning theme consisted of students' wishes about increasing their academic knowledge, and providing professional development. Within the context of these aims, they stated that the reasons for their preferences as:

> *"Distance education provides me with continuing education, and I'm improving myself academically as well as in my work life"* [P-13]. *"I believe in lifelong learning, but I am dealing with a high tempo work life. I couldn't attend a traditional program because of my workload, so I choose distance education. Distance education is a very useful system for busy people like me"* [P-46]. *"I choose distance education because it was the most appropriate method with which I can continue with minimum loss elsewhere. Besides, I believe that, after completing this program, I will be in a better position in my work life"* [P-53].

When looking over the order of the themes, having a full time job was the most important, as was the case in the undergraduate program students' data. Effective time management, and accessibility and flexibility were the next themes in terms of importance. Also being married, having children, living outside of the city or country, and being a part of a leading university were the other reasons mentioned.

4. CONCLUSION

The results of this study indicate the importance of distance education, which can provide the equality of opportunity independent of graduation level. Every person has the right to obtain a quality education, regardless of whether it is a graduate or undergraduate degree. Sometimes life obstacles can be a barrier in front of people's choices. In this study, the researchers aimed that identify the differences between students' reasons for their preferences for distance learning. It was found that, generally, these reasons were parallel between these two degrees, but also there were some differences regarding certain points.

The common themes for both of the groups were having a full time job, accessibility and flexibility, individual responsibility, effective time management, physical distance, institutional prestige, and disability. The differences were in terms of preferences at graduate degree level, individual difficulties, features of the learning environment, academic preference, obtaining a second degree and the aging process. For graduate students, the predominant difference was the desire for lifelong learning. Actually, these themes tend to represent the students' characteristics. Undergraduate degrees are fundamental for finding a job, so this is an obligation for most students. Because of this, people who have difficulties regarding their budget, health issues or special conditions prefer distance education to a greater extent. Similar difficulties aren't observed at graduate level. Graduate level is not an obligation for a job; it depends much more on intrinsic motivation.

This is why these seven themes weren't evident in the data analysis. According to the analysis, people who enroll on a graduate level program are seeking more professional development.

According to both qualitative and demographic data, those people who can't complete or even start their education due to family responsibilities are, generally, the female students. Consequently, with distance education female students are able to find their place in social and work life much more effectively than before. Social roles and/or cultural expectations can bring about certain disadvantages to females, but it is shown that distance education can play an important role in overcoming these issues.

Hence, although this research does not add any specific new findings to the field, it was important to revisit the underlying factors influencing learner preferences, since technology and pedagogy should be shaped according to these needs. Providing education services to all the people who need them, and also increasing the quality of education in an accessible way provides numerous benefits to people's lives. With the use of regular tracking systems, educational practitioners can better understand students' reasons for preferring distance learning, as well as their expectations. Thus, institutions can provide a more enhanced and comprehensive service.

REFERENCES

Bertea, P., 2009. Measuring students' attitude towards e-learning: A case study. *The 5th International Scientific Conference E-Learning and Software for Education*. Bucharest, Romania. Retreieved at February 28, 2016 from https://adlunap.ro/else2009/papers/979.1.Bertea.pdf

Conrad, R. M., & Donaldson, J. A., 2010. *Engaging the Online Learner: Activities and Resources for Creative Instruction*. Wiley, San Francisco, USA.

Çağlar, E. S. & Turgut, T., 2014. Factors Effecting E-Learning Preference: An Analysis on Turkish University Students from Government and Private Institutions. *Emerging Markets Journal*, Vol. 4, No. 1, pp. 42-48.

Chyung, S. Y., 2001. Systematic and systemic approaches to reducing attrition rates in online higher education, *American Journal of Distance Education*, Vol. 15, No.3, pp. 36-49.

Creswell, J.W., 2007. *Qualitative inquiry and research design: Choosing among five approaches (2nd ed.)*. Sage Publications, Thousand Oaks. CA, USA.

Dabbagh, N., 2007. The online learner: Characteristics and pedagogical implications. *Contemporary Issues in Technology and Teacher Education*, Vol. 7, No. 3, pp. 217- 226.

Kearsley, G., 2002. Is online learning for everybody? *Educational Technology,* Vol. 42, No. 1, pp. 41–44.

John K. & Katsuaki S., 2004. Learner motivation and E-learning design: A multinationally validated process. *Journal of Educational Media*, Vol. 29, No. 3, pp. 229-239.

Krippendorff, K., 2004. *Content analysis: an introduction to its methodology (2nd ed.)*. Sage Publications, Thousand Oaks. CA, USA.

Landis, J. R. & Koch, G. G., 1977. The Measurement of Observer Agreement for Categorical Data. *Biometrics*, Vol. 33, No. 1, pp. 159-174.

Lee, Y. & Choi, J., 2011. A review of online course dropout research: implications for practice and future research. *Educational Technology Research & Development*. Vol. 59, No. 5, pp. 593-618.

Liaw, S.S., Huang, H.M. & Chen, G.D., 2007. Surveying instructor and learner attitudes toward e-learning. *Computers & Education*. Vol. 49, No. 4, pp. 1066-1080.

Lim, D. H., & Morris, M. L., 2009. Learner and Instructional Factors Influencing Learning Outcomes within a Blended Learning Environment. *Educational Technology & Society*, Vol. 12, No. 4, pp. 282–293.

Moskal, P. D., & Dziuban, C. D., 2001. Present and future directions for assessing cybereducation: The changing research paradigm. *Cybereducation: The future of long-distance learning*. Mary Ann Liebert, New York, USA.

Navarro, P., & Shoemaker, J., 2000. Performance and perceptions of distance learners in cyberspace. *American Journal of Distance Education*, Vol. 14, No. 2, pp. 15–35.

Nogueira, J. &Machado, C., 2008. Teams in virtualclasses: An experiential perspective. Technology, Education, and Development. Retrieved at February 28, 2016 from http://www.intechopen.com/books/technology-education-and-development/teams-in-virtual-classes-an-experiential-perspective

Park, J.-H., & Choi, H. J., 2009. Factors Influencing Adult Learners' Decision to Drop Out or Persist in Online Learning. *Educational Technology & Society*, Vol. 12, No. 4, pp. 207–217.

Rovai, A. P., 2003. In search of higher persistence rates in distance education online programs. *Internet and Higher Education*, Vol. 6, No. 1, pp. 1–16.

Sun, P.; Tsai, R.J.; Finger, G.; Chen, Y. & Yeh, D., 2008. What drives a successful e-Learning? An empirical investigation of the critical factors influencing learner satisfaction. *Computers & Education*, Vol. 50, No. 4, pp. 1183-1202.

Yudko, E., Hirokawa, R. & Chi, R., 2008. Attitudes, beliefs, and attendance in a hybrid course. *Computers & Education*, Vol. 50, No. 4, pp. 1217-1227.

Zawacki-Richter, O. & Naidu, S., 2016. Mapping research trends from 35 years of publications in Distance Education. *Distance Education*, Vol. 37, No. 3, pp. 1-20.

ENHANCING INTERCULTURAL COMPETENCE OF ENGINEERING STUDENTS VIA GVT (GLOBAL VIRTUAL TEAMS)-BASED VIRTUAL EXCHANGES: AN INTERNATIONAL COLLABORATIVE COURSE IN INTRALOGISTICS EDUCATION

Rui Wang[a], Friederike Rechl[a], Sonja Bigontina[a], Dianjun Fang[b], Willibald A. Günthner[a] and Johannes Fottner[a]

[a]*Institute for Materials Handling, Material Flow and Logistics, Technical University of Munich, Munich, Germany*

[b]*Jungheinrich-Chair for Technical Logistics, Sino-German School for Postgraduate Studies, Tongji University, Shanghai, China*

ABSTRACT

In order to enhance the intercultural competence of engineering students, an international collaborative course in intralogistics education was initiated and realized between the Technical University of Munich in Germany and the Tongji University in China. In this course, students worked in global virtual teams (GVTs) and solved a concrete case study in the field of intralogistics in a virtual setting via modern communication tools. This paper introduced the course in detail and reported lessons learned from conducting the course and student feedback. The findings of this study suggested that teaching using GVT-based virtual exchange is effective in improving intercultural competence of engineering students.

KEYWORDS

Global virtual teams; virtual exchange; international collaborative course; intralogistics; engineering education

1. INTRODUCTION

In order to succeed in today's working environment, engineers need not only to have excellent "hard" technical skills, but also to develop their "soft skills" which is also known as interpersonal skills, people skills or personal attributes that one possesses (Berglund and Heintz, 2014; Robles, 2012). A lack of soft skills will cost time and money (SitePoint, 2016). Therefore, in almost every job listing, soft skills are required, and candidates who posses both technical and non-technical skills are preferred by employers (Tong, 2003).

With the increasing globalization, the cross-border collaboration is more and more common in the industry. Intercultural competence has been becoming one of the most important soft skills which engineers need to develop today. According to a survey of the German Chambers of Industry and Commerce (DIHK) in 2013, every second German corporation was planning to invest in foreign countries and the most favourite ones are China and the USA (von Borstel, 2013). Alone in China, the number of the affiliates operated by German investors achieved 5200 in 2015 (Germen Chamber of Commerce in China, 2015). Against this background, global engineers need not only to be able to communicate in foreign languages, but also, just as importantly, to develop their cross-cultural competence which will assist them in working collaboratively in their expatriate assignments.

In the working area of logistics in a globalized context, this competence has become indispensable. While people usually emphasize this competence in the area of supply chain management, corporations also need more and more employees with intercultural abilities in the working field of intralogistics. The term „intralogistics" is defined by the German Mechanical Engineering Industry Association (VDMA) as the organization, control, execution and optimization of the internal material flow, information streams and goods handling in industrial, commercial and public facilities (Friedrich, 2012). In the survey of DIHK, one third of the companies with investment intentions were planning to expand their production capacities in foreign countries (von Borstel, 2013). These companies usually face the challenges where to build their factories, how to design their factories and how to optimize their material flows of their production in the foreign countries.

In order to prepare students for their jobs in a global market, the Institute for Materials Handling, Material Flow and Logistics (fml) at the Technical University of Munich (TUM) has initiated und designed an international course in cooperation with the endowed chair of the Jungheinrich Foundation at the Tongji University in Shanghai. The goal of the course "Planning intralogistics systems in an international context" is on the one hand to teach students the most important methods for the planning of material flow and logistics processes in the intralogistics, on the other hand it aims to strengthen their international und cross-cultural competence.

In this paper we present the findings from conducting the course. Section 2 presents the related work and activities regarding international exchanges especially virtual exchanges in engineering education. After that, we introduce the design and the execution of the course in section 3. In section 4, student feedback and lessons learned are discussed. Our paper closes with a conclusion and future perspectives in section 5.

2. RELATED WORK AND ACTIVITIES

Realizing that it is important to address and develop the intercultural competence of engineering students before they are sent off to the working world, universities increasingly offer and promote different kinds of programs to provide students opportunities to train this skill. International travel-based experiences such as study abroad or international internships are the most popular programs in the recent years (Parkinson, 2007). These programs have the benefit that students learn first hand about a different culture during their study visit or working stay in the foreign countries. Studies show that students who participate in longer study abroad programs demonstrate a positive change on intercultural competence, language proficiency and also on intellectual and cognitive development (Custer, 2016). However, because of the high cost und time issues, not all of the students, especially the undergraduate students, are able to afford such a travel-based program (Ball, 2012; Maldonado et al., 2014). According to a report of the German Academic Exchange Service (DAAD) in 2015, only about half of the enrolled students in Germany have studied abroad or are planning a study abroad period. In the engineering field, this proportion is even lower (Woisch and Willige, 2015). In addition to the cost and time challenges, an unprepared study in foreign countries could also be less effective or even fail. Studies found out that students become more confident and learn more productively if they have the awareness of cultural differences before they go abroad (Del Vitto, 2008). Under these circumstances, universities are beginning to search for additional ways to enhance the intercultural competence of their students.

With the rapid development of computer and Internet technology, global virtual teams (GVTs) have become a business necessity in multinational organizations. A GVT is a "temporary, culturally diverse, geographically dispersed, electronically communicating work group"(Jarvenpaa and Leidner, 1999). People of the groups are distributed in different countries and "rarely meet in person, conducting almost all of their interaction and decision making using communications technology"(Chudoba and Maznevski, 2000). As GVTs are increasingly common and important in the working world, some universities have also launched GVT-based courses or trainings to provide an international virtual exchange for the students. Compared to study abroad programs, virtual exchanges are not associated with high cost and investment. Moreover, they are scalable and timely more flexible and can therefore be adopted as an alternative or supplement to study abroad programs (Custer, 2016; Taras et al., 2013).

Virtual exchanges are often used in language or intercultural communication courses (Custer, 2016; Lamy and Goodfellow, 1999; Munkvold et al., 2011). In management education or MBA courses, where teamwork is needed, GVT-based virtual exchanges are becoming increasingly popular (Taras et al., 2013). In the working field of software development, GVT is increasingly used, especially in large IT companies who have numerous software development groups residing in different countries around the world. Therefore, some GVT-based courses are found in software engineering education which are mainly aimed at helping students better understand the distributed collaborative software development process (Edwards and Sridhar, 2003;

Richardson et al., 2006). However, in other engineering fields, there exist only few courses based on virtual exchanges. “Engineering the future: A global Endeavour” was a joint transnational course between the Technical University of Dortmund in Germany and the University of Virginia in the USA. This course contained a section with a role-playing simulation which focused on nuclear energy. Students had to work in multinational teams and played the roles of different stakeholders such as government representatives, nuclear company representatives, environmental activists, journalists and so on. In the end, a nuclear energy policy based on the group discussion had to be developed by each team. The course was a pilot project for improving intercultural competence of engineering students using online role-playing simulation and it mainly focused on social-technical systems and cross-cultural contact (May et al., 2015).

The course we have developed provides an innovative and inspiring possibility in engineering education. In this course, students have to work in GVTs and solve together a concrete case study in the field of intralogistics.

3. DESIGN AND EXECUTION OF AN INTERNATIONAL COLLABORATIVE COURSE FOR INTRALOGISTICS PLANNING

3.1 Course Content

The international collaborative course between the Technical University of Munich und the Tongji University was entitled “Planning of intralogistics systems in an international context” and it was primarily designed for graduate students with a background in intralogistics. In this course, students learn the relevant planning methods and procedures in the working field of intralogistics by solving a case study. In the case study, students play the roles being employees of a planning office, who is commissioned by a renowned German company in Shanghai to plan a new factory due to an ongoing increase in demand. For this reason, current intralogistics systems and processes need to be investigated and analysed. Based on the analysis, the new factory as well as its logistics systems are to be planned. Although the story which is told in the case study is fictional, a big part of the data which are used in the case study was collected from the company, so that the insight into the real-world industrial processes could be guaranteed. Figure 1 shows the typical planning phases for the intralogistics planning. The planning process principally consists of four phases: the preparation phase, the gross planning, the detailed planning and the final implementation. In each phase, different sub tasks need to be handled. The case study is split into three parts and each part contains different tasks. Part 1 deals with the tasks in the preparation phase and the gross planning phase. Students are asked to carry out a comprehensive material flow analysis of the current factory based on the given information. Furthermore, a site selection using benefit analysis for the new factory is to be performed and a layout for the new factory is to be developed. In part 2, a more detailed planning is carried out. Based on given information, students are asked to design two possible system alternatives for the central warehouse of the new factory: 1) a multi-bay racking warehouse with narrow-aisle stacker and 2) a high racking warehouse with stacker cranes. In part 3, both of the two prepared variants need to be compared by means of a benefit analysis as well as different methods of capital budgeting. By solving the case study, students get to know the typical tasks which occur in different phases of intralogistics planning and learn the methods to solve the tasks.

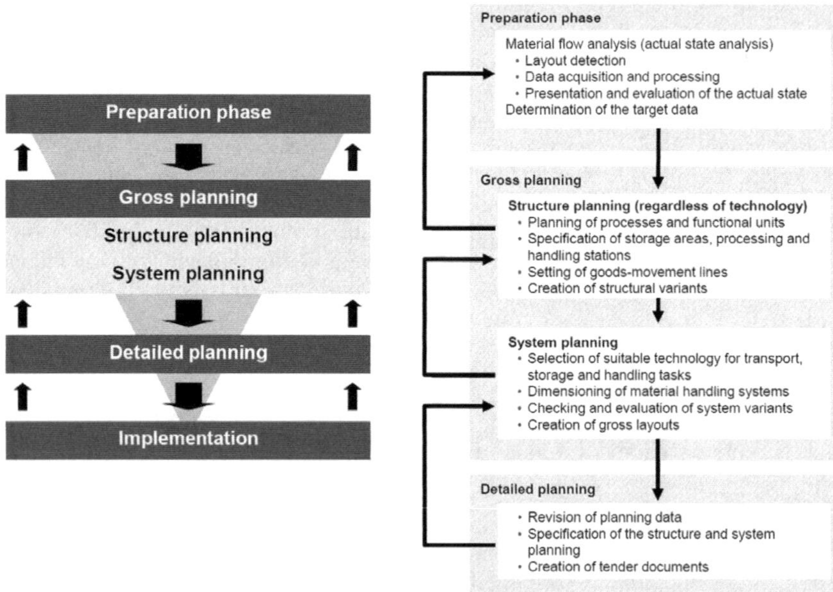

Figure 1. Phases and the related tasks of the intralogistics planning (course content)

3.2 Course Organization

The different curricular structures and study schedules present major challenges for joint transnational courses (May et al., 2015). For example, a lot of the graduate students from Tongji University are doing internships or are participating in study abroad programs during the summer semester. Therefore, the course had to be arranged in the winter semesters. Furthermore, the German lecture period in winter semester usually starts in the middle of October and ends in the middle of February, whereas the Chinese lecture period lasts from the beginning of September to the end of December. Therefore, we had to arrange the course with respect to the different academic calendars. Furthermore, the big difference of the time zones (seven hours in winter) also needed to be considered while planning the course. The course had totally 4 obligatory dates (Figure 2): Kick-off and part 1, part 2, part 3 and the closing session. Each date took about 2 hours. In each obligatory date, theories as well as methods to solve the tasks of the respective part of the case study were presented to all of the students via live broadcasting between TUM and Tongji. After that, the students needed to organize their teamwork with their team members to solve the tasks of the case study together. They had to submit their solution in a written document to the supervisors via email the day before the next course date. Besides, selected student teams had to present their results in front of the class in the next course date. In the winter semester 2016/2017, we had totally 40 students from both universities in the course: 22 from the TUM and 18 from the Tongji University. We built 9 teams, each team consisting of 4-5 students (2-3 from the TUM and 2 from the Tongji university). For each part of the case study, we selected 3 teams to present their results. The teams were asked to choose one or more team members as representatives to do the presentation. However, most of the students decided to present the results as a team, splitting the speaking time equally among all of the team members.

Because of the time difference between Germany and China and the different study schedules, we gave the students the freedom to organize their teamwork by themselves according to their individual needs. However, we provided consultation hours twice a week, for each part of the case study. The consultation hours were non-obligatory. Yet students had the possibility to consult the supervisors when they had questions or difficulties to solve the tasks. During consultation hours, computers with Internet connection were provided so that the students also had the possibility to carry out their teamwork under supervision.

There was also a short written test for each part of the case study. The short written tests, the written documents as well as the presentation made up the final overall grade of the students.

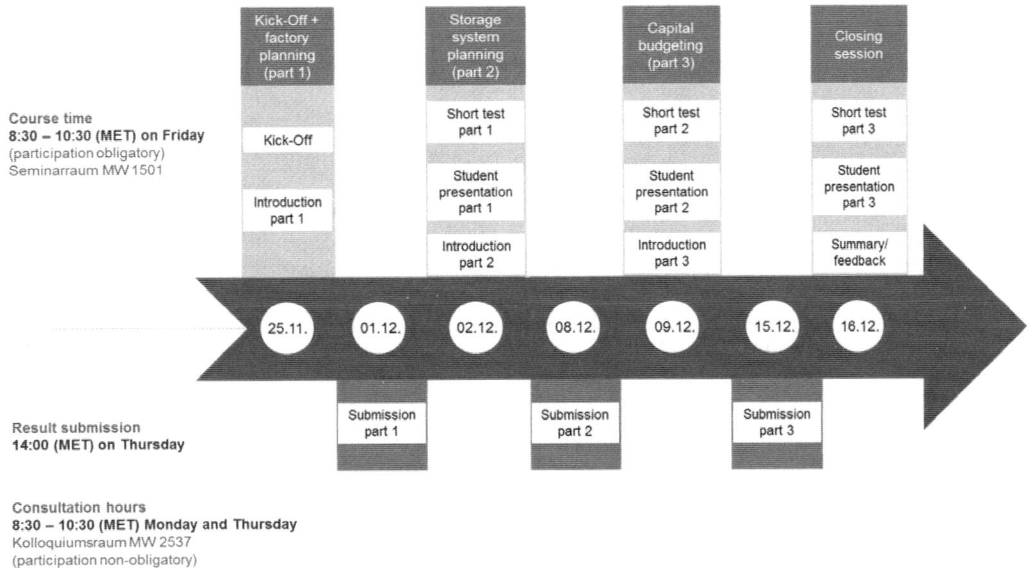

Figure 2. Course schedule and organization (Winter semester 2016/17)

3.3 Communication Tools

As already introduced, the four obligatory course dates were conducted via live broadcasting. We used the web conferencing tool from the German National Research and Education Network, DFN, a non-profit association for promoting communications networks for science and research in Germany. The tool supports multipoint audio and video conferences, whiteboard and document sharing, archive for PowerPoint presentations, role management e.g. moderator or participant, chat discussion and much more (https://www.vc.dfn.de/en.html). For each obligatory course date, the lectures were presented in PowerPoint and broadcasted via this tool, including a bidirectional audio-visual webcast. Student presentations were also live broadcasted in the same way (Figure 3).

As introduced previously, students were asked to organize their teamwork by themselves. We conducted a research regarding possible teamwork and communication software and listed the features of these software in the kick-off meeting. Besides DFN, Skype, WhatsApp and WeChat (the most popular chatting App in China) can also be used for live communication. However, there are still some differences in the features. OneDrive is a file hosting service of Microsoft. The biggest advantage of OneDrive is that it supports online collaboration. People have the possibility to edit Word or PowerPoint documents at the same time online and any change of the documents can be seen by all in real time. The above mentioned software were introduced by the lecturers. However, students had the freedom to decide which software they use according to their own needs.

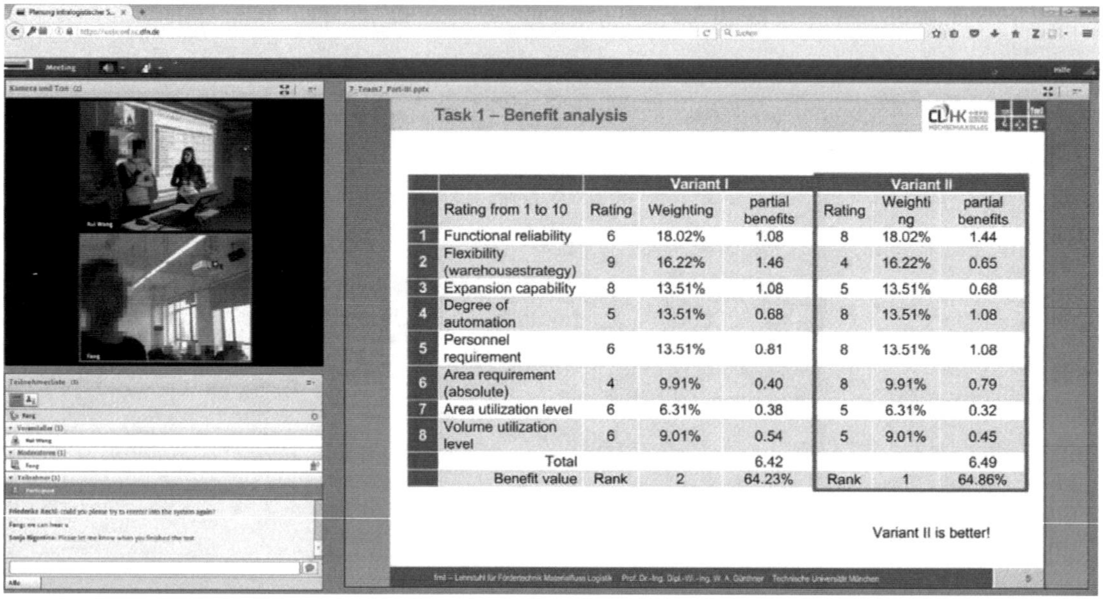

Figure 3. Live Broadcasting via DFN-tool

3.4 Teaching Methods

We applied different teaching methods in this course. The first part of the case study (factory planning) was set up as a role play. Students in a team played different roles of the planning office and got different information about the factory. To get the complete information for solving the case study, they had to work closely together and exchange information with each other. For the second and third part of the case study, we suggested task division with subsequent discussion. In part 2, students were asked to design two system alternatives for the central warehouse. They were suggested to divide the tasks inside their teams. For example, in some teams, students at TUM designed one alternative and students at Tongji designed another alternative. After that, they compared their results and conducted a subsequent discussion. In part 3, the benefit analysis as well as different methods of capital budgeting could be carried out in the same way.

4. FEEDBACKS AND LESSONS LEARNED

At the conclusion of the course, students were asked to complete an anonymous online survey designed to get their feedbacks regarding the design, execution and effectiveness of the course. We had totally 40 students and got 26 responses from the online survey.

The key results of the student feedback are shown in Figure 4. Most of the students are very satisfied with the course. More than half of the survey participants rated the course as "excellent" or "very good". Regarding teaching methods, most students preferred task division with a subsequent discussion. However, there are also some participants who preferred roleplay or both. Students used different software to conduct their teamwork, including OneDrive, Skype, WhatsApp and WeChat. Among them, OneDrive and WhatsApp were mostly used and students are principally satisfied with the software. While most students had no problems with their teamwork, some students still had difficulties in working with their teammates. According to the opinions of the surveyed students, the main reasons were the cultural difference and limited language skills. Time difference, lack of team spirit and also different prior knowledge also played a role. Almost all of the students stated that the course has helped them to improve their intercultural competence and that they would recommend the course to other students.

The results of the survey proved that a GVT-based course is effective to improve the intercultural competence of engineering students. Not only from the student feedback but also from the conduction of the course and the consultation hours, there are the following important lessons we have learned.

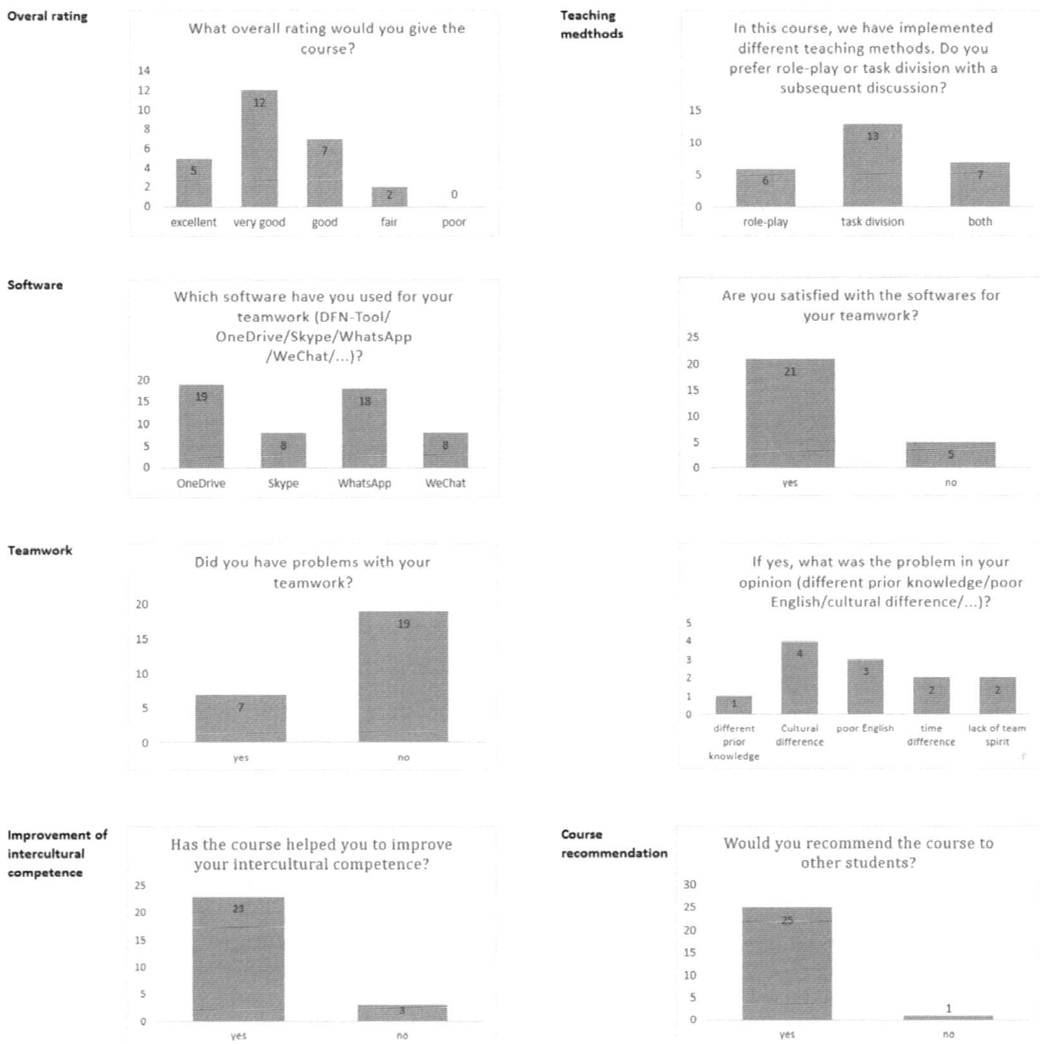

Figure 5. Student feedback

4.1 Organization

A course for students who are situated in different places needs to be very well and carefully organized. It is recommended to structure the entire course thoroughly and think ahead about possible problems which may arise and their solutions before the course starts. Organizational information needs to be clear and precise. In our course, we have prepared a document with all of the organizational information such as submission deadlines, scope and time of the written tests, etc. and have sent it to all of the students at the beginning of the course so that the students have always had a clear instruction to follow throughout the course. In order to avoid unnecessary problems or work, it also requires a good coordination between the instructors at both universities to exchange information and clarify teaching tasks and to-dos for every course date.

4.2 Technologies

For a GVT-based course, broadcasting and communication software plays a very important role. Especially for an international cross-country course, improper IT-settings or unstable Internet connections dramatically influence the course quality. Therefore, it is important to set up and test the IT and Internet environments before the course starts and also before every course date. The tool we have chosen (DFN) has proved to be a very effective tool for the course. However, we still have tested it every time before the course started and adjusted the video and audio settings in the most appropriate way so that a live broadcasting with a fine quality could be guaranteed.

As mentioned in the last part, we have given the students the freedom to choose the software for their teamwork themselves. OneDrive has proved to be a very useful tool for the teamwork, especially when team members would like to work on a specific document in real time together. However, some students in China have complained that the OneDrive connection in China is very unstable, which has influenced their working progress a lot. Alternatives to OneDrive need to be found in the future. Since there are a lot of possible software tools for audio and video conferences, students had no problems with this kind of communication.

4.3 Teamwork

It is usually reported that Asian students are reticent and passive learners in classrooms (Braddock et al., 1995; Jones, 1999). Many researchers think that this behaviour results from certain cultural attributes of Asian societies (Griffiths et al., 2014; Turner and Hiraga, 1996). However, some researchers have argued that this allegations of reticence and passivity set up against Asian learners are over-generalizations (Cheng, 2000; Liu and Littlewood, 1997). Although this behaviour may be true for some Asian students, the causes are situation specific which are more likely related with the teaching methodologies and the lack of language proficiency.

In the designing phase of the course, we have considered this factor which could potentially influence the teamwork. Therefore, we have implemented various strategies to promote the motivation and willingness of the students to better participate in the teamwork. Firstly, we introduced diverse teaching methods to this course, including role play and task division. Secondly, considering the time difference, we allowed the students to organize their teamwork outside the course by themselves. In this way, they could find a suitable time frame and place and might feel more at ease to conduct their discussion. Thirdly, we introduced a presentation part to the course. Students might be more motivated for the teamwork when they know that they are going to present the results in front of the class. Fourthly, we kindly asked the students to give a short summary about the collaboration within their team including the following key questions: 1) How often did your team (all members) meet virtually? 2) Did you split the tasks within the team? If so, please state in this document who worked out which task. In this way, students felt more obliged to better participate in the teamwork. Finally, through the entire course, we encouraged the students to inform us if they had problems with their teamwork so that we could help them to solve the problems or conflicts right away.

By deploying the above mentioned strategies and methodologies, most of the students were motivated and participated actively in their teamwork and most of them were also satisfied with their teammates. It has been proven that potential problems resulting from cultural differences and the difference in time can be compensated or even avoided through appropriate and thoughtful teaching methodologies.

5. CONCLUSION AND FUTURE PERSPECTIVES

The course we have developed provides an innovative possibility to improve the intercultural competence of engineering students. A course in this form is a first attempt not only at the TU Munich but also at the Tongji University. By building up GVTs using modern communication technologies and platforms, students distributed in geographically distant locations have the opportunity to communicate with each other, carry out teamwork on concrete engineering issues, jointly work out solutions and make decisions. In this paper, we have introduced the course in detail including the course content, the course organization, the teaching methodologies as well as the deployed communication tools. Furthermore, student feedback and lessons learned were discussed extensively. We hope to provide inspiring ideas to other institutions or educators in engineering education by sharing our experiences. According to the student feedback, a course in this way is proved to be effective in improving the intercultural competence of engineering students. We think GVT-based virtual exchanges could be used as an alternative way or as a supplement as well as a preparation for study abroad programs or internships abroad. Furthermore, it also indeed promotes the international exchange of students from different countries and universities. The students got to know our partner institute and university better by taking part in the course. Some have asked about possible study abroad or internship possibilities at the partner university and one student has even already applied for it directly after the course.

As mentioned, a big part of the data which are used in the case study was collected from a German company in China. In the future, we will further expand the collaboration between academic institutions and industry and hope to be able to put more practical elements or real-world cases into the course. Moreover, by interacting with the industrial partners, we also hope to be able to arrange industrial internship positions for students in the context of the course. In this way, students could also gain more practical experiences while improving their technical knowledge and intercultural competence, which is particularly important in today's engineering education.

ACKNOWLEDGEMENT

The authors are grateful for the support of the Jungheinrich Foundation.

REFERENCES

Ball, A., 2012. *A Comparative Evaluation of an Educational Program Designed to Enable Mechanical Engineering Students to Develop Global Competence.* Department of Mechanical Engineering, Brigham Young University, Provo.

Berglund, A., Heintz, F., 2014. Integrating Soft Skills into Engineering Education for Increased Student Throughput and more Professional Engineers. *LTHs 8:e Pedagogical Inspirationskonferens*, Lund, Sweden, 17 December 2014, Lunds university.

Braddock, R., Roberts, P., Zheng, C., Guzman, T., 1995. Survey on Skill Development in Intercultural Teaching of International Students. *Asia-Pacific Research Institute (APRIM)*, <Macquarie University.

Cheng, X., 2000. Asian students' reticence revisited. *System*, Vol. 28, No. 3, pp. 435–446.

Chudoba, K., Maznevski, M., 2000. Bridging Space over Time: Global Virtual Team Dynamics and Effectiveness. *Organization Science.* Vol.11, No. 5, pp. 473–492.

Custer, L., 2016. Using Technology to Promote Intercultural Competence: An Exchange between Japanese and U.S. College Students. *Jpn. Womens Univ. Stud. Engl.* No. 51, pp. 49–67.

Del Vitto, C., 2008. Cross-Cultural "Soft Skills" and the Global Engineer: Corporate Best Practices and Trainer Methodologies. *Online Journal for Global Engineering Education.* Vol.3, No. 1, pp. 1-10.

Edwards, H.K., Sridhar, V., 2003. Analysis of the effectiveness of global virtual teams in software engineering projects, in: 36th Annual Hawaii International Conference on System Sciences, 2003. *Proceedings of the. Presented at the 36th Annual Hawaii International Conference on System Sciences, 2003.*

Friedrich, J., 2012. Was ist eigentlich Intralogistik? *URL: https://foerd.vdma.org:443/article/-/articleview/11195643*

Germen Chamber of Commerce in China, 2015. Deutsche Unternehmen in China 2015. *URL:http://china.ahk.de/fileadmin/ahk_china/Marktinfo/Studies/2015_BCS_China_Report_DE.pdf*

Griffiths, C., Oxford, R.L., Kawai, Y., Kawai, C., Park, Y.Y., Ma, X., Meng, Y., Yang, N., 2014. Focus on context: Narratives from East Asia. *System, Language Learning Strategy Research in the Twenty-First Century: Insights and Innovations*, Vol.43, No. 4, pp.50–63.

Jarvenpaa, S.L., Leidner, D.E., 1999. Communication and Trust in Global Virtual Teams. *Organization Science*, Vol. 3, No. 4, pp. 791–815.

Jones, J.F., 1999. From Silence to Talk: Cross-Cultural Ideas on Students Participation in Academic Group Discussion. *English for Specific Purposes.* Vol.18, No.3, pp. 243–259.

Lamy, M.-N., Goodfellow, R., 1999. "Reflective conversation" in the virtual language classroom. *Language Learning & Technology.* Vol.2, No.2, pp. 43-61.

Liu, N.-F., Littlewood, W., 1997. Why do many students appear reluctant to participate in classroom learning discourse? *System.* Vol.25, No.3, pp. 371–384.

Maldonado, V., Castillo, L., Carbajal, G., Hajela, P., 2014. Building international experiences into an engineering curriculum – a design project-based approach. *European Journal of Engineering Education*. Vol.39, No.4, pp. 377–390.

May, D., Wold, K., Moore, S., 2015. Using interactive online role-playing simulations to develop global competency and to prepare engineering students for a globalized world. *European Journal of Engineering Education*. Vol.40, No.5, pp. 522–545.

Munkvold, B., Zigurs, I., Khazanchi, D., 2011. Augmenting Online Learning with Real-Time Conferencing: Experiences from an International Course. *Proceedings of Norsk konferanse for organisasjoners bruk av informasjonsteknologi 2011*. Norway.

Parkinson, A., 2007. Engineering Study Abroad Programs: Formats, Challenges, Best Practices. *Online Journal for Global Engineering Education*. Vol.2, No.2, pp. 1-17.

SitePoint, 2016. Soft-Skills für Ingenieure: Was wirklich wichtig ist. *Ingenieurkarriere.de. URL: http://www.ingenieurkarriere.de/magazin/karrierestrategie/soft-skills-fuer-ingenieure-was-wirklich-wichtig-ist.*

Richardson, I., Milewski, A.E., Mullick, N., Keil, P., 2006. Distributed Development: An Education Perspective on the Global Studio Project. *Proceedings of the 28th International Conference on Software Engineering*. New York, NY, USA, pp. 679–684.

Robles, M.M., 2012. Executive Perceptions of the Top 10 Soft Skills Needed in Today's Workplace. *Business and Professional Communication Quarterly*. Vol.75, No.4, pp. 453–465.

Taras, V., Caprar, D.V., Rottig, D., Sarala, R.M., Zakaria, N., Zhao, F., Jiménez, A., Wankel, C., Lei, W.S., Minor, M.S., Bryła, P., Ordeñana, X., Bode, A., Schuster, A., Vaiginiene, E., Froese, F.J., Bathula, H., Yajnik, N., Baldegger, R., Huang, V.Z., 2013. A Global Classroom? Evaluating the Effectiveness of Global Virtual Collaboration as a Teaching Tool in Management Education. *Academy of Management. Learning and Education*. Vol.12, No.3, pp. 414–435.

Tong, L.F., 2003. Identifying essential learning skills in students' Engineering education. *Research and Development in Higher Education: Learning for an Unknown Future. 26th HERDSA Annual Conference Christchurch*. New Zealand.

Turner, J.M., Hiraga, M.K., 1996. Elaborating Elaboration in Academic Tutorials: Changing cultural assumptions, in: Change and Language. *British Association for Applied Linguistics in association with Multilingual Matters*, Clevedon, pp. 131–140.

von Borstel, S., 2013. DIHK-Umfrage: Deutsche Firmen drängen ins Ausland wie nie zuvor. *DIE WELT. URL: http://www.welt.de/wirtschaft/article114879286/Deutsche-Firmen-draengen-ins-Ausland-wie-nie-zuvor.html.*

Woisch, A., Willige, J., 2015. Internationale Mobilität im Studium 2015 - Ergebnisse der fünften Befragung deutscher Studierender zur studienbezogenen Auslandsmobilität. *DAAD*. Germany.

Short Papers

EXPLORING CHARACTERISTICS OF FINE-GRAINED BEHAVIORS OF LEARNING MATHEMATICS IN TABLET-BASED E-LEARNING ACTIVITIES

Cheuk Yu Yeung[1], Kam Hong Shum[2], Lucas Chi Kwong Hui[1], Samuel Kai Wah Chu[2], Tsing Yun Chan[1], Yung Nin Kuo[1] and Yee Ling Ng[1]

[1]Department of Computer Science, The University of Hong Kong, Pokfulam, Hong Kong

[2]Faculty of Education, The University of Hong Kong, Pokfulam, Hong Kong

ABSTRACT

Attributes of teaching and learning contexts provide rich information about how students participate in learning activities. By tracking and analyzing snapshots of these attributes captured continuously throughout the duration of the learning activities, teachers can identify individual students who need special attention and apply different pedagogical actions to them. This paper describes the results of the work-in-progress study in exploring characteristics of fine-grained behaviors of learning mathematics in tablet-based e-learning activities. An experimental platform called SkyApp is built. Through SkyApp, teachers can create e-learning activities and track learning records of students after the delivery of the activities. SkyApp supports capturing, storing and analyzing of fine-grained behaviors of students. Pilot tests have been done in two primary schools for eight months. The review of the tests demonstrates the potential in performing learning analytics. By applying clustering algorithms on multiple learning metrics of marks, time and number of attempts for students in solving mathematics questions, classification of students by learning characteristics of performance and engagement can be formulated.

KEYWORDS

Fine-grained Behaviors, Tablet-based E-learning Activities, Learning Analytic, Learning Metrics, Learning Traits

1. INTRODUCTION

The infrastructure of e-learning in recent years allows teachers, school administrators, students and parents to monitor learning records that are generated during the delivery of learning activities, through which the insights of learners' behaviors can be obtained by learning analytics (Becker, 2013). Learning analytics (Siemens, 2010) is defined as the use of intelligent data, learner-produced data, and analysis models to discover information and social connections, and to predict and advise on learning. Based on the results of learning analytic, teachers can identify students with learning difficulties so that strategic interventions can be made (Dawson, 2010). Researchers explore different technology and data sources to discover digital footprints of learners, such as sensors for capturing and analyzing eye-tracking, heartbeat, skin conductivity, gesture, voice and etc. Blikstein (2013) called this approach as multimodal learning analytics. Through automated, fine-grained and high-frequency data collection, this approach allows measurement of affective factors which include emotions of the learners. Rienties and Rivers (2014) review more than 100 recent studies of learning analytics in which the role of emotions is considered as one of the key drivers of e-learning. They identify approximately 100 different emotions that may have different levels of impact on learners' attitude and cognition. In addition to learning emotion, researchers measure students' behaviors of engagement (Richards, 2011) and motivation (Hershkovitz, & Nachmias, 2008) in e-learning activities.

RELATED WORK: As classified by Wise (2014), learning analytics can be applied by the stakeholders at macro and micro level. At macro level, learning analytics supports the decision making process of administrators that are related to the institutional level and beyond. Siemens and Long (2011) refer this type of learning analytics as Academic Analytics. Based on the records stored in learning management systems (LMS) and virtual learning environment (VLE), visual graphical tools are built to show activity information of students, which include frequency of using resources, time spent per student in each resource, etc. Notable examples of learning analytics tools that explore the records in LMS such as Matep (Zorrilla & Álvarez, 2008). These platforms help monitoring learning records that are generated by the LMS that is adopted by the school for delivering learning activities. More recently, tools of learning analytics have been developed to perform analysis of log data in VLE (Agudo et al., 2013) and Khan Academy platform (Ruipérez et al., 2014). These analytic tools are often used to determine summative learning data and identify "at risk" students, but they are pedagogy-neutral. As for supporting teaching and learning at the micro level, tools require addressing the challenges of capturing, analyzing and displaying learning data for improving pedagogical practices. For example, LOCO-Analyst (Jovanović et al., 2008) obtains learning data from the online learning environment and presents the feedback data to teachers for evaluation.

However, it is a heavy burden for the teachers of primary and secondary schools if they need to carry out the works of design, development, and delivery of e-learning activities by themselves. To tackle this challenge, teachers need a tool to capture, analyze and present the learning data. There are currently very few tablet-based mobile apps that keep track of on the fine-grained data about students' inputs during e-learning activities. This paper introduces a new app, called SkyApp, as a platform to explore the possibility of using learning analytic to enhance the outcome of teaching and learning. Some parts of our work have been presented in CITERS 2016 (Shum et al., 2016), and a detail technical report is posted on our university's website (Hui et al., 2015).

2. METRICS OF LEARNING BEHAVIORS

SkyApp aims at helping mathematics teachers to deliver tablet-based e-learning activities. It allows teachers to import teaching and assessment contents in developing e-learning activity simply by file upload or photo-taking based on their existing teaching materials. The mathematics teachers of the participating schools create learning activities such as worksheets, quizzes, competitions, and homework for primary 4 to 5 (Ages 9-10) classes with the help of SkyApp. The objectives of these e-learning activities align with the curricular goals defined in the schools' teaching plan and annual subject plan. By measuring students' input on tablet computers, it is possible to examine fine-grained students' behaviors in detail. SkyApp offers facilities for students to provide answers or responses to the questions or assessment by typing, handwriting and adding emojis. SkyApp captures inputs such as time spent on each part of the e-learning activity and the details of the handwriting which are essential in supporting data analysis.

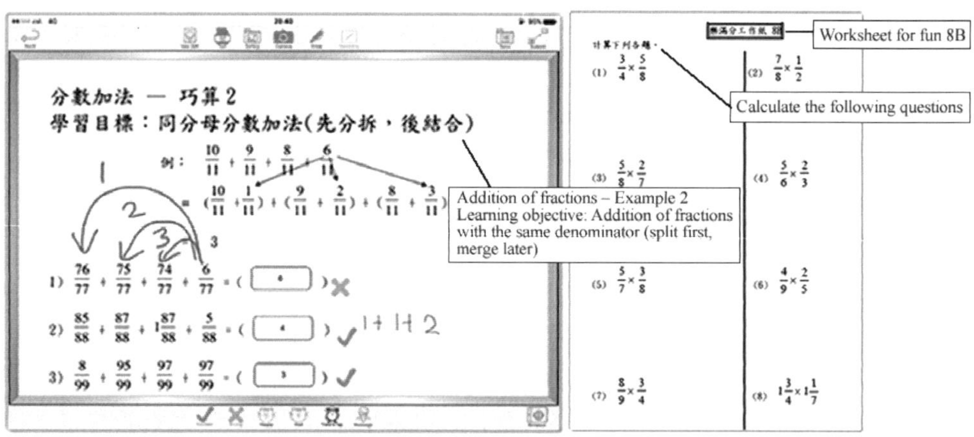

Figure 1. Left - Entering Answer Box, Adding Emoji and Handwriting Inputs, Right - Worksheet 31

The facility of Answer Boxes (Figure 1 –Left) helps to capture the inputs of learners. SkyApp captures the answers entered by students and performs automatic matching with the modeled answers. In addition, students can select and add emojis to the SkyApp, to express common emotions in participating the e-learning activity (Figure 1 - Left). In the form of worksheets presented in SkyApp, students can finish the questions under a specific topic, such as arithmetic operations of fraction, in each e-learning activity. Through the event logs of SkyApp, the inputs of users can be captured. There are two types of event logs, namely independent and dependent events. An independent event occurs only at one specific instance in time, for example inserting an emoji by a student is recorded as an independent event. A dependent event whereas records information at multiple instances of time, starting by a start of event action and following a series of in-process actions until ending by the end of event action. For example, during inputting answers in the Answer Boxes of the questions Q1 and Q2 in a worksheet, inputs are recorded as dependent events. Idle Times and Answer Times of a user can be measured in answering the first two questions of the worksheet (Figure 2).

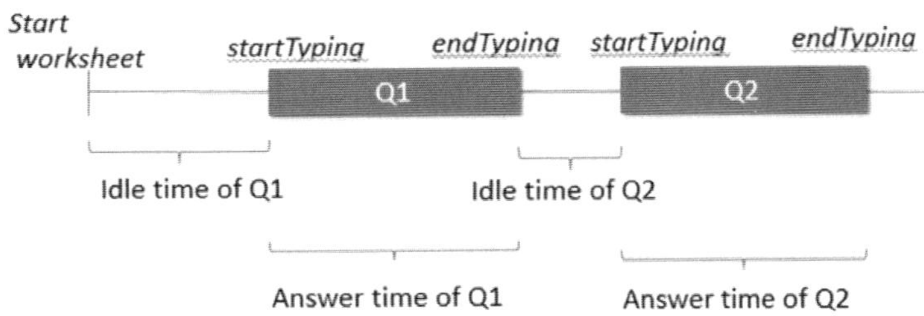

Figure 2. Example of Idle Times and Answer Times

The learning metrics of *Time, Attempts* and *Marks* are used to perform analysis of learning data. Based on event logs, the measuring metric of *Time* is formulated as the sum of Idle Times and Answer Times of all the questions in a worksheet. By taking the maximum number of attempts in answering the same question in a worksheet, the measuring metric of *Attempts* is formulated. For the measuring metric of *Marks*, it is determined by the sum of marks assigned in each correctly answered question.

3. DISCOVERING LEARNING BEHAVIORS BY CLUSTERING

With the infrastructure of mobile learning in place, which includes WiFi network, tablet computers and educational mobile apps, primary and secondary schools can now adopt new models of e-learning that unleash the potential of applying new technology in education. Pilot tests are conducted with the participation of the mathematics teachers in the classes of two local primary schools. The tests were conducted mainly by a total of 64 students. All students are from one class of primary 4 and another class of primary 5 separately in the two primary schools. The test lasted 8 months in the academic year 2015-2016. The e-learning activities essentially include mathematics questions in the form of worksheets that are delivered as class exercises.

To conduct the experiments, tablets of all the students and the teachers in the class are running SkyApp which are connected to the WiFi available in their schools. SkyApp is written in Objective-C that runs in iOS tablets. The data captured by SkyApp is structured in JSON format before sending to the back-end system for learning analytics. To perform analysis of the records captured, an analytical tool is built in Python to extract raw data from the database and convert them into CSV files. Data analytics can then be performed by calling statistical libraries through R programming. Analysis reports and classification results are then presented graphically in the dashboard by HTML. Clustering algorithms (Rokach, 2009) are used to find the data points represented in specific learning metrics that group together into a set of clusters. Patterns of learning characteristics can be identified by applying clustering algorithms on one or multiple learning metrics. The clustering method is called Complete-linkage clustering, which is one of the agglomerative hierarchical clustering. Literally, agglomerative method means that each object starts out as its own cluster, and close individuals or clusters are gradually merged until all individuals are grouped into a single cluster or any certain termination conditions are satisfied. Four criteria are used for identifying the best number of clusters, namely Silhouette, KL, CH and C-Index. A scientific way to study the relationship of clusters is to calculate the Euclidean distance between the center points of the clusters. However, the most straightforward way is to generate a graph that can visually observe the distance between clusters.

A typical experiment of one of the participating schools is described in this paper to demonstrate the effects of exploring fine-grained learning behaviors by using SkyApp in mathematics classes. Figure 3 shows the results of the students of the school in using SkyApp to complete Worksheet 31 (Figure 1 - Right) which consists of 8 questions of fraction multiplication. Clustering algorithms are performed based on the metrics of *Time*, *Attempts* and *Marks*. The results in Figure 3 are presented in four quartiles of ranges of *Marks*, which are the most common ranges used by teachers and schools to represent students' performance. The clusters identified in Figure 3 can be considered as meaningful patterns of learning characteristics of engagement and performance. As shown in Figure 3, Cluster D splits into two groups, one includes students 478, 484, & 503 and the other includes Students 497 & 499. The students in this Cluster scored relatively low marks, tried relatively fewer attempts and took relatively short time in answering the questions. These students show possible signs of relatively low learning engagement and performance. Students of Cluster A and Cluster E show efforts in making extra attempts and spending more time in answering the questions, whereas the students of Cluster B and Cluster C show relative strength in learning performance among other students. To further distinguish the difference between Clusters B and C, different ranges of *Marks* can be applied to the presentation of Figure 3. The benefits of clustering of students' learning characteristics to teachers are twofold: teachers can have an overview picture of the learning outcomes of the whole class in each e-learning activity, and teachers can have insights of the traits of learning of individual students.

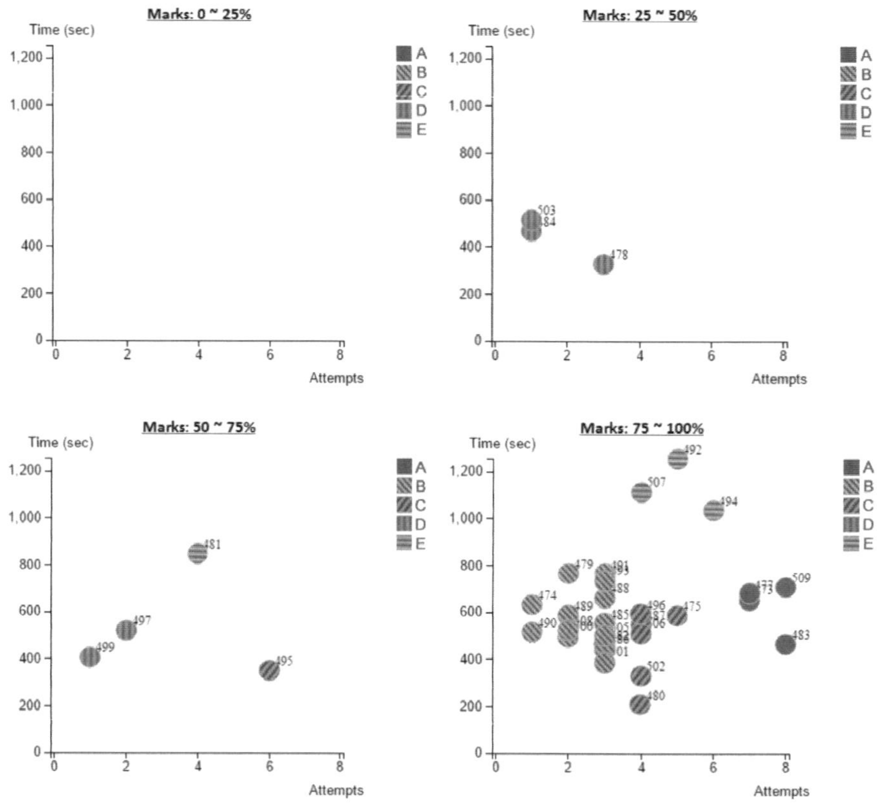

Figure 3. Clustering by Attempts and Time in different ranges of Marks

4. EVALUATION

Based on the results of student surveys on 64 students at the end of test period, around 80% of students want to continue to use SkyApp in Math classes and around 69% of them agree that SkyApp makes the learning in Math classes more interesting to them. 10 students are interviewed to collect detailed comments on the usability of SkyApp. Besides the suggestions of new functions to SkyApp and improvements required to make SkyApp more effective, students expressed keen interests in the interviews that teachers can use SkyApp to offer incentives to them by giving out cartoon icons upon completion of e-learning activities. This shows that student engagement can potentially be enhanced by elements of gamification.

5. SUMMARY AND FUTURE WORK

An experimental platform called SkyApp is developed to support tablet-based e-learning activities in learning mathematics with the capabilities in supporting learning analytics based on the fine-grained learners' behaviors due to students' inputs and responses. Initial efforts have been made in classifying learning characteristics of performance and engagement based on the results of the pilot tests. The next critical step is to investigate whether learning analytics can be applied to classify other learning characteristics such as motivation and emotion. Rigorous evaluations by quantitative and qualitative research methods are required.

This study also brings up some questions that deserve further investigation: **1) Real-time learning analytics:** the results show that it is technically feasible to perform clustering algorithms on learning metrics in real-time. The most time demanding part of the analysis is the computation time of running clustering algorithm and generating graphs. The time required is 6 to 10 seconds. It is feasible for teachers to view the results of the learning analytics right after each e-learning activity so that the results can help the teacher to revise the pedagogical actions of subsequent activities. **2) Personalized supports to students**: through real-time analytics, teachers can revise their pedagogies and introduce specific design elements such as gamification elements to engage students, and provide scaffolding supports according to the pace and style of learning of individual students. We believe that with more participation in using SkyApp by teachers, more concrete personalized e-learning pedagogical strategies can be discovered.

REFERENCES

Agudo-Peregrina, Á.F., et al., 2014. Can we predict success from log data in VLEs? Classification of interactions for learning analytics and their relation with performance in VLE-supported F2F and online learning. *Computers in human behavior*, *31*, pp.542-550.

Becker, B., 2013. Learning analytics: Insights into the natural learning behavior of our students. *Behavioral & Social Sciences Librarian*, *32*(1), pp.63-67.

Blikstein, P., 2013, April. Multimodal learning analytics. In *Proceedings of the third international conference on learning analytics and knowledge* (pp. 102-106). ACM.

Dawson, S., 2010. 'Seeing'the learning community: An exploration of the development of a resource for monitoring online student networking. *British Journal of Educational Technology*, *41*(5), pp.736-752.

Hershkovitz, A. and Nachmias, R., 2008, June. Developing a log-based motivation measuring tool. In *Educational Data Mining 2008*.

Hui, C. K., et al., 2015. A Mobile App Platform for Discovering Learning Profiles and Analytics. *Technical Report TR-2015-08*, Department of Computer Science, The University of Hong Kong

Jovanovic, Jelena, et al. 2008. LOCO-Analyst: semantic web technologies in learning content usage analysis. *International journal of continuing engineering education and life long learning*, *18*(1), pp.54-76.

Siemens, G. and Long, P., 2011. Penetrating the fog: Analytics in learning and education. *EDUCAUSE review*, *46*(5), p.30.

Rienties, B. and Rivers, B.A., 2014. Measuring and understanding learner emotions: Evidence and prospects. *Learning Analytics Review*, *1*, pp.1-28.

Richards, G., 2011. Measuring engagement: Learning analytics in online learning. *electronic Kazan, 2011.*

Rokach, L., 2009. A survey of clustering algorithms. In *Data mining and knowledge discovery handbook* (pp. 269-298). Springer US.

Ruipérez-Valiente, José A., et al., 2015. ALAS-KA: A learning analytics extension for better understanding the learning process in the Khan Academy platform. *Computers in Human Behavior*, *47*, pp.139-148.

Shum, K. H., et al., 2016. SkyApp: a tablet-based e-learning design tool for mathematics teachers to cater for learning diversity. In *CITE Research Symposium, CITERS 2016*.

Siemens, G., 2010. What are learning analytics? *Elearnspace*, August 25, 2010.

Wise, A.F., 2014, March. Designing pedagogical interventions to support student use of learning analytics. In *Proceedings of the Fourth International Conference on Learning Analytics And Knowledge* (pp. 203-211). ACM.

Zorrilla, M.E. and Álvarez, E., 2008, July. MATEP: Monitoring and analysis tool for e-learning platforms. In *Advanced Learning Technologies, 2008. ICALT'08. Eighth IEEE International Conference on* (pp. 611-613). IEEE.

BREAKING THE GENDERED-TECHNOLOGY PHENOMENON IN TAIWAN'S HIGHER EDUCATION

Ya-Hsuan Wang
Institute of Education, National Chung Cheng University, 168, University Road, Ming-Hsiung, Chia-Yi, Taiwan

ABSTRACT

Addressing the policy of gender mainstreaming in response to the gendered-technology phenomenon, this study aims to explore the contemporary change of the gender-technology relation. Drawing the female discourses on technology, gender, and success, this study collected qualitative data by individual interviews from 28 women in technology who were asked about their experiences of doing technology, doing gender and performing femininity or/and masculinity. This paper demonstrates women success in relation to their gender identity and gender-technology discourse of gendered technology. Based on the cross-generation females' accounts on their context of family, schools and society, this paper explores how female technologists constitute their gender role and how they articulate the formation of gendered technology phenomenon. It concludes a vase-breaking theory that elite female technologists can break gender boundary by individual characteristics, masculinity, family support, school empowerment from female role-model and single-gendered school, and social support from university. Although mostly the female co-constructed and deconstructed simultaneously the gendered technology, there is seen changing culture among three generations that younger generation get more advantages on gender mobility by breaking gender boundary. There is also a phenomenon of elite female develops technology well by appropriating all sorts of resources and eventually gender mobility is achieved with the help from men and women so that they have broken the strict boundary of gendered technology.

KEYWORDS

Female technologist, feminism, gender mobility, gendered technology, masculinity

1. INTRODUCTION

As individuals cannot be detached from his/her living environment, education should take four aspects of individual, family, school and society into consideration. So do science education. How do people learn about science and technology? Learning does not only take place in school but also in family and society. Taiwan is well-known as a kingdom of technology but there are very few female technologists. Since*2004 Gender Equality Education Reform* started, it had corresponded to the revolution of gender structure in the field of technology and science. This study focuses on the gender-technology relations. It questions the "technology as a masculine culture" and "technology as a male institution". This study aims to explore the contemporary discourse of gender boundary and gender mobility in technology, drawing the girl discourses on technology, gender, and success. Thanks to the policy of *Gender Equality Education*, more female technologists workin universities and more girls get into technology in universities. However, according to previous research, female technologists are rather corresponding to the patriarchic society than challenging gender inequality (Wang, 2010). Empirical study shows that female technologists have advantages in successfully demonstrating both femininity and masculinity. While they succeed in technology, they experience failure in female identity. Gender mobility is seen in those who survive in the social structure of strict gender boundary (Wang, 2012).Followed by the above study on the gender discourses of woman technologists in Taiwan's universities that reflect a masculine technology which intensifies masculinity yet mitigates femininity, this research focuses on the female gender discourses on learning technology and science, by exploring if they were aware of gender equality or are they just corresponding to the patriarchic society? This paper aims to analyze the gender-technology discourse of girls into technology and explore female success to the gender-technology relation and gender identity (femininity/masculinity).

2. BREAKING GENDER-TECHNOLOGY RELATIONS

The methodology and methods used in this study and the research findings for breading gender-technology relations are discussed as follow.

2.1 Methodology and Methods

A feminist approach was selected for this study in order to uncover the rich details and in-depth descriptions of the female experiences. Individual interviews were conducted on 28 elite women, including 12 female university teachers &16 female university students majoring in technology in Taiwan's top universities. They were based on five top universities in Taiwan and represented the mainstream of Taiwan's diverse ethnic backgrounds. Empirical data were collected by individual interviews and oral historical interviews from 28 selected females (teachers and students majoring in technology in Taiwan's top universities). They were asked about their life experiences of doing technology, doing gender and performing femininity or/and masculinity. Interviewing items were focused on their learning experiences on technology and its dilemma, motivation and social model, the successful self of the elite girls in the field of technology, how they perceive their success linking with their personal femininity or masculinity, how they make use/transform/discard their femininity during their career in technology, and how they interpret gender boundary and gender mobility by mapping the gendered culture in the technology field. In total, interview for each participant was done during 1.5~2.5 hours. In order to double check the quality of data, this study employs a follow-up investigation by Bem's (1974) Gender Role Scale. The scale is to investigate the type of gender role for the researched females--masculinity, femininity, undifferentiated, or androgynous.

2.2 Research Findings and Discussions

Based on the 28 qualitative interviews, this study categorized the contextual data into four aspects of their technology-learning experiences: individual, family, schooling and society.

2.2.1 Transforming Femininity into Masculinity

The participants' stories show that femininity is not welcome in technology. Most of the researched females in this study gradually transform their femininity into masculinity as long as they figure out the masculine culture in the university campus, especially in their Department of SECT. The technology females were not born masculine but becoming masculine. The individual femininity was shaped by the disciplinary culture of *Engineering*, gradually transforming into masculinity, as Huihsuan said:

> *I become more robust and strict as long as I study in this subject. I was so shy in childhood. However, my college classmates judge me a strong woman. They see a very firm and masculine temperature in me. Therefore, I think, doing technology is somehow redoing gender (Huihsuan, 20 years old, undergraduate student, Department of Electrical Engineering)*

However, the researcher was curious of this special articulation from the technology females. Are they masculine women? An investigation of masculinity/femininity provided quantitative evidence based on Bem's Gender Role Scale which was employed to figure out the types of gender role as Table 1.

Table 1. The investigation of BEM's Gender Role Scale on the researched females

Gender role type	Masculinity	Femininity	Undifferentiated	Androgynous	Sum
Teachers	5 (46%)	3 (27%)	3 (27%)	0 (0%)	11(100%)
Students	2 (14%)	5 (36%)	7 (50%)	0 (0%)	14(100%)
Sum	7(28%)	8(32%)	10(40%)	0 (0%)	25(100%)

Table 1shows that 25 scales were returned in which only 7 women in the type of masculinity. The result was very different from what they thought they were. Many of them thought of androgynous type and some thought of masculine type. None thought of feminine type, yet there are 8 women in the type of femininity in the scale result. There could be two interpretations. One is that the self-perception of technology females is changed by the organizational climate of the environment where they are. The other interpretation is that Bem's scale is inappropriate for the females in Taiwan due to cultural difference.

Above all, females in technology performed masculinity more than femininity, preferring thinking and understanding to memorizing or recitation, and preferring reading natural scientific mystery books to romantic fictions. Younger generation desires female models more than older generation although mostly they identify with male role models and adorn masculinity. Younger generation can escape from the anxiety of being 'strong woman' easily than older generation, though the stigma of strong women is still in place.

2.2.2 Growing in a Non-Patriarchic Family with Female Models

According to their family data, most females grew up in a non-patriarchic family. They were supported from their parents by providing good education, unisex toys, cultural capital, and high educational expectation. The most important support is family models in technology and science. They identified with male role models like uncles or fathers working as engineers, medical doctors or professors. Fewidentified with female role models in family whom inspired the interest of exploration, as Yinching said:

> My parents are both technology professors but I'd say I was influenced significantly by my grandmom and my mom. Probably I should say the females in my family have more impact on me than males. They are all very independent with their own thoughts. Even if my unties are housewives, they encouraged me to take a breakthrough to develop my own career. I believe women are able to accomplish a great business (Yingching, Assistant Professor, 32, 20100127).

Regarding their family support, gender-free family climate is also a key to develop girls'potentiality in technology. Most girls were growing up in an open environment without gender differentiation. Some parents even treat their daughter as a son, as Huana said:

> *My father is a SECT professor. He works for technical production for marketing. My uncle works in medicine. He is very good at medicine improvement. I have two younger brothers, but my parents have quite high expectation in me, probably inspired by my uncle's achievement. They don't treat me differently from my brothers. I'd say they somehow dominate the way which I stand now (Huana, 24 years old, graduate student, Department of Communications Engineering)*

Above we can see younger generation take advantage of the gender equality family. Elder daughters were trained to do housekeeping, yet the youngest daughter had the freedom. Younger generation was protected by their parents who even strongly suggest the future way to go, as Huiting said:

> *My parents were against Humanity which for them is not promising at all. They suggest me study for natural science or technology. The whole family prefer technology career...my uncles and my sisters,all doctor and electronically engineer,are against social science or humanity (Material Science, Huiting, undergraduate, 20111019).*

Females were impacted mostly by technology family full of male or female models. Younger generation benefits from gender-free family. Older generation benefits from patriarchic family subject to the youngest daughter within a group of children. Even if their family situation is quite good for developing technology, most women were unconfident with the possible dilemma between family and career in the future.

2.2.3 Studying in a Single-Sex School with Masculine Schooling

Single-sex schools and talented classes were advantageous for girls into technology. Twenty of the 28 researched were from single-sex high school. In a classroom full of female students, they received less gender stereotypes and were expected for good scientific performance as Chiahsuan said:

> *I was selected into the talented class in our girl school. The talented class is honored for studying natural science or technology. We study the materials much earlier than general classes. Obviously as soon as you were in, you cannot out as it is a one-way road to Science and Technology (Mechanical Engineering, Chiahsuan, Associate Professor, 37, 20100121).*

All the older-generation female chose Science and Technology as their career in high school because they had been in the track and there is no way out. It is obviously that single-sex school and talent class is the key streaming to technology for older generation. The situation is quite the same in the younger generation.

Moreover, thanks to the single-sex school and the talented class, these girls fortunately have female role models in SECT. Many of them were encouraged or inspired by their female teachers of physics in schools or university. However, in most cases, teachers' gender discrimination is the worst harm to them. The situation was worse in junior high school than in high school because single-sex school provide pertection against gender discrimination, as Luiwen said:

> *...to me boys are better than girls in Math and Science when I was junior high school where my class is mixed with boys and girls. I scored the top in the class, yet teachers teased at me why I could beat boys. It seemed to him I should be left behind boys. However, my high school is a girl school where everybody is distinguished. I found teachers never treat us with gender discrimination. I never heard that boys are superior to girls or girls should focus their conduct more than achievement (Mechanical Engineering, Luiwen, researched student, 24, 20100918).*

Above all, the schooling was perceived mostly unfriendly to girls' exploration into science and technology. Gender discrimination from the male gaze threatens girls' potentiality in technology. The females spent much time on crashing the stigma of beauty, detaching the weakness-label, and moving beyond the teachers' Pygmalion effect. However, these constrains cannot beat girls' involvement in technology as long as they have female models and freedom in the single-sex school.

2.2.4 Society Embracing Feminism

What is the social impacton gender-technology relations? Mostyoung generation had positive experiences of being female. For example, recently more organizations in SECT desire gender equality. In this circumstance, women majoring in technology are much more welcome than men.

> *Some companies claiming gender equality would recruit female technologists than male. Women in technology are welcome than ever. Now that most members in this company are male, why not recruit female? Women can take a balance of the masculine culture in SECT. It's an advantage for me (Chiaching, 22 years old, graduate student, Department of Electronics Engineering)*

The field of technology desires women in order to develop female technologies. Above all, female can break the gendered technology by establishing the advantageous forces and overcoming the disadvantageous forces. Women can accomplish big business such as doing technology or doing science distinguishably. The masculine ideology may be no longer penetrated the technological fields through the positive gender discourses.

3. CONCLUSION

Based on the qualitative data from 28 woman university technology females, they broke gender boundary supported by personal interest, family support, school empowerment from which they gained power in technology. Responding to the changing economy, there are more market needs for female technology instead of male technology. It seems that technological girls have promising future. It is worth to mention that the stigmatized woman for female technologist is a trap door (Guy, 1994) that could crackdown female mobility to technology. As we all know, the patriarchic gendered structure can reproduce its corresponding gender ideology that male is superior to women in the public field and in the wider society (Massy, 1994). It turns out that woman can only act as a vase with the function of decoration. Now that women can perform masculinity and do the business of SECT as well as men, this result explicates an alternative pattern of gender hierarchy that masculinity is superior to femininity. It is somehow corresponding to Vaerting's (1923) research that those who perform masculinity become the dominant sex, yet that performs femininity is subordinate. Technology females can become the dominant sex thanks to their control of technology. However, masculinity may not be so omnipotent in relation to technology. Current university isfriendlytoward females in technology without demanding for masculinity. Although females in technology are quite minor numerously, they felt more advantages because they can demonstrate both masculinity and femininity. If so, hopefully women don't have to become man (masculine) in order to get access to the stage of success and we can hence challenge what Weinstein (1988) relates femininity to an empty space and silent object.

REFERENCES

Barone, C. (2011). Some things never change: Gender segregation in higher education across eight nations and three decades.*Sociology of Education, 84* (2), 157-176.

Bem, S. L. (1974). The measurement of psychological androgyny.*Journal of Consulting and Clinical Psychology, 42*, 155-162.

Blackmore, J.(1999) *Troubling Women: Feminism, Leadership and EducationalChange.*Buckingham: Open University Press.

Brickhouse, N. (1994). Bringing in the outsiders: Reshaping the sciences of the future.*CurriculumStudies, 26,* 401–416.

Connell, R. (2006). Glass ceilings or gendered institutions?Mapping the gender regimes of public sector worksites.*Public Administration Review, November/December*, 837-849.

Danielsson, A. T. (2012). Exploring woman university physics students''doing gender' and 'doing physics'. *Gender & Education, 24* (1), 25-39.

Department of Statistics (2009). College Students' Numbers and Percentage by Gender and Three Disciplines over the Years, 2009, retrieved fromhttp://140.111.34.54/statistics/content.aspx?site_content_sn=8168, 2010/1/19.

Gill, R. &Grint, K. (1995).The gender-technology relation: Contemporary theory and research. In Keith Grin t and Rosalind Gill (ed.),*The gender-technology relation: Contemporary theory and research*. London:Taylor & Francis.

Guy, M. E. (1994).Organizational architecture, gender and women's careers.*Review of Public PersonnelAdministration,14* (2), 77-90.

Kleinman, S. S. (1998). Overview of feminist perspectives on the ideology of science. *Journal of Research in Science Teaching, 35* (8), 837- 844.

Lather, P. (1991). *Getting smart: Feminist research andpedagogy with/in the postmodern*. New York: Routledge.

Massey, D. (1994). *Space, place, and gender*. Minneapolis, MN: University of Minnesota.

McCarthy, R. (2009). Beyond Smash and Crash: Gender-Friendly Tech Ed. *The Technology Teacher, 69*(2), pp.16-21.

McCarthy, R. R. & Berger, J. (2008). Moving beyond cultural barriers: Successful strategies of female technology education teachers. *Journal of Technology Education, 19*(2), pp.65-79.

McDowell, L. (1999). *Gender, identity and place: Understanding Feminist geographies*. University of Minnesota Press

McNeil, M. (1987). It's a man's world. In McNeil, M. (Ed.), *Gender and expertise.* London: Free Association Books.

Phipps, A. (2008). Women in science, engineering and technology: Three decades of UK initiatives. Trentham Books.

Reimer, D. & Steinmetz, S. (2009). Highly educated but in the wrong field? *European Societies, 11* (5), 723-746.

Smyth, E. (2005). Gender differentiation and early labour market integration across Europe. *European Societies, 7* (3), 451-479.

Vaerting, M. (1923). *The dominant sex: A study in the sociology of sex differentiation*. Translated from the German by Eden and Cedar Paul. 2008/12/15 retrieved from Electronic Text Center, University of Virginia Library http://etext.virginia.edu/toc/modeng/public/VaeDomi.html

Wajcman, J. (1991). *Feminism confronts technology*. Cambridge: Polity. Waller, W. (1965). *The sociology of teaching.* New York: Russell & Russell.

Wang, Y-H (2012). Still gender boundary? Exploring woman university technology students' doing gender and doing technology. International Journal of e-Education, e-Business, e-Management and e-Learning, 2 (1), 34-39

Weinstein, M. (1988). Computer advertising and the construction of gender. In Bromley, H. & Apple, M. W. (Eds.), *Education/Technology/Power: Educational computing as a social practice* (pp.85-100). Albany: State University of New York Press.

ONTOLOGY-BASED LEARNER CATEGORIZATION THROUGH CASE BASED REASONING AND FUZZY LOGIC

Sohail Sarwar[1], Raul García-Castro[2], Zia Ul Qayyum[3], Muhammad Safyan[1] and Rana Faisal Munir[4]
[1] *Department of Computing Iqra University Islamabad,Pakistan*
[2] *Universidad Politecnica de Madrid (UPM), Spain*
[3] *University of Gujrat Gujrat, Pakistan*
[4] *University Politecnica de Catalunya, Barcelona, Spain*

ABSTRACT

Learner categorization has a pivotal role in making e-learning systems a success. However, learner characteristics exploited at abstract level of granularity by contemporary techniques cannot categorize the learners effectively. In this paper, an architecture of e-learning framework has been presented that exploits the machine learning based techniques for learner categorization taking into account the cognitive and inclinatory attributes of learners at finer level of granularity. Learner attributes are subjected to a pre-processing mechanism for taking into account the most important ones out of initial attribute set. Subsequently, couple of machine learning techniques namely Fuzzy Logic and Case Based Reasoning was employed on attributes selected for learner categorization. To best of our knowledge, these techniques have not been employed so far in learner categorization with quality of data and adaptivity while targeting semantic web.

KEYWORDS

E-learning, Learner Categorization, Case based Reasoning, Fuzzy Logic

1. INTRODUCTION

Internet has redefined every aspect of human life and hence the methods of educating the learners. Phenomenon of e-learning has greatly prevailed through ubiquity and universality in educating diverse communities of knowledge. Despite of all the benefits, e-Learning needs to prevail much in addressing content personalization for the learners (Sarwar, 2016). Learner is one of the key stake holders in an E-learning system along the Instructor and System Administrator. Instructor, an educationist with supervisory role, designs the learning contents, exercises/assignments and exams to educate and assess the learners.

Learner on the other hand, consumer of learning contents, undergoes the learning cycle of learning, assessments and corrections to master certain course(s). System Administrator, with a role of facilitator, harnesses the platform for instructor and learner in performing their respective roles. An e-learning system with its stakeholders is illustrated in Fig. 1 where focus of our work is pertinent to "Learner" (i.e. "Learner Categorization"). Learner categorization through learner profile aids in personalized recommendation of learning contests and subsequent adaptivity of these contents. Our current work focuses on learner categorization since typical techniques may not completely consider both academic (CGPA, Pre-Requisite score, Pre-Test score) taken implicitly and cognitive characteristics (learning style, aptitude and age) acquired explicitly for learner categorization at finer level of granularity. Few learner categorization techniques, after categorizing the learners, do not retain current information of categorization to take advantage of reusing information for future classifications. Others lack in having comprehensive set of axioms in categorizing the learners rightly. Lastly, few techniques claim to target the semantic web but explicit description of domain i.e. ontologies seem missing.

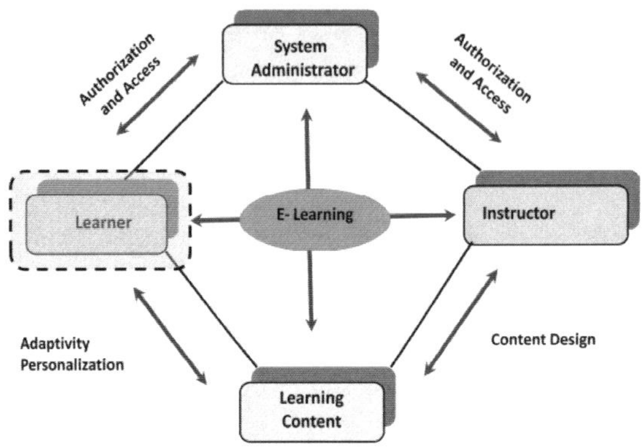

Figure 1. Stakeholders of-Learning System

Keeping above in view, phenomenon of machine learning techniques is employed for learner categorization that targets e-learning systems by modeling learner profile through ontology. It is dynamic enough to build learner's profile automatically with implicit parameters from real time data sources and explicit parameters acquired from the learner. Profile of learner is modeled by considering academic and cognitive aspects of learner using "LearnerOntology" coupled with "LearningContentOntology" to benefit from underlying technologies of semantic web. Once profile of learner is built, Case Base Reasoning (CBR) conjuncted with Majority vote classification (Agnar, 1994; Sankar, 2004) and Fuzzy Logic (FL) (Ying, 2004) is used to categorize the learners as illustrated in figure 2. Learners are categorized into one of the categories of 'Novice', 'Easy', 'Proficient' or 'Expert' based on their profiles. These learner categories have been introduced after consulting seasoned educationists, psychologists and literature (Agnar, 1994; Sankar, 2004; Thakaa, 2014; Ying, 2004).

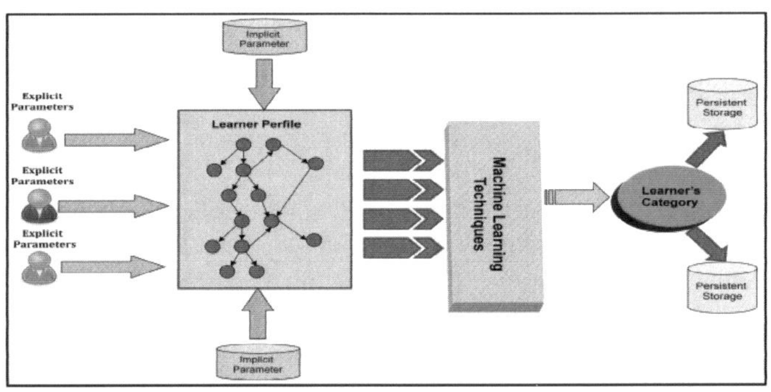

Figure 2. Learner Categorization using Machine Learning Techniques

The rest of the paper is organized as given in the follows: section 2 provides an overview of state of the art followed by section 3 describing the architecture. Section 4 elaborates implementation details followed by directions to for results and evaluations.

2. LITERATURE SURVEY

Educational Data Mining (Shute, 2010) termed as an emerging discipline is claimed to have a great room for developing methods and exploring unique types of data that come from educational settings. Using these methods has potential to facilitate better understanding of contents for students. Data mining techniques (Minaei, 2003) are employed for formative assessment of learners in order to provide a way for classifying the slow learners by identifying relation between academic achievements and his behavior in course of English language. Evaluation of learner is carried out through modes of listening, speaking and writing that helps in respective classification of learners.

Data mining techniques (Romero, 2007) have been used to predict failure ratio of students in two classes (Portuguese and Mathematics) while exploiting 25-29 predictive variables. Support Vector Machine, Decision Tree, Neural Network and Random Forest were employed on student dataset comprising of 800 students who appeared in final examination. Neural Nets and Decision Tree algorithms showed a predictive accuracy of 91% and 93% respectively for two-class dataset (pass/fail).

Any e-learning system has three mandatory components as suggested by experts of educational psychology; the content model (domain model), the learner model (user model) and the adaptive engine (Brusilovsky, 2010). Here adaptivity of learning contents based upon learner profile is discussed for recommending suitable contents.

3. OVERVIEW OF IMPLEMENTATION APPROACH

Modular architecture of proposed approach is presented in figure 3. There are three modules namely: Learner Ontology, Case base Reasoning (CBR) and Fuzzy Logic (FL).

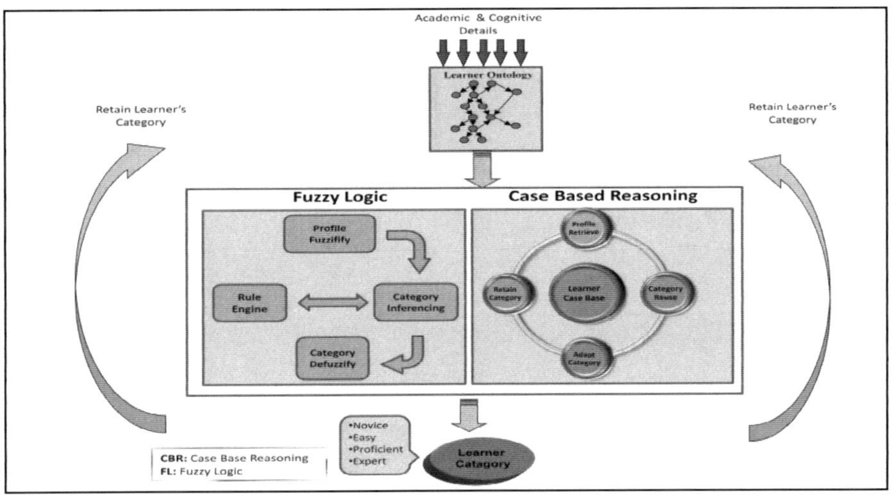

Figure 3. Proposed Architecture for Learner Categorization

3.1 Case Base Reasoning and Neural Networks

Case based reasoning targets to resolve the problems based on prior knowledge maintained in case base. Whenever new learners were enrolled in certain course, their profile was created by taking their personal details and ones pertinent to their aptitude and academics. Based upon this information, each learner was assigned a category reference to his cognitive strengths i.e. easy, novice, proficient and expert. This category was maintained along with rest of the profile details of learner in a repository. This repository serves as a "Case base" for our CBR model that not only plays a key role in categorizing new learners but is evolving over time. Phenomenon of how new learner is assigned a category using our CBR model is elaborated below:

Case Retrieval: provides query specific solution given the profile attributes of new learner (query case). Level of similarity is computed for the 'query case' vs 'cases in the case base'. This similarity index is computed using 'Tversky Ratio model (Sankar, 2004)' among query case and ones in case base. If cases retrieved from case base appear with exact similarity i.e. learner attributes in query case and cases in case base are same then new learner is assigned same category as that of similar learner in case base (termed as Reuse in CBR).

On the other hand, if retrieved cases are not exactly similar but similarity index falls between thresholds of 60 %-90 %), Case Adaptation is triggered (It is also called Revision). There may be another scenario where multiple cases are retrieved falling within stated range. Here decision of which case to adapt is made on the basis of 'Rank' assigned to each of the retrieved case through similarity index.

Case Revision aids in provision of possibly nearest solution to assign a category to certain learner, if exact match for new learner case is not found. Case adaptation is carried out through 'Majority Voting Classifier (MVC)'.

In MVC, occurrences of certain solutions are considered among the retrieved cases for classifying a certain learner. The learner category having a maximum number of occurrences is considered as the category of the new learner. In other words, the value of the nth element is considered for selecting the most probable candidate. For example, if the case retrieval process returns 10 cases (each case corresponding to 10 learners); 4 with category 'easy', 3 with category 'proficient', 2 with category 'novice' and 1 with category 'expert'; the category 'easy' is assigned to the new case (learner).

3.2 Fuzzy Logic

Fuzzy logic can be considered as knowledge-based systems incorporating human knowledge into their knowledge base through fuzzy rules and fuzzy membership functions (Ying, 2006) by manipulating the linguistic data of learner such as ("Novice", "Easy", "Proficient" and "Expert"). This module exploits the "Fuzzy Control Logic (FCL)" in order to categorize the learner.

Whenever a new learner comes in, input variables (feature attributes selected) corresponding to learner's profile are fed to the FL model in crisp form scaled over a numeric range. For example PreTestScore is an input variable with four ranges for Fuzzification through membership function i.e. poor (0-1.9), fair (2-4.9), good (5-7.9) and very good (8-10). These variables are fuzzified using the "Gaussian" membership function and represented in fig 3.

The Rule base of the fuzzy logic model aids in deciding the category of the learner. The knowledge required for the reasoning purpose is greatly dependent upon rules in the rule engine. Few of these rules (if-then-else) are given in the following:

RULE 1 : IF PreTestScore IS poor OR CGPA IS fair OR LearningStyle is belowAverage THEN LearnerCategory IS novice;

RULE 2 : IF CGPA IS average OR PreTestScore IS fair OR LearningStyle is average THEN LearnerCategory IS easy;

After rule engine yields certain value for the learner, it needs to be transformed into human-understandable format i.e. defuzzification. "Center Of Gravity" method is used to defuzzify the output of rule inference engine with other options of weighted average (Dipiti, 2001) and singleton methods.

Another important aspect of architecture is the representation of data pertinent to learner's profile. Since goal of presented system is to serve as component of semantic web based e-learning system, so learner's profile is maintained in ontology along with learning contents to benefit technologies of web 3.0. The learner's profile is modeled in the "Learner ontology". This ontology has been developed in a semi-automatic fashion where some of the concepts have been acquired implicitly from institute's repositories and others were incorporated manually in consultation with domain expert. The concepts in the learner ontology are envisaged to have reason among attributes learners, instructors and course contents through standard properties (associative, reflexive or transitive) or user-defined predicates. For example, if student 'A' has specialization of 'AI' and Instructor 'I' is teaching course of 'AI' the 'I' is likely to be supervisor of 'A'(assuming student and instructors have 1-1 relation).

4. EVALUATION AND DISCUSSION

In order to evaluate the proposed techniques, profiles of 400 students from different institutes and universities were used. The input for the evaluation of the given techniques consisted in four sets of new learners' profiles each having 20 profiles of learners. These profiles were subjected as input to all the ML models of CBR, and Fuzzy Logic for evaluating performance of ML techniques in terms of accurately categorizing the learners. The degree of accuracies exhibited by two machine learning techniques has been furnished in table 1.

Table 1. Percent Comparison of Accuracy in Learner Categorization

Technique	FL	CBR
Average (%)	49.67	67.35

In order to compare and analyze the accuracy of recommendations made by the CBR and Fuzzy Logic keeping in view the profiles of the learners. Domain experts have also suggested the categories given the profiles of the learners. Kappa coefficient (Sim, 2005) has been used to assert the relationship among recommendations by machine learning techniques and domain expert (DE).

An average of contents recommended by domain experts was taken as shown in table 2. This average was used alongside the contents recommended by CBR and FL for calculating the Kappa's coefficient. These results assert that CBR has better performance than FL due to its capacity of utilizing the profiles in the case base and dynamic nature of adaptive technique i.e. MVC. On the other side, FL has static rule base whose performance may be improvised with dynamic manipulation of if-else rules in fuzzy inference engine.

Table 2. Kappa Coefficient based Comparison of Accuracy in Learner Categorization

Set of Learner Profiles	% Recommendations		Accuracy Validation by DE		Kappa 's Coefficient
	FL	CBR	DE 1	DE 2	
Set 1	15	13	72%	81%	74%
Set 2	9	14	83%	77%	79%
Set 3	7	11	80%	85%	81%
Set 4	8	16	83%	68%	72%

5. CONCLUSION

Learner categorization targeted for e-learning systems is carried out through couple of machine learning ML techniques in this work. A comparative analysis for deciding the best one among Fuzzy Logic and Case Based Reasoning. CBR module uses similarity metrics in retrieving the relevant cases from the case base. The similarity metrics used with CBR seem trivial and static. So, different similarity metrics such as clustering or fuzzy logic would be employed to experiment unsupervised and supervised techniques for dynamic retrieval of relevant cases.

REFERENCES

Agnar A., Enric P., (1994), *Case-Based Reasoning: Foundational Issues, Methodological Variations, and System Approaches*. AI Communications. IOS Press USA, pp. 39-59.

Brusilovsky, P., (1996), Methods and techniques of adaptive hypermedia, Journal of user modeling and user-adapted Interaction, Vol 6(3), pp. 87–129.

Dipiti S., Cheu L., (2001), Hybrid Fuzzy Logic-Genetic Algorithm technique for automated detection of traffic incidents on freeways, IEEE Intelligent Transportation Systems, pp 7194-7201.

Minaei B., Punch W., (2003), Using genetic algorithms for data mining optimization in an educational web-based system. *In Genetic and Evolutionary Computation, LNCS,* Vol 4(3), pp. 2252-2263.

Romero C., Ventura S., (2007), Educational Data Mining: A Survey from 1995 to 2005, *Expert Systems with Applications*, Vol. 33(1), pp. 135-146.

Sankar K., Simon C., Shiu K., (2004), *Foundations of Soft Case based Reasoning* by John Wiley & Sons, Inc.

Sarwar, S., Qayyum, Z.,Safyan, M., & Munir, F., (2016), Ontology based Adaptive, Semantic E-Learning Framework (OASEF), *Springer LNEE ICISA*, vol 376, pp. 1199-1212.

Shute V., & Towle B., (2010), Adaptive e-learning, *Educational Psychologist*, Vol. 38(2), pp. 105–114.

Thakaa Z., Mohammad A. and et al, (2014), Classification Model of English Course e-Learning System for Slow Learners: Recent Advances in Information Science, *International Journal of Computer Science (IJCS)*, Vol 4(7), pp. 474-486.

Van S., Ossevroot and et al, (2012), Influence of student characteristics on use of adaptive e-learning material, *International Journal of Computers & Education* Vol. 58(3), pp. 942–952.

Ying B., Dali W., (2006), *Fundamentals of Fuzzy Logic Control – Fuzzy Sets, Fuzzy Rules and Defuzzifications*, Advanced Fuzzy Logic Technologies in Industrial Applications.

Sim, J., Wright, C. (2005). The Kappa Statistic in Reliability Studies: Use, Interpretation, and Sample Size Requirements. Physical Therapy. 85 (3): 257–268.

LEARNING FACTORY – INTEGRATIVE E-LEARNING

Peter Steininger
FOM – Hochschule für Oekonomie und Management gGmbH, Steubenstraße 12, 68163 Mannheim, Germany

ABSTRACT

Integrative E-Learning (IEP): The goal of the project is the development and testing of an integrative teaching format for the assembly of imported, tried and tested (classic) teaching elements (e.g. wallboard and flipchart, screen walls and other visualization aids, Projector, manuscripts, and workbooks, etc.), with contemporary, innovative elements "new media". The solution to be developed in this project involves comprehensive, interrelated elements in an integrative holistic approach. The elements of the solution do not lie in isolation next to each other, but are tuned to one another and are used per the target, using and integrating results of LEARNING FACTORY a predecessor project. The intention is the "integrative e-learning environment" of the presence theory. The target group is every student.

KEYWORDS

E-Learning integrative, content, production, learning factory

1. INTRODUCTION

Integrative e-learning (IEP): The aim of the project is the development and testing of an integrative teaching format for the integration of imported, tried and tested (classical) teaching elements (e.g.: wallboard and flipchart, screens and other visualization aids, overhead projector, manuscripts etc.) (see Döring, Ritter-Mamczek 1998, p.133) of the university course with contemporary, innovative elements "new media" (see Klimsa 1993, p. 19). This is the target group of every student.

The solution to be developed in this project involves comprehensive, interrelated elements in an integrative holistic approach. The elements of the solution do not lie in isolation next to each other, but are tuned to one another and are used per target (Lehmann, Bloh 2002, p. 14). The intention is the "integrative e-learning environment" of the presence theory. The current state of research shows that this has become very strong in industrial sectors, which are strongly characterized by professionally developed products, that integrative approaches to teaching at universities are scarce. The approach is a combination of learning and working. This will encourage students to apply their knowledge about production processes gained during traditional class room lectures and to transfer it to computer supported learning on the web. Our syllabus is divided in two parts: The first part is content presentation via internet or intranet (within the university) for students; the second part is self study of special topics, concerning detailed process knowledge, and to apply lessons learnt in scenarios provided by inter-/intranet. This combination of traditional forms of learning ("class room learning") and e-learning is called "hybrid learning". Hybrid learning describes learning or training activities where traditional forms of training such as "class room learning" are combined with e-learning supplements.

There are many ways of combining these two principles of teaching and for every situation the right composition must be found. Also, the integration of hybrid learning into organizational settings poses challenges.

2. THE IDEA

The conceptual combination "integrative e-learning" is characterized by a didactic combination of methods, in which the individual elements are related and coordinated with each other. In the context of e-learning, the term "integrative concept" was used by Euler and Seufert (2005) as a further development of the "blended learning" approach (Wissenschaftskommission 2008, p. 57), but the focus is on the interchange, effective complementation and change of methods in the sense of an overall concept. Integrative means more than an "enrichment" or "mixture", as the blended learning approach implicitly expresses - for example, it is assumed that the integration of computer-assisted teaching/learning offers also changes the pedagogy and learning and no longer (see Schulmeister 2001, p. 221 ff.).

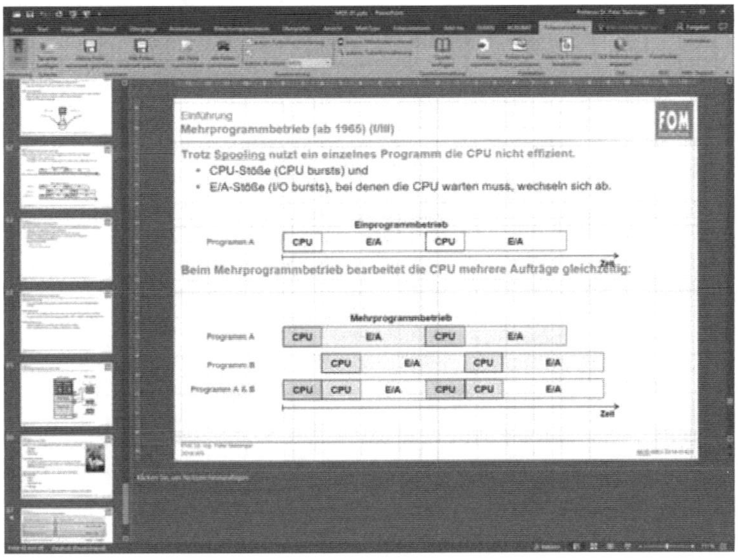

Figure 1. Microsoft PowerPoint with template and Extensions (for detailed menu, see Figure 2)

Therefore, one of the aims of the project is to merge previously separated solutions into a "solution landscape". Teachers should be taught the implementation, further development and maintenance of the processes for the creation of teaching materials per the conception of the pedagogy by means of information technology tools (see Figure *1* and Figure *2*). In the same way as the ERP systems pursue the value-adding process of the industry, the focus is on the actual task of the teacher at the centre and accompanying processes (if possible) are to be automated.

Figure 2. Extensions Toolbar inside Microsoft PowerPoint

Classical teaching elements, such as those used in presence events (for example, a wall panel, overhead projector, electronic presentation, etc.), are now usually supplemented with scripts. These scripts are, as a matter of experience, the result of a previous lecture which has been prepared "digitally". Today's (educational) offerings, such as iTunes-U or iBook's, create an expectation for students regarding learning materials, which can not be fulfilled by the classical methods and means.

IEP aims to create a prototypical process and system landscape based on common digital media (such as Microsoft PowerPoint, Web technologies, etc.), which enables an integrated approach, high-quality learning/teaching materials as a direct result of the preparation of the primary medium (presentation). Based on the methods used, students should be provided with learning materials, which can be derived directly from the teaching materials of the lecturer and achieve a qualitative standard that would not be achievable for the individual teacher without the process integration (see Figure *3*). The goal is to provide students with teaching and learning materials with similar quality as iBook's marketed by Apple (see Figure *3*).

All aspects of a multimedia teaching/learning scenario can be the object of the evaluation: learning software, learning environment and teaching scenario, authors, lecturers, learners and, finally, the interaction between the different persons and aspects.

The project "Integrative E-Learning" is to be evaluated continuously based on all the objects mentioned, even after completion of the grant. The evaluation results are to be used repeatedly during the project promotion to influence the further development and thus to the success of the project and a high acceptance with apprentices and learners (continuous improvement process (CIP)). This is also the reason for the planned early use of the software developed in the project, to be able to go through several semester evaluations during the project run-up and, thus, to draw attention to faulty developments early on.

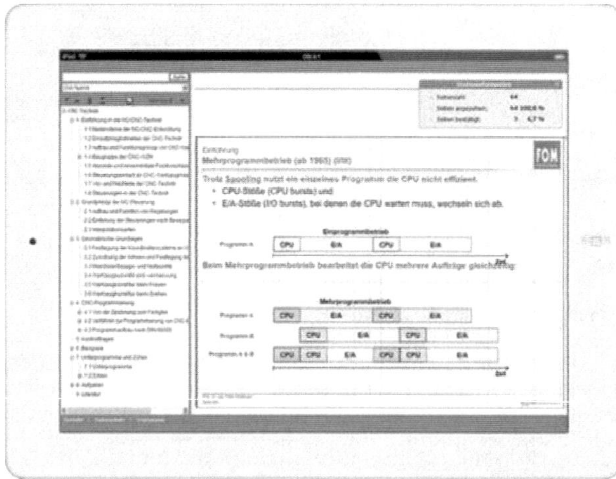

Figure 3. IEP viewed with an Apple iPad

2.1 Didactical Concept and Methods

To improve professional competence, curricula which have been, up now, handled individually should be combined. The holistic nature of production processes and the interconnections of individual sections should thereby be made apparent. In addition to the central question of how knowledge should be imparted, the question as to the means to be used, regarding the media for the transportation of knowledge, is also affiliated. Independent planning, execution and controlling of an operation are decisive for the training. Operation oriented methods are well suited to bringing this aspect across to the students. They differ from traditional instruction forms through a combination of target, content, methods and media areas, which is why one refers to multi-dimensional teaching learning-arrangements or hybrid learning.

One of the challenges facing the curriculum development was how to integrate technological applications into the curriculum. As the course goals and objectives were developed, it became evident that a textbook-based curriculum would not be effective. Furthermore, with the commitment made to internet technologies a multimedia-based curriculum was deemed more effective for students.

However, the curriculum could not take the form of a standard online course, where students would work independently of a teacher-facilitator in completing assignments. Instead, the focus shifted to a hybrid e-Learning course. The concept of hybrid e-learning incorporates online applications into the "live" arena of the class room. Such a course offers some of the conveniences of all-online courses without the complete loss of face-to face contact. Moreover, because the course would include students of differing abilities and differing learning styles, written and graphical materials could be presented in a range of formats to help make sure every student is fully engaged at least in the class activities.

2.2 Hybrid Learning

A mix of traditional teaching and e-learning has a lot of promising advantages compared to pure e-learning or pure traditional teaching. For example, one serious problem of e-learning is the loss of learners' motivation. Through recurrent class room meetings the teachers can better build up relationships with their students and are thus able to support them better during their e-learning sessions. Traditional teaching in turn cannot offer the time- and location-related flexibility of e-learning. If the students are distributed among many different locations, the number of physical meetings can significantly be reduced with the help of additional e-learning units. If active learning materials must be used or traditional methods of organisational education must be applied, hybrid learning can also be the right choice. It can also be applied if there are topics in a syllabus of an organisational education plan that are practically impossible to be taught with electronic means like for instance how to apply social skills, how to carry on negotiations or other soft skills.

2.3 Interaction

Both the theory of transactional distance and the theory of equivalence view the dialog as a fundamental element of distance education. Teachers within this field must pay a lot of attention to get the students involved in the learning process. Hence, the distance education courses need to be designed and organized adequately to ensure dialog and interaction suitable for the various teaching tasks for different subjects for learners at different stages of studies. As a minimum, MOORE (1993) distinguishes between three types of interaction that must be practiced by distance teachers. He labels these as learner-content interaction, learner-instructor interaction and learner-learner interaction.

The first one, the learner-content interaction, is the intellectual interaction the student has with the subject of study. This type of interaction shapes the basis of all distance education, since it results in changes in the learner's understanding and contributes to his construct of knowledge. Without this specific interaction, there cannot be a distance education. In Moore's (1993) opinion the concept also includes internal didactic conversation, per Holmberg (1986) the oldest form of distance education aimed to facilitate learner-content interaction. At that time, distance education was based on didactic texts, printed material, in the shape of letters, assignments and gradually accompanying study guides. There was little or nearly no contact, neither with the instructor nor with other learners. With the evolvement of new media, computer software with interactive multimedia like CD-ROM and the Internet, the learner-content interaction expanded and got a new dimension. The concept is now used to describe computer-based learning programs designed as one-way communication programs with a subject expert, intending to help the lonely distant learner in their study of a specific topic. Moore and Kearsley (1996) regard some of these learning programs as solely content-interactive in nature. As the learner-content interaction is an absolute condition for all types of distance education, this is not the case of the learner-instructor interaction. Most learners regard this second type of interaction as desirable, but not necessary. It is however seen as important by most educators (for e.g. effective learning). Per Moore (1993), this is a way to increase the teacher's influence: "The frequency and intensity of the teacher's influence on learners when there is a learner-teacher interaction is much greater than when there is only learner-content interaction. The learner-instructor interaction is referred to as the "interaction between the learner and the expert who prepared the subject material or some other expert acting as instructor".

After having presented the content, the educator tries to stimulate and motivate the student in interacting with the subject and organize their application of what they have learned. Evaluation, counselling, encouragement and student support are important features of this interaction. The two-way interaction between learner and instructor requires however a high degree of learner autonomy and a feeling of confidence. To build this confidence, a tight communication between teacher and learner is provided, thus causing an additional workload on the teacher compared to traditional learning, where this can be handled during the class room presentation. The instructor's role as respondent to the learners' application of knowledge thus especially valuable, but must be perform in written form (e.g. via e-mail) instead of the less time-consuming oral form during class room lectures.

The third type of interaction, the learner-learner interaction, is, as the concept indicates, the interaction between one learner and another learner or learners, as a pair or in group settings, with or without the real-time presence of an instructor. Whereas learner-learner interaction among members of a class or a group is a resource of great value for learning, sometimes essential, his type of interaction is often considered desirable of pedagogical reasons. Research has shown that group interaction sometimes is used as strategy for learning. Not only face-to-face communication can be used to facilitate this type of interaction - also modern educational technology like e-mail, computer conferencing, distribution lists and virtual class rooms may contribute to reach this target. To decide when inter-learner interaction is desirable and effective depends however on the learning environment, the learner's age, their experiences and their learner autonomy. Moore (1993) proclaimed that just this third form of interaction, characterized as a new dimension of distance education, would be a challenge to our thinking and practice in the next years. Looking at different learning environments, both in academia and in the workplace this prophesy proved. Most authors stress the importance to commit to all three types of interaction within one and the same distance education program types, not only to one of them. This implies to plan for the application of different types of medium and to develop a learning environment that fits different learning styles. On the internet, the students get feedback related to the actual studied pages, the reached learning goals and the topics they still must work through. Feedback means that the headings of pages seen and acknowledged by the student get a blue colour (colour is changeable by the course editor) in the course outline. The actual page is in red and the box on top of the pages (cf. Figure 3 in German: "Status information") gives information about the "performance", meaning total pages and pages worked through. These values are stored per user in the database for reuse.

For the next version of the hybrid learning system an "adaptive" content systems should be developed, which builds the curriculum on the knowledge of the students, who first completes an interactive query system. This query system was developed in another e-learning project and shall then be integrated into the herein mentioned system. The questionnaire data is transferred between the servers and the front-end with XML which uses SCORM DTD "QTIv1p1" (cf. Scorm 2002). This format was chosen since it receives direct support within the authoring system and since a possibility for data exchange with other systems implemented per this standard can take place. Furthermore, possibilities for transfer to other curriculum are provided within the query system itself. An interface has been defined which offers the possibility to exchange content with other query systems which use this standard, since the storage of the questionnaire content is not stored per SCORM DTD.

3. CONCLUSION

In conclusion, the development and implementation of a hybrid e-learning course is a complex work. We hope that Student enrolment will be high and that the variety of learning activities and opportunities in different media will promote better student performance and better student learning. Students should feel that they have ownership over their own learning process using more participatory and student centred learning activities. As a teacher, venturing into hybrid e-learning will change the way to teach as well. The goal is to integrate multimedia applications, internet applications and differing learning activities in all offered courses. Hybrid e-learning, though, is not for every class or for every student. Care and diligence must be taken in adapting any course to this format. However, with the right course, the proper learning goals, the right teacher, students and with a little creativity and risk-taking, any teacher would soon find that the imagination is the limit.

REFERENCES

Döring, Klaus W.; Ritter-Mamczek, Bettina, 1998. Medien in der Weiterbildung. Beltz, Weinheim.

Euler, D.; Seufert, S, 2005. *Nachhaltigkeit von eLearning-Innovationen: Fallstudien zu Implementierungsstrategien von eLearning als Innovationen an Hochschulen. SCIL Arbeitsbericht 4.* Universität St. Gallen, St. Gallen.

Holmberg, Börje, 1986. *Growth and structure of Distance Education.* Croom Helm, London.

Klimsa, Paul, 1993. *Neue Medien und Weiterbildung.* Dt. Studien-Verlag, Weinheim.

Lehmann, Burkhard; Bloh, Egon, 2002. *Online-Pädagogik.* Schneider Hohengehren, Baltmannsweiler.

Moore, Michael G., 1993. *Three types of interaction.* In: Distance Education: New Perspectives Eds.: Harry, Keith; John, Magnus; Keegan, Dermond. Routledge, London.

Moore, Michael Grahame, 1993. *Handbook of Distance Education.* Taylor & Francis Ltd, Abingdon.

Moore, Michael G.; Kearsley, Greg, 1996. *Distance Education. A Systems View.* Wadsworth Publishing, London.

Scorm, 2002. *Advanced Distributed Learning, Advanced Distributed Learning Initiative, Sharable Content Object Reference Model (SCORM™), Version 1.2.* Scorm White Paper, February 15, 2002. http://www.adlnet.org.

Schulmeister, Rolf, 2001. *Virtuelle Universität - Virtuelles Lernen.* De Gruyter Oldenbourg, München.

Steininger, Peter; Zülch, Gert, 2003. *Editing and Visualization of NC-Code in an E-Learning Project.* In: C# and .NET Technologies for Graphics, Visualization and Computer Vision. Hrsg.: Skala, V. Pilsen, Czech Republic: Union Agency – Science Press, (CD-ROM).

Wissenschaftskommision, 2008. Gesamtkonzept für die Informationsinfrastruktur in Deutschland. Berlin.

INTERCULTURAL SENSIBILITY IN ONLINE TEACHING AND LEARNING PROCESSES

Eulalia Torras[1] and Andreu Bellot[2]
[1]*OBS Business School*
[2]*UNIBA*

ABSTRACT

Attention to cultural diversity is a necessity for online higher education in management. Beamer (2004) postulated the Model of Intercultural Sensitivity to conceptualize the intercultural competence dimensions that can develop. The Complementary, Intercultural Learning Model (Beamer, 2016) emphasizes the importance that students are able to encode and decode the differences in messages emitted by people of various cultures. The aim of this research is to analyze the verbalization of intercultural content of online students participation and their learning products for an online masters in human resources direction. The content of participation and the learning products of 108 participants based on the system of categories proposed by the Model of Intercultural Sensitivity and enriched by Intercultural Learning Model has been analyzed. The most frequent category found is adaptation, so cultural difference is the state in which the experience of another culture yields perception and encourages behavior appropriate to that culture.

KEYWORDS

Online Teaching and Learning, Higher Education, Management, Intercultural, Higher Education Institutions, Content Analysis

1. INTRODUCTION

As Zhu, Handford and Johnstone Young (2016) noticed, culture and interculturality is framed in online promotional discourse at higher education programs. "*There have been paradigm shifts and theoretical debates within the field of study of intercultural communication with regard to what culture is*" (Zhu, Handford and Johnstone, 2016, p. 3). Interculturality is used as an umbrella term covering a plethora of terms referring to, for example, cultural diversity, cultural differences, hybridity, cultural identity and even multiculturalism: a term which has a distinct connotation. Nonetheless, two theoretical frameworks stand out for their acceptance of the analysis of interculturality.

Bennett (1986, 1993, 2016) and Bennett and Bennett (2003, 2004) highlight the importance of being more interculturally competent. Move from ethnocentrism to ethnorelativism seems to be very relevant for intercultural competence and the major change in the quality of the cultural experience. Bennett (2004) postulated a framework for conceptualizing dimensions of intercultural competence in his Development Model of Intercultural Sensitivity (DMIS). The DMIS constitutes a progression of worldview with orientations toward cultural difference that understand the potential of increasingly more cross-culturally complete experiences. Three ethnocentric orientations, where culture is a central experience in reality (denial, defense, minimization) and three ethnorelatives orientations, where culture is considered an experience (acceptance, adaptation and integration) are postulated.

The Intercultural Learning Model (Beamer, 1992, 2004) emphasizes the importance that participants are able to encode and decode the differences in messages emitted by people of different cultures. The model proposes spiral learning, which is characterized by the ability of students to go deeper into cultural differences. Building knowledge from this model involves engaging repeatedly with the same issues to structure increasingly complex mental representations (Abdallah-Pretceille, 2001; Bernal, 2003; Blignault & Ritchie, 2009; Boksberger & Melsen, 2011). The assimilation and accommodation of new concepts is part of this learning process. The construction of new meanings around diverse cultures appears fundamental (Hofstede, 1984; Koschman, Hall & Miyake, 2002; Koschman, Suthers& Chan, 2005; Juwah, 2006;

Garrison& Arbaugh, 2007; Kanuka, 2011). This construction implies that students are competent to generate other cultural messages, analyze communication, challenge stereotypes, pose questions and understand diversity. Cultural values and practices influence business communication. Beamer (2004) analyzes the relationships among the cultural environments of firms and the structure of these firms. He examines how companies and individuals communicate and concentrates on the underlying cultural reasons for behaviour.

Complementarily, Hofstede (1984, 2005) proposes four dimensions to simplify the analysis of the intercultural fact. These dimensions have been commonly used in analysis from a management perspective. Every person carries within him or herself patterns of thinking, feeling, and potential ways of acting that were learned throughout their lifetime. "Culture consists of the unwritten rules of the social game. It is the collective programming of the mind that distinguishes members of a group or category from people of others." (Hofstede, 1984, p.3). The first of these dimensions is the power distance index. The power distance index measures the degree of inequality in society: power distance can be defined as the extent to which the less powerful members of institutions and organizations within a country expect and accept that. Secondly, individualism and collectivism, which measure the degree of individualism in society: individualism pertains to societies in which the ties between individuals are loose; while collectivism, as its opposite, pertains to societies in which people from birth onward are integrated into strong and cohesive in-groups, which throughout people's lifetimes continue to protect them in exchange for unquestioning loyalty. Thirdly, role stereotypes, which highlight key differences between feminine and masculine societies and general norms and family. Finally, the uncertainty avoidance, the extent to which the members of a culture feel threatened by ambiguous or unknown situations (Torras and Mayordomo, 2011; Mok, 2015; Piyush, Jackie, Tamand Kim, 2015; Porto and Byram, 2015;Prats, 2007). The aim of this research is to analyze the verbalization of intercultural content in the online students' participation and in their learning products for an online masters in human resources direction. According to the theoretical model described, this research focuses on the analysis of behaviors that students display in an online learning environment in relation to their intercultural sensibility. The objectives of this study are to describe:

1. The intercultural sensibility verbalizations, that is, the behaviors that students exhibit in online learning environments according to ethnocentrism and ethnorelativism positions.

2. The intercultural sensibility verbalizations of the students that increases functionality and adjusts to the educational content.

2. METHODOLOGY

2.1 Procedure

The nature of the aim leads us to use a qualitative methodology based on observations. This methodological option has been selected because the subject of the study involves attitudes for which experimental manipulation and strict control is difficult for various theoretical reasons. We needed to consider attitudes in their context, and this process required a limited period. We needed to obtain data on the interaction between participants. Finally, this complex process was too lengthy to be reduced to a mere set of variables. The units of analysis were related to the categories of previously established dimensions, in accordance with the level of analysis proposed. An online masters course was analyzed. In the context of an e-learning platform, Blackboard, used by 108 students, we observed the teaching–learning processes of four learning activities that corresponded to one subject in online higher education. This course involved an online learning environment activity. Learning activities were selected based on two criteria. The first criterion consisted of choosing types of activities that included knowledge socialization (conversation forum, debate forum, team work, and individual work): these types of activities are found frequently in electronic learning environments based on asynchronous written communication.

2.2 Participants

The contributions and learning products of 108 participants, 82 women and 26 men, from OBS Business School's online masters in human resources direction have been analyzed. All the students participate online. The students featured are from Spain (26.68%), Colombia (21.6%), Ecuador (34.56%), Mexico (7.56%),

Peru (5.4), El Salvador (1.08%), Nicaragua (1.08%), Argentina (2.16%), Equatorial Guinea (1.08%), Albania (1.08%), Bolivia (1.08%) and Uruguay (1.08%). The participants are students enrolled in the subject: the new role of the human resources director. This subject reflects on the role that a HR Director should play at companies in the future and moves towards a new vision of the human resources management role. This new role implies the director as the strategic partner, promoter of organizational transformations, discoverer of talent and facilitator of effective competency trainings. The didactic sequence analyzed involves a month of student work.

2.3 Analysis

This analysis will focus on the methodology of analyzing online interaction. As dialogue and interaction are seen as important drivers of interculturality, researchers often want to analyze the interactive processes. Thus, a holistic approach is needed, allowing researchers to analyze the whole process of interaction and online discussion (Gee and Handford, 2012; Glaser and Strauss, 2012; Ravithand Mittenfelner, 2016).

The course will take quantitative content analysis of transcripts of asynchronous discussions (discussion boards/for a) as a starting point: data which could open up the discussion of content analyses of other types of interaction (online wiki work, interaction in video data, etc.) will be analyzed. The main purpose of this analysis is to provide categories of how to analyze student-student interactions and products in order to make evidence denial, defense, minimization, acceptance, adaptation, integration, power distance, individualism-collectivism, role stereotypes and ambiguous or unknown situations. The content analysis was carried out in a total of 314 verbalizations and 108 learning products. A four-phase procedure was established:

Phase 1 consisted of captured data: copied from boards, saved as text files, and ordered chronologically. This data corresponded to 1 teacher and 108 students, (electronic messages, students' and teachers' documents), during the time they carried out the activities being considered.

Phase 2 consisted of developing the intercultural sensibility protocol for observational methodology. The protocol is a document that collects the results of discussion between researchers around the theoretical integration of Zhu, Handford and Johnstone Young (2016), Bennett (1986, 1992, 1993, 2014, 2016), Bennett & Bennett (2003, 2004) and Hofstede (1984, 2005). The protocol defines, characterizes and exemplifies intercultural sensibility based on references. The development of the protocol involved two researchers. This phase was critical to ensure rigor in data analysis.

Phase 3consisted of establishing a procedure for inter-observer reliability based on the Cohenk index. Researchers worked in pairs to guarantee the precision of the observation protocol, which we considered to be very important in relation to the research objectives. Reliability was calculated by fragments and by the dimensions and obtained adequate results: activity one's fragments' Cohen k index¼1.00; activity one's dimensions' Cohen k index¼1.00; activity two's fragments' Cohen k index¼1.00; activity two's dimensions' Cohen k index¼1.00; activity three's fragments' Cohen k index¼0.85; activity three's dimensions' Cohen k index¼0.89; and activity four's fragments' Cohen k index¼0.79; activity four's dimensions' Cohen kindex¼0.78.

Phase 4 consisted of the implementation of intercultural sensibility protocol. The deployment meant that researchers shared criteria of fragmentation, concept, characteristics, and examples set in two protocols. The text fragments emerged codified into dimensions and factors. Finally, we obtained frequencies for each of the dimensions and factors.

From these frequencies, percentages were calculated to find the proportion of each size and frequency over the total. Therefore, despite using the qualitative methodology, the final results are presented as frequencies and percentages. The complexity of the procedure was aimed at ensuring the methodological rigor of the investigation.

2.4 Results

The results show that ethnorelativism values have been verbalized in 12% of student contributions. The category that appears most in the verbalization of the participants is integration (51%) followed by adaptation (40%) and acceptance (9%).

Table 1. Categories development of cultural sensitivity

Cultural sensitivity	Definition	Percentage
Denial	The verbalizations of the participants demonstrate the lack of positive aspects in forming groups with participants of different nationalities. The importance of interculturalism is disdained and therefore it is not considered necessary to develop cultural sensitivity.	0%
Defense	Participants activate the protection mechanism verbalizing reasons or motives to distort the contribution of peers. The participants act in defense of their own person, group or institution considering that there is risk with the participation of people from other countries.	0%
Minimization	The verbalizations evidenced a reduction of the importance of the contributions of the participants related to their belonging to another culture. Also included in this category are reducing the number of significant contributions in this regard.	0%
Acceptance	Interculturality is qualified as positive and adequate. It includes verbalizations in which the participant clearly expresses an opinion in favor of cultural diversity.	9%
Adaptation	The verbalizations show accommodation or adjustment to the companions of other nationalities. The adjustment is adequate and works for the benefit of the teaching-learning process.	40%
Integration	There are elements that show the approach of the participants and their configuration as a cohesive working group.	51%

3. CONCLUSION

The results show that awareness of cultural differences and willingness to integrate participants from other cultures emerges in online education. In spite of this, it is necessary that the institutions of online higher education promote interculturality to reach levels closer to cultural integration. Even in the contents in which cultural sensitivity is necessary for understanding, interculturality does not appear unless it is approached explicitly in the classrooms. At the era of global information, ethnorelativism values are relevant for the understanding of the manager's work.

ACKNOWLEDGEMENT

This paper has been written in the framework of the research supported financially by OBServatory. International Observatory on Online Higher Education in Management by OBS Business School.

REFERENCES

Abdallah-Pretceille, M., 2001. *La educación intercultural*. Barcelona, Idea Books

Arbaugh, J.B., Dearmond, S. and Rau, B. L., 2013. New Uses for Existing Tools? A Call to Study On-line Management Instruction and Instructors. *Academy of Management Learning & Education*, Vol. 12, 4, pp. 635–655. http://dx.doi.org/10.5465/amle.2011.0018A

Ayuste, A. Escofet, A., Obiols, N. and Masgrau, M., 2016. Aprendizaje-servicio y codiseño en la formación de maestros: Vías de integración de las experiencias y perspectivas de los estudiantes. *Bordón. Revista de pedagogía*, Vol. 68, 2, pp. 169-183.

Beamer, L., 1992. Learning Intercultural Communication Competence. *The Journal of Business Communication*, Vol. 29(3), 285-303.

Beamer, L., 2004. *Intercultural Communication in the Global Workplace*. New York, McGraw Hill Higher Education.

Bennett, M. J., 2004. Becoming interculturally competent. In J.S. Wurzel (Ed.) *Toward multiculturalism: A reader in multicultural education*. Newton, MA: Intercultural Resource Corporation. (Originally published in The diversity symposium proceedings: An interim step toward a conceptual framework for the practice of diversity. Waltham, MA: Bentley College, 2004). Additional information at www.idrinstitute.org

Bernal, A., 2003. La educación entre la multiculturalidad y la interculturalidad. *ESE*, Vol. 4, pp. 85-100.

Blignault, I. and Ritchie, J., 2009. Revealing the wood and the trees: reporting qualitative research. *Health Promotion Journal of Australia*, Vol. 20, 2, pp. 140-145.

Boksberger, P. E. and Melsen. L., 2011. Perceived value: A critical examination of definitions, concepts and measures for the service industry. *Journal of Services Marketing*, Vol. 35(3), pp. 229-240.

Briones, E. y Lara, L., 2016. Educación ética en la Universidad a través del diálogo multicultural online. *Comunicar*, Vol. 47, XXIV, pp. 99-107.

Consejo de Europa. Libro Blanco sobre el Diálogo Intercultural, 2009. *Vivir juntos con igual dignidad*. Estrasburgo, Ministros de Asuntos Exteriores del Consejo de Europa en su 118ª Sesión Ministerial

Fraser, J. W., 2016. Debating teacher education in the united states universities and their critics. *Bordón. Revista de pedagogía*, Vol. 68, 2, pp. 35-49.

Gallarza, M. G., Gil-Saura, I. and Holbrook, M. B., 2011. The value of value: Further excursions on the meaning and role of customer value. *Journal of Consumer Behaviour*, Vol. 10(4), pp. 179-191.

Garrison, A. and Arbaugh, J. B., 2007. Researching the community of inquiry framework: Review, issues, and future directions. *Internet and Higher Education*, Vol. 10, pp. 157–172.

Gee, J. P. and Handford, M., 2012. *Handbook of Discourse Analysis*. London, Routledge.

Glaser, B. G. and Strauss, A. L., 2012. *The Discovery of Grounded Theory: Strategies for Qualitative Research*. New York, Seventh paperback printing.

Hammera, M. R., Milton, J. Bennett, J and Wiseman, R., 2016. Measuring intercultural sensitivity: The intercultural development inventory. *International Journal of Intercultural Relations*, Vol. 27, pp. 421–443.

Hofstede, G., 1984. Cultural dimensions in management and planning. *Asia Pacific Journal of Management*, Vol.1, 81. DOI:10.1007/BF01733682

Juwah, C., 2006.*Interactions in online education: Implications for theory and practice*. New York, Lawrence Erlbaum.

Kanuka, H., 2011. Interaction and the online distance classroom: Do instructional methods effect the quality of interaction? *Journal of Computing in Higher Education*, Vol. 23, pp. 143-156

Koschman, T. D., Hall, R. and Miyake, N., 2002.*CSCL 2, carrying forward the conversation*. New Jersey, Lawrence Erlbaum Associates.

Koschman, T. D., Suthers, D. D. and Chan, T. W., 2005. Computer supported collaborative learning 2005: the next 10 years! *Proceedings of the International Conference on Computer Supported Collaborative Learning 2005*, Taipei, May 30-June 4.

Lavonen, J., 2016. Educating professional teachers through the master's level teacher education programme in Finland. *Bordón. Revista de pedagogía*, Vol. 68 (2), pp. 51-68.

Mok, J., 2015. A case study of developing student-teachers' language awareness through online discussion forums. *Language Awareness*, Vol. 22 (2), pp. 161–175.

Onrubia, J., 2005. Aprender y enseñar en entornos virtuales: actividad conjunta, ayuda pedagógica y construcción del conocimiento. *RED. Revista de Educación a Distancia*, Número monográfico II.

Piyush, S., Jackie, S., Tam, L. M. and Kim, N., 2015. Service role and outcome as moderators intercultural service encounters. *Journal of Service Management*, vol. 26 (1), pp. 137 - 155. http://dx.doi.org/10.1108/JOSM-03-2013-0062

Porto, M. and Byram, M., 2015. A curriculum for action in the community and intercultural citizenship in higher education. *Language, Culture and Curriculum*, vol. 28, 3, pp.226-242. DOI: 10.1080/07908318.2015.1087555

Prats, E., 2007. Multiculturalismo y educación para la equidad. *Colección Educación en Valores, Octaedro-OEI*, vol. septiembre, pp. 166.

Ramilevna Kayumova, A. and Vasilevna Sadykova, G., 2016. Online collaborative cross-cultural learning: students' perspectives. *Journal of Organizational Culture, Communications & Conflict*, Special Issue, Vol. 20, pp. 248-256.

Ravith, S. and Mittenfelner, M., 2016. *Qualitative Research: Bridging the Conceptual, Theoretical, and Methodological*. New York, SAGE.

Suanet, I. and van de Vijver, F.J.R., 2009. Perceived cultural distance and acculturation among exchange students in Russia. *Journal of Community & Applied Social Psychology*, Vol. 19(3), pp. 182-197.

Thompson, D. L. and Thompson, M. J., 2014. Knowledge, instruction and behavioural change: building a framework for effective eczema education in clinical practice. *Journal of Advanced Nursing*, Vol. 70 (11), pp. 2483–2494.

Topping, K. E., Smith, F., Swanson, I. and Elliot, A., 2000. Formative peer assessment of academic written between postgraduate students. *Assessment & Evaluation in Higher Education*, Vol. 25(2), pp. 149-169.

Torras, E and Mayordomo, R., 2011. Teaching presence and regulation in an electronic portfolio. *Computers in Human Behavior*, Vol. 27, pp. 2284–2291.

Van Merrienboer, J. G. and Kirschner, P. A., 2007. *Ten steps to complex learning: A systematic approach to four-component instructional design*. New Jersey, Lawrence Erlbaum Associates.

Watt, C., Angelis, J. and Chapman, D., 2012. Customer value and lean operations in masters education. *Proceedings of the 14th International Conference on Engineering and Product Design Education: Design Education for Future Wellbeing. EPDE 2012*, pp. 699-704.

Zhu, H., Handford, M. and Johnstone Young, T., 2016. Framing interculturality: a corpus-based analysis of online promotional discourse of higher education intercultural communication courses. *Journal of Multilingual and Multicultural Development,*pp. 1-18. DOI: 10.1080/01434632.2015.1134555

MOBILE LEARNING ON THE BASIS OF THE CLOUD SERVICES

Tatyana Makarchuk
Saint-Petersburg state university of economics, 21, Sadovaya street, 191023 St. Petersburg, Russian Federation

ABSTRACT

Spreading of interactive applications for mobile devices became one of the trends of IT development in 2015-2017. In higher education mobile applications are being used to advance the productivity of professors and students, which raises the overall quality of education. In the article SkyDrive, GoogleDisk mobile applications' features for group academic activities with the help of mobile devices are described. Integration technology of cloud services and education management system is described. The article includes an example of educational content management system building in frames of master's semester (September-December 2016).

KEYWORDS

mobile learning, learning management systems

1. INTRODUCTION

Wide spreading of interactive applications for mobile devices became one of the trends of IT development in 2015-2017, which is proved by Gartner, Inc. analytical data (Rivera, 2015). Such trend finds its reflection in educational process management of professional education as mobile learning that is becoming popular nowadays (Stefan, et al, 2005; Makarchuk, 2013). One of the features of mobile learning are classes with the application of interactive methods with the quota of 10-20% of all the classes (Makarchuk, et al, 2014). All higher education institutions included in the academic rating of world universities, pay specific attention to the development of interactive methods and teaching environment (Stevens and Kitchenham, 2011).

Recently, the rising of Web 2.0, the online knowledge-sharing community formed by interpersonal interaction is now a major character of mobile learning (Huang, et al, 2010). According to annual «Mobile World Congress» 2015, 2016 (URL: www.mobileworldcongress.com) among the manufacturers of mobile devices emerged a trend of mobile devices and technologies prices' reduction for «democratization» of access to them given the fact that they are in high demand in the sphere of mobile learning.

Delivery options for mobile learning are increasing, however new technologies alone will not improve the experience of mobile learners. Learning content must be adapted to meet the unique and personal needs of that learner within their current context (Al-Hmouz and Freeman, 2010).

2. ACTIVE LINKS CREATION TECHNIQUE IN THE SYSTEM OF MOBILE LEARNING MANAGEMENT ON THE BASIS OF PERSONAL CLOUD

Learning management system (LMS) is one of the main instruments of mobile learning (Cashell, 2011). LMS is a cross platform, web-oriented environment accessible from mobile devices with multi language support. Traditional approach to the work with LMS includes data storage on the program server, which creates difficulties with learning content editing. Thus, the process of editing means the execution of a certain chain of actions. You need to download the document from the server; save it on the computer; edit it; upload a new version of the document to the LMS server; delete the old link; add new link to the new version of the document. From the side of a student file editing is even more complicated process as quite often professor's actions are needed in order to delete old version of the task and upload the new one. In learning process when joint work of professor and students (200+) is in action, repeating of redundant actions leads to students' and professors' time losses. Creation of active links to the learning content on the basis of personal cloud of every participant of the learning process with the uploading of the link to the LMS reduces time in the management of the learning content. Integration of the cloud services with the LMS facilitates publishing and management of the content developed and saved in different software environments and data storage systems.

3. TECHNOLOGY OF OPERATION IN LMS ON THE BASIS OF THE CLOUD SERVICES

Learning Management System (LMS) is high-level strategic decision for planning, conduction and management of the studying course (Mtebe, 2011). In the work (Birkenkrahe, et al, 2012) mentions that the content published in LMS has to comply with the principles of Web 2.0:

interactivity - filling of content with visual elements like graphics, animation, video clips, 3D models etc.;

openness - availability of the content to the big amount of users regardless of the organization it belongs to;

community - open exchange of opinions according to the focus of the course;

Control in the process of the work with educational content.

There is a decent amount of LMS-platforms ready for usage which are published on the web-servers, multilingually supported and possess its own data bases.

Nowadays there exist three options of learning management system acquisition by the organizations:

-LMS are developed by the organizations themselves;

-LMS is purchased as a platform which is adjusted and published on the server of the organization;

-LMS is spread by subscription by the model Software as a service on the basis of cloud services.

Development of the LMS by the organization is a laborious and long-term process and today represents unpopular decision.

Among LMS-platforms published on the server of the organization Open Source software is one of the popular ones. It is open for view, usage, analysis and editing. These LMS-platforms include:

-LMS eFont (www.)

- LMS Moodle
- LMS Blackboard Learn

Nowadays LMS spread by subscription are getting more popular. Among the leading developers of cloud-based learning management software are:

- Docebo LMS (//www.docebo.com/)
- Litmos LMS (www.litmos.com/)
- Torch LMS (torchlms.com/)
- Mirapolis (mirapolis.ru)

Analysis of the popular LMS-platforms conducted by the authors does not contradict the conclusions from Centre for Learning & Performance Technologies in 2009-2103 (Hart, 2016.).

In the frames of «IT in management» course for the training of the bachelors of economics the authors chose LMS Moodle published on the server of the university. This option was chosen because of several reasons: friendly interface, variety of management elements, open source product etc. Cloud LMS option was not possible because of the subscription fee for 250 students. As cloud SaaS-services of mobile learning support were used applications developed by Google, Microsoft, Youtube etc. which provide variety of possibilities for the work with learning content including interactive access, storage, preview and editing services and organization of the general access to them.

In order to create folders with general access to the documents with the opportunity of collaborative editing the professor provided students with his/her e-mail and the name of the cloud service which is recommended for the future operation. Students' personal clouds were created in Onedrive, Microsoft. With the help of Office Web Apps it is possible to preview and edit Office documents in web-browser with

Internet access. Performance capabilities of Onedrive can be enlarged in case of the operation with Microsoft Office applications package, which was available for students and professors in terms of A2 plan for educational institutions for free.

As a result, of LMS building on the basis of cloud services it was possible to solve following tasks:

-creation of educational groups with the name of address like @groups.live.com;

-organization of the calendar with academic tasks with the possibility of automatic notification of the group about the tasks and its completion;

-discussion of specific lectures with the help of OneNote Web Apps;

-Collaborative editing of the document by several members of the group (the best results were achieved in the process of collaborative tasks completion, as file exchange was not needed for the discussion of the results between members of the groups and professors);

-Learning materials publishing with an opportunity of its update in the current file (additions; comments to the specific elements; inaccuracies editing);

-distribution of tasks and its completion reports in case of the absence of the student for a reasonable excuse, except for the tests, with the help of services accessible 24/7 from any location and mobile devices;

-Monitoring of educational tasks completion during the semester.

Figure 1 shows the elements of interactive methods of learning available with LMS Moodle on the basis of Ondrive, DropBox, Youtube cloud services.

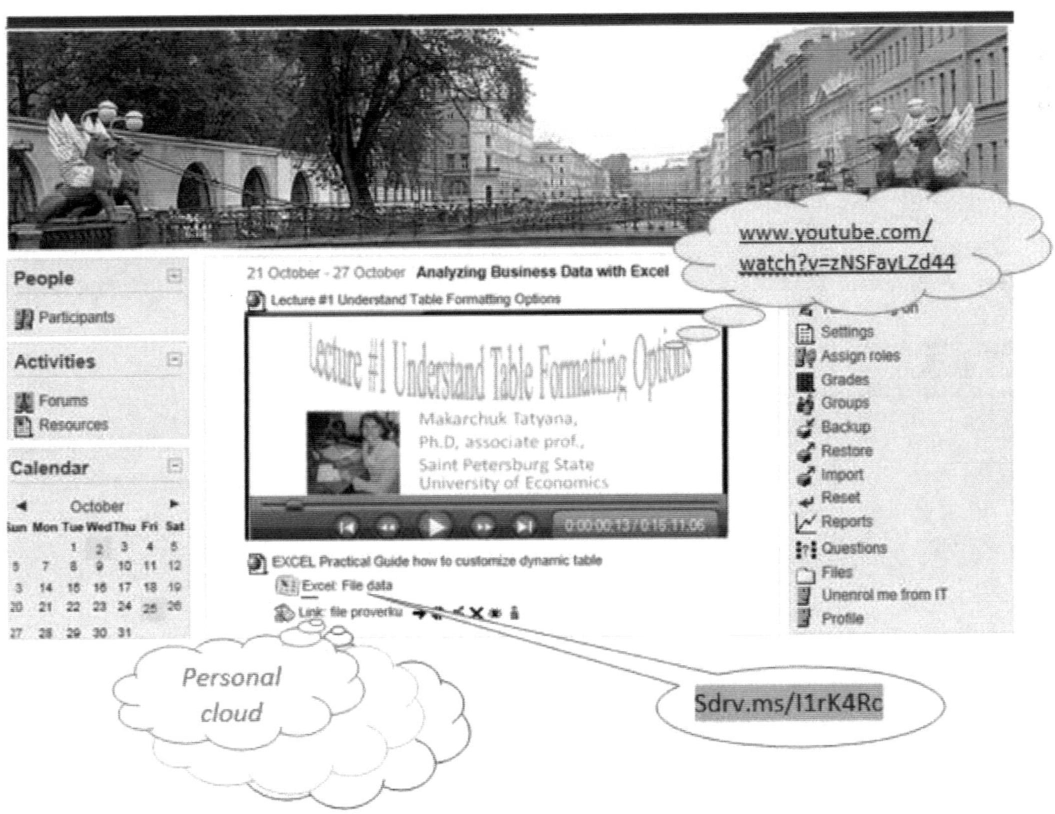

Figure 1. Scheme of interaction of LMS and personal clouds accessible from mobile devices

Mobile learning organization on the basis of cloud services allowed to make educational content active, up-to-date and accessible; to raise the quality of education and to minimize costs of professors.

4. CONCLUSIONS

The article describes a new way to form educational content, which is edited and stored outside of the LMS. Composed and published in different environments, the content becomes «active». Changes in the informational resource are shown automatically in the LMS virtual environment. Thus, the biggest part of professor's and student's activities is conducted in mobile applications with the results of these activities available to the course students on active links in LMS.

REFERENCES

Al-Hmouz, A. and Freeman, A., 2010. Learning on location: an adaptive mobile learning content framework. *Proceedings of IEEE International Symposium on Technology and Society: Social Implications of Emerging Technologies, ISTAS'10*. Wollongong, Australia, pp. 450-456.

Birkenkrahe, M. et al, 2012. UNIVERSITY 2.0. *Proceeding of IADIS International conference on computer science and information systems*. Madrid, Spain, pp. 505-509.

Cashell, P., 2011. Rankings and the Reshaping of Higher Education: The Battle for World-Class Excellence. *In Tertiary Education and Management*, Vol.17, No 4, pp. 373-375.

Hart, J., 2016. *Modern Workplace Learning*. Centre for Learning & Performants Technologies Publishers, USA.

Huang, J. et al, 2010. Social learning networks: build mobile learning networks based on collaborative services. *In Educational technology and society*, Vol. 13, No 3, pp. 78-92.

Makarchuk, T. et al, 2013. Mobile learning based on cloud services. *In Modern problems of science and education*, Vol 2, No 46, pp. 319.

Makarchuk, T., 2014. Mobile applications for interactive teaching methods. *Proceedings Information technologies in business*. Saint-Petersburg, Russia.

Mtebe, J., 2011. *Strategies for managing virtual learning environment*. Lambert Academic Publishing, Saarbrücken, Germany.

Rivera, J., 2015. Gartner Identifies the Top 10 Strategic Technology Trends for 2015. *Proceedings of Gartner Symposium ITxpo 2014*. Orlando, USA.

Stefan, R. et al, 2005. *Mobile IP Technology and Applications*. Cisco Press, Indianapolis, USA.

Stevens, D. and Kitchenham, A., 2011. *An analysis of mobile learning in education, business and medicine*. IGI Global Publishers, Hershey, USA.

PERSONALIZATION OF LEARNING ACTIVITIES WITHIN A VIRTUAL ENVIRONMENT FOR TRAINING BASED ON FUZZY LOGIC THEORY

Fahim Mohamed, Jakimi Abdeslam and El Bermi Lahcen
Software Engineering & Information Systems, Engineering Team, Computer Sciences Department, Moulay Ismaïl University, FST Errachidia, Morocco

ABSTRACT

Virtual Environments for Training (VET) are useful tools for visualization, discovery as well as for training. VETs are based on virtual reality technique to put learners in training situations that emulate genuine situations. VETs have proven to be advantageous in putting learners into varied training situations to acquire knowledge and competencies, especially when these situations are taking place in uncontrolled circumstances, or when they are dangerous, unrealizable, or expensive to establish in reality. However individual learners find it difficult to select suitable activities for their particular situations because there is no personalized service to respond to the user needs. The solution is to generate learning activities based on learner's profile. Yet, a learner's profile may contain uncertain data (such as the desired level of difficulty, etc). This paper presents an attempt to introduce the concepts of fuzzy set theory the design of an online educational module. Such a module can deal with uncertainties in the knowledge acquisition, representation and decision making. The fuzzy logic principles are used to create the learner profile and to provide the appropriate learning activities to each learner according to his/her profile.

KEYWORDS

Virtual Environments for Training, learning activities, fuzzy logic

1. INTRODUCTION

Some learning contexts have such a complexity that classical trainings cannot prepare trainees to handle every kind of situation they might face. VETs have proven to be a very useful alternative to deal with complex, dangerous and expensive or just sometimes unrealizable situations. VETs are also used to promote trial and error as an effective strategy for learning. A VET can be defined as a computer-supported environments for human learning (CSEHL) which; applies virtual reality technologies in order to immerse learners in a virtual environment enabling them to learn by doing (Nicolas, 2010). Virtual reality (VR) is a scientific and technical field that applies computer science and behavioral interfaces in order to simulate in a virtual world the behavior of 3D entities which interact in real time with each other and with a user (or users) in pseudo-natural immersion (Fuchs and Moreau, 2006).

Learning in open environments like a VET, demands even more personalization approaches to provide learners with individualized learning activities in order to assure the quality of learning. A learning activity contains several features of information necessary to achieve the objective of training, such as content description, lecture information, prerequisite information and so on. In a VET, the excellence of learners can be improved by recommending suitable learning activities (personalization), based on each learner's profile. Personalization of learning activities (PLA) relies on the fact that the learning ability of each individual can depend on several factors such as age, gender, duration of training, personal preferences, content of the material etc. However PLA is an issue with the uncertainty and imprecision of data that may contain a learner's profile. This paper is an attempt to integrate the fuzzy logic theory into the process of the personalization of learning activities is presented.

The general architecture of the approach in question consists of three fundamental elements namely, *Fuzzifier*, *Inference engine* and the *fuzzy rule base*. In the following, we first present the related works to the personalization of learning activities (adaptation). Then, we present our methodology. Finally, we conclude and reflect on the future of the present work.

2. RELATED WORK

The learning ability of each individual can depend on several factors such as: age, gender, etc. The question of adapting to different learning activities is one of the main interests of current research about E-learning in general. The goal is to associate suitable learning activities, pedagogical resources, for instance, to each learner based on his/her profile. A profile may include information such as: learner 's knowledge level, as well as the desired difficulty level. To allow this personalization of learning, many solutions have been suggested. Current methods for personalization of learning can be divided into three groups: (i) oriented activities approaches (Naji and Ramdani, 2013) : where the learning process is represented by a graph in which the activities are identified and decomposed. (ii) oriented resources approaches (Karampiperis and Sampson, 2006; De-Marcos et al, 2008; Valigiani et al, 2007): in which case the learning process returns to select, assemble and present contents, (iii) oriented objectives approaches (Bouhdidi et al, 2013; Talhi et al, 2007): the learning process is seen as a process of satisfaction of pedagogical objectives already defined. These approaches use a set of algorithms and techniques from Artificial Intelligence and Web Semantics such as ant colony optimization (Kardan et al, 2014; Kumar et al, 2007; Pushpa, 2012; Valigian, 2007) Bayesian networks (Bouhdidi et al, 2013) the algorithm of Support Vector Machines (SVM) (Ouraiba, 2009), ontologies (Ghailani et al, 2014), to name a few. However, these methods are quite limited in term of handling uncertain and inacurate data.

3. FUZZY LOGIC THEORY

The human brain can deal with imprecise concepts. For instance, to answer a question about a hotel services, most answers could be likely "Not Very Satisfied" or "Quite Satisfied", which are also fuzzy or ambiguous answers. To what extent exactly is one satisfied or dissatisfied with some hotel services? These vague answers can only be created and implemented by human beings, but not machines. so, how can computers and machines handle those vague data?. Based on this observation, Lotfi A. Zadeh (Zadeh, 1965; Zadeh, 1975) developed fuzzy set theory that generalizes classical set theory to allow the notion of partial membership. This invention was not well recognized until Dr. E. H. Mamdani, who is a professor at London University, applied the fuzzy logic in a practical application to control an automatic steam engine in 1974(Mamdani, and Assilion, 1974). The use of fuzzy logic allows working with quantitative and qualitative descriptions. In the fuzzy set theory, an element can belong entirely to a set (degree of belonging is 1), or "almost" belong to it (with a degree of belonging equal to, say, 0.9). Fuzzy logic has been successfully employed in a variety of applications in recent years (Lin et al, 2006; Lin et al, 2006; Wallace et al, 2006). Let consider, μ_A the membership function of the set A, U a reference, in the classical set theory:

$$\forall x \in U,\ \mu_A(x) = 0 \text{ if } x \notin A$$
$$\mu_A(x) = 1 \text{ if } x \in A$$

In the context of fuzzy set theory, a fuzzy set A of U is characterized by a membership function μA defined by:

$$\mu_A : U \rightarrow [0.1]$$
$$x \rightarrow \mu_A(x)$$

μ_A : Associates to each object x of U a value in the interval [0,1] which represents the degree of membership of x to A.

There is many application of fuzzy logic and fuzzy sets : Fuzzy Inference Systems(FIS), Fuzzy Decision Trees(FDT), etc. We have chosen FIS, because it seems to be the most suitable for our approach of personalization of learning activities.

4. PROPOSAL

The architecture of the system we are developing is shown in the figure 1. The first step in the task of our system is to collect user's data to build a learner profile. Information which form a learner profile are the following:

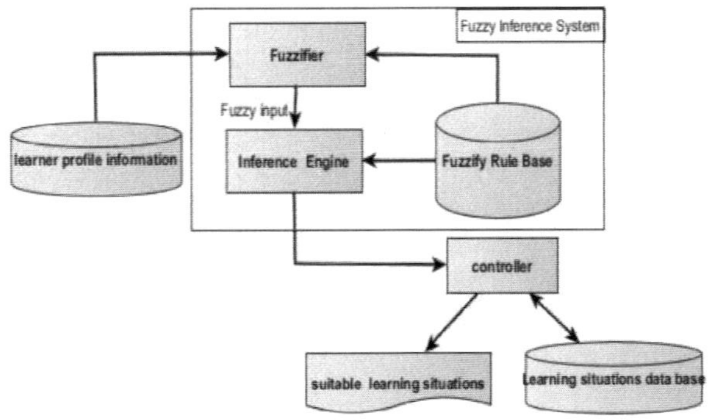

Figure 1. Overview of our approach

-Learning session duration
-Gender
-Level of difficulty
-Desired language
-Current knowledge level
-Age

The second step is fuzzification which involves a domain transformation where crisp inputs are transformed into fuzzy inputs. To do this, the fuzzy system designer must create membership functions. A membership function is a function that defines the degree of membership of a numerical data to a linguistic variable. Depending on their shapes, membership functions can take different form of representations, the most commonly used membership functions in fuzzification processes are Trapezoidal, Triangular, Bell curves, Gaussian and Sigmoid membership functions. The figure 2 comprises of half left trapezoidal, two triangular and half right trapezoidal functions.

To more understand the fuzzification step, let's take for example a mark obtained by a leaner after passing a test. That mark will reflect for instance his/her current knowledge level. We want to transform this numerical data into a linguistic variable. We can find several linguistic variables qualifying a mark: "weak", "average", "good", and "very good". In the figure 2, if we take a mark as equal to 17, after fuzzification, the grade will be good at 30%, very good at 70 %, weak at 0%, and average at 0%.

Now that we have linguistic variables, we will be able to pass them into the inference engine, which is the kernel of decision making process. Each rule of the inference engine is written by the fuzzy system designer according to the knowledge it possesses. The first thing to do for this second part is to list all the rules that we know and that apply to the system. The fuzzy rule base composed of expert **IF** antecedents **THEN** conclusions rules. These rules transform the input variables (The learner profile information) to an output that will tell us know the suitable learning activity. The following rule is an example of a fuzzy **If-Then** rule:

If (Age is young) And (gender is female) And (Level of difficulty is Medium) And (Current knowledge is Low) And (Learning session duration is Long) Then Learning activities are the "*LA set 3*".

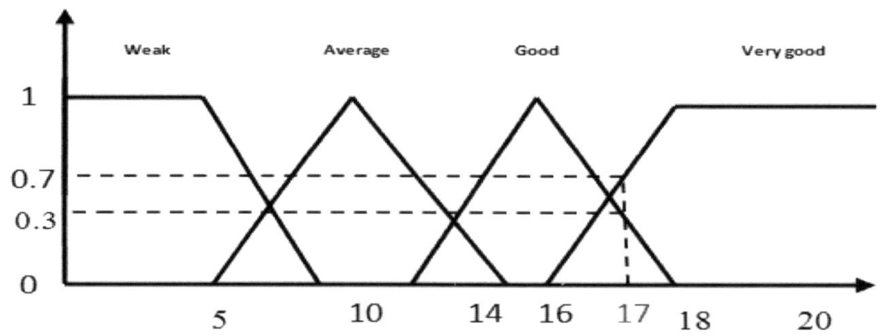

Figure 2. Graphical representation of the linguistic variable "Mark

Finally, the controller, based on the value given by the inference engine, picks up from the " learning activities data base", the suitable learning activities set appropriate for the learner profile of the input.

5. CONCLUSION

This paper has outlined the development of a fuzzy based approach for the generation of learning activities within a virtual environment for training. The main advantage of this proposed methodology is that it is efficient in handling the uncertainty in the learner's profile. The fuzzy inference engine used the fuzzy rule base to generate suitable learning activities for each learner. However, a number of further data, in particular, learner's feedback information is required to promote the functionality of the system. The ongoing work aims at including this proposed approach in our previous (Fahim et al, 2016), in order to generate adaptable and effective pedagogical scenarios for VET.

REFERENCES

A. A. Kardan, M. A. Ebrahim, and M. B. Imani. 2014. A new personalized learning path generation method: Acomap. *Indian Journal Science Research*. 5(1), 17–24.

A. Kumar, J. Nalavade, V. Yeola, V. Vivek, and Y. Srivastava. An adaptive learning system based on ant colony algorithm. *International Journal of Soft Computing and Engineering (IJSCE)*. (2013).

A. Naji and M. Ramdani, 2013. Using the ant colony algorithm to establish the best path of learning activities. *Applied Mathematical Sciences*, 7(78), 3873–3881.

C. T. Lin, K. W. Fan, C. M. Yeh, H. C. Pu, and F.Y. Wu, 2006. High-accuracy skew estimation of document images, *International Journal of Fuzzy Systems*, 8(3), 119–126.

C. T. Lin and C. L. Chin, 2006. Using fuzzy inference and cubic curve to detect and compensate backlight image,*International Journal of Fuzzy Systems,* 8(1), 2–13.

E.-A. Ouraiba, A. Chikh, A. Taleb-Ahmed, and Z. E. Yeb dri. 2009. Automatic personalization of learning scenarios using svm. In : Proc. *International Conference of Advanced Learning Technologies*.

E. H. Mamdani, S. Assilion, 1974. An Experiment in Linguistic Synthesis With a Fuzzy Logic Controller, *Intl J. Man-Machine Stud*. 7, 1–13.

G. Valigiani, E. Lutton, C. Fonlupt, and P. Collet, 2007. Optimisation par hommilire de chemins pdagogiques pour un logiciel d'e-learning. RSTI TSI, 26(10), 1245–1268.

J. E. Bouhdidi, M. Ghailani, and A. Fennan, 2013. An intelligent architecture for generating evolutionary personalized learning paths based on learner profiles. *Journal of Theoretical and Applied Information Technology* (JATIT).57(2), 294–304.

L. A. Zadeh, Fuzzy set, 1965. Information and Control. 8 ,338–353.

L. A. Zadeh, 1975. The concept of a linguistic variable and its application to approximate reasoning, Information Sciences.8, 199–249.

L. De-Marcos, J.-J. Martinez, and J.-A. Gutierrez. 2008. Swarm intelligence in e-learning: a learning object sequencing agent based on competencies. In : Proc. *The 10th annual conference on Genetic and evolutionary computation*. 17–24

M. Ghailani, J. E. Bouhdidi, and A. Fennan.2014. Towards an adaptive e-learning solution based on ontologies and competencies approach. International Journal of Computer Applications, 98(21).

M. Fahim, A. Jakimi and L. El bermi,2016. Pedagogical Scenarization for Virtual Environments for Training: Towards Genericity, Coherence and Adaptivity. *International Journal of Advanced Engineering Research and Science* (IJAERS). 12(3), 96–103.

M. Pushpa. 2012. Aco in e-learning: Towards an adaptive learning path. *International Journal on Computer Science and Engineering (IJCSE)*. 4(3).

M. Wallace, S. Ioannou, K. Karpouzis, and S. Kollias, 2006. Possibilistic rule evaluation: A case study in facial expression analysis, *International Journal of Fuzzy Systems*. 8(4), 219–223.

N. Marion, 2010. Modlisation de scnarios pdagogiques pour les environnements de ralit virtuelle d'apprentissage humain, Phd thesis, universit de Bretagne Occidentale, france.

P. Fuchs And G. Moreau, 2006. Le trait de la ralit virtuelle. Les Presses de lEcole des Mines de Paris.

P. Karampiperis and D. Sampson, 2006. Automatic learning object selection and sequencing in web-based intelligent learning systems. Idea Group Inc..

S. Talhi, M. Djoudi, S. Ouadfel, and S. Zidat. 2007.Un canevas de tuteur intelligent hypermdia pour l'apprentissage distance universitaire. In : Proc. *4th International Conference on Computer Integrated Manufacturing*.

.

PROMOTING BEST PRACTICES IN TEACHING AND LEARNING IN NIGERIAN UNIVERSITIES THROUGH EFFECTIVE E-LEARNING: PROSPECTS AND CHALLENGES

Grace Ifeoma Obuekwe, Ph.D[1] and Rose-Ann Ifeoma Eze, Ph.D[2]
[1]*Department of Adult Education, University of Lagos, Akoka, Lagos, Nigeria*
[2]*Department of Educational Psychology, University of the Western Cape, Cape Town, South-Africa*

ABSTRACT

The importance of e-learning in our educational system as well as the nation's development cannot be over-emphasized. The use of e-learning in impartation and acquisition of knowledge by lecturers and students is becoming a vital tool in meeting the demands of education in the 21st century. The paper is aimed at exploring the prospects and challenges of e-learning towards promoting best practices in university education in Nigeria. It was discovered that effective communication between lecturers and students is enhanced through e-learning which has the potential to make learning to be realized faster and more efficiently than existing learning methods. However, literature revealed that the major challenges to e-learning remain that the various technologies used do not make provision for people who are visually impaired; unavailability of the equipment such as computers, digital technology, and internet for proper utilization due to cost; irregular supply of electricity, lack of both technical and social skills required for the implementation of e-learning. Recommendations made include the development of voice based e-learning applications for the visually impaired faculties and learners; recruitment of indigenous IT professionals for the development of low cost software packages; provision of incentives for private and non-governmental organisations that contribute to e-learning in Nigerian universities; Webinars, drills and workshops that engage participants in the active use of and development of e-learning technologies should be instituted at intervals.

KEYWORDS

E-learning, Multi-media learning, Information Communication Technology (ICT), Audio-visual, Virtual learning, Massive online open courses (MOOCs)

1. INTRODUCTION

The present age is the era of information revolution driven by e-learning. In many countries of the world, different fields of life such as business, travel, banking, entertainment, governance, security have witnessed rapid revolution as a result of the emergence of ICT. It is worthy to note that education is not left out as through ICT, teachers can now access a lot of information which they can transmit to the students. Dames (2001) notes that ICT motivates people to learn; enrich and deepen skills, promote individualised instruction, strengthen teaching by bringing the world into a classroom, relate school experiences to work practices and create economic viability for tomorrow's workers.

With a population of more than 170 million and a literacy rate of 72%, Nigeria has 153 universities, 40 Federal universities, 44 state universities and 69 private owned universities. The total acceptance rate into these universities is about 10% (JAMB, 2016). Few universities in Nigeria employ e-learning effectively in the teaching and learning process. These universities are mostly privately owned, one notable exception of government owned university is National Open University of Nigeria (NOUN).

It is widely accepted that teaching and learning of most courses in the university will be more effective with the use of ICT as it has the capacity to aid the students to construct knowledge by themselves through generating information via internet.

2. BODY OF PAPER

E-learning with the aid of information and communication technology (ICT), has the potential to expose a larger audience to improved learning opportunities. Omofaye (2007) opines that one of the easiest ways of making a nation become a successful economy is by turning such nation into a learning society. For effective impartation and retention of knowledge in learners, there must be a paradigm shift from teacher centeredness to learner centeredness which can be enhanced with the adoption of e-learning.

E-learning simply entails the use of ICT, electronic media and educational technology in education. It is synonymous with some learning platforms such as Internet-Based Training, Web-Based Training, Computer Assisted Instruction, Multimedia learning, Technology Enhanced Learning, Virtual Learning Environment, Virtual Education and M-Learning (Tawangarian, Leypold, and Nolting, 2012; Bates and Poole, 2013). E–learning can take place in and out of classroom. It may be. The pioneer of e-learning, Bernard Luskin interprets "e" outside electronic to mean exciting, enthusiastic, emotional, extended, excellent and educational while Parks (2013) suggested that "e" should refer to "everything, everyone, engaging and easy" in addition to 'electronic'.

E-learning may be instructor led /synchronous learning or self-paced/asynchronous learning. **Synchronous learning** connotes the instructor-led type of learning where there is collaboration and exchange of ideas and knowledge among participants at the same time. It could be in the form of face to face discussion, video conferencing, chat room or virtual classrooms that bring all participants online working collaboratively at the same time in real-time for instruction and feedback (Robinson, 2008; Murali, 2010). **Asynchronous learning** which is self-paced uses e-mail, blogs, wikis, discussion boards, web-supported textbooks, audio, video courses, web networks, hypertext documents (Manprit, 2011). It allows participants to still exchange ideas and information without necessarily involving all participants at the same time. According to Johnson (2007), asynchronous learning affords people the time to complete their work in a less stressed environment and is especially beneficial to students who cannot participate in class activities in real time. Students can access and participate in variety of university courses online while working and still graduate with the class. Such e-learning resources afford students the opportunity to listen to lectures multiple times and reflect on the material without holding back the rest of the class.

2.1 Challenges

E-learning has been met with increased enthusiasm, however it is not without challenges in Nigerian Universities.

I. Due to the fact that the options available for most learning environments are face to face, electronic mail, chat room, instant messaging, students with visual impairments have been left behind due to the lack of an accessible content delivery system to aid their disabilities. Lack of provision for voice in the existing learning methods has excluded support for the visually impaired as no blind person can see or communicate through mail or electronic means that require sight to see the board or computer screen and manipulate the computer keyboard for either data entry. There is paucity of research dedicated to the design and implementation of e-Learning for the disabled. However, some researchers (Azeta *et* al., 2010) from Covenant University, Ota, Ogun State, Nigeria developed a prototype voice-based e-Learning application using the VoiceXML application development life cycle to proffer a solution that will complement the existing learning methods in a case study involving a school for the blind in Lagos, Nigeria. The assistive technology developed has the ability to fundamentally change the way teaching and training is delivered to the students of the school for the blind as proven in their case study and other schools alike. The voice-based e-Learning technology will improve accessibility to education, including distance learning for learners who are visually impaired in the school for the blind. By doing so, the group will not be completely neglected in the scheme of promoting ICT in education and learning.

II. Another challenge is lack of both technical and social skills required for the implementation of e-learning which contributes to failure of e-learning projects. Some lecturers and students are not trained to make use of some of the e-learning equipment. This affects e-learning programme in our universities as a combination of connectivity, equipment and software will achieve anything if people are not trained to use them. Aduke (2008) reported that the gross inadequacy of trained personnel is a challenge to the use of ICT in most Nigerian higher institutions and that this is also evident in NOUN which is a public university in Nigeria known for ICT use.

III. There is also inability of teachers to assist the students develop the ability and knowledge necessary to make them use the e-learning effectively. Some e-learning studies conducted in developing countries show lack of vision and framework in implementing e-learning leading to failure of these e-learning projects (Kizito & Bijan, 2006; Pal, 2006).

IV. Limited or lack of internet connectivity in many developing countries including Nigerian Universities impedes access to e-learning. Cost of Internet connectivity which is a major driver of ICT in education in Nigeria is so high, thus most students make use of pay-as-you-surf Cyber cafes whose charges are very high despite their poor service and slow rate of their server.

V. Lack of funds to acquire cutting-edge equipment needed for implementing e-learning. The high cost of ICT gadgets is a major barrier to the success and adequate employ of e-learning in the country. The government bears a greater percentage of the economic costs of education in Nigerian federal and state universities most of which have significantly larger student populations than private institutions. With the annual increase in number of applicants and matriculants, the expenditure on education is becoming a huge burden to the government. Economic costs of implementing e-learning would fall on the students many of which are already below the poverty line.

VI. Epileptic power supply: The abysmal state of electric power supply is a major setback in the implementation of e-Learning. Irregular and interrupted power supply in Nigeria is a perennial problem that affects every aspect of the economy including education. Ajadi, Salawu and Adeoye (2008) argued that it has been a major setback for technological advancement in the country. Most rural areas in Nigeria are not even connected to the national grid which makes it difficult for students residing in such areas to use ICT effectively.

VII. There is also the problem of conservative attitude displayed by both faculties and students in resisting to change from traditional pedagogical methods to a more innovative, technology based teaching and learning methods. E-learning faces a major bottleneck in our institutions as most of the universities do not inculcate ICT based courses in their curriculum and the equipment such as computers, digital technology and internet which are required to facilitate learning are not available for proper utilization.

2.2 Prospects

The contributions of e-learning as proposed by several scholars include cost-effectiveness, enhanced responsiveness to change, consistency, timely content, flexible accessibility, and providing customer value (Olomo, 2001); Personalized instruction, Content standardization, Accountability, On-demand availability (Bhuasiri, Xaymoungkhoun, Jeung and Cigenek, 2011). E-learning should be seen as a tool to ameliorate several challenges facing higher education including the move towards lifelong learning, demand for continuous professional development, and the drive to wider participation.

E–learning based on the benefits it provides to stakeholders in educational sector is valuable in ways such as:

I. Increase in accessibility to information: we are at the edge of a wave of innovation in tertiary education. Massive online open courses (MOOCs) have gained much attention. ICT based MOOCs hosted by companies such as edX, Coursera, Udacity, Alison courses, MIT open courseware, Khan Academy among others can engender novel approaches to teaching and learning in Nigerian universities. It is expected that with the formal introduction of MOOCs in the university education program, there would be transition of learning to a transformative and remarkably informative process involving flipped classrooms, interactive problem identification and increased capacity building via problem solving while sustaining increased peer interaction not just with students in one lecture hall but between students across various time zones of the world.

II. On-demand availability because learning can take place anytime and anywhere which increases retention of knowledge. The application of e-learning can achieve just-in-time learning with greater reach irrespective of location (whether on the move, at home or work), speed of response and consistency of message. The sequence of lecture and homework assignments can be reversed, online materials can be administered as assignments before peer and tutor interactions with the purpose of enhancing the learning process and improving preceptorship.

III. Self- pacing allows fast and slow learners to go on their speed in any course respectively without slow learners being neglected. Every learner is engaged to progress at his/her own pace without any feeling of frustration.

IV. E-learning, fuelled by the use of sophisticated learning tools, media and ICT is aimed at augmenting the learners' experience thus making education learner-centred. It also builds confidence in learners as it increases retention due to hands on application unlike in traditional teaching and learning methods. This motivates and sustains the learners' interest to a large extent as well as makes them to be actively involved in learning.

V. Ease of accessibility to e–learning facilities provides opportunities for professional development of workers. This can be possible through web-based courses, webinars and tutorials.

VI. Nigerian higher education system currently has 153 universities, 40 Federal universities, 44 state universities and 69 private owned universities. Every year, about a million students apply to enrol into these universities but barely 10% of them are enrolled (JAMB, 2016). One of the reasons for which candidates are not admitted into the degree programs for which they applied is limited space and inadequate infrastructure. E-learning platforms for degree programs in which students can participate in class activities online could be instituted. A significant number of candidates can be admitted into such online programs where they can still obtain a degree under the terms of the university.

2.3 Recommendation for Improvement

I. Inadequate power supply and funding remains a bottleneck to the development of e-learning in Nigerian Universities in the public sector. The tertiary education system stands to benefit immensely from cutting-edge ICT equipment, stable power supply and an increased budget allocation for e-learning initiatives. There is need to increase the annual allocation on education by the government at both the federal and state cadre to facilitate adequate provision of e-learning equipment and steady power supply in the universities.

II. Indigenous IT professionals could be recruited for the development of software packages for e-learning which can be made affordable at a low cost to students in the universities.

III. Paramount to the success of e-learning is a basic understanding of computer function and ICT literacy. Provision should be made for routine training of faculty, IT operators and students on the operation and use of functional e-learning systems in place. Webinars, drills and workshops that engage participants in the active use of and development of e-learning technologies should be instituted on a periodic basis.

IV. There is a need for incentives for private and non-governmental organisations to contribute to e-learning in Nigerian universities. For instance, a moderate tax reduction benefit could be offered to institutions that contribute to the development of e-learning in Nigerian universities. Such private-government partnerships are needed to ameliorate challenges associated with sole funding by the government.

V. At the centre of e-learning is equitable accessibility to the internet. Fast internet with a wide bandwidth that allows for connection of multiple users at the same time which would be of tremendous benefit to e-learning in Nigerian universities should be made available at an affordable cost.

VI. Custom-designed ICT subjects should be incorporated into the curriculum at the secondary school level. Exposure at the pre-varsity stage would help get students acclimatized to and interested in e-learning and prepare them ahead of time. This principle of *the earlier the better* would also contribute to reduction of cost of training in the long run.

VII. Voice based e-learning applications for the visually impaired faculties and learners must be developed so that this group will not be completely neglected in the scheme of promoting e-learning.

3. CONCLUSION

E-learning in education remains an evolving trend in Nigeria. Nonetheless, it has tremendous potential to improve productivity in the educational sector. With the challenges facing e-learning in the Nigerian university education system notwithstanding, e-learning demonstrates a huge potential if employed and utilised adequately. The prospects, challenges and recommendations as regarding e-Learning in Nigerian universities has been elucidated in the paper. It is therefore expedient to focus attention towards factors that will promote the effectiveness and enhance delivery of e-learning in Nigerian universities so as to satisfy the needs of all stakeholders to a large extent.

REFERENCES

Aduke, A.F., 2008. Usage and challenges of information and technology (ICT) in teaching and learning in Nigerian universities. *Asian Journal of Information Technology,* Vol. 7, No. 7, pp. 290-295.

Ajadi, T.O., Salawu, I.O. and Adeoye, F.A., 2008. E-learning and distance education in Nigeria. *The Turkish Online Journal of Educational Technology,* Vol. 7, No. 4, p. 769.

Azeta, A. A., Ayo, C.K., Atayero, A.A. and Ikhu-Omoregbe, N. A., 2010. *Application of VoiceXML in e-Learning Systems* in: *Cases on Successful E-Learning Practices in the Developed and Developing World: Methods for the Global Information Economy* by Olaniran, B. Published by Information Science Reference (an imprint of IGI Global), United States of America.

Bates, A. and Poole, G., 2013. *Effective teaching with technology in higher education.* Bass/John Wiley, San Francisco.

Bhuasiri, W., Xaymoungkhoun, O.Z., Jeung, J.R. and Ciganek, A.P., 2011. Critical Success Factors for E-learning in Developing Countries: A Comparative Analysis between ICT Experts and Faculty. *Computers and Education* Vol. 58, pp. 843-855.

JAMB, 2016. JAMB Statistics: Application and Admission (UTME), Retrieved February 26, 2017 from http://www.jamb.gov.ng

Johnson, H.M., (2007). *Dialogue and the construction of knowledge in e-learning: exploring students' perceptions of their learning while using blackboard's asynchronous discussion board.* Chandos Publishers, Cambridge.

Kizito, B.J. and Bijan, K., 2006. An Empirical Study on Education Strategy to E- learning in Developing Countries. *Proceedings of 4th IEEE International Workshop on Technology for Education in Developing Countries.*

Manprit, K., 2011. *Using online forums in language education*. Kogan Page Publishers, Gilly Salmon.

Murali, R., 2010. *Web-enabled user support system*. ICDE, New-Delhi.

Olomo, R.O., 2001. Mapping and the Internet; challenges and opportunities in Nigeria. *Journal of the Nigerian cartography association,* Vol. 17, pp. 8-12.

Omofaye, J.O., 2007. Challenges facing ICT infrastructure and successful online education in Africa, Retrieved February 27, 2017.

Pal, J., 2006. Early Stage of Practical of Implementing Computer Aided Education Experience from India. *Proceedings of 4th IEEE International Workshop.*

Parks, E., 2013. *"What's the "e" in e-learning?"* askinternational.com, Retrieved November 22, 2016.

Robinson, B., 2008. Using distance education and ICT to improve access, equity and the quality in teachers' professional development in Western China. *International Review of Research in Open and Distance Learning,* Vol. 9, No. 1, pp. 24-34.

Reflection Papers

A CONCEPTUAL FRAMEWORK FOR WEB-BASED LEARNING DESIGN

Hesham Alomyan
University of Petra, Jordan

ABSTRACT

The purpose of this paper is to provide a coherent framework to present the relationship between individual differences and web-based learning. Two individual difference factors have been identified for investigation within the present paper: Cognitive style and prior knowledge. The importance of individual differences is reviewed and previous work on the effect of individual differences on Web-based learning is examined. Problems associated with Web-based learning are identified and discussed in relation to cognitive style and prior knowledge. Possible solutions to these problems are suggested and presented in the form of a conceptual framework that can be used for developing web-based learning systems.

KEYWORDS

Web-based learning, instructional design, individual differences

1. INTRODUCTION

The vast majority of the early research into web-based learning falls outside the area of instructional design in fields long involved in human-computer interaction. With the rapidly increasing use of the Web in our educational systems, a need for *instructional* design for web-based learning has become a necessity. That is, there is a need for guidelines to design effective web-based learning. A suitable approach to such guidelines would be investigating learners' individual differences to identify their needs and preferences. Adaptive web-based learning programs can be then created to meet such needs and preferences.

Among a variety of individual differences aspects, cognitive style and prior knowledge are considered to be viable factors that may influence the effectiveness of teaching and learning. Thus, the aim of the present paper is to review and evaluate how these individual difference factors might influence learning in Web-based learning environments and provide guidelines for instructional designers of web-based learning systems in the form of a conceptual framework. These factors are discussed in depth in the next sections.

2. COGNITIVE STYLES

Cognitive style is defined as an individual's preferred and habitual approach to organizing and representing information (Riding and Rayner, 1998). Research has identified different types of cognitive style. Among these, field dependence/field independence appears to be the most researched cognitive style within education. Witkin, Moore, Goodenough, & Cox (1977) used the term, field independence, to describe individuals who are individualistic, internally directed and accept ideas through analysis. On the other hand, field dependent individuals prefer working in groups, are externally directed, influenced by salient features and they accept ideas as presented. Owning to their characteristics field independent learners outperform field dependent learners in various web-based learning settings (Nozari, Siamian, 2015; Onyekurum, 2015).

Since Web-based learning systems feature the potential for flexibly displaying information in many different ways, characteristics of field-dependent and field-independent individuals described above seem to have instructional and design implications that might influence the quality of Web-based learning. Thus, instead of asking how Web-based material affects student learning, the question to be asked is how

Web-based learning is used by learners with different cognitive styles? The following subsections discuss this issue within three areas: (a) field dependence and hypermedia structure; (b) field dependence and learning behaviour; and (c) field dependence and learning outcomes.

2.1 Field Dependence and Hypermedia Structure

Research has investigated how learners with diverse cognitive styles cope with different hypermedia structures. Empirical studies (e.g. Graff, 2003; Ipek, 2010; Reed & Oughton, 1997) revealed that:

a) field-independent learners are relatively capable of directing their learning by themselves in hypermedia programs with non-linear presentation.
b) field-dependent learners appear to prefer more structured paths to follow in linear learning programs. That is, they prefer to be externally directed.

2.2 Field Dependence and Learning Behavior

Learning behaviours can be considered as learners' interaction patterns with learning materials, instructors, tutors, and peers. In the context of hypermedia learning systems, Research (e.g Ford & Chen, 2000; Somyurek, Guyer, & Atasoy, 2008) indicated that field-dependent students preferred navigational tools such as global maps, which provided an overall picture of the contents, whereas field-independent students preferred tools such as an index or find options, designed for searching for specific information. In addition, other studies (Palmquist & Kim, 2000; Wang, Hawk, & Tenopir, 2000) showed that field-dependent learners navigate the Web in a more linear mode and they get lost more frequently. However, among individuals with substantial online search experience, their cognitive style did not seem to influence any of the search performance or tool usage. Therefore, it might be argued that cognitive style appears as an important factor in designing navigation tools which should be presented in the user interface for learning and teaching.

2.3 Field Dependence and Learning Outcome

The field dependent/independent cognitive style has been identified as an influential factor in academic achievement in both traditional and hypermedia learning settings. In traditional learning settings, field-independent students frequently perform better than field-dependent students in various subject matters (Jamieson, 1992).

In hypermedia learning settings, although research is still inconclusive, the majority of works available indicate that field-independent students will score significantly better than field-dependent students (Noble, Miller, & Heckman, 2008; Nozari & Siamian, 2015). This outperformance of the field-independent students can be attributed to their ability to impose their own organization of structure on learning materials. However, research showed that when sufficient structure and support are provided in hypermedia learning environments (e.g., menu of contents, back/forward navigation buttons, indexes etc.) field-dependent students may overcome the limitations of imposing effective structure on their learning enabling them to perform as good as their peers. The remaining subsections discuss problems field-dependent learners, may encounter whilst learning in hypermedia systems. These problems are: (a) disorientation, (b) learner control, and (c) cognitive overload.

2.4 Problems Field-Dependent Learners Experience in Web-Based Learning

2.4.1 Disorientation

Disorientation refers to users not knowing their position in hypermedia space (Murray, Piemonte, Khan, Shen, & Condit, 2000). It has been observed that field-dependent learners, as opposed to field-independent learners, are more likely to become disoriented during navigation in hyperspace and non-linear hypermedia systems (Palmquist & Kim, 2000; Wang et al., 2000).

It is possible that the ability of field-independent individuals to take an active approach, apply organization on information and extract relevant cues helps them find their way in non-linear learning environments. Conversely, field-dependent students tend to adopt an approach where they prefer guidance and attend to the most salient cues regardless of their relevance. Therefore, to learn effectively, field-dependent learners need to be provided with more instructional guidance in Web-based learning, which can direct them to the relevant information and reduce disorientation.

2.4.2 Cognitive Overload

Cognitive overload described as the additional effort and concentration necessary to maintain several tasks or trails at one time (Conklin, 1987). This problem can be caused by a large number of choices and decisions the user has to make in a hypermedia system. For field-dependent learners, freedom of navigation could mean confusion and their attention may be diverted from content and relationships as they attend to navigational decision making, especially when accessing large quantities of information. Cognitive overload could also be a result of the ability of hypermedia to present content material in various textual as well as static and dynamic pictorial representations which might become a burden on learner cognition. Such multiple representations might make specific demands on learners. That is, learners have to process different representations simultaneously to construct a coherent mental representation which, in turn, might cause learnersto experience cognitive overload. No published studies have directly investigated the relationship between cognitive style and cognitive overload in Web-based learning environments. However, a number of researchers (Palmquist & Kim, 2001; Wang et al., 2000) have suggested that field-dependent learners are more likely to experience cognitive overload.

2.4.3 Learner Control

Learner control can be defined as the amount of control a learner can have, in an individualised learning environment on the leaning material (Lin & Hsieh, 2001). With regard to cognitive style, empirical studies have suggested that field-dependent learners tend to perform better in program-controlled instruction and prefer to be externally guided, whereas field-independent learners often tend to do well in independent learning (Chen & Macredie, 2002). It can be argued that field-dependent individuals might gain benefit from hypermedia learning systems when less learner control and more guidance are provided. On the other hand, relatively, field-independent individuals enjoy independent learning in hypermedia systems provided with high levels of learner control.

Solutions offered to help learners, in particular field-dependent learners, overcome the mentioned problems and perform well in hypermedia learning environments are presented in section 4. The next section illustrates and discusses the importance of prior knowledge in hypermedia learning.

3. PRIOR KNOWLEDGE AND WEB-BASD LEARNING

Prior knowledge is considered to be a key factor underlying successful learning. Jonassen and Grabowski (1993, p. 417) defined prior knowledge as "the knowledge, skills, or ability that students bring to the learning process. A number of educators and researchers (e.g., Chen, Fan & Macredie, 2006; Chen & Paul, 2003) have recognised prior knowledge as a potent factor that might help them analyse the way in which learners navigate and perform in a non-linear learning environment. Empirical studies in hypermedia learning settings (e.g., Calisir & Gurel, 2003; Chen, 2015; Song, Kalet, & Plass, 2016; Tabatabai & Shore, 2005) showed that learners with high prior knowledge frequently outperform learners with limited prior knowledge and learners with varying levels of prior knowledge show different navigational behaviour and their performance is often affected by types of content structure.

With regard to navigation, research (e.g., Calisir & Gurel, 2003; Chen, Fan, & Macredie, 2006) shows that students with high prior knowledge of the content do not experience disorientation with hypermedia and seem to experience much less frustration while performing their tasks. On the other hand, students with low prior knowledge often suffer from disorientation, exhibited little awareness of where they had been, or where they could go to find the information that they needed.

Regarding content structure, research suggests that experts and novices differ in their performance depending on content structure in hypermedia learning systems (Calisir & Gurel, 2003). It was found that low prior knowledge students benefited more from a hierarchical and linear structure than from a network linking structure. Whereas, High prior knowledge students were able to function equally well in both conditions. In summary, prior knowledge appears to be a viable factor that predicts the way learners react to hypermedia learning system.

4. A PROPSED FRAMEWORK FOR WEB-BASED LEARNING DESIGN

Drawn from the preceding analysis of the literature, a conceptual framework is developed, as shown in Figure 1 and 2, and suggests several techniques that can be used to address the problems field-dependent and low prior knowledge learners encounter in web-based learning environments. The conceptual framework illustrates the basic characteristics of individuals with field-independent and field-dependent cognitive style and individuals with high and low levels of prior knowledge and their requirements for Web-based learning systems. The proposed framework can help designers to develop web-based learning systems that address effectively the needs of learners with different types of cognitive style and levels of prior knowledge.

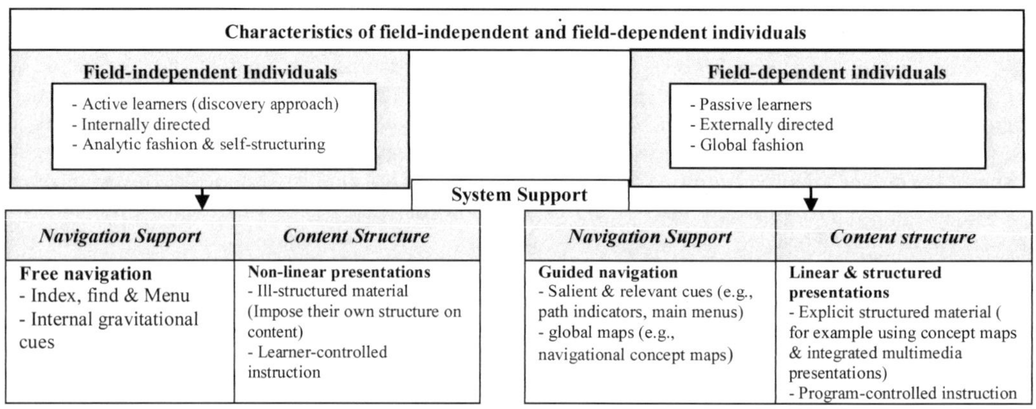

Figure 1. Characteristics of field-independent and dependent-individuals and their implications for Web-based learning

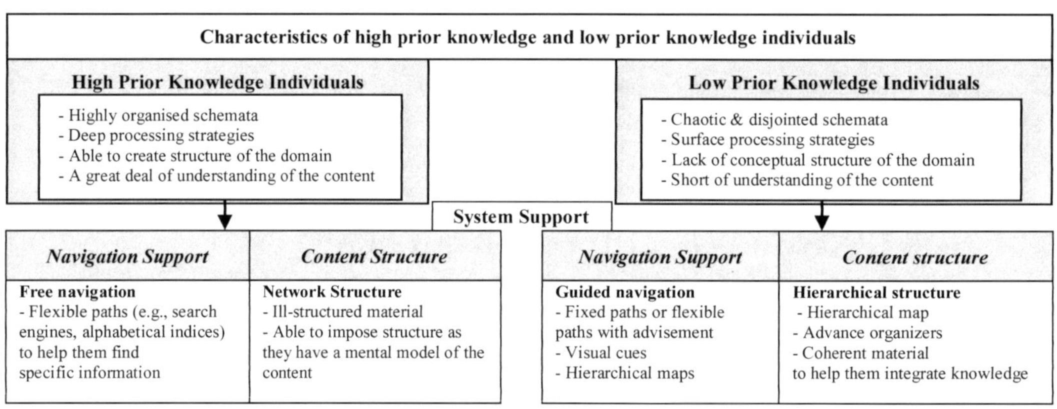

Figure 2. Characteristics of high and low prior knowledge individuals and their implications for Web-based learning

5. CONCLUSION

The manner in which individual differences may interact with web-based material is the major topic of this paper. In particular, it is noted that field-independent individuals do appear to have certain advantages over field-independent peers in many learning situations, especially situations where learners need to impose structure upon a relatively incomplete or disorganised input. However, under certain conditions and with stronger (more organised, more direct) instructional cues field-dependent individuals may learn at similar levels to field-independent individuals.

Prior knowledge seems to operate in a similar manner as cognitive style. Individuals with high levels of prior knowledge appear to be better able to learn and perform in less structured domains, through using their existing knowledge as an effective learning tool. On the other hand, this is not the case with low prior knowledge learners, whose knowledge cannot assist them in dealing with new information. Such learners cannot rely on their prior knowledge to help them determine the underlying structure of the new learning material. Like field-dependent individuals, individuals with low prior knowledge need more guidance in their learning process. Consequently, the framework proposed in the present paper suggests several techniques that can be used in web-based learning systems to assist both field-dependent students and students with low prior knowledge in their learning experience and improve learning outcomes.

REFERENCES

Calisir, F., & Gurel, Z. (2003). Influence of text structure and prior knowledge of the learner on reading comprehension, browsing and perceived control. *Computers in Human Behavior, 19*, 135–145.

Chen, L. (2015). Web-based learning programs: Use by learners with various cognitive styles. *Computers & Education, 54, 4,* 1028-1035.

Chen, S. Y., Fan, J., & Macredie, R. D. (2006). Navigation in hypermedia learning systems: Experts vs. novices. *Computers in Human Behavior, 22,* 251–266.

Conklin, J. (1987). Hypertext: An introduction and surveys. *IEEE Computer*, *20*, 17-41.

Ford, N., & Chen, S. Y. (2000). Individual differences, hypermedia navigation and learning: An empirical study. *Journal of Educational Multimedia and Hypermedia*, *9*, 281– 312.

Graff, M. (2003). Cognitive style and attitudes towards using online learning and assessment methods. *Electronic Journal of e-Learning, 1*, 21-28.

Ipek, I. (2010). The effects of CBI lesson sequence type and field dependence on learning from computer-based cooperative instruction in web. *Turkish Online Journal of Educational Technology*, *9,* 221-234.

Jamieson, J. (1992). The cognitive styles of reflection/impulsivity and field independence/dependence and ESL success. *Modern Language Journal*, *3*, 491-501.

Jonassen, D. H., & Grabowski, B. (1993). *Individual differences and instruction*. New York: Allen & Bacon.

Murray, T., Piemonte, J., Khan, S., Shen, T., & Condit, C. (2000). Evaluating the need for intelligence in an adaptive hypermedia system. In Frasson & Gautheir (Eds.), *Proceedings of Intelligent Tutoring Systems* (373-382), Springer-Verlag, New York.

Noble, K. A., Miller, S. M., & Heckman, J. (2008). The Cognitive Style of Nursing Students: Educational Implications for Teaching and Learning. *Journal of Nursing Education, 47,* 6, 245-253.

Nozari. A., & Siamian. H. (2015). The relationship between field dependent-independent cognitive style and understanding of English text reading and academic success. *Mater Sociomed. 27,* 39-41.

Onyekuru, B. (2015). Field dependence-field independence cognitive style, gender, career choice and academic achievement of secondary school students in Emohua local government area of rivers state. *Journal of Education and Practice. 6*, 76-86

Palmquist, R. A., Kim, K.-S. (2000). Cognitive style and on-line database search experience as predictors of Web search performance. *Journal of the American Society for Information Science*, *51*, 558–566.

Reed, W. M., & Oughton, J. M. (1997). Computer experience and interval based hypermedia navigation. *Journal of Research on Computing in Education*, *30*, 38–52.

Somyurek.S., Guyer.T., & Atasoy.B,. (2008). the effects of individual differences on learner's navigation in a courseware. *The Turkish Online Journal of Educational Technology*, *7*, 39-41.

Song, S.; Kalet, L., & Plass, L. (2016). Interplay of prior knowledge, self-regulation and motivation in complex multimedia learning environments. *Journal of Computer Assisted Learning,* 32, 1, 31-50.

Tabatabai, D., & Shore, B. M. (2005). How experts and novices search the Web. *Library & Information Science Research, 27*, 222–248.

Wang, P., Hawk, W. B., & Tenopir, C. (2000). Users' interaction with World Wide Web resources: An exploratory study using a holistic approach. *Information processing & Management*, *36*, 229–251.

Witkin, H. A., Moore, C. A., Goodenough, D. R., & Cox, P. W. (1977). Field dependent and field independent cognitive styles and their educational implications. *Review of Educational Research, 47*, 1-64.

Riding R. J., & Rayner, S. (1998). *Cognitive styles and learning strategies: Understanding style differences in learninand behaviour*. London: David Fulton.

Lin, B & Hsieh,C.(2001).Web-based teaching and learner control:A research review.*Computers & Education,37*,377-386

THE KEY TO SUCCESS IN ELECTRONIC LEARNING: FACULTY TRAINING AND EVALUATION

Warren Matthews and Albert Smothers
University of Phoenix, USA

ABSTRACT

Over the past thirty years, higher education for adult students has emerged to help prepare the labor force for the 21st century in a world of globalization. At the same time, there have been massive advances in computing and the internet that provide many tools useful in higher education. Most universities now offer some form of electronic learning (EL), and many offer complete EL degree programs tailored for the working adult student. Now it is essential that managers of these new educational programs act to select and train faculty to fit the special needs of the adult student. More importantly, program managers need to use the new technology and learning theory to monitor program delivery and insure their program goals are achieved.

KEYWORDS

Andragogy, faculty evaluation, adult students

1. INTRODUCTION

Pedagogy is the theory of teaching children. Andragogy is the theory of teaching adults. In recent years, more attention has been paid to andragogy because many more adults are seeking higher education. New technologies related to computers and the internet have made available new possibilities in higher education, and educators have worked to understand and apply these new technologies in new ways to support the creation and dissemination of knowledge to adult students. See Scoppio and Covell, 2016. We are constantly learning new ways to teach adults, and we now understand that the theories and methods of pedagogy do not always apply to the adult student. See Boshier, 1998.

Traditionally secondary and higher education has been conducted in a small group setting in a classroom. In a "one room schoolhouse", the one room was a classroom. Over the last thirty years, education, especially higher education, has evolved to include electronic learning (EL) at a distance. Students work online, and the room in the one room schoolhouse is the server room – or the home office. These monumental changes in how we can best serve the adult student create new challenges and opportunities for the academy. See Wang, 2015.

2. FACULTY RECRUITING AND SELECTION

Teaching the adult student is different from teaching the traditional age secondary school or college student. The main difference is that the working adult student has experiences and perspectives based on work experience and practical knowledge. The adult student needs to know why certain learning objectives are presented and how they will add value. Younger students often do not have this perspective, and tend to accept guidance from an effective teacher. This unique aspect of the adult student has been documented around the world. See Gordivenko, 2013.

Not only is the adult student different, but the student in an electronic or distance learning environment is different and require a different approach in teaching. See Keller, 2014. This difference also has been found in many cultures and settings. See Baptista, 2013 and Alalshaikh, 2015.

The adult student will accept and respect the teacher (faculty) only to the extent that the teacher shows knowledge, experience, and respect. Adult students must find purpose and meaning in the material presented to them. The role of teacher in the electronic learning (EL) environment is to clarify the purpose and meaning based on professional experience. Student motivation must come from both the technical knowledge and the personal and professional experience of the teacher. Teachers for the EL environment should be selected based on their academic qualifications, their professional experience, and their ability to conduct a dynamic and effective EL experience for adult students. Continuing faculty training and evaluation can improve learning outcomes and program success. See Lakin, 2016.

Student retention and persistence are strongly influenced by the teacher-student relationship. Deans and Program Managers can increase the success of their educational programs by training and evaluating faculty in the use of modern teaching practices sought by and needed by the adult student. See Howell, 2012 and Binti, 2014.

Those who plan and manage EL programs should encourage and monitor the sharing of professional experience with students in EL courses. Learning Management Systems (LMS), such as Blackboard, eCollege, Canvas, Accenture, and others provide the tools to assure the EL classroom is a positive learning experience for all. In some cases, managers do not use these tools and do not provide an effective learning environment.

3. EFFECTIVE TEACHING PRACTICES

Faculty in the EL environment need to use techniques that are appropriate to the adult student, such as active learning. Active learning methods are those which engage the student and encourage application of concepts by analysis, reasoning, and exploration. Much research in active learning theory shows valuable benefits for students. See Chen, 2014. Faculty with relevant professional experience can find opportunities to apply concepts to real-world situations and motivate students to learn. Sharing of professional experience by faculty helps students see the relevance and usefulness of basic concepts and theory. See Knowles, Holton, & Swanson (2011).

Higher education should involve critical thinking. Proactive faculty in the EL setting should lead students to take basic concepts and apply them to different situations. Students should search for cause and effect, and they should be led to examine their assumptions and biases. Adult students learn by observation and by solving problems. The successful EL faculty will challenge students to stretch their perspectives by investigating new ideas and applying theory in new ways. Problem-based learning is one example of a teaching practice that fully engages the student. In problem-based learning, the student or a team of students face a practical problem and must deliver a solution. For excellent examples, see Romero, 2014.

Faculty can achieve excellence in the EL setting by engaging all students in a process of exploration. Students can be asked to identify their assumptions. They can be faced with a new case or situation to compare with others. The faculty can share personal experience when appropriate to illustrate a problem solved or a goal accomplished. Such activity is likely to resonate with the adult student and may lead them to identify additional real world problems and opportunities that apply to the learning objectives.

Because participants in the EL setting are not meeting face to face, it is possible for some students to be disengaged and not participate. Faculty should use LMS tools to monitor the activity of each student and encourage all students to participate in the discussions. Participation can be increased by posing questions to individual students, often based on their own experience or occupation. Faculty may ask one student to respond specifically to the discussion of another student, applying their experience or perspective. In addition, team assignments encourage students to participate and collaborate with each other.

A friendly and professional tone in the Electronic Learning (EL) course is a very important. An important difference in the EL course compared to a traditional course in a physical classroom is that the faculty and students do not see each other. Body language is not available to convey meaning, and faculty must be careful and avoid using language or tone that may be interpreted as abrupt, insensitive, condescending, or disrespectful. Faculty should maintain an atmosphere of openness and inclusion, and encourage active participation by all students to achieve an effective and collaborative learning environment.

Often faculty will find that students post discussions that are correct and complete. In such cases, the class discussion may proceed with little faculty intervention. In other cases, students may post incorrect information or may omit important considerations. In such cases, the faculty must intervene promptly and provide clarity. This correction and reorientation of the discussion need to be positive and encouraging – not punitive or disrespectful.

A positive and professional tone should be maintained by faculty in responding to student discussions. A faculty response should start with a positive statement acknowledging the student's post and efforts. Next, a correction or omission should be mentioned (once only) and documented. Cite personal experience if appropriate. Finally, a positive motivational statement should suggest future applications of the concepts involved related to the learning objectives. This approach makes corrections while still motivating and respecting the student.

These teaching practices have been found to enhance learning and take full advantage of the experience of the faculty. Managers should have methods in place to encourage and measure the use of these techniques.

4. STRATEGIES AVAILABLE IN THE EL COURSE

The technology available today offers many tools to promote learning in the EL setting. The widespread availability of computing devices makes higher education accessible to many non-traditional students. Innovative educators can apply this technology in many ways to promote learning, as we see in this conference. Much recent research informs us on useful strategies. See Chang, 2014.

There is a wide range of learning styles among adults, and higher education can best serve this audience with a broad range of teaching methods and strategies. Some students learn best by reading. Some learn best by interacting with other people. The new technology related to the internet makes possible the concurrent use of multiple approaches in higher education in the electronic learning environment. See Ghost-Bear, 2012.

Online discussions are the most common feature of the EL classroom. Asynchronous online discussions allow students to respond on their own schedule, and their comments are preserved for others to read and reply. When well written, discussions keep the comments on topic, they build on prior learning, and they set the stage for future learning objectives. They encourage students (and faculty) to share experiences and insights, and they help all students learn by applying textbook theory to real world situations.

In many courses case studies are useful. Cases can be analyzed as individual or team assignments, and then they can be discussed and dissected. Some cases are carried over throughout a course. The case approach to teaching was pioneered at Harvard Business School many years ago. Some medical schools use a case approach in a clinical setting. The case approach can enhance learning by creating an interactive learning environment. Students that are actively engaged in a learning activity, rather than passive, have been shown to learn more effectively. See Peshal, 2014.

Individual papers play an important role in most EL courses. The written assignment allows the student to research and review concepts, and then present creative work to address the assigned topic. The LMS platform provides an efficient mechanism to receive and host papers and check for plagiarism and format. It may be useful for students to read and critique the papers of other students as a learning activity. Individual papers also provide a record of student accomplishment and may be suitable to build a portfolio to document academic progress.

There also is a role for team assignments that lead to papers or presentations. Many employers cite the ability to work in teams as an important skill they seek. In completing team assignments, team members collaborate with each other, draw on their experience, plan and execute research, and critically evaluate their assumptions and beliefs. Most important team members present their ideas to each other and justify their conclusions. This process of first learning and then explaining to others is the highest form of active learning.

Quizzes have always been used in education to measure learning and identify areas needing more emphasis. The LMS platforms provide means to administered timed tests, and random selection of questions from large problem sets can be used. Some programs use monitored quizzes to insure validity. Quizzes give students prompt feedback on which concepts they have mastered and which concepts need more attention.

Some academic programs use live video conferencing or videotaped lectures to increase student involvement and possibly replicate the traditional classroom. In some cases, these techniques have been successful. See Malinovski, et al, 2015.

These strategies have been shown to add value for adult students. They suggest approaches that Deans and Program Managers can use to manage programs and evaluate faculty performance. See Pulkka, 2013.

5. OVERSIGHT OF FACULTY TO ACHIEVE EFFECTIVE LEARNING

Deans and Program Managers can monitor their EL programs for effectiveness, consistency, and proper implementation of local policies. Some faculty may be practitioners from industry rather than full-time professors. So, monitoring can insure that students in an EL program have consistency across their courses. Monitoring can help guide a program by identifying areas for improvements to the curriculum and faculty training. The consistent evaluation of courses and faculty help to insure the courses are presented in a way that supports program goals and policy.

LMS provide many tools to monitor and evaluate the presentation of courses. One essential requirement in the EL environment is that faculty are present and active in the online classroom. Faculty and student frequency and duration of engagement by day and hour can help to identify any shortcomings. Such measures can identify problems with faculty or student participation in time to make proper adjustments. As faculty and students learn that frequency of participation is monitored, performance should improve.

LMS provide a mechanism for students to post assignments and for faculty to post grades. The time required for this process in each case can be measured to verify compliance with local policy. Students submitting late assignments can be identified and counseled. In addition, analysis of the pattern of assignment submission and grading may assist in program review and development.

6. CONCLUSIONS AND RECOMMENDATIONS

Higher education programs for working adult students need to be planned and executed in accordance with recent advances in education theory. The adult student has unique needs and experience, and faculty needs to be trained for this challenge. Most important, program managers need to insure programs are monitored to insure that they are presented properly to achieve the goals of students and institutions.

REFERENCES

Adler, R. B., Procter, R. F., & Towne, N. (2005). Looking Out/Looking In (11th ed). Belmont, CA. Thompson/Wadsworth.

Alalshaikh, Sultan (2016). Cultural Impacts on Distance Learning, Online Learning Styles, and Design, Quarterly Review of Distance Education, Vol 16, Issue 3.

Baptista, Ana V. (2013). Non-traditional Adult Students: Who Are They and What Are the Implications for Higher Education? Cypriot Journal of Educational Sciences, Vol 8, Issue 2.

Binti, Liyana (2014). Motivating Adult Learners Using Blended Learning in Higher Education, Researchers World, Vol 5, Issue 3.

Boshier, Roger (1998). Malcolm Bowles, Archbishop of Andragogy, Adult Education Quarterly, Vol 48, Issue 2.

Chang, Eunice and Hannafin, Michael (2015). The Uses and Misuses of Collaborative Distance Education Technologies, Quarterly Review of Distance Education, Vol 16, Issue 2.

Charles, C. M. (2005). Building classroom discipline (8th ed). Boston, MA. Pearson A & B.

Chen, Joseph C., (2014). Teaching Nontraditional Adult Students: Adult Learning Theories in Practice, Teaching in Higher Education, Vol 19, Issue 4.

Ghost-Bear, Anne A (2012). Technology, Learning, and Individual Differences, Journal of Adult Education, Vol 41, Issue 2.

Gordivenko, N. G., (2013). Adult Students in the European Educational Environment, Obrazovanie I Nauka, Vol 1, Issue 4.

Howell, George and Buck, Jeffrey M. (2012). The Adult Student and Course Satisfaction: What Matters Most? Innovative Higher Education, Vol 37, Issue 3.

Keller, Gary F. (2014). Comparing Differences Between the Learning Outcomes of Adult Students, Traditional Students, and Online Students, International Journal of Arts & Sciences, Vol 7, Issue 3.

Lakin, Amy (2016). Effective Faculty Evaluation at the Teaching-centered University, International Journal of Educational Management, Vol 30, Issue 6.

Malinovski, Toni; Vasileva-Stojanovska, Tatiana; and Jovevski, Dobri; (2015). Adult Students' Perceptions in Distance Education Learning Environments Based on Videoconferencing Platforms, Journal of Information Technology Education Research, Vol 14.

Peshal, Khanal, (2014). Making Virtual Learning Interactive and Meaningful: Implications of Constructivism for Adult Students, International Journal of Research Studies in Education, Vol 3, Issue 1.

Pulkka, Antti-Tuomas and Niemivirta, Markku, (2013). Adult Students' Achievement Goal Orientations and Evaluations of the Learning Environment: A Person Centered Longitudinal Analysis, Educational Research and Evaluation, Vol 19, Issue 4.

Romero, Liz; Orzechowski, Agnes; and Rahatka, Ola (2014). Teaching Problem Solving and Critical Thinking Skills Online Using Problem-based Learning, Educational Technology, Vol 54, Issue 1.

Schermerhorn, Jr., J. R., Hunt, J. G., & Osburn, R. N. (2003). Organizational Behavior (8th ed). New York, NY. Wiley.

Scoppio, Grazia and Covell, Leigha (2016). Mapping Trends in Pedagogical Approaches and Learning Technologies, The Canadian Journal of Higher Education, Vol 46, Issue 2.

Wang, Victor C. and Torrisi-Steele, Geraldine (2015). Online Teaching, Change, and Critical Theory, New Horizons in Adult Education and Human Resource Development, Vol 27, Issue 3.

USING GAMES, COMIC STRIPS, AND MAPS TO ENHANCE TEACHER CANDIDATES' E-LEARNING PRACTICE IN THE SOCIAL STUDIES

Nancy B. Sardone Ph.D.
Georgian Court University, 900 Lakewood Avenue, Lakewood, New Jersey 08701, USA

ABSTRACT

This article reports on teacher candidates' use of e-learning tools and activities designed for their future students. Candidates offered comments to give an idea of the strengths and challenges of each. Suggestions are made for teacher educators on the types of technology-integrated activities that lend themselves to both traditional and e-learning environments, offering an updated perspective on teaching and learning in the Social Studies.

KEYWORDS

e-Learning, Social Studies, games, comic books, maps

1. INTRODUCTION

When thinking about instruction, preservice teachers tend to follow the teaching methods experienced in their own K-12 education. Those experiences tend to be traditional in nature, such as worksheet-based assignments and textbook-based readings, especially in Social Studies. Yet, numerous studies on teachers' use of technology and students' desire to use technology in school advise us to reassess our views. We need to take into consideration that today's classrooms are filled with students whose daily media exposure is almost eleven hours (Kaiser Family Foundation, 2009). In addition, we need to consider the *National Council of Social Studies* Position Statement regarding curriculum suggests that social studies programs should engage students directly and actively in the learning process and such programs should use several kinds of media technology (NCSS, 2010). Through the use of technology, teachers begin to recognize the strong positive effects it's use has on student learning and engagement (Educators, 2010). Under four headings related to themes in social studies (digital citizenship, geographic competency, raising awareness of current events, and social consciousness), a brief commentary follows offering perspective on teaching and learning in the social studies using the technology-integrated projects and describes teacher candidate experiences.

2. DEVELOPING DIGITAL CITIZENSHIP

"Students aren't getting enough instruction in school on how to use technology and the Internet in a safe and responsible manner" (National Cyber Security Alliance, 2011). Keeping children safe while engaged in online activities is a critical concern of parents, teachers, and policymakers (Thai, 2009). Other aspects to digital citizenship are responsibility and collaboration. The International Society for Technology in Education states, that advances in technology have drastically changed the way we interact with the world and each other. The digital age requires that we understand and are able to harness the power of technology to live and learn (2012). There are many well-constructed digital games designed to teach cyber safety, cyber security, and cyber ethics.

Candidate use: Candidates played online game *Privacy Playground: The First Adventure of the CyberPigs*, which aims to teach elementary students how to navigate the Internet and to identify Internet marketing ploys. In this game, each time the game characters' face a decision, players answer questions as to whether or not the characters are making the right decision. Through this game, elementary students learn techniques to avoid online predators. Candidates explored *Privacy Playground*, and many expressed surprise at the depth and complexity of thought required to ensure online safety. A few candidates reported that they got a couple of game questions wrong, indicating to them that K-12 students are not the only ones who need to be educated in these topics. Lycoming College's online module teaches college age students what constitutes plagiarism and how to avoid it in the online game, *Goblin Threat*. Players are asked a series of questions such as "Tara can use an article in an online database without citing it if:" (A) It only contains information found in other articles; (B) She only uses the abstract; (C) She can never do this; or (D) It was used in a class discussion. Candidates remarked that it was a good review of material. Keeping oneself in check as to current copyright laws is a prudent plan to share with students. Australian Web Site, *Teaching Treasures* offers ways to ensure cyber safety through a self-check activity.

2.1 Developing Geographic Competency

It is remarkable that Americans are relatively uninterested in geography (Fritzer et al, 2010). In one study, 50 percent of American participants (n=510) between the ages of 18 and 24 indicated it important, but not necessary to know where countries in the news are located or to speak a language other than English (47%). Three-quarters believe English is the most commonly spoken native language in the world, rather than Mandarin Chinese (National Geographic & Roper Public Affairs, 2006, p. 4). The American Geosciences Institute cites gaps in geographic competencies in students (2015). These findings suggest that U.S. youths are unprepared for an increasingly global future.

Candidate use: Using maps and National Geography (2015) standards - *How to use maps and other geographic representations, geospatial technologies, and spatial thinking to understand and communicate information,* and *The physical and human characteristics of places*, candidates worked in triads to design a game that could help to develop the geographic skills of students. Each team was provided with three different countries as the context of their game. For example, one team received the grouping of Egypt, the Netherlands, and Argentina and another Namibia, Peru, and Iceland. All ten groups created board games that used a variety of maps (both online and paper-based). A few teams also asked players to use the Web to answer specific game questions.

In another semester, the assignment guidelines tasked candidates with finding an authentic geography problem that K-6 students could explore through a game interface. Twenty board games were developed; twelve contained interactive components where players would use the Internet to answer specific questions asked during game play. An example of an interactive game is *Citrus-opoly*, focused on an authentic problem where, since 2005 Florida citrus groves have been infected with citrus greening (Harmon, 2013; Voosen, 2014). Players are asked to consider relocating the farmers' Florida groves, limiting choices to Texas, Arizona, or California. Players round the board game and using a computer to locate specific Web-based maps, they would compare and contrast the physical, political, climate, and agricultural characteristics of these three U.S. states.

2.2 Raising Awareness about Current Events

During the fall of 2014, world news agencies reported on Iran's growing nuclear ability. Those talks were aimed at curbing Iran's ability to put two elements (uranium and plutonium) to use in weapons (Broad & Pecanha, 2015). Since nuclear weapons are the most dangerous weapons known to man, it is important to be aware of and give deep attention and consideration to the countries stockpiling radioactive materials. Today, there are over 16,000 known nuclear warheads (Kristensen & Norris, 2014) possessed by nine countries reduced from an all-time high of 60,000 during the Cold War. Nuclear weapon development began as a struggle between Communism and anti-Communism until 1986 when then Soviet leader, Mikhail Gorbachev floated the idea of a "nuclear-weapon-free world" (Rotblat, Steinberger, & Udgankar, 1993). Since that time, the debate and consideration of nuclear weaponry has ensued.

Candidate use: Seventeen candidates played online game, *Peace Doves*, whose objective is to use the dove as a worldwide symbol of peace to disarm nuclear weapons possessed by nations. Each player is given eight peace doves. Once players identify the country possessing nuclear weapons based on provided clues, they launch a dove to that specific country to disarm it. If correctly identified, the mission is deemed successful as the nation is disarmed. If not, the player gets another chance. Candidates completed the same questions post play as they did pre-play, revealing significant improvement in knowledge gained through game play (Sardone, 2017). We then discussed the then news headlines involving Iran nuclear ability. Candidates wanted to know if, for example, Iran encroached on the 1970 Non-Proliferation Treaty agreement when constructing a nuclear energy plant. The long-term impact of Iran as holder of nuclear materials on the other Gulf States was discussed and debated. After discussion, candidates understood that possession of nuclear weaponry was a strategy countries used to keep potential attacks at bay. However, they did not understand why the United States was involved in the talks and what the U.S. hoped to gain by such involvement.

2.3 Developing a Critical Social Consciousness

Bullying and harassment, most often by peers, are the most frequent threats that minors face, both online and offline (Internet Safety Technical Task Force Report, 2008). The proliferation of cyberbullying cases in our society is of concern, and gaming is one tool to help students develop both awareness and skills to advert or confront such instances. Cyberbullying is being cruel to others by sending or posting harmful material or engaging in other forms of social aggression using the Internet or other digital technologies (Willard, 2007).

Candidate use: Candidates played *Allies and Aliens: A Mission in Critical Thinking*, designed to develop middle school students' awareness of stereotyping and prejudice. The game's content asks students to examine their values as scenarios of increasing degrees of prejudice and discrimination are presented. The game setting is the year 3065 and Earth considers joining an intergalactic alliance and players decide the benefits of joining such an organization. Teacher candidates remarked how quickly, silently, and insidiously discrimination spreads. One discussant stated that it is important for children to experience through game interfaces the way people think and act toward others when they feel threatened so they can evaluate their own feelings, if found in a similar situation.

Another assignment equipped candidates with Web-based tools like *Toon Doo* and *Story Board That* to develop comic strips on topics such as bullying, racism, conflict resolution, and the environment with the purpose to help K-12 students develop a social consciousness. Researchers and educators promote the use of comics as an effective and powerful way to get students engaged in their own learning (McVicker, 2007).

3. CONCLUSION

We are in the midst of exciting changes in education that can enrich and extend the learning of social studies well beyond class time. The candidates involved in this experience reported that they did not use digital games in their own K-12 educational experiences but did use review games like *Jeopardy*. Further, their past experiences learning social studies are no different than that reported in many studies, where social studies is often the most disliked subject taught in schools due to the use of stagnant instructional strategies (Leming et al, 2006).

Facilitation of instruction by teaching content through application demands a fundamental change in teachers' roles. In the role of facilitator, teachers are no longer the purveyors of facts; instead, they are asked to guide activities that help students exercise their skills and knowledge (Sawchuk, 2009). Today's teachers are being asked to develop and/or select learning activities that aim to develop students' critical thinking skills. The technology-based activities designed, guided, and recommend in this article are fairly easy for the motivated teacher to organize. Most tools used in these projects are free and Web-based. Assigned readings or discussions may seem an easy fit for social studies topics but have found that active engagement by blending concepts with a technology integrated activity to be worth the effort.

REFERENCES

American Geosciences Institute. 2015. Retrieved from https://www.americangeosciences.org/sites/default/files/currents/Currents104_GCMaPS_GeographyTechSkills_0.pdf

Broad, W. & Pecanha, S. 2015, July 14. The Iran nuclear deal: A simple guide. *The New York Times.* Retrieved from http://www.nytimes.com/interactive/2015/03/31/world/ middleeast/simple-guide-nuclear-talks-iran-us.html.

Educators, Technology and 21st Century Skills: Dispelling Five Myths: A Study on the Connection Between K–12 Technology Use and 21st Century Skills. 2010, June. Retrieved from http://www.waldenu.edu/Documents/Degree-Programs/Full_Report_-_Dispelling _Five_Myths.pdf

Fritzer, P. et al, 2010. *Social studies content for elementary and middle school teachers*. Boston: Allyn & Bacon.

Harmon, A. 2013. A race to save the orange by altering its dna. *The New York Times*, Retrieved from http://www.nytimes.com/2013/07/28/science/a-race-to-save-the-orange-by-altering-its-dna.html?pagewanted=all

International Society for Technology in Education. 2012. *Expanding Horizons 2011-2012 Annual Report.* Retrieved from https://www.iste.org/docs/documents/annualreportfin.pdf?sfvrsn=2

Internet Safety Technical Task Force Report. 2008. *Enhancing child safety and online technologies.* Final Report of the Internet Safety Technical Task Force to the Multi-State Working Group on Social Networking of State Attorneys General of the United States. Retrieved from http://cyber.law.harvard.edu/pubrelease/isttf/

Kaiser Family Foundation. 2009. *Generation M2: Media in the Lives of 8- to 18-year olds.* Retrieved from http://slides.kff.org/chart.aspx?ch=1351

Kristensen, H. & Norris, R. 2014, August 26. Worldwide deployments of nuclear weapons. *Bulletin of the Atomic Scientists.* Retrieved from http://bos.sagepub.com/content/ early/2014/08/26/0096340214547619.full.pdf+html.

Leming, J. et al, 2006. The state of social studies: A national random survey of elementary and middle school social studies teachers. *Social Education*, Vol. 70, pp. 322-327.

McVicker, C. 2007. Comic strips as a text structure for learning to read. *The Reading Teacher,* Vol. 61, No. 1, pp. 85-88.

National Council for the Social Studies. 2010. *Position Statement.* Retrieved from http://www.socialstudies.org/system/files/Curriculum_Guidelines_SocialStudies_Teaching_and_Learning.pdf

National Geographic and Roper Public Affairs. 2006. *National geographic and roper public affairs 2006 geographic literacy survey.* Retrieved from http://www.nationalgeographic.com/roper2006/pdf/FINALReport2006GeogLitsurvey.pdf

National Cyber Security Alliance 2010. *National survey: Online safety is a personal priority for American.* Retrieved from http://staysafeonline.mediaroom.com/index.php?s=43&item=62

Rotblat, J., Steinberger, J. & Udgankar, B. (Eds). 1993. *A nuclear-weapon-free world.* Boulder, CO: Westview Press.

Sardone, N. (2017). Game-based learning to raise awareness of nuclear proliferation. In Y. Baek (Ed.), *Game-Based Learning: Theory, Strategies and Performance Outcomes,* (Chapter 21, pp. 409-420). Hauppauge, NY: Nova Science Publishers, Inc.

Sawchuk, S. 2009. 21st-Century Skills' Focus Shifts W.Va. Teachers' Role, *eSchool News*, Vol. 28, No. 16, pp. 1,12-13.

Thai, A. 2009. *Game changer: Investing in digital play to advance children's learning and health.* New York: The Joan Ganz Cooney Center at Sesame Workshop. Retrieved from http://www.joanganzcooneycenter.org

Voosen, P. 2014 "Can genetic engineering save the Florida orange?"*National Geographic*, Retrieved from http://news.nationalgeographic.com/news/2014/09/140914-florida-orange-citrus-greening-gmo-environment-science/

Willard, N. 2007. Cyber-safekids, cyber-savvy teens: Helping young people learn to use the internet safely and responsibly. San Francisco: John Wiley & Sons, Inc.

SCANNER BASED ASSESSMENT IN EXAMS ORGANIZED WITH PERSONALIZED THESIS RANDOMLY GENERATED VIA MICROSOFT WORD

Romeo Teneqexhi[1], Margarita Qirko[2], Genci Sharko[3], Fatmir Vrapi[4] and Loreta Kuneshka[5]
[1]Director of Distance Education Centre
[2]Lecturer of Numerical Analysis
[3]Lecturer of Electrical Measurements
[4]Lecturer of Foreign Languages / English
[5]Lecturer of Statistics
[1,2,3,4]Tirana Polytechnic University, Albania, Universiteti Politeknik i Tiranës, Sheshi "Nënë Tereza", No 4. Tirana, Albania
[5]Medical University of Tirana, Albania , Universiteti i Mjekësisë i Tiranës, Rruga e Dibres, Tirana, Albania

ABSTRACT

Exams assessment is one of the most tedious work for university teachers all over the world. Multiple choice theses make exams assessment a little bit easier, but the teacher cannot prepare more than 3-4 variants; in this case, the possibility of students for cheating from one another becomes a risk for "objective assessment outcome". On the other hand, even when the exams are organized with multiple-choices, the time for student's outcome takes up relatively too much time. We have developed a platform which tries to eliminate the time-range and is appropriate for big-sized classrooms testing. It works as follows: The teacher prepares for every exam-question, a JPG file, in simple words precisely an e-picture, preferably with the same dimensions for all photos. It is easy to make use of sniping tool from windows. Let us consider the exam-paper will contain 60 questions / exercises (can be up to 100). Every student will have all these 60 questions / exercises in his/her thesis, in a uniquely personalized version, but randomly ordered by computer. This means that every thesis / exam-paper has the corresponding unique solution key for the outcome, and only the computer knows it, by using the same combine logic with every generated variant of exam-paper. Consequently, the teacher prepares 60 JPG photos which are saved in USB memory stick folder. With this USB, teacher presents to the faculty secretary (printing center) the number of students he/she has and the folder where the photos are stored in the relevant USB. An operator, at teacher's presence, automatically generates and prints 60 different versions of the exam - papers, using Microsoft Word with a special macro code written in Visual Basic in order to design the proper page making. The secretary also prints a personalized answer sheet, with a student photo for everyone. It is very important for e-students, because minimum time is needed for student's authentication during exams. All answer-sheets are automatically scanned via "SEKRETAR" software (Copyright Romeo Teneqexhi, ZSHDA) and the outcome is generated immediately after the exam procedures. The process could also be handled by the secretary, but it can be used by the teacher himself in the exam classroom. The teacher only needs a laptop and a simple scanner in exam classroom. For the future, we plan to substitute this laptop-scanner-system with the teacher's smart phone. All the above services and provisions can be offered to all teachers by logging to a web platform.

KEYWORDS

Scanner based assessment, personalized thesis, personalized answer sheet

1. INTRODUCTION

The authors are teachers in different universities in Tirana, Albania. We all like our profession and are very dedicated to teaching. There are two main reasons why we started working on this project: For many years in Albania entering the university as a student has been arranged through a competition process. This process is similarly like organizing exams with considerable numbers of students. Every faculty used to organize its own test, by occupying its teachers for assessment. For objective assessment reason, these kind of exams have been organized by using secrete barcodes. Many university teachers were involved into the assessment process, because the assessment has been performed manually. A pretty long time was needed to announce the results to the students. In some cases, we have encountered corruption problems. Most of the time, the tests have been multiple choice question type. Preserving the secrecy of the "solution key" has been a big problem. The second reason for initiation of this project is the fact that even in the course of the normal exams, at times students try to copy from each other. To avoid the negative phenomena, we have developed a full system for preparing individual (personalized) theses with the same set of questions for all students. Students give the answers by completing the personalized answer sheet and the outcome is given immediately after the exam. This is carried out by the teacher himself in exam-classroom by using a simple scanner and a laptop. The system we have set up is an infrastructure offered to the teachers to help them prepare, organize and successfully finalize the exams. We have conceived the whole aligned process as a chain where the first and the last link is the teacher. With the other links in between, common infrastructure used to help in the process. Let us clarify the following steps.

2. PREPARATION OF THESIS

Let us suppose you represent the teacher and want to use our infrastructure to organize a multiple choice question exam with randomly, 60 questions (the system provides exams up to 100 questions). All you have to proceed is just to put in a USB folder 60 JPG files (or photos with other words). It does not matter on how you produce these files by scanning, taking pictures by smart phone, grabbing from computer screen, exporting from a graphic software, etc. (the easiest way is by cropping a piece of computer screen using "sniping tool" in windows 7 or later version). It is important to name these files like this: "exercise01+10-3.jpg", "exercise02+3-1.jpg", "exercise03+6-2.jpg", and on. If you see between "exercise" and ".jpg", there is the information included in the name of the file. What does it mean? The number immediately after "exercise" means the number of exercise (in our case study, 01 to 60). This number is very important for future reference during the whole process. The information "+3-1" for example in "exercise02+3-1.jpg" conveys this meaning: If the student finds the right answer he/she takes 3 points plus. If the student gives the wrong answer he/she takes 1 point minus. The "minus number" in the name of the file is optional, but "plus number" is obligatory. By leaving all options empty or giving more than one answer, is also penalized by "negative number". Option "I don't know" must be in all exercises (zero point resulting for this answer). This system is preferably chosen to avoid passing the exam, by giving random answers from the students. On the other hand, this gives the possibility to have in exam, exercises of graded difficulty and weight. The information "plus number" / "minus number" must be visible for the student for every exercise, certainly, according to the information in the file name. If the teacher wants, he/she can add notice inside the exercise image for example (with explanation). This means that the students must have written in the notebook, the explanation of the corresponding answer. In this case, after computer assessment, the teacher can review the outcome checking for randomly finding the right answer by the student. All these 60 exercises are ordered, as mentioned in the name of the file make so-called "VARIANT ZERO". All the students have to answer these 60 exercises, but they will have them ordered in different manner. Nobody will have "variant zero" in exams. This is only for the teacher. According to "variant zero", the teacher must prepare the so-called "solution key" which will be used later for the assessment.

3. VARIANTS GENERATION

After the teacher has saved all exams images in a separated folder in a USB memory stick, he/she has to go to the printing center of the Faculty, where the system of theses generation is available. The number of students and the folder where the photos are located in USB as mentioned above, is the only information the operator wants to know for preparing different variants for every student. The operator, at teacher's presence, automatically generates and prints for each student a different version of the exam thesis, using Microsoft Word equipped with a special macro code written in Visual Basic. Only the computer knows how the thesis is mixed in each version. Every version of thesis is named automatically as "version 001", "version 002", "version 070" etc. The operator also prints a "variant zero" of the thesis and this is only for the teacher. He will use it to prepare the KEY solution of these. In figure below are shown variant 491 and 492 of a thesis, with 14 exercises. The composition of the page is flexible and easily configured by the operator.

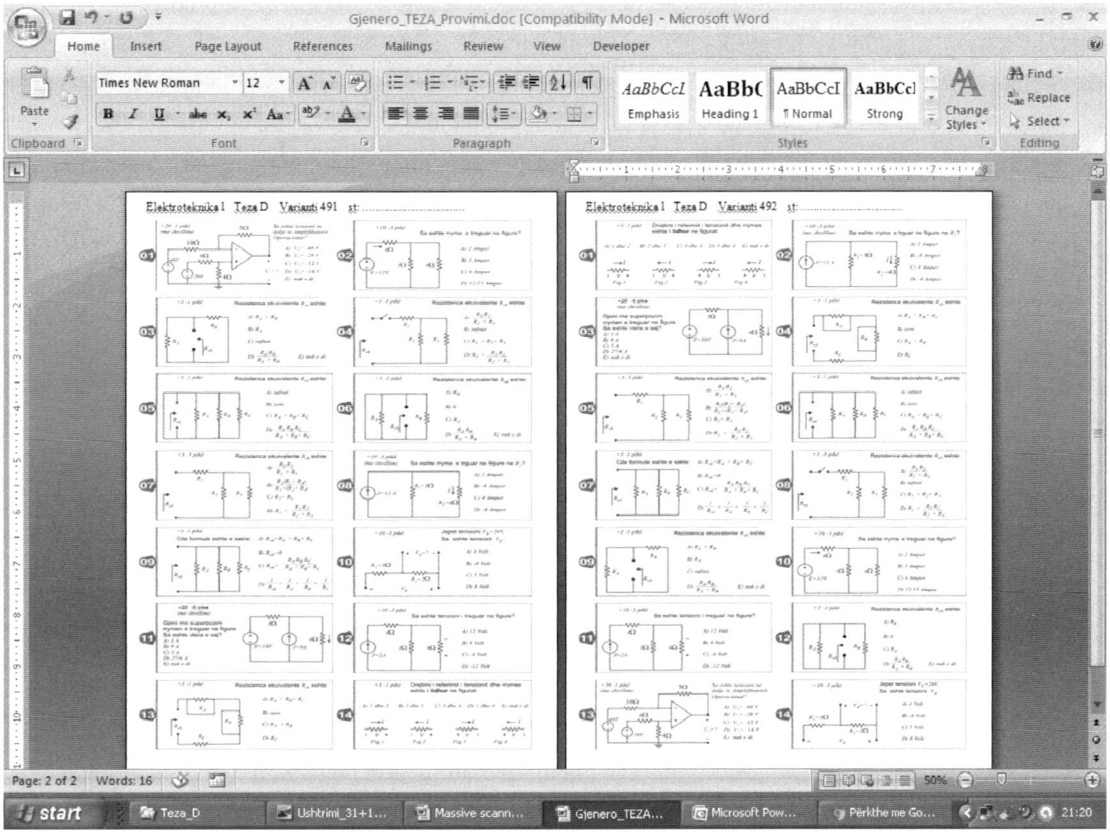

Figure 1. Two exam thesis automated generated via Microsoft Word

4. PRINTING PERSONALISED ANSWER SHEETS

The system we have developed is closely related with the secretary of the university. The teacher informs the secretary for the exams, at least, two hours before the exam takes place. The "SEKRETAR" software which is installed in our university is capable to print in minutes the personalized answer sheets, with student's photo, for every student of the Study Course. Every answer sheet is a unique one, with a unique serial number. It contains graphic elements for identification by the scanner and spaces for putting personal data by the student. The student has to fulfill this sheet according to the personal thesis. By using this answer sheet, you can arrange up to 4 different subject exams in one classroom (Thesis A, B, C, D). Student has to declare on the answer sheet his/her variant number of thesis, give the answer of the question and sign next to his name.

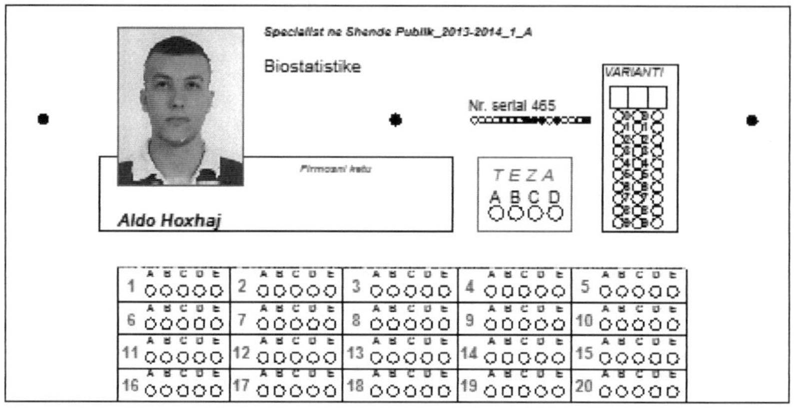

Figure 2. Personalized answer sheet

5. SCANNER BASED ASSESSMENT

As it is mentioned above, every student has in the exams, his personalized answer sheet, one thesis and the notebook. He has to give all the answers of exercises to the answer sheet by making a black spot inside the corresponding circle. When he finishes the exam, he gives to the teacher the answer sheet which is scanned by the software "SEKRETAR". If there are problems while completing the answer sheet, they can be corrected by the student before he leaves the exam room. After the last student completes the exam, the teacher is ready to give the preliminary result / outcome to the student immediately. It means every student knows the points he/she has collected. The final assessment can be arranged by the teacher later, or immediately after the exam. It is up to the teacher. All data generated by the scanning process are automatically saved, in an excel file. Teachers can make use of them for different statistical purposes and conclusions in assessments.

6. CONCLUSION

The authors of this article and several colleagues have used this system in their exams, and the results have been nearly the same with the traditional exams assessment. The students are very much satisfied with this technique and we recommend this soft system to be spread into other Albanian universities. For the future, we plan to substitute this laptop-scanner system with teacher's smart phone. All services for the teachers, as mentioned above, can be also offered by a web platform.

REFERENCES

1. MICROSOFT WORD (User Manual): https://www.tutorialspoint.com/word/
2. "SEKRETAR" software, Copyright registration in ZSHDA: www.zshda.gov.al
3. VISUAL BASIC 6 (Programming Language): http://www.vbtutor.net/vbtutor.html

DESIGNING A WEB-BASED ASYNCHRONOUS INNOVATION / ENTREPRENEURISM COURSE

Parviz Ghandforoush
Virginia Tech, 7054 Haycock Road, Falls Church, Virginia U.S.A. 22043

ABSTRACT

Teaching an online fully asynchronous information technology course that requires students to ideate, build an e-commerce website, and develop an effective business plan involves a well-developed and highly engaging course design. This paper describes the design, development, and implementation of such a course and presents information on students' learning effectiveness and challenges associated with managing a course using this approach.

KEYWORDS

Online Instruction, Asynchronous, Innovation and Entrepreneurism

1. INTRODUCTION

Teaching fully asynchronous courses online requires faculty expertise, a well-developed course plan, and the required technology to enable effective communication between faculty and students. Unlike highly technical courses teaching students to engage in creative projects and to build a functioning enterprise online has many challenges associated with it and thus requires further attention given to the development of an effective course design. In a course involving examination of the concepts, technologies, and applications of electronic commerce with topics including the World Wide Web as a platform for electronic commerce; mobile networks; electronic banking and payment systems; security and firewalls; software agents; and the social, legal, and international issues of electronic commerce we need a carefully planned set of foundational topics to be shared with learners plus a technology platform that will allow for individual and group communication and teamwork.

2. COURSE DESIGN

Two approaches can be taken to integrate e-commerce website and platform building: 1) Teaching a standardized process, so students all acquire the skills by watching the instructor demonstrate and the students emulate or 2) Creating the framework for students to fathom their own ideas and experiment with building out their own implementation. Option 2 will require more time, empathy, and attention as students should be given autonomy, but be closely monitored to ensure certain levels of productivity and forward trajectory. Students should also be primed to think innovatively and entrepreneurially, which will take additional time and energy from the instructional team.

Several tactics to promote innovation and entrepreneurism include:

a. Cultivate creativity by encouraging students to experiment, fail, and obtain feedback. This must be a controlled process.

b. Use guest speakers to encourage and motivate students. Bringing in actual practitioners to complement professor teachings would only reinforce concepts and show the realm of possibilities to students.

Enter the text here.

c. Mandate entrepreneurial book readings and articles. Students can learn the intricacies of e-commerce, the internet, and business principles through the textbook; however, integrating short, practical books can help invigorate students' entrepreneurial ambitions. Some of the material in this field provide an atypical framework to creating a business that is currently not being taught in conventional textbooks. Exposing students to both perspectives expands their horizon for thinking.

d. Provide timely feedback to students. Give ample feedback and provide early and often to help steer students in the correct direction early. Additionally, early feedback allows students to take corrective measures or to stifle the onset of bad habits.

e. Allow students to focus on the "big picture" problem. Give students the opportunity to formulate a strategy to solve a "big picture" issue, then remove encumbrances that may inhibit the creativity process. Inundating students with too many smaller level tasks or "Level C" tasks prevents them from accomplishing "Level A" tasks. It will be up to the instructor to design the course to create primary "Level A" tasks / objectives rather than to generate a series of constant "Level C" deliverables.

2.1 Learning Mediums

All students learn differently and require different modes of exposure to content. The five learning mediums used are described below:

1. Learning Communities- The purpose of advanced level educational degrees is to become producers of information rather than consumers of information. Another benefit to pursuing these degrees is the networking. To facilitate networking in an Online program may seem difficult, which is why Learning Communities are being used more often.

Through the use of learning communities, students foster relationships with peers by moving from a large sized class to a smaller segmented group of individuals. The formation of learning communities should be well-thought out to prevent too many like-minded individuals from congregating together and possibly creating groupthink. Diversity of group members' perspectives and backgrounds should be considered when curating groups. These individuals will work within the Learning Community together, which creates this illusion of a smaller class. This removes the fear and intimidation or the feeling of being a "lost voice" in the sea of many when in a large class.

If a degree program encourages more group work in subsequent classes, many students in Learning Communities will have already established working relationships and can leverage these relationships in future courses. In an introductory core course and predecessor to many other courses in various modules, this would be a good course for students to establish networks and relationships, and promote strong work ethics due to the rigors of the course. Furthermore, Learning Communities can encourage students to learn or improve rapport building skills as they navigate the course together and negotiate tasks and team contributions with one another.

Within Learning Communities, prompts must be provided to facilitate discussion. The discussion prompts used in the class pertain to entrepreneurism concepts. Since students read the material on their own with very minimal oversight or compliance enforcement, the discussion prompts are used to serve as the mechanisms to instill student accountability. Students are asked to read two (2) chapters from the book every week, then required to create three (3) possible exam questions to posit to their peers. Peers are then obligated to answer three (3) of their peers' questions. Essentially, students became the solutions architects of possible final exam questions. Since students have to devise their own examination questions, this would incentivize them to do the readings, ask the questions, and answer other questions. Professors can conduct quality control of the questions by monitoring the types of questions posited. If key concepts are not sufficiently covered, then the professor has the right to intervene and reorient the types of questions asked or generate his/ her own final exam questions. This further incentivized students to ask deep, profound questions covering essential topics and concepts to ensure insertion into the final exam.

2. Hands-on Application- In such a course students are required to build an e-commerce website. Each student is required to learn the necessary skills to build his/her own website. Later, they will assemble into groups to build one larger application. In order to get students ready for the build, each has to complete a series of individual assignments. Once completed, they work together to formulate a business plan for ideation and planning purposes, then seek to implement the plan.

Steps to getting students ready for the build:

Students are exposed to Library Resources such as business databases, government statistics, and industry analyses to understand how to conduct market research on a superficial level.

Students then are asked to analyze two existing e-commerce businesses and determine their business models. This would help not only with writing business plans, but also to nurture the creative thinking process.

Students are then required to build their own WordPress websites for hosting. Customization of WordPress websites is restricted in some hosting sites; however, students are exposed to the principles of what comprised a website. The subject matter of the website is up to the student. This is another tool to allow for student's creativity to flourish and thrive.

Students peer review each other's websites to learn practices undertaken by others, but also to ease the grading burden for the Instructors. The more peers can do to grade one another, the less workload imposed on the graders.

Students create an Ecwid.com site to understand the simplicity of creating an E-commerce storefront in the matter of minutes.

Students engage in two rounds of business plan writing: 1) Initial business plan and 2) Final business plan. The initial business plan is required to structure groups' to first plan out the product or service they would unveil to the marketspace. This is to be written before building the e-commerce site. The Final business plans is written in conjunction with the build. If groups find it implausible to build the site, they could pivot and change course. They could amend the business plan or abandon it and create something entirely new. The business plan is not intended to become a restrictive device to bind students to an untested product or service. It is not until they started the build and obtained feedback that they could amend or change accordingly.

Teach website development skills. These are the skill sets students need to separate themselves from other peers. Once the skill is attained, students can create an online portfolio of projects they've built in school to showcase to employers, investors, family, and friends. In fact, every student should have his / her own website to serve as a dynamic resume. This could be construed to be the same as a LinkedIn account, but this site could be leveraged to demonstrate his or her creativity. They could also integrate social media accounts onto their websites to create a repository of a person's web presence and social footprint.

In school, students learn how to create PowerPoints for presentations. Students can learn how to create websites and use websites for presentations, too. This can be used as a communication tool. Creating websites is simply a functional skill to have.

3. Live Q & A sessions- Live Q&A sessions are administered every week. instructors teach requisite skills students need in order to propel forward motion. For example, the Instructors can teach how to setup a WordPress website and how to navigate through the dashboard. This frees students from fumbling around in the backend to focus more on what they intended to build and how to convey the content.

4. Lectures, Textbooks, and Examinations- Lectures and examinations are the traditional vehicles to convey and indelibly imbue key concepts and takeaways. These methods should still be the staples in any course. There are other vehicles to complement lectures and textbooks, but those methods should be combined synergistically. For example, examinations are accountability tools to ensure students are attending lectures and reading materials. Without exams, students may not attend class nor read materials on their own without some sort of enforcement mechanism.

In reference to student readings, students can lose fervor to engage reading materials if the reading materials are located in various locations. Some online courses provide links to online content for reading. Some courses provide journal articles for reading. When textbooks are used for a course, these act as centralized repositories to reduce the amount of "moving parts" in a class. This is akin to website browsing. Web surfers would like to obtain all their content from a single website. When websites begin directing users to different sites that is when users get lost in the shuffle. They begin reading topics outside the webpage and can become distracted from the main purpose of visiting the initial website.

Also, textbooks can facilitate a standardized routine for students. When an online class has multiple aspects to it, such as Learning Communities and Hands-on Applications, for students to know that every week they will have certain amount of material to read, they can read or plan ahead. They can count the amount of weeks that have elapsed to know how many chapters they should have read. By routinizing their reading schedule, students can free up their conscious mind to think creatively for projects and hands-on applications.

5. Discussion Forum- Students need lively discussions. Students will ask the same questions and it's best to create a centralized repository for them to seek when needed. Being this is asynchronous, some students get a preemptive jump and start at the beginning of the week. If they encounter a problem, they ask the question in the forum. These are similar to the early adopters. Then the early majority swoops in and asks more questions. By the time the late majority and laggards begin their work, all the questions and answers will dwell within a discussion forum.

Instructors need to create the discussion forums from which all the data can be accumulated. If the professor does not, students can create their own discussion forums. When students begin creating their own discussion forums, then randomness takes place and it becomes more difficult to figure out where to start. If not, there just becomes an abundant amount of prompts with few responses and it becomes so overwhelming to click through each post read. We must still think about user navigation and user interface. The less clicks they have to make the better.

Concepts described in this paper are currently being implemented in an information technology course with 86 students enrolled. The results of this experimental study will be available at the conclusion of the course.

REFERENCES

Arbaugh, J. B. (2005). Is there an optimal design for online MBA courses? Academy of Management Learning & Education, 4(2), 135-149.

Arbaugh, J. B., Rau, B. L. (2007). A study of disciplinary, structural, and behavioral effects on course outcomes in online MBA courses. Decision Sciences Journal of Innovative Education, 5(1), 65-95.

Brower, H.H. (2003). On emulating classroom discussion in a distance-delivered OBHR course: creating an online community. Academy of Management Learning and Education, 2(1), 22-36.

Clouse, S. F., & Evans, G. E. (2003). Graduate business students' performance with synchronous and asynchronous interaction e-learning methods. Decision Sciences Journal of Innovative Education, 1(2),181-202.

Dellana, S. A., Collins, W. H., et al. (2000). Online education in a management science course -- effectiveness and performance factors. Journal of Education for Business, 76(1), 43-47.

Liaw, S. S., Chen, G. D., and Huang, H. M. (2008). Users' attitudes toward web-based collaborative learning systems for knowledge management. Computers & Education, 50(3), 950-961.

Ries, E. (2011). The lean Startup: How Today's Entrepreneurs use Continuous Innovation to Create Radically Successful Businesses. Crown Publishing, New York.

Rovai, A. P. (2001). Building classroom community at a distance: A case study. Educational Technology Research and Development, 49(2), 33-48.

Scifres, E. L., Behara, R. S. (1998). An ampirical investigatin of electronic groups in the classroom. Journal of Education for Business, 73(4), 247-250.

Seo, K. K. (2007). Utilizing peer moderating in online discussions: addressing the controversy between teacher moderation and non-moderation. American Journal of Distance Education, 21(1), 21-36.

Sonner, B. S. (1999). Success in the capstone business course -- assessing the effectiveness of distance learning. Journal of Education for Business, 74(4), 243-247.

Swan, K. (2002). Building learning communities in online courses: the importance of interaction. Education, Communication, & Information, 2(1), 23-49.

Williams, E. A., Duray, R., & Reddy, V. (2006). Teamwork orientation, group cohesiveness, and student learning: a study of the use of teams in online distance education. Journal of Management Education, 30(4), 592-616.

SEMANTIC ANNOTATION OF RESOURCES TO LEARN WITH CONNECTED THINGS

Aymeric Bouchereau and Ioan Roxin
ELLIADD laboratory, Franche-Comté University, France

ABSTRACT

Computer systems tend to be ubiquitous as they become more integrated in our everyday activities, embedded in tables, shoes, watch and plenty of others connected things (CT). In the e-learning field, the transformations induced by the Internet of Things (IoT) allow individuals to learn whenever they want, accessing a quantity of diverse digital learning resources (DLR) and experiencing new interaction modes paired with innovative pedagogical methods. In the perspective of ubiquitous learning in line with the IoT paradigm, accessibility and interoperability of the DLRs became critical for accessing knowledge. The growing volume of online data scattered in heterogeneous repositories restrains these DLR characteristics. In these conditions, we think semantic Web technologies can be used to face these challenging issues enhance DLR accessibility and interoperability to sustain ubiquitous learning.

KEYWORDS

Digital learning resource, Internet of Things, Linked Open Data, semantic web, ubiquitous learning

1. INTRODUCTION

The pervasiveness of connected things (CT) and the ubiquity of communication networks have given rise to the ubiquitous computing (Weiser, 1999) and contribute to the Internet of Things (IoT) development. In education, the digital convergence—i.e. the digitalization and integration of various media (e.g. voice, picture, video, text) into one architecture—and the explosion of Internet-based services have stimulated new ways of learning and teaching. The IoT paradigm tends to continue and emphasise these transformations, leading to ubiquitous learning (u-learning): individuals can learn throughout everyday activities (Yahya et al., 2010). The ATAWADAC acronym (AnyTime, AnyWhere, AnyDevice, AnyContent)[1] illustrates the fact that learning activities can occur without constraints of time, space, device and content (Derycke, 2006). The CT multiplication is combined with a diversification of presentation forms, interaction modes (provided by ubiquitous user interfaces (Krumm, 2010)) and pedagogical methods (e.g. flipped classroom, blended learning). These elements echo with learning theories like constructivism (Piaget, 1969) and socio-constructivism (Vygotski, 1997), suggesting that learners construct knowledge by means of involvement, social interaction and collaboration.

Beyond the implementation of u-learning in relation to the IoT, the main issues are accessibility and interoperability of Digital Learning Resources (DLR, like books, videos, pictures, Open Educational Resources (OER) and Massive Open Online Courses (MOOC)). These DLR characteristics are critical to access knowledge, to the design of learning platforms and to the Open Learning movement (Barker and Campbell, 2016). Nonetheless, obstacles are reducing access to relevant DLRs and are negatively impacting the e- learning sector.

The aim of this paper is to give an overview on DLR accessibility and interoperability issues and solutions regarding to the IoT development. In section 2, we highlight obstacles to u-learning generated by evolution's intrinsic effects of technologies and by the adopted model of e-learning actors. In section 3, we will describe semantic Web technologies as a possible solution to face these challenging issues and their potential to sustain u-learning.

---

[1] Extension of ATAWAD, a term registered by Xavier Dalloz in 2003.

2. LEARNING HINDRANCES

In an "everything's connected" world individuals are bombarded with a mass of information that exceeds individuals' capacity to treat all. When it comes to learning the phenomenon becomes problematic because individuals are facing a growing volume of DLRs scattered in distinct silos that tend to isolate resources from each other.

2.1 Data Volume

In the form of dictionaries, encyclopaedias, MOOCs, learning systems, videos, blogs, records, video games, and interactive devices, individuals have access to a vast amount of DLRs. Like (IDC, 2014; Kanellos, 2016) numerous studies demonstrated the gigantism of the data volume produced and its exponential growth. The digital convergence and the explosion of the Internet have initiated a systematic process of knowledge dematerialization and publication on the Web. In so doing, the World Wide Web (WWW) has evolved into a virtual library hosting countless books. Learner's questions are no longer about the existence of a specific DLR, but about the localization. The Web looks like a library in which finding the corresponding book to a specific need becomes complex and requires the support of specialized tools (e.g. vertical search engines, MOOC platforms, databases, Virtual Learning Environments (VLE)). In these conditions, the identification of relevant DLR becomes time-consuming and the success may depend on variables such as time spent on the task, search channels used, and the ability to discern what is appropriate and what is not. In other words, the volume limits the effectiveness of DLR searching activities and restraints DLR accessibility.

2.2 Data Silos

The limited accessibility of the DLRs is also amplified by their dissemination in different repositories (e.g. OER repository, VLE, MOOC platform) (Dietze et al., 2013); which engenders DLR isolation. The plurality and heterogeneity of repositories make critical the interoperability characteristic of DLR as formats and structures vary from one repository to another. Plus, within the Web 2.0, learning platforms have been built upon closed environment using proprietary technologies and architectures (Christian Bizer et al., 2009; Piedra et al., 2017). As a consequence, the visibility and discovery of the DLRs are lessened (Piedra et al., 2017) and learners have no choice but to adapt and adopt specific strategies to find relevant DLR (e.g. using vertical search engine, repeating investigation on each repository). To improve interoperability, standards have been developed to provide a common and structured description of DLR: Dublin Core (DC), Learning Object Metadata (LOM), Tin Can API (the successor of Sharable Content Object Reference Model (SCORM)) (Abdullah and Abdel Aziz Ali, 2016; Klašnja-Milićević et al., 2017). Nevertheless difficulties are persisting to express all possible contexts, use cases and DLRs (Allert, 2004). The coexistence of standards sharing the same purpose limits the interoperability because learning platforms are implementing different one. Despite this, several projects aim to enhance the DLR visibility and discovery by manually indexing and listing them into a single repository. For example, the "search engine for pedagogical resources" set up by the French government is indexing DLR according to the SupLOMFR standard (Sup-Numérique, 2017). More widely with the Open Learning movement where several repositories and resource aggregators have been created to index and list OERs (Barker and Campbell, 2016). Yet, operation modes and standards used to describe DLR differ from one project to another (Dietze et al., 2013). In a general way, we can state that the visibility and the discovery of the DLRs are limited by the lack of interoperability among platforms and resources.

3. RESOURCE INTERCONNECTION

DLR accessibility and interoperability needs to be improved so individuals can easily find relevant resources without searching in a quantity of information and multiple repositories. In this context, we think semantic Web technologies and more specifically the Linked Open Data (LOD) can enhance the visibility and discovery of the DLRs and, therefore, can support u-learning.

3.1 Semantic Web and Linked Open Data (LOD)

Initiated by Tim Berners-Lee and the World Wide Web Consortium (W3C), the semantic Web (also called Web of data, which is sometimes used in reference to the Web 3.0) is an extension of the Web of documents designed for data (Berners-Lee et al., 2001). More precisely, the semantic Web gives computer systems the capacity to understand the "meaning" of data and make them searchable like current Web documents. This can be achieved thanks to the description of knowledge and relationships between data in accordance with a structured language. In order to undertake the semantic Web goals, the LOD concept (called Linked Data without the notion of openness) aims at formally describing data, creating connections among themselves and enabling readability as if it was web documents. When publishing data on the Web, the following principles should be applied to be compliant with LOD: formal description of data using the Resource Description Framework (RDF) language, unique identification via the Uniform Resource Identifier (URI) protocol, linking with existing online data, and open exploitation of data with the HyperText Transfer Protocol (HTTP) (Christian Bizer et al., 2009). The semantic description and the creation of connections among data and datasets lead to the creation of a global graph, composed of data (respecting the LOD principles) across the Web. From the point of view of learning, the LOD principles are promoting an open access to DLR from any computer without the need of specific and proprietary programs. The use of a common description language and the DLR interconnection ensure their interoperability so that learners can easily access to a DLR and navigate from one to another (d'Aquin, 2012).

3.2 Exploitation of Semantic Resources

In addition to technologies for describing, identifying and accessing DLR, the W3C also standardized tools to query and handle resources with semantic annotation. Thus, thanks to the SPARQL Protocol and RDF Query Language (SPARQL), it is possible to build and execute complex queries on a graph of RDF described resources: to select, modify, update, or delete information[2]. Besides SPARQL, the standard Linked Data Platform (LDP) achieves the same goals but with an approach turned towards Web services production (Nandana Mihindukulasooriya, 2016). LDP behaves like an extension of HTTP and defines an architecture to read and write data on the Web. The LDP operationalization is close to the REpresentational State Transfer (REST) architecture on which are based numerous Web services. These standards can be used as a basis for the design of tools to speed up the identification of relevant DLR and recommendation systems can enhance their suggestions to the learners. The creation of a resource graph reduces silos negative effects and fosters the accessibility and interoperability of the DLRs. The implementation of systems able to correlate the meaning of the resource and the meaning of the query ensures efficient DLR identification. Moreover, the identification process can also be fine-tuned by considering the learner's profile (e.g. age, knowledge level, learning style) and contextual information (e.g. localisation, time, device). The development of semantic learning tools allowing relevant DLR identification can sustain learning activities within the IoT paradigm outlined in the introduction. On the one hand, CT supports mobility, interactivity and peer collaboration and, on the other hand, visibility and discovery of suitable DLR are ensured by semantic Web Technologies. We think these conditions make possible the operationalization of opportunities offered by the IoT and can support the advancement of u-learning—i.e. providing the right DLR, at the right time and the right place.

4. CONCLUSION

Transformations involve by the IoT progress are changing practices and tools for learning and teaching. The increasing number of CT and the ubiquitous aspect of communication networks contribute to the diversification and multiplication of DLRs. Perspectives brought by the IoT suggest u-learning whose main features are ubiquity, the diversity of presentation forms, new interaction modes, the application of innovative pedagogy, and personalization. However, the progress of IoT adapted learning is hampered by a limited DLR accessibility and interoperability. Individuals are searching DLRs in a large volume of resources in which the most relevant DLRs are drowned. DLR visibility and discovery are also reduced by a silos

[2] https://www.w3.org/TR/rdf-sparql-query/

model created both by proprietary platforms, and by the heterogeneity of standards and repositories. In these circumstances, we proposed to use semantic Web technologies, which are endowed with properties that allow answering DLR accessibility and interoperability issues. On one side, computer systems became able to understand the meaning of data they handle due to the semantic annotation of DLR in line with a structured description language. On the other side, the creation of a link between a DLR and an existing online data leads to the development of a global graph that can be explored like we used to with documents on the Web. Both mechanisms improve the accessibility and interoperability of resources by implementing a more efficient DLR organization and by providing effective tools to query and identify relevant DLR. Therefore, we think u-learning can be sustained by semantic Web-based systems that enable to relevant identification and provide rapid access to a DLR in relation to a context. Our future works should focus on modelling such a system and reflecting on these following concerns: means for semantically annotated DLR in distributed repositories, DLR indexation, semantic kernel for querying resources, and management of contextual data and learner's profile.

REFERENCES

Abdullah, M. and Abdel Aziz Ali, N., 2016. E-learning standards. *Proceedings of the International Conference on Communication (ICCMIT 2016)*. Cosenza, Italy, pp. 639–648.

Allert, H., 2004. Coherent Social Systems for Learning: An Approach for Contextualized and Community-Centred Metadata. *Journal of Interactive Media in Education*. Vol. 2004, No. 1, p.Art.7.

Barker, P. and Campbell, L.M., 2016. 3. Technology Strategies for Open Educational Resource Dissemination. *Open Education: International Perspectives in Higher Education*. Open Book Publishers, pp. 51–72.

Berners-Lee, T., Hendler, J. and Lassila, O., 2001. The Semantic Web. *Scientific American*. May 2001, pp. 28–37.

Bizer, C., Heath, T. and Berners-Lee, T., 2009. Linked Data - The Story So Far. *International Journal on Semantic Web and Information Systems (IJSWIS)*. Special Issue on Linked Data.

d'Aquin, M., 2012. *Linked data for open and distance learning*. Commonwealth of Learning, Burnaby, Canada.

Derycke, A., 2006. Du E-Learning au Pervasive-Learning: Concepts, Exemples et Questions de Recherche. *Conférence UBIMOB'06*. Paris, France.

Dietze, S., Sanchez-Alonso, S., Ebner, H., Qing Yu, H., Giordano, D., Marenzi, I. and Pereira Nunes, B., 2013. Interlinking educational resources and the web of data: A survey of challenges and approaches. *Program*. Vol. 47, No. 1, pp. 60–91.

IDC, 2014. The Digital Universe of Opportunities: Rich Data and the Increasing Value of the Internet of Things. *EMC*.

Kanellos, M., 2016. 152,000 Smart Devices Every Minute In 2025: IDC Outlines The Future of Smart Things. *Forbes*.

Klašnja-Milićević, A., Vesin, B., Ivanović, M., Budimac, Z. and Jain, L.C., 2017. *E-Learning Systems*. Springer International Publishing, Switzerland.

Krumm, J. (Ed.), 2010. *Ubiquitous computing fundamentals*. Chapman & Hall/CRC Press, Boca Ragon.

Nandana Mihindukulasooriya, 2016. Introduction to W3C Linked Data Platform (LDP). 4th Linked Data in Architecture and Construction Workshop. Madrid, Spain.

Piaget, J., 1969. *Psychologie et pédagogie*, Denoël ed., Paris, France.

Piedra, N., Chicaiza, J., Atenas, J., Lopez-Vargas, J. and Tovar, E., 2017. Using Linked Data to Blended Educational Materials With OER—A General Context of Synergy: Linked Data for Describe, Discovery and Retrieve OER and Human Beings Knowledge to Provide Context. *Open Education: From OERs to MOOCs*. Springer, Berlin, Heidelberg, pp. 283–313.

Sup-Numérique, 2017. Moteur des ressources pédagogiques - sup-numerique.gouv.fr. Ministère de l'éducation nationale, de l'enseignement supérieur et de la recherche.

Vygotski, L.S., 1997. *Pensée et langage*, La Dispute ed., Paris, France.

Weiser, M., 1999. The Computer for the 21st Century. *SIGMOBILE Mobile Computing and Communications Review*. Vol. 3, No. 3, pp. 3-11.

Yahya, S., Arniza Ahmad, E. and Abd Jalil, K., 2010. The definition and characteristics of ubiquitous learning: A discussion. *International Journal of Education and Development using Information and Communication Technology (IJEDICT)*. Vol. 6, No. 1, pp. 117–127.

Posters

DEVELOPMENT OF A FRAMEWORK FOR MOOC IN CONTINUOUS TRAINING

Carolina Amado and Ana Pedro
Instituto de Educação, Universidade de Lisboa, Alameda da Universidade, 1649-013 Lisboa, Portugal

ABSTRACT

Inserted in the area of education in the field of specialty of the technologies of information and communication in the education, the focus of this research is the production of knowledge about the MOOC (Massive Open Online Courses) within the educational community, through the formulation of a conceptual framework for the continuous training.
The accelerated expansion and spread of digital technologies has made the Massive Open Online Course (MOOC) a mass distribution of knowledge, providing access to a more open and flexible education. Nevertheless, being a relatively recent phenomenon, it is still not considered properly or excessively clarified, thus motivating us to carry out this study, seeking to know this reality more deeply. Thus, the focus of the future study is to develop a framework for MOOC in the context of continuing teacher education.

KEYWORDS

MOOC, Framework, Continuous Training

1. INTRODUCTION

This article reports research developed within the PhD Program Technology Enhanced Learning and Societal Challenges, funded by Fundação para a Ciência e Tecnologia, FCT I. P. – Portugal, under contracts # PD/00173/2014 and # PD/BI/127984/2016.

Inserted in the area of education in the field of specialty of the technologies of information and communication in the education, the focus of this research is the production of knowledge about the MOOC (Massive Open Online Courses) within the educational community, through the formulation of a conceptual framework for the continuous training.

Our research fits into the field of education and training, specifically in the recent modality of massive and open distribution of knowledge. We consider that the theme Massive Open Online Courses is relevant, evidencing and attending to the national and international adhesion of this type of courses, signaled by the growing number of studies that have arisen. Nevertheless, being a relatively recent phenomenon, it is still not considered properly or excessively clarified, thus motivating us to carry out this study, seeking to know this reality more deeply.

In this line, we understand a possible gap in the construction of courses of this format: the lack of a solid and justified structure in the construction of a MOOC. Thus, this work intends to contribute to the construction of courses in this format, within the framework of continuous teacher training, showing how this typology of courses can be adjusted to the training offer for teacher training.

2. WORK IN PROGRESS

Several distance education, open education and online educational service delivery programs have been developed to promote accessibility and personalized learning in higher education (Perifanou, 2014). Currently, with the advent of MOOC, new educational models have emerged that offer flexibility and completion of the course for free or low cost (Yuan & Powell, 2013).

A Massive Open Online Courses is a recent phenomenon that has emerged, particularly in the field of higher education. Distinguishing from more traditional online courses, the MOOC are new learning environments based on the connectivist learning theory of Siemens and Downes (2008). These courses support a large number of participants, intermediated by online, interactive and collaborative application models and in open access, with shared knowledge freely without restrictions (geographical and economic) of access.

As regards the development of frameworks, several works have been done in this area, highlighting the work of Rosselle, Caron and Heutte (2014) and Schneider (2013). However, we consider it necessary to know works done a priori in this area, whose purpose is to know the empirical field to later define it. Defining the field, is relevant make a bridge between the same and the area of MOOC, allowing meet the links shared of the two concepts.

We pretend to research, especiafically, a field low explored due to the potencial as work and in order to give fill the gap of have scarce information in that area. Thus, we intend know in-depth a field, develop and definy it based in research done for others.

2.1 Problem, Research Questions and Objectives

The present work is based on the following research problem: What criteria should be established for the creation of a framework for MOOC in the context of continuous training?

This problem arose due to the need to (i) study a recent educational phenomenon, (ii) to clarify a gap identified by us and to establish clear lines regarding the construction and development of MOOC, and (iii) to apply empirical methodologies and techniques that May be favorable to our study.

Having stated our research problem, we have set out four questions that we intend to answer in the course of our research, and we consider it essential to achieve the goals set by us.

Q1: What dimensions are identified in the various types of frameworks for existing MOOCs and how are they implemented?

Q2: What factors are related to MOOC implementation success?

Q3: Are there any specifications based on the context or audience for which the MOOC is directed?

Q4: Are there particular factors and / or dimensions depending on the context or the target audience for which the MOOC is directed?

Through the exposition of the problem and research questions, the present research has as general objective to structure a solid framework of the development of MOOC, applied in the scope of continuous training. According to the situation identified as problematic, the following specific objectives were defined:

(i) Carry out the literary review and existing works on the topics to be studied, defining and highlighting the key concepts;

(ii) Analyze multiple framework typologies for MOOC (through scoping literature review) and verify the various dimensions of these frameworks, in order to consider the key elements to create a supportive framework for MOOC;

(iii) Structuring a framework for MOOC, stating the dimensions that constitute it and indicating how these dimensions can be applied in the context of continuous training.

3. FUTURE WORK

In this research we need to establish the methodology that fits and meets our objectives and which respond to our questions, opting maybe to a qualitative or mixed methodology. However, this parameter is not definitively defined, being one of the characteristics to establish in future work.

Besides that, we intend to understand MOOC vision and building process behind it, through the knowledge and concepts acquired in a literature review. This study aims to establish a literary systematization through foundations based on reality and knowledge and services, serving as support for the research problem. In other words, it is intended to find a clear explanation through the collection of data in the empirical reality, carrying out an in-depth study through the systematization of existing knowledge and new findings based on research.

In this way, it will be sought to determine and establish potential typologies and plausible and credible dimensions for the development of a framework that sustains a more recent reality, theoretically and socially justified, in order to be followed and applied by other specialists. We intend to make a critical exhaustive analysis of existing typologies, stipulating a set of dimensions that fulfill all the requirements for us intended. For this, we will take into consideration all the important angles for the construction of a MOOC, a simple structure that preserves the complexity of the formative process, versatility in teaching-learning process methods, diversity in interactive and collaborative tools, among others. This analysis will focus on continuous training as well as other areas of research in order to compare and perceive possible and potential differences between disparate contexts and target audiences.

In order to delineate the dimensions for the framework, a validation by specialists of different areas will be carried out after the definition of the dimensions, with the purpose of obtaining recommendations by the same ones for the implementation and application of the framework. With this data collection, it is intended to support the construction and consolidation of the developed framework, so that conclusions can be drawn to reach the final product.

REFERENCES

Perifanou, M. A. (2014). PLEs & MOOCs in Language Learning Context: A challenging connection. In Proceedings of the PLE Conference 2014. Tallinn, Estonia;

Rosselle, M., Carron, P. & Heutte, J. (2014). A typology and dimensions of a description framework for MOOCs. Paper presented at the European MOOCs Stakeholders Summit 2014. Lausanne, France;

Schneider, E. (2013). Welcome to the moocspace: a proposed theory and taxonomy for massive open online courses. In Proceedings of the 1st Workshop on Massive Open Online Courses at the 16th Annual Conference on Artificial Intelligence in Education. Memphis, Tennessee;

Yuan, L. & Powell, S. (2013). MOOCs and Open Education: Implications for Higher Education. Cetis White Paper. The University of Bolton. Retrieved from: http://publications.cetis.org.uk/wp-content/uploads/2013/03/MOOCs-and-OpenEducation.pdf.

INFORMATION LITERACY IN THE 21ST CENTURY: USEFULNESS AND EASE OF LEARNING

Patricia Fidalgo[1] and Joan Thormann[2]
[1]*Emirates College for Advanced Education, P.O. Box. 126662, Abu Dhabi, UAE*
[2]*Lesley University, 29 Everett St., Cambridge, MA 02138, USA*

ABSTRACT

This study of teachers in training in UAE addresses Information Literacy skills including ease of learning, usefulness and instructional preferences. Most teachers in training found that IL skills are both useful and ease to learn. Multiple instructional strategies were preferred by the teachers in training. The study also shows that although most teachers in training found IL skills easy to learn there are areas such as online safety and privacy that they want to learn more about.

KEYWORDS

Information literacy, Online environments, Teaching strategies, Teacher training

1. INTRODUCTION

According to Schubert et al (2013) a way to explore and improve pedagogies is by measuring and assessing the Information Literacy skills (IL) that students are taught. In a technology-based environment, IL skills are becoming essential, not only as a part of formal learning but also as part of lifelong learning. According to Partnership for 21st Century (2009) the knowledge, skills and expertise the 21st century student must master are: knowledge in key subjects (such as English, reading or language arts, world languages, arts, mathematics, economics, science, geography, history and government and civics), think and work creatively with others, being able to think critically and solve problems, communicate and collaborate, have life and career skills and finally have information, media and technology skills. Twenty-first century schools have to take into consideration the requirements expected by educational agencies, society and the labor market (Raish & Rimland, 2016; Thonney, & Montgomery, 2015).

The purpose of our research was to assess the usefulness and ease of learning Information Literacy (IL) skills, from the view point of teachers in training. We also wanted to assess what are the preferred methods for learning and developing IL skills and what other IL skills they would like to learn. It is very important that K-12 teachers in training learn IL skills as well as understand its importance for their future career. This study will allow further knowledge about how to provide IL skills training as well as it will allow college programs to adapt and evolve their curriculum for the challenges that future teachers have to face in the 21st century.

2. METHODS

This research was conducted at the completion of the undergraduate course titled Information Literacy offered for 15 weeks in the fall semester of 2016 at a teacher education college in the UAE. Thirty one students were enrolled in two separate sections of this course. The course is designed to provide students with the opportunity to become information literate by using Information and Communication Technology (ICT). IL skills taught included using the school's portal, email and learning management system, digital ethics, online privacy and security, searching for information online, podcasting, screencasting, editing video and audio, evaluating sources and resources of information and using technology to present information. The teaching strategies used during the course were: teacher demonstration, video demonstration, colleague's instruction, in class practice and teacher support during in class practice.

Twenty one of the 31 students responded to the survey. To collect data we used a survey developed specifically for this study that contained open and closed questions and was completed online by students. The survey included 11 items about students' opinions regarding the usefulness and the ease of learning information literacy skills and demographics. Descriptive statistics of the closed questions of the survey are presented in graphic format and provide summaries of the items. Qualitative content analysis of the open questions of the survey were also performed.

The research questions for this study were:

1. What is the opinion of teachers in training regarding the usefulness and the ease of learning information literacy skills?

2. What are the teachers in training preferred methods for learning and developing information literacy skills?

3. What other information literacy skills would teachers in training like to learn more about?

2.1 Results and Discussion

Most of the students found the IL skills easy to learn and/ or moderately easy. Just a few found it difficult. The relative ease of learning the IL skills may be attributed to several factors. Teachers in training may have been introduced to these skills previously. Another factor may be that this generation of students feels more comfortable with technology.

The data also shows the skills taught in the course were perceived as useful or very useful by the teachers in training. This response may be due to their understanding of what technology skills primary school teachers need to know. In addition, these teachers in training are aware that numerous aspects of their lives involve technology and having technology skills can help them in many areas.

The participants in this study indicated that multiple learning strategies were beneficial. Classroom instruction and in class practice were cited a little more often, than video demonstration and peer instruction. However the number of responses for each learning strategy was similar which may indicate that the use of many teaching strategies by the instructors is advantageous. The reason for this may be that the skills taught are varied and that this requires multiple ways to teach. Some skills may be better taught, for example, through demonstration and others by in class practice.

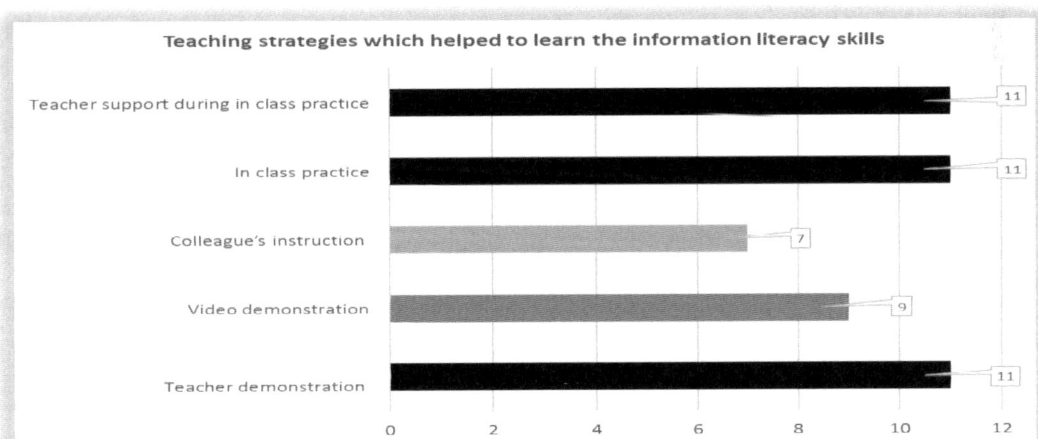

Figure 1. Student preferences regarding teaching strategies

The participants were also asked what additional IL skills they would like to learn. The skill with most responses was related to how to protect themselves and their data in online environments.

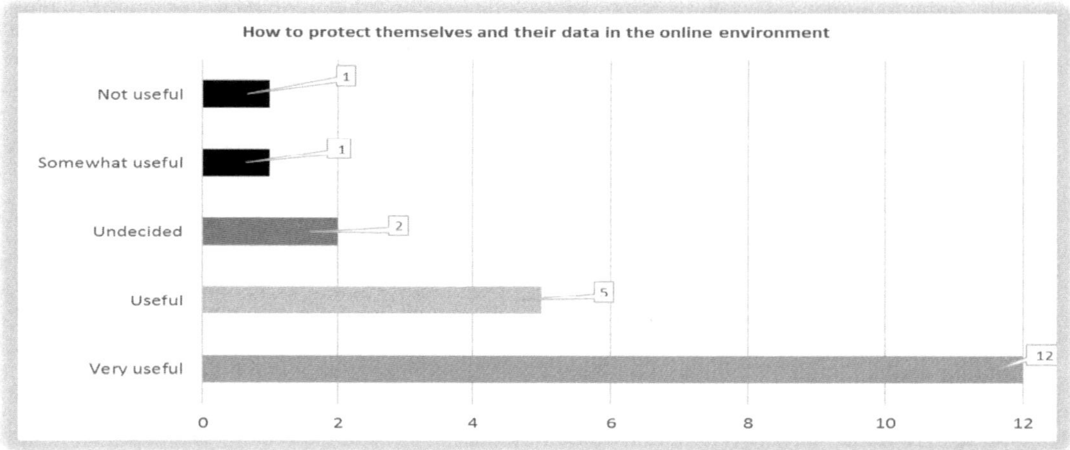

Figure 2. Student preferences regarding online safety

These skills that were taught include online behaviors as well as measures to protect their data and devices. Both of these aspects, that often are connected, might make them feel that these are valuable skills and greater understanding is better. They might also be aware that new dangers to their privacy are being deployed and they need ongoing defenses. Furthermore, personal privacy is important and though they learned some ways to be protected, the participants may be particularly sensitive to this issue. Thus they feel the need to learn additional skills to protect themselves and their data.

3. CONCLUSION

The literature indicates that IL skills are found generally useful for diverse purposes (personal and work related). Our study shows that most teachers in training find IL skills easy to learn. Using multiple teaching strategies (in particular classroom instruction) seems beneficial as it addresses the diverse nature of the information resources and learner needs. Thus good classroom instruction may also account for the general ease of learning IL skills. Despite the fact that the current generation of students feel more comfortable using technology there are still some areas, such as safety and privacy, where more knowledge and experience is desirable.

REFERENCES

Raish, V., & Rimland, E., 2016. Employer Perceptions of Critical Information Literacy Skills and Digital Badges. *College & Research Libraries*, Vol. 77, No.1, pp 87-113.

Schubert F. et. al, 2013. Information Literacy Skills of Humanities, Arts, and Social Science Tertiary Students in Singapore. *Reference & User Services Quarterly*, Vol. 53, No. 1, pp 40–50.

Thonney, T., & Montgomery, J. C., 2015. The Relationship between Cumulative Credits and Student Learning Outcomes: A Cross-Sectional Assessment of Information Literacy and Communication Skills. *Journal of the Scholarship Of Teaching And Learning*, Vol. 15, No. 1, pp 70-87.

Partnership for 21st Century, 2009. P21 Framework Definitions. Partnership for 21St Century Skills.

Doctoral Consortium

E-LEARNING RESEARCH AND DEVELOPMENT: ON EVALUATION, LEARNING PERFORMANCE, AND VISUAL ATTENTION

Marco Rüth
Department of Psychology, University of Cologne, Germany

ABSTRACT

Digital learning is becoming a prevalent everyday human behavior. Effective digital learning services are integral for educational innovation and constitute competitive advantages for education businesses. Quality management in e-learning research and development is thus of utmost importance and needs both strong conceptual and empirical underpinnings. On the one hand, this work delineates a new model that conceptualizes main critical issues in e-learning research and development projects. The model will foster substantial progress in evaluation and theory development of digital learning. On the other hand, the evaluation of how central features of digital learning services affect learning is indispensable. Here, empirical studies will investigate three key stages of learning: the initial situation, the learning procedure, and the assessment procedure. With regard to the initial situation, how do existing learner characteristics relate to learning performance in digital learning modules? Second, how do visual features of the digital learning content affect the visual attention, cognitive load, and learning performance of the users? Third, how do additional information in textual feedback affect the learning performance in digital multiple-choice quizzes? Overall, this work presents a new model for the systematic evaluation of e-learning and investigates key learning stages to illustrate the importance of developing evidence-based guidelines. Turning both approaches into common practice in e-learning research and development will substantiate theory development, quality management, and project success.

KEYWORDS

e-learning, evaluation, theory development, learner characteristics, eye tracking, e-assessment

1. INTRODUCTION

Many educational institutions offer electronic services for learning (e-learning) and teaching (e-teaching), e.g., to improve education, to develop new learning spaces, to enhance mobility, to foster international outreach, or to gain more evidence on the quality of teaching and learning processes. Common arguments for choosing digital learning services (i.e., products of e-learning projects) can be found in various existing guidelines on e-learning of educational institutions and companies. On the one hand, these guidelines often list pros and cons of digital learning services per se (e.g., more flexibility and less social interaction, respectively). However, neither does this approach enable to explain failure or success, nor does it consider that e-learning projects are often very different. Thus, including the pros and excluding the cons does not appear to be a satisfying heuristic for e-learning project teams. On the other hand, building new projects based on best practices is also not necessarily a promising approach. Some of these practices might include insights that highly depend on contextual or unknown factors. Obviously, one should not replicate successful concepts in different contexts, e.g., in higher education and in high schools, without adapting to the context. Still, it will remain less clear how to handle missing information during adaptation, e.g., if best practices do not explain how the teams decided on implementing specific features in digital learning services. Project teams and researchers need such essential information to determine and to discuss educational effectiveness and efficiency. In turn, e-learning project teams could clarify promises and pitfalls of digital learning services by providing comprehensive documentations including empirical evidence based on scientific inquiry.

First, only if e-learning project teams continuously monitor and explicitly document the quality of their project, they will be able to revise the route of the project when necessary. To monitor the quality of e-learning projects, they may adapt evaluation criteria to some degree, e.g., from international standard frameworks on e-learning quality management (ISO/IEC DIS 40180), on human-centered design for interactive systems (ISO 9241-210), or on usability (ISO 9241-11). However, they should carefully integrate such standards with systematic evaluation strategies and frameworks that consider features specific to e-learning projects. Digital learning services become increasingly available and their use may become necessary in realizing some contexts of learning. Consequently, this work formulates conceptual solutions to current critical problems with regard to the evaluation of e-learning.

Second, e-learning projects fail or succeed depending on how much the resulting digital learning services are used (i.e., users will usually accept or decline them) and depending on how well they enable learning. Hence, e-learning project teams should aim for an entire understanding of the target audience from the very start. Does the digital learning service satisfy the users' needs? Does it facilitate their learning process? What do the users actually learn? The project teams need to evaluate their products based on empirical investigations to answer such essential questions. Only then, they can formulate valid statements on how their service affects learning and teaching in comparison with other (technology-enhanced) implementations. In line with the aforementioned three questions, this work focuses on particular effects during three key stages of common learning procedures. First, the initial stage of learning, where users bring along prior knowledge, motivation, and other learner characteristics. Second, the stage of learning processes, here focusing on learners that visually perceive some learning content. Third, the assessment stage, which usually follows learning processes to assess the learning performance. Studying these key learning stages intends to clarify the role of personality, visual learning behavior, and feedback in digital learning services. E-learning project teams that consider such evidence could knowingly adjust their project routes to success.

Overall, this work aims to enhance the effectiveness and the (understanding of the) user performance in digital learning services and endorses that evidence-based evaluations increase the success rate of e-learning projects. The following section focuses on theory development in e-learning and on the evaluation of e-learning projects. Then, in accordance with the three key learning stages, empirical investigations on learner characteristics, visual learning behavior, and learning performance of e-learning users will be outlined.

2. E-LEARNING EVALUATION AND THEORY DEVELOPMENT

Digital learning services can be used in almost any context of learning. Unique and discipline-specific factors are often inherent to many of these contexts. Therefore, the related e-learning projects are often neither easy to compare nor to replicate. Unique projects can yield innovative outcomes, but scientific inquiries aiming for comprehensive theories of e-learning need a way to accumulate the generated knowledge. This strategic deficit hampers progress in e-learning evaluation and theory development. To enhance progress in evaluation and theory development, e-learning project teams could consider the eleven critical issues that Rüth and Kaspar (2017) formulated in the E-Learning Setting Circle. Accordingly, the next two paragraphs present the rationale and the two most important critical issues from that already published part of this work.

With regard to evaluation, it is important to understand that the assessment of the main goals of e-learning projects – to actually, effectively, and efficiently enhance learning – is not a simple task. One reason for this is that traditional learning theories – e.g., behaviorism, cognitivism, constructivism, and active theory (cf. Pange and Pange, 2011) – are compatible with some approaches of e-learning, but do not fully capture the scope of e-learning. The discrepancy between traditional learning and e-learning is due to the fact that e-learning projects are highly artificial phenomena (cf. Phillips, Kennedy, and McNaught, 2012). To generalize natural phenomena such as gravitation, one can refer to and build on multiple comparable experimental evidence. In contrast, e-learning projects are necessarily co-determined by situational factors. These range from general boundary conditions to specific, partly inherent aspects of technological processes. Situational factors lead to a vast amount of decision routes e-learning project teams might take, which in turn complicates comparisons across the projects' processes and products. Nevertheless, each team needs solid arguments that go far beyond method novelty or technological advance to create effective implementations. Further, the teams that realize e-learning projects often consist of experts from different disciplines that temporarily collaborate. Consequently, performing and documenting decision-making comprehensibly is essential, e.g., to allow each team to trace how another team worked out an effective combination of technological features. Since project routes typically vary, it is of particular importance that the teams carefully monitor which routes are promising for goal achievement – decisions at each stage of the project might co-determine its failure or success. During each project, many feedback loops and iterations are conceivable and many technological features enable user interaction. Overall, more situational factors co-determine e-learning projects further than in case of traditional learning projects. Comprehensible project work referencing to theory will hence distinctly facilitate the generalization of e-learning project results. Importantly, the most important issues in e-learning projects are to elucidate the role of decision-making and to assess the goal attainment level.

On the one hand, due to the artificial nature of e-learning projects, decision-making is integral to all project activities. The project teams always need to explicate in what regard stakeholders, project deliverables, and other situational factors drive their decision-making. Importantly, if the influence of situational factors is not considered, neither will it be easy to compare evidence from e-learning projects, e.g., for benchmarking of project results, nor will it be straightforward to generalize such evidence, e.g., for companies or educational institutions aiming to formulate comprehensible best and worst practices.

On the other hand, the primary goal of e-learning projects – to enhance learning – and other existing goals should be defined from the start. Similarly, only if the methodology and quality metrics are clearly formulated, e-learning projects will become comparable and will be eligible for benchmarking. Consequently, only if project outcomes and project goals are clearly related within and across projects, there will be systematic and substantial progress in the area of e-learning research and development.

Hence, Rüth and Kaspar (2017) defined decision-making and the assessment of the goal attainment level as the universal element and the guiding element of the E-Learning Setting Circle, respectively. The E-Learning Setting Circle provides a practical solution for all e-learning project teams that aim to enhance the validity of their e-learning project evaluations. It is thus essential that e-learning project teams document the relevant decision routes and project results meticulously. The scientific purpose of the model is to enhance comparability and generalizability of evidence from e-learning projects. In practical terms, those teams that apply the model could identify and anticipate decision routes that actually lead to failure or success of e-learning projects more systematically.

3. UNDERSTANDING LEARNING PERFORMANCE IN E-LEARNING

The empirical part of this work scrutinizes the impact of learner characteristics, visual attention, and feedback on learning performance in e-learning. Each of the next three paragraphs only presents the rationale of the planned studies. The full methodology will be specified in the prospective publications.

First, to illustrate the importance of learner characteristics, picture two extreme versions of how digital learning could take place. On the one hand, one e-learning project team decides to implement one standardized learning path that forces each learner to complete the same learning module. One the other hand, another team decides to investigate differences between their users first to then deliver the learning content in a customized way. Since uniform and customized digital learning services provide different degrees of freedom, the users might show different levels of learner motivation (see, e.g., Keller, 2016; Keller and Suzuki, 2004) and self-regulation (see, e.g., Liaw and Huang, 2013). Nakayama, Mutsuura, and Yamamoto (2014) highlighted the important relation between personality and learning performance in an online course. Köster et al. (2015) showed that users recognized personalized content more often than non-personalized content in the context of digital online advertisements. Accordingly, this study tests if digital learning services tailored to specific personal learner characteristics improve learner motivation and learning performance. In an experimental setup, the users will complete a digital learning sequence at their own speed. The learning modules will differ with respect to customization, i.e., the degree to which the learning content meets the users' needs. To assess the memory performance of the learners, they will complete computer-based tests constructively aligned to the learning content. Computer-based questionnaires will quantify the learner motivation. Main demographical characteristics (e.g., age and gender) and the learners' expectations (Paechter, Maier, and Macher, 2010) will be measured alike and will be included as covariates in the data analysis. The results will show if personalized digital learning content increases or decreases the learner motivation and the learning performance. Potential pitfalls of personalized learning will be discussed, e.g., if customized learning reduces the learners' opportunities to learn how to learn. In practical terms, the results of this study might help to explain when customization of digital learning services could enhance learning performance in general.

Second, with regard to the learning procedure, it is specifically important to evaluate how visual features of the learning content (e.g., textual and pictorial multimedia components) affect the learning performance and user experience of the learners. There is much evidence that design choices in multimedia content can systematically influence visual attention and learning amongst other cognitive mechanisms (for an overview see, e.g., Mayer, 2014). First, according to the cognitive theory of multimedia learning (cf. Mayer, 2014), learners actively process the digital learning content by attending, selecting, organizing, and integrating relevant information. Second, they use two distinct channels to process textual and pictorial information. Third, learners only process up to some quantity of information at once, because the capacity to learn is limited. Nevertheless, particular designs of multimedia learning content might reduce the cognitive load of the learners (Mayer and Moreno, 2003). Accordingly, this study will compare how different visual features of digital learning content reduce the cognitive load and if they enhance the subsequent learning performance. To assess the learning performance, the learners will complete a computer-based test constructively aligned to the learning content. First, an online experiment will test for differences in learning performance and will allow estimating the effect size. If learners actually perform differently, a second experiment will test for similar effects under laboratory conditions. If this is the case, a third experiment will implement the same procedure while also assessing the gaze behavior of the learners by means of eye tracking. This enables to identify those visual features of the digital learning content that are potentially relevant for the difference in learning performance of the users (cf. Rakoczi and Pohl, 2012). In all experiments, the learners will indicate their subjective cognitive load based on self-reported difficulty. In the third experiment, objective eye tracking measures will also be used to quantify the cognitive load (cf. Zagermann, Pfeil, and Reiterer, 2016). In addition, all experiments will test if the subjective evaluation of the digital learning service in terms of user experience affects the learning performance. These additional data will increase the validity of the measures of visual attention. Together, the related data might indicate how visual features of digital learning content elicit beneficial or malign effects on learning performance.

Third, as to the assessment procedure, digital tools are especially powerful in providing opportunities for formative assessments for learning (cf. Brown, 2004) – in contrast to summative assessments of learning such as final examinations. Importantly, formative assessments need to include effective feedback. A frequently used tool for formative assessments are multiple-choice quizzes. However, the reported testing effects in digital quiz-like environments are mixed (Little and Bjork, 2015). To close this gap, three subsequent experiments will assess how feedback in digital multiple-choice quizzes affects the learning performance. More specifically, it is expected that learners that receive feedback including additional textual information outperform learners that only receive information about the correctness of their answers. The aim of the first laboratory experiment is to test how the feedback affects immediate learning performance for content relevant for an upcoming exam. The second laboratory experiment will focus on the immediate and delayed (i.e., one week later) effects of the feedback on learning general knowledge. The third experiment will test for feedback effects on learning general knowledge in an unsupervised online setup. Importantly, the feedback might also affect metacognition and the subjective evaluation of the quiz. Therefore, all experiments will also test for differences in the learners' response certainty and user experience. Response certainty is a metacognitive estimate based on prior knowledge (cf. Kulhavy and Stock, 1989) that contributes to an understanding of how feedback is processed. Prior experiments have shown that response certainty is related to the duration of feedback reception and learning performance in subsequent tests (e.g., Kulhavy and Stock, 1989; Mory, 1994). In sum, these experiments will provide multiple evidence from different learning contexts, which facilitates evaluating the effectiveness and efficiency of two feedback types frequently used in digital multiple-choice quizzes.

4. CONCLUSION

Conceptual and empirical progress in the area of digital learning is crucial to unravel the critical factors that make for effective digital learning services. First, conceptual progress in e-learning research and development needs progress in theory development. To achieve this, e-learning project teams could foster project comparability and generalizability by approaching the critical issues of their projects outlined in the

E-Learning Setting Circle. Second, e-learning teams usually aim at improving the learning performance when deciding for or against the implementation of particular features in digital learning services. Thus, e-learning teams should consider empirical investigations on how these features affect the learning performance before implementing them in digital learning services. Overall, systematic conceptual and empirical progress substantiates effective digital learning services and shapes the future of learning.

REFERENCES

Brown, S., 2004. Assessment for learning. *Learning and Teaching in Higher Education*, *1*(1), pp.81–89.

International Organization for Standardization/International Electrotechnical Commission, 2010. ISO/DIS 9241-210. Ergonomics of human-system interaction -- Part 210: Human-centred design for interactive systems. International Organization for Standardization.

International Organization for Standardization/International Electrotechnical Commission, 2016. ISO/IEC DIS 40180. Information Technology - Learning, Education, and Training - Quality for learning, education and training - Fundamentals and reference framework. International Organization for Standardization.

International Organization for Standardization/International Electrotechnical Commission, 2016. ISO/DIS 9241-11. Ergonomics of human-system interaction -- Part 11: Usability: Definitions and concepts. International Organization for Standardization.

Keller, J.M. and Suzuki, K., 2004. Learner motivation and E-learning design: A multinationally validated process. *Journal of Educational Media*, 29(3), pp.229-239.

Keller, J.M., 2016. Motivation, Learning, and Technology: Applying the ARCS-V Motivation Model, *Participatory Educational Research*, 3(2), pp.1-13.

Köster, M., Rüth, M., Hamborg, K. C. and Kaspar, K., 2015. Effects of personalized banner ads on visual attention and recognition memory. *Applied Cognitive Psychology, 29*(2), pp.181-192.

Kulhavy, R.W. and Stock, W.A., 1989. Feedback in Written Instruction: The Place of Response Certitude. *Educational Psychology Review*, 1(4), pp.279–308.

Laugwitz, B., Held, T., and Schrepp, M., 2008. Construction and Evaluation of a User Experience Questionnaire. In *Proceedings of the 4th Symposium of the Workgroup Human-Computer Interaction and Usability Engineering of the Austrian Computer Society on HCI and Usability for Education and Work*, pp.63–76.

Liaw, S.S. and Huang, H.M., 2013. Perceived satisfaction, perceived usefulness and interactive learning environments as predictors to self-regulation in e-learning environments. *Computers & Education*, 60(1), pp.14-24.

Little, J.L. and Bjork, E.L., 2015. Optimizing multiple-choice tests as tools for learning. *Memory & Cognition*, 43(1), pp.14–26.

Mayer, R.E. and Moreno, R., 2003. Nine ways to reduce cognitive load in multimedia learning. *Educational psychologist*, *38*(1), pp.43-52.

Mayer, R.E., 2014. *The Cambridge handbook of multimedia learning*. Cambridge university press, New York, USA.

Mory, E.H., 1994. Adaptive feedback in computer-based instruction: Effects of response certitude on performance, feedback-study time, and efficiency. *Journal of Educational Computing Research*, 11(3), pp.263-290.

Nakayama, M., Mutsuura, K., and Yamamoto, H., 2014. Impact of Learner's Characteristics and Learning Behaviour on Learning Performance during a Fully Online Course. *Electronic Journal of e-Learning*, *12*(4), pp.394-408.

Paechter, M., Maier, B., and Macher, D., 2010. Students' expectations of, and experiences in e-learning: Their relation to learning achievements and course satisfaction. *Computers & education*, *54*(1), pp.222-229.

Pange, A. and Pange, J., 2011. Is E-learning Based On Learning Theories? A Literature Review. *International Journal of Social, Behavioral, Educational, Economic, Business and Industrial Engineering*, 5(8), pp.932-936.

Phillips, R., Kennedy, G., and McNaught, C., 2012. The role of theory in learning technology evaluation research. *Australasian Journal of Educational Technology*, *28*(7), pp.1103-1118.

Rakoczi, G. and Pohl, M., 2012. Visualisation and analysis of multiuser gaze data: Eye tracking usability studies in the special context of e-learning. *In 2012 IEEE 12th International Conference on Advanced Learning Technologies (ICALT),* Rome, Italy, pp.738-739.

Rüth, M. and Kaspar, K., 2017. The E-Learning Setting Circle: First Steps Toward Theory Development in E-Learning Research. *The Electronic Journal of e-Learning,* 15(1), pp.94-103.

Zagermann, J., Pfeil, U., and Reiterer, H., 2016. Measuring Cognitive Load using Eye Tracking Technology in Visual Computing. In *BELIV'16: Proceedings of the Sixth Workshop on Beyond Time and Errors on Novel Evaluation Methods for Visualization*, pp.78-85.

AUTHOR INDEX

Aladjem, R. 161, 195
Abdeslam, J. 179
Alhasan, K. 71
Alomyan, H. 191
Amado, C. 219
Aristovnik, A. 113
Barata, A. 55
Bellot, A. 169
Bigontina, S. 137
Bonne, T. 3
Bouchereau, A. 213
Carvalho, P. 55
Champagnat, R. 63
Chan, T. 149
Chen, F. 71
Chen, H. 97
Chen, L. 71
Choosri, N. 80
Chu, S. 149
Cilliers, L. 32
De Castro-Santos, A. 25
Debabi, W. 63
Dinicu, A. 105
Escudeiro, P. 55
Eze, R. 184
Fajardo, W. 25
Fang, D. 137
Fidalgo, P. 222
Fottner, J. 137
García-Castro, R. 159
Ghandforoush, P. 209
Gulbahar, Y. 130
Günthner, W. 137
Hui, L. 149
Ilgaz, H. 130
Kaul, M. 3
Keržič, D. 113
Kilar-Magdziarz, E. 47
Kilroy, J. 89
Kless, A. 3
Kuneshka, L. 205
Kuo, Y. 149
Lahcen, E. 179
Makarchuk, T. 175
Marques, B. 55
Matthews, W. 196
Mohamed, F. 179
Molina-Solana, M. 25
Munir, R. 159
Ng, Y. 149
Oancea, R. 105
Obuekwe, G. 184
Ogawa, N. 121
Pedro, A. 219
Peng, Y. 39
Pookao, C. 80
Qirko, M. 205
Queiros, S. 55
Rechl, F. 137
Rieke, A. 3
Roxin, I. 213
Rüth, M. 227
Sadeghi, S. 13
Safyan, M. 159
Sardone, N. 201
Sarwar, S. 159
Seekoe, E. 32
Sharko, G. 205
Shimizu, A. 121
Shum, K. 149
Silva, A. 55
Smothers, A. 196
Steininger, P. 164
Teneqexhi, R. 205
Thormann, J. 222
Tomaževič, N. 113
Torras, E. 169
Ul Qayyum, Z. 159
Umek, L. 113
Van Niekerk, E. 32
Vrapi, F. 205
Wang, R. 137

Wang, Y. 97
Wang, Y. 154
Wright, G.. 32
Yan, W. 39
Yeung, C... 149